Naturalizing Epistemology

Naturalizing Epistemology

Second Edition

edited by Hilary Kornblith

A Bradford Book
The MIT Press
Cambridge, Massachusetts
London, England

This book was set in Palatino by The Maple-Vail Book Manufacturing Group and was printed and bound in the United States of America.

Library of Congress Cataloging-in-Publication Data

Naturalizing epistemology / edited by Hilary Kornblith. — 2nd ed.
  p. cm.
"A Bradford book."
Includes bibliographical references and index.
ISBN 0–262–11180–2. — ISBN 0–262–61090–6 (pbk.)
1. Knowledge, Theory of. I. Kornblith, Hilary.
BD161.N29 1993
121—dc20   93–23976
                                                                      CIP

Contents

Preface to the
Second Edition

Much has happened in the field of epistemology since the first edition of this volume appeared in 1985. Choosing a selection of papers for the first edition was relatively easy; making the choices for the second edition was much more difficult. I have been faced with an embarrassment of riches. If the size and price of this volume were not constraints, it would have been substantially larger and more wide ranging. While I find operating under real-world constraints congenial to epistemological theorizing, such constraints on editorial practice are far less to my liking. For reasons of space and thematic unity, I have had to leave out pieces I judged to be excellent, in spite of the fact that the collection would have been richer were they included. Such decisions were never pleasant. I am especially sorry that I had to delete some chapters that appeared in the first edition, and that I was unable to include Philip Kitcher's paper "The Naturalists Return" because of its size. Anyone who is interested in naturalistic epistemology would profit from adding this work of Kitcher's to their reading list.

I have also been faced with the question of what to do with my introduction to the first edition. Many people have commented that this introduction was helpful to them and that it offered a useful perspective on the field. I have therefore resisted the temptation to redo the introduction completely, and have instead left it largely as it was, with only minor additions to reflect the new table of contents. This has the added benefit that those who found my perspective on the field misguided in some way will not be presented with a moving target.

I have adopted an unusual system of citation for this volume as a result of the structure of the bibliography. As with the first edition, the bibliography for this edition is divided thematically. While this proved exceptionally useful for certain purposes, it made it extremely time consuming to look up sources that were cited by author and year of publication: each section of the bibliography had to be examined until the relevant entry was located. In order to address this problem, citations now include not only author and year of publication but a number indicating location in the bibliography as well. Thus, the Kitcher article mentioned above is cited as Kitcher 1992 [217]. This indicates that the article was published in 1992 and appears as item number 217 in the bibliography. This will, I hope, make the volume easier to use, even if it does result in a rather baroque system of citation.

I have received a good deal of help in putting together this second edition. Constructive comments and suggestions were provided by Alvin Goldman, Gilbert Harman, James Maffie, and Stephen Stich. Fred Schmitt, who suggested in the early 1980s that I put this collection together, has done a wonderful job of updating his bibliography, this time with the aid of James Spellman. The idea for a second edition is due to Betty Stanton of Bradford Books, and I am grateful to Teri Mendelsohn for her help in every phase of production. Leslie Weiger has been exceptionally helpful in preparing the manuscript.

Naturalizing Epistemology

Introduction: What Is Naturalistic Epistemology?

Hilary Kornblith

In recent years the naturalistic approach to epistemology has been gaining currency. The goal of this introduction is to answer my title question and at the same time to place the essays that follow in appropriate perspective.

Three Questions

Consider the following three questions.

1. How ought we to arrive at our beliefs?

2. How do we arrive at our beliefs?

3. Are the processes by which we do arrive at our beliefs the ones by which we ought to arrive at our beliefs?

Different theorists will answer these questions differently. The topic I wish to deal with here has to do with the relations among these three questions. If we wish to answer all of these questions, which should we deal with first? Can any of these questions be answered independently of the others, or will the answers to each constrain the range of answers we might give to those remaining? Just as different theorists disagree about answers to questions 1, 2, and 3, there are disagreements about the relations among these questions. What I want to suggest here is that what is distinctive about the naturalistic approach to epistemology is its view about the relations among these three questions.

The Traditional View

One view, which I will label the *traditional view*, suggests a strategy of divide and conquer. Question 1 is to be assigned to philosophers, question 2 to psychologists. Each of these groups is to conduct its research independently of the other. When both groups have completed their work, they must get together to answer question 3. It is permissible, of course, for philosophers and psychologists to meet prior to each group's completion of its assigned task. Such meetings will allow them to check progress on question 3. These meetings will not, however, have any effect on work on questions 1 or 2. Question 1 is in the bailiwick of philosophers; question 2 in the bailiwick of psychologists; and the answer to question 3 is produced by comparing the answers to questions 1 and 2.

Most research in philosophy as well as psychology seems to be guided by the traditional view. On the philosophical side consider one kind of answer that has been offered to question 1: the coherence theory of justification. Coherence theorists hold, roughly, that in deciding whether to accept or reject any statement, one ought to consider how well it fits in with or coheres with one's other beliefs; one ought to adopt beliefs cohering with beliefs one already has. Whatever the merits of this view, it seems to have nothing to do with any possible answer to question 2. Suppose that psychologists were to discover that people actually arrive at their beliefs by some kind of nonconscious mechanism that measures the coherence of candidate beliefs with the body of beliefs already held; candidates that cohere are adopted and those that do not are rejected. What bearing would this psychological theory have on the merits of the coherence theory of justification as an answer to question 1? None, it seems. How we actually arrive at our beliefs need have nothing to do with how we ought to arrive at them. By the same token if we are evaluating the merits of some psychological account of belief acquisition, a purported account of how people actually arrive at their beliefs in some situation, theories about how we ought to arrive at our beliefs seem to be irrelevant.

An analogy with ethics seems apt here. Consider the following three questions about human action:

A. How ought people to act?

B. How do people act?

C. Do people act the way they ought?

These questions bear the same relations to each other as questions 1, 2, and 3. Moreover it seems clear that it is the job of ethical theorists to answer question A and psychologists concerned with human motivation to answer question B. Only by comparing the results of these two independent investigations will the answer to C emerge. Note how absurd it would be for a philosopher to object to a psychological account of how people act on the grounds that action of that sort is immoral. It would be equally absurd if a psychologist were to object to a philosophical account of how we ought to act on the grounds that people do not act that way. There is a straightforward explanation of the absurdity of these challenges. The normative questions that philosophers ask are completely independent of the descriptive questions psychologists ask. This seems to be true not only in the case of questions A and B but also in the case of questions 1 and 2.

I do not mean to endorse the arguments of this section for the traditional view, nor do I mean to suggest that no other arguments for it are available. Instead I hope only to have presented enough of the traditional view and its motivation so that it may clearly be distinguished from a naturalistic approach to questions 1, 2, and 3.

The Replacement Thesis

I take the naturalistic approach to epistemology to consist in this: question 1 cannot be answered independently of question 2. Questions about how we actually arrive at our beliefs are thus relevant to questions about how we ought to arrive at our beliefs. Descriptive questions about belief acquisition have an important bearing on normative questions about belief acquisition.

There are, of course, different camps within the naturalistic approach; naturalistic epistemologists differ on how direct a bearing psychology has on epistemology. The most radical view here is due to Quine:

Epistemology still goes on, though in a new setting and a clarified status. Epistemology, or something like it, simply falls into place as a chapter of psychology and hence of natural science. It studies a natural phenomenon, viz., a physical human subject. This human subject is accorded a certain experimentally controlled input—certain patterns of irradiation in assorted frequencies, for instance—and in the fullness of time the subject delivers as output a description of the three dimensional external world and its history. The relation between the meager input and the torrential output is a relation that we are prompted to study for somewhat the same reasons that always prompted epistemology; namely, in order to see how evidence relates to theory, and in what ways one's theory of nature transcends any available evidence.[1]

I will speak of the view that epistemological questions may be replaced by psychological questions as the *replacement thesis*.

Quine's argument for the replacement thesis in chapter 1 is this: the history of epistemology is largely the history of the foundationalist program. Foundationalists tried to show that there is a class of beliefs—typically beliefs about our own sense experience—about which it is impossible to be wrong. These beliefs were held to be sufficient to justify the rest of our beliefs; thus, in addition to identifying those beliefs that would serve as the foundation of knowledge, foundationalists sought to show how foundational beliefs provide us with good reason for adopting the remainder of our beliefs. The history of epistemology shows that the foundationalist program has faced one failure after another. The lesson to be learned from these failures, according to Quine, is not just that foundationalists had mistakenly answered question 1 in claiming that the appropriate way to arrive at one's beliefs is to begin with beliefs about which one cannot be wrong and build upon that foundation. Rather, according to Quine, foundationalists were asking the wrong questions. Once we see the sterility of the foundationalist program, we see that the only genuine questions there are to ask about the relation between theory and evidence and about the acquisition of belief are psychological questions. In this view question 2 is relevant to question 1 because it holds all the content that is left in question 1. The relation between these two questions is much like the relation atheists believe to hold between questions about God's act of creation and questions about the details of, for example, the big bang; the latter questions exhaust all the content there is in the former questions.

One illustration of the way in which traditional epistemological questions have become transformed through our newly gained understanding forms the heart of chapter 3. Philosophers have long asked, how is knowledge possible? This question has been understood for centuries as a request for a response to the skeptic, and the result has been the various attempts to work out the details of the foundationalist program. What we are now in a position to understand is precisely how foundationalists misinterpreted this important question. If the question about the possibility of knowledge is interpreted as a request to respond to the skeptic on his or her own terms, then any attempt to answer the question is doomed to failure. Quine argues, however, that this interpretation mislocates the very worries that gave rise to the question in the first place. It is through the rise of science that we were first led to question the limits and possibility of knowledge. As science made clear the falsity of our former beliefs and our susceptibility to illusion, the question naturally arose as to whether the beliefs we arrive at, even under the best of conditions, are likely to be true. In short the question arose as to whether knowledge is possible. Insofar as this question arises from within science, we may call on the resources of science to answer it. Far from making epistemology a necessary prerequisite to doing science, this makes epistemology continuous with the scientific enterprise.

Fortunately, when we turn to science to answer our question, we are not disappointed. As Quine suggests, "There is some encouragement in Darwin." Creatures whose belief generating mechanisms do not afford them cognitive contact with the world "have a pathetic but praiseworthy tendency to die before reproducing their kind." Since believing truths has survival value, the survival of the fittest guarantees that our innate intellectual endowment gives us a predisposition for believing truths. Knowledge is thus not only possible but a necessary by-product of natural selection.

This Darwinian argument may be thought to provide a motivation for the replacement thesis quite different from that offered by Quine in chapter 1. If the Darwinian argument can be worked out in detail, it may provide a way of tackling the original three questions by taking on question 3 first. If nature has so constructed us that our belief-generating processes are inevitably biased in favor of true beliefs, then it must be that the processes by which we arrive at beliefs just are those by which we ought to arrive at them. Question 3 is thus answered with an emphatic affirmative, and we may move on to the remaining two questions. If we know in advance, however, that we arrive at beliefs in just the way we ought, one way to approach question 1 is just by doing psychology. In discovering the processes by which we actually arrive at beliefs, we are thereby discovering the processes by which we ought to arrive at beliefs. The epistemological enterprise may be replaced by empirical psychology.

Notice that the attempt to defend the replacement thesis by way of the Darwinian argument requires that the conclusion of that argument be given a very strong reading. Someone who concludes on the basis of natural selection that the processes by which we acquire beliefs must be roughly like the processes by which we ought will not be in a position to defend the replacement thesis. If psychological investigation is to be able to replace epistemological theorizing, there must be a perfect match between the processes by which we do and those by which we ought to acquire beliefs. Without such a perfect match, the results of psychological theorizing will only give an approximate answer to question 1, and epistemology will be called on to make up the slack. Psychology would thus be strongly relevant to epistemology, and this version of the Darwinian argument would thus motivate a version of naturalistic epistemology, but the resulting view would be far weaker than the replacement thesis.[2]

Still a third argument for the replacement thesis is to be found in such writers as Davidson,[3] Dennett,[4] Harman,[5] and, once again, Quine.[6] In Harman's version, the argument is as follows:

We normally assume that there are basic principles of rationality that apply to all normal human beings. . . . We come to understand someone else by coming to appreciate that person's reasons for his or her beliefs and actions, or by seeing how that person made a mistake. Someone who reasoned in a fundamentally different way from the way in which we reason would really and truly be unintelligible to us. . . . In assuming, as we normally do, that we can make sense of other people, given sufficient information about them, we presuppose that everyone else operates in accordance with the same basic principles as we do.[7]

As Harman makes clear, he does not mean to be arguing only for the conclusion that we all arrive at our beliefs in the same way but rather that rational belief acquisition consists of arriving at beliefs in the way we all do. In Harman's view since individuals who reason in a way different than we do would be unintelligible to us, we would not count them as rational; the only rational individuals are thus ones who reason as we do. Once again this allows us to approach the original three questions by answering question 3 first, and in answering it in the affirmative, the way is paved for the replacement of epistemology by psychology. It should also be noted that the conclusion of Harman's argument must be interpreted in quite a strong way if it is to serve as an argument for the replacement thesis. When Harman argues that someone who reasons in a fundamentally different way would be unintelligible to us, he cannot simply mean that large differences in the way individuals reason would result in mutual uninterpretability, for this view is compatible with the claim that individuals differ from one another in minor respects in the way they reason. Psychology could then describe the different ways in which individuals reason but it would be impotent to pick out which of these ways (if any) were rational. Harman must therefore be arguing for the conclusion that any difference whatsoever in the ways individuals reason would result in mutual uninterpretability. Weaker conclusions than this will not support the replacement thesis.

We are now in a position to distinguish between a strong and a weak version of the replacement thesis. The strong version of the replacement thesis is argued for by Quine in chapter 1. Quine argues not only that epistemological questions may be replaced by psychological questions but also that this replacement must take place; psychological questions hold all the content there is in epistemological questions. On this view psychology replaces epistemology in much the same way that chemistry has replaced alchemy. The other two arguments examined for the replacement thesis, however—the Darwinian argument and the argument from mutual interpretability— suggest a weak version of the replacement thesis. In this view psychology and epistemology provide two different avenues for arriving at the same place. Psychology may replace epistemology because the processes psychologists identify as the ones by which we do arrive at our beliefs will inevitably turn out to be the very processes epistemologists would identify as the ones by which we ought to arrive at our beliefs. Thus even if all epistemologists were to give up their trade and turn to auto mechanics, the questions they tried to answer would nevertheless be addressed, in a different guise, by psychologists. This view is carefully scrutinized in chapter 15 by Stephen Stich, "Could Man Be an Irrational Animal?"

The Autonomy of Epistemology

There is a world of difference between the strong and the weak version of the replacement thesis. The question at issue is the autonomy of epistemology. Are there legitimate epistemological questions that are distinct in content from the questions of descriptive psychology? Advocates of the strong version of the replacement thesis answer this question in the negative, advocates of the weak version answer it in the affirmative. The consequences of the strong version of the replacement thesis for the study of epistemology are clear: epistemology must go the way of alchemy and be absorbed into another science. In this section I examine some of the consequences of the weak replacement thesis for epistemological theorizing. If epistemology is an autonomous discipline but subject nevertheless to the constraints of the weak replacement thesis, what will epistemology look like? What kind of relationship does this dictate between psychology and epistemology?

If the weak replacement thesis is true, epistemologists need not fear that they will be replaced by descriptive psychologists. The weak replacement thesis is a two-way street. If psychologists and epistemologists inevitably will receive the same answers to the different questions they ask, psychologists are just as subject to replacement by epistemologists as epistemologists are by psychologists. We may leave the unemployment issue aside, however, for if the weak replacement thesis is true, no kind of replacement is likely to go on. Either discipline could replace the other, but there are extremely good pragmatic reasons why they should not.

If the thesis under discussion is true, the psychology of belief acquisition and epistemology are two different fields, which ask different but equally legitimate questions and have different methodologies. In spite of these differences a complete (and true) psychology of belief acquisition will describe the same processes that a complete (and true) epistemology will prescribe. That these two fields will, when complete, single out the same processes of belief acquisition does not, however, suggest that at stages short of completion, the processes singled out by philosophers and those singled out by psychologists will match perfectly. Indeed it is clear that if pursued independently of one another, anything short of a complete psychology would look very different from anything short of a complete epistemology, in spite of their ultimate convergence. Because the two fields deal with different questions and because these questions are approached with different methodologies, processes that are easily identified by psychologists as ones that occur in us may not easily be identified by philosophers as ones that ought to be used; by the same token processes easily identified by philosophers as ones we ought to use need not be easily identified by psychologists as processes we actually make use of. The upshot is that even if the weak replacement thesis is true, no actual replacement can occur until each field has completed its work. Moreover, in order to hasten progress, philosophers and psychologists ought to be eagerly examining each other's work. If philosophers correctly identify some process as one by which we ought to arrive at our beliefs, psychologists will thereby know, even if they have not independently discovered it, that it occurs in us. Similarly if psychologists identify some process as one that occurs in us, epistemologists can be confident that this is a process by which we ought to arrive at our beliefs, even if they have not yet reached that conclusion independently. Thus if the weak replacement thesis is true, we can look forward to rapid progress in both psychology and epistemology as a result of their interaction, rather than either field being co-opted by the other.

Psychologism

Psychologism is the view that the processes by which we ought to arrive at our beliefs are the processes by which we do arrive at our beliefs; in short it is the view that the answer to question 3 is "yes." If the weak replacement thesis is true, then so is psychologism. Nevertheless it may be that psychologism is true and yet the weak replacement thesis is false. In this section I explain how that might be so.

Consider Alvin Goldman's answer to question 1 in chapter 5. Goldman suggests that we ought to arrive at our beliefs by processes that are reliable, that is, by whatever processes tend to produce true beliefs. Let us assume that Goldman is correct, and let us also assume, as Goldman does not, that psychologism is true. It thus follows that the processes by which we actually arrive at our beliefs are reliable. Even though, as we are assuming, a complete psychology of belief acquisition would describe the same processes Goldman's theory prescribes, a completed psychology would look nothing like a completed Goldman-style epistemology. It would not do for a psychologist to say merely that the processes by which we arrive at our beliefs are reliable and leave it at that. Obviously a complete psychological theory must be far more detailed and specific. The added specificity of the psychological account is not merely unnecessary, however, to answering the epistemological question, if anything like Goldman's theory is correct; the psychological theory is simply spelled out in terms at the wrong level of generality to do epistemological work. Imagine that we have a complete list of all the belief acquisition processes that take place in human beings. This list, it seems, will not answer our epistemological question (even assuming psychologism to be true), for we wish to know what all these processes have in common in virtue of which we ought to acquire beliefs by way of them. Our psychological theory will not answer this question. By the same token our philosophical theory, even if given in full detail, will not answer all our psychological questions.

I have used Goldman's theory only by way of illustration; what I say about Goldman's account is doubtless true of many rival accounts as well. If a proper epistemological theory must be cashed out at a different level of generality than psychological theories, then even if psychologism is true, the weak replacement thesis is false; no replacement could ever occur, even in completed theories, if they are not couched in terms of the same generality. Psychologism is thus still weaker that the weak replacement thesis.

What implications does psychologism have for the relation between philosophy and psychology? If psychologism is true and the weak replacement thesis false, we will not be able to read our epistemology directly from our psychology nor psychology directly from epistemology. In spite of this there will be significant constraints cast on each theory by the other. If our epistemological theory tells us that we ought adopt only beliefs arrived at by processes that have a certain property, then we know that our psychological theory must attribute to believers only belief acquisition processes with that property. If our psychological theory isolates a number of different processes of belief acquisition, then an epistemologist would do well to consider what these processes have in common. This mutual readjustment will allow each discipline to advance at a more rapid rate than it would were it to proceed independently of the other. We may thus look forward to a long and fruitful relationship between philosophy and psychology.

Antiskepticism and Ballpark Psychologism

Many philosophers who reject psychologism nevertheless believe that the processes by which we arrive at beliefs are at least roughly like the processes by which we ought to arrive at our beliefs; the one set of processes is in the same ballpark as the other. I will speak of this view as *ballpark psychologism*. It will be difficult to give a precise statement of this view; it is, for example, compatible with the suggestion that some of the processes by which we arrive at our beliefs are nothing like processes by which we ought to arrive at our beliefs. It is also compatible with the view that different people arrive at their beliefs in different ways. In spite of this vagueness it will be clear that this view has important implications for the relation between philosophy and psychology.

Anyone who rejects skepticism should embrace ballpark psychologism. To know something, it seems, is to arrive at a true belief in the way one ought, or, at the very least, in a way very much like the way one ought. If most people know a great many things, then many of their beliefs are arrived at by processes at least roughly like the processes by which they ought to arrive at their beliefs. In short antiskepticism implies ballpark psychologism.

If ballpark psychologism is true, there may be a fruitful interaction between epistemology and psychology, although the connection between the two will be weaker than that just outlined for psychologism. To the extent that psychologists are successful in describing some of the processes by which paradigm cases of knowledge are produced and to the extent that epistemologists are successful in describing certain general features of some belief acquisition processes, useful interaction between the disciplines will be likely.

Some are bound to object to this conclusion. I anticipate the following sort of objection:

You insist that once we reject skepticism we are committed to the mutual relevance of psychology and epistemology. Suppose epistemological questions can be answered *a priori;* that is, suppose it is possible to figure out, independent of any experience, which the processes are by which we should arrive at our beliefs. In this case, there would be no reason for epistemologists to consult with psychologists, for psychological work is unnecessary to reaching epistemological conclusions. There may be some sense in which psychology is relevant to epistemology, but there is no sense in which epistemologists must consult with psychologists in order to answer the questions they wish to have answered.

I want to deal with this objection. Most naturalistic epistemologists will reject the suggestion that anything is knowable a priori.[8] I do not wish to enter that debate here. Rather I will argue that the issue of a priority is a red herring. Whether the answers to epistemological questions can be known a priori in principle, epistemologists would do well to consult psychologists in practice.

It will be useful to begin by considering an example from the theory of probability.[9] Suppose I decide to start an insurance company and after lengthy actuarial calculations determine the rates to charge for various policies. I determine the rates in the following way. First, I write out the part of the probability calculus relevant to my problem. Then I gather information about mortality rates. By combining the abstract statements of the probability calculus with the data about

mortality rates, I can determine how much I need to charge for policies to make a profit. With this information in hand, I go about the
business of selling policies.

After many years I find that my company is losing large sums of
money. It may be that I am simply unlucky. It may also be that I have
made mistakes in my attempt to gather information about mortality
rates. There is, however, a third possibility: I may have mistakenly
formulated the theory of probability. It would be foolish for me to
ignore this third possibility.

Now the theory of probability is a priori knowable if anything is.[10]
I may be led, however, to revise my formulation of the probability
theory by empirical tests. Although it may be true that in the absence
of this or any other experience, a priori reasoning alone could have
straightened out my errors, the fact remains that a posteriori testing
may contribute to locating my errors. Indeed empirical test may be
the most efficient means of discovering errors.

What is important here is not whether the theory of probability is a
priori knowable but how obvious it is. A priority and obviousness do
not go hand in hand. Once we recognize that in the light of the difficulty of determining some of the statements of the probability theory
we are liable to err in arriving at them, we may subject our theory to
test by conjoining it with obviously empirical bits of information to
yield a prediction. If the prediction is falsified, it may well have been
that our attempt to formulate the a priori theory was mistaken.

What is true of probability theory is also true in the theory of
knowledge. Even granting for the sake of argument that in principle
it is possible to answer epistemological questions a priori, epistemological truths are anything but obvious. It would thus be foolhardy
not to subject epistemological theories to empirical tests. If skepticism
is to be rejected, then epistemology and psychology impose significant constraints on each other. The best way to develop epistemological theories is thus to employ these constraints in a way that allows
us to prod the theory along by confronting it with empirical tests.

An epistemological example is in order here. Consider again Goldman's suggestion that justified beliefs are beliefs that are reliably produced. It does not matter whether one regards this suggestion as
arrived at by a priori means; in any case we may subject it to empirical
test. Let us consider a paradigm case of justified belief: beliefs obtained by induction. It surely seems that everyone has a great deal of
inductive knowledge. If Goldman's account is correct and we are not

skeptics about induction, we should expect that when psychologists investigate human induction, they will find that inductive beliefs are reliably produced. Chapter 12 by Richard Nisbett and Lee Ross discusses some of the processes by which inductive beliefs are formed. The processes described do not seem to be reliable. In the light of this result, we have three choices: (1) to give up our antiskepticism and simply say that beliefs formed in the way Nisbett and Ross describe are not justified, (2) to deny that Nisbett and Ross accurately describe the way in which inductive beliefs are acquired, or (3) to revise or reject reliabilism.

It would be unreasonable to refuse even to consider option 3 on the grounds that epistemological truths are a priori knowable. In the end we may have good reason for maintaining reliabilism but we must seriously entertain the possibility that we have erred. Even if we want to insist that revisions in our epistemological theories are always the product of a priori recognition of previous errors even when prompted by empirical results, it would be foolhardy to ignore this additional check on our a priori reasoning.

Goldman's theory is used only as an example. The kinds of test I have described may apply to any other epistemological theory. In particular the Nisbett and Ross results provide an interesting test for any epistemological theory.

Exactly how epistemology will look if we allow it to be shaped by psychology remains to be seen. Quine's approach to epistemology is critically examined by Jaegwon Kim in chapter 2. Ellen Markman provides some interesting psychological work on our understanding of natural kinds in chapter 4; her account here is quite different from the Quinean account provided in chapter 3. The notion of observation is placed in a naturalistic perspective by Jerry Fodor in chapter 9. Fred Dretske suggests in chapter 10 that we will receive important illumination if we draw on work in the mathematical theory of communication. Christopher Cherniak shows how work in the theory of computational complexity bears on the very form of an epistemological theory in chapter 11. Chapter 6, which I wrote, attempts to resolve the dispute between foundationalists and coherence theorists. More general arguments for the relevance of empirical work for epistemology are presented in chapter 8 by Michael Friedman. Chapter 14 by Gilbert Harman is part of a larger project: a defense of psychologism. Alvin Goldman examines the relationship between our ordinary epistemological concepts and those of a scientific epistemology in chapter

13. The prospects for improving our inductive inferences are examined by John Holland, Keith Holyoak, Richard Nisbett, and Paul Thagard in chapter 16. And Stephen Stich suggests one way in which normative concepts may be integrated into a naturalistic epistemology in chapter 17.

Conclusion

If the arguments of the last section are sound, any epistemologist who rejects skepticism ought to be influenced in his or her philosophical work by descriptive work in psychology. The chapters in this book are a product of this influence. My hope is that this book will encourage a careful evaluation of the prospects and problems of naturalizing epistemology.[11]

Notes

1. See below, Quine 1969 [101].

2. This weaker view, which I call ballpark psychologism, is discussed below.

3. See, e.g., Davidson 1973 [703].

4. Dennett 1978 [562], pp. 3–22.

5. Harman 1982 [742].

6. E.g., Quine 1960 [100], chapter 2.

7. Harman 1982 [742], pp. 570–571.

8. For a naturalistic reconstruction of the concept of a priori knowledge, see chapter 7.

9. For a historical discussion of probability theory in which the interaction between putatively a priori reasoning and a posteriori reasoning is beautifully illustrated, see Hacking 1975 [588].

10. I do not mean to suggest that the theory of probability is a priori knowable.

11. I have received helpful suggestions from John Heil, Philip Kitcher, Linda Polson, Fred Schmitt, George Sher, and especially Louis Loeb.

1   Epistemology Naturalized

W. V. O. Quine

Epistemology is concerned with the foundations of science. Conceived thus broadly, epistemology includes the study of the foundations of mathematics as one of its departments. Specialists at the turn of the century thought that their efforts in this particular department were achieving notable success: mathematics seemed to reduce altogether to logic. In a more recent perspective this reduction is seen to be better describable as a reduction to logic and set theory. This correction is a disappointment epistemologically, since the firmness and obviousness that we associate with logic cannot be claimed for set theory. But still the success achieved in the foundations of mathematics remains exemplary by comparative standards, and we can illuminate the rest of epistemology somewhat by drawing parallels to this department.

Studies in the foundations of mathematics divide symmetrically into two sorts, conceptual and doctrinal. The conceptual studies are concerned with meaning, the doctrinal with truth. The conceptual studies are concerned with clarifying concepts by defining them, some in terms of others. The doctrinal studies are concerned with establishing laws by proving them, some on the basis of others. Ideally the obscurer concepts would be defined in terms of the clearer ones so as to maximize clarity, and the less obvious laws would be proved from the more obvious ones so as to maximize certainty. Ideally the definitions would generate all the concepts from clear and distinct ideas, and the proofs would generate all the theorems from self-evident truths.

The two ideals are linked. For, if you define all the concepts by use of some favored subset of them, you thereby show how to translate all theorems into these favored terms. The clearer these terms are, the likelier it is that the truths couched in them will be obviously true, or derivable from obvious truths. If in particular the concepts of mathematics were all reducible to the clear terms of logic, then all the truths of mathematics would go over into truths of logic; and surely the truths of logic are all obvious or at least potentially obvious, i.e., derivable from obvious truths by individually obvious steps.

This particular outcome is in fact denied us, however, since mathematics reduces only to set theory and not to logic proper. Such reduction still enhances clarity, but only because of the interrelations that emerge and not because the end terms of the analysis are clearer than others. As for the end truths, the axioms of set theory, these have less obviousness and certainty to recommend them than do most of the mathematical theorems that we would derive from them. Moreover, we know from Gödel's work that no consistent axiom system can cover mathematics even when we renounce self-evidence. Reduction in the foundations of mathematics remains mathematically and philosophically fascinating, but it does not do what the epistemologist would like of it: it does not reveal the ground of mathematical knowledge, it does not show how mathematical certainty is possible.

Still there remains a helpful thought, regarding epistemology generally, in that duality of structure which was especially conspicuous in the foundations of mathematics. I refer to the bifurcation into a theory of concepts, or meaning, and a theory of doctrine, or truth; for this applies to the epistemology of natural knowledge no less than to the foundations of mathematics. The parallel is as follows. Just as mathematics is to be reduced to logic, or logic and set theory, so natural knowledge is to be based somehow on sense experience. This means explaining the notion of body in sensory terms; here is the conceptual side. And it means justifying our knowledge of truths of nature in sensory terms; here is the doctrinal side of the bifurcation.

Hume pondered the epistemology of natural knowledge on both sides of the bifurcation, the conceptual and the doctrinal. His handling of the conceptual side of the problem, the explanation of body in sensory terms, was bold and simple: he identified bodies outright with the sense impressions. If common sense distinguishes between the material apple and our sense impressions of it on the ground that the apple is one and enduring while the impressions are many and fleeting, then, Hume held, so much the worse for common sense; the notion of its being the same apple on one occasion and another is a vulgar confusion.

Nearly a century after Hume's *Treatise*, the same view of bodies was espoused by the early American philosopher Alexander Bryan Johnson.[1] "The word iron names an associated sight and feel," Johnson wrote.

What then of the doctrinal side, the justification of our knowledge of truths about nature? Here, Hume despaired. By his identification of bodies with impressions he did succeed in construing some singular statements about bodies as indubitable truths, yes; as truths about impressions, directly known. But general statements, also singular statements about the future, gained no increment of certainty by being construed as about impressions.

On the doctrinal side, I do not see that we are farther along today than where Hume left us. The Humean predicament is the human predicament. But on the conceptual side there has been progress. There the crucial step forward was made already before Alexander Bryan Johnson's day, although Johnson did not emulate it. It was made by Bentham in his theory of fictions. Bentham's step was the recognition of contextual definition, or what he called paraphrasis. He recognized that to explain a term we do not need to specify an object for it to refer to, nor even specify a synonymous word or phrase; we need only show, by whatever means, how to translate all the whole sentences in which the term is to be used. Hume's and Johnson's desperate measure of identifying bodies with impressions ceased to be the only conceivable way of making sense of talk of bodies, even granted that impressions were the only reality. One could undertake to explain talk of bodies in terms of talk of impressions by translating one's whole sentences about bodies into whole sentences about impressions, without equating the bodies themselves to anything at all.

This idea of contextual definition, or recognition of the sentence as the primary vehicle of meaning, was indispensable to the ensuing developments in the foundations of mathematics. It was explicit in Frege, and it attained its full flower in Russell's doctrine of singular descriptions as incomplete symbols.

Contextual definition was one of two resorts that could be expected to have a liberating effect upon the conceptual side of the epistemology of natural knowledge. The other is resort to the resources of set theory as auxiliary concepts. The epistemologist who is willing to eke out his austere ontology of sense impressions with these set-theoretic auxiliaries is suddenly rich: he has not just his impressions to play with, but sets of them, and sets of sets, and so on up. Constructions in the foundations of mathematics have shown that such set-theoretic aids are a powerful addition; after all, the entire glossary of concepts of classical mathematics is constructible from them. Thus equipped, our epistemologist may not need either to identify bodies with impressions or to settle for contextual definition; he may hope to find in some subtle construction of sets upon sets of sense impressions a category of objects enjoying just the formula properties that he wants for bodies.

The two resorts are very unequal in epistemological status. Contextual definition is unassailable. Sentences that have been given meaning as wholes are undeniably meaningful, and the use they make of their component terms is therefore meaningful, regardless of whether any translations are offered for those terms in isolation. Surely Hume and A. B. Johnson would have used contextual definition with pleasure if they had thought of it. Recourse to sets, on the other hand, is a drastic ontological move, a retreat from the austere ontology of impressions. There are philosophers who would rather settle for bodies outright than accept all these sets, which amount, after all, to the whole abstract ontology of mathematics.

This issue has not always been clear, however, owing to deceptive hints of continuity between elementary logic and set theory. This is why mathematics was once believed to reduce to logic, that is, to an innocent and unquestionable logic, and to inherit these qualities. And this is probably why Russell was content to resort to sets as well as to contextual definition when in *Our Knowledge of the External World* and elsewhere he addressed himself to the epistemology of natural knowledge, on its conceptual side.

To account for the external world as a logical construct of sense data—such, in Russell's terms, was the program. It was Carnap, in his *Der logische Aufbau der Welt* of 1928, who came nearest to executing it.

This was the conceptual side of epistemology; what of the doctrinal? There the Humean predicament remained unaltered. Carnap's constructions, if carried successfully to completion, would have enable us to translate all sentences about the world into terms of sense data, or observation, plus logic and set theory. But the mere fact that a sentence is *couched* in terms of observation, logic, and set theory does not mean that it can be *proved* from observation sentences by logic and set theory. The most modest of generalizations about observable traits will cover more cases than its utterer can have had occasion actually to observe. The hopelessness of grounding natural science upon immediate experience in a firmly logical way was acknowledged. The Cartesian quest for certainty had been the remote motivation of epistemology, both on its conceptual and its doctrinal side; but that quest was seen as a lost cause. To endow the truths of nature with the full authority of immediate experience was as forlorn a hope as hoping to endow the truths of mathematics with the potential obviousness of elementary logic.

What then could have motivated Carnap's heroic efforts on the conceptual side of epistemology, when hope of certainty on the doctrinal side was abandoned? There were two good reasons still. One was that such constructions could be expected to elicit and clarify the sensory evidence for science, even if the inferential steps between sensory evidence and scientific doctrine must fall short of certainty. The other reason was that such constructions would deepen our understanding of our discourse about the world, even apart from questions of evidence; it would make all cognitive discourse as clear as observation terms and logic and, I must regretfully add, set theory.

It was sad for epistemologists, Hume and others, to have to acquiesce in the impossibility of strictly deriving the science of the external world from sensory evidence. Two cardinal tenets of empiricism remained unassailable, however, and so remain to this day. One is that whatever evidence there *is* for science *is* sensory evidence. The other, to which I shall recur, is that all inculcation of meanings of words must rest ultimately on sensory evidence. Hence the continuing attractiveness of the idea of a *logischer Aufbau* in which the sensory content of discourse would stand forth explicitly.

If Carnap had successfully carried such a construction through, how could he have told whether it was the right one? The question would have had no point. He was seeking what he called a *rational reconstruction*. Any construction of physicalistic discourse in terms of sense experience, logic, and set theory would have been seen as satisfactory if it made the physicalistic discourse come out right. If there is one way there are many, but any would be a great achievement.

But why all this creative reconstruction, all this make-believe? The stimulation of his sensory receptors is all the evidence anybody has had to go on, ultimately, in arriving at his picture of the world. Why not just see how this construction really proceeds? Why not settle for psychology? Such a surrender of the epistemological burden to psychology is a move that was disallowed in earlier times as circular reasoning. If the epistemologist's goal is validation of the grounds of empirical science, he defeats his purpose by using psychology or other empirical science in the validation. However, such scruples agains circularity have little point once we have stopped dreaming of deducing science from observations. If we are out simply to understand the link between observation and science, we are well advised to use any available information, including that provided by the very science whose link with observation we are seeking to understand.

But there remains a different reason, unconnected with fears of circularity, for still favoring creative reconstruction. We should like to be able to *translate* science into logic and observation terms and set theory. This would be a great epistemological achievement, for it would show all the rest of the concepts of science to be theoretically superfluous. It would legitimize them—to whatever degree the concepts of set theory, logic, and observation are themselves legitimate—by showing that everything done with the one apparatus could in principle be done with the other. If psychology itself could deliver a truly translational reduction of this kind, we should welcome it; but certainly it cannot, for certainly we did not grow up learning definitions of physicalistic language in terms of a prior language of set theory, logic, and observation. Here, then, would be good reason for persisting in a rational reconstruction: we want to establish the essential innocence of physical concepts, by showing them to be theoretically dispensable.

The fact is, though, that the construction which Carnap outlined in *Der logische Aufbau Der Welt* does not give translational reduction either. It would not even if the outline were filled in. The crucial point comes where Carnap is explaining how to assign sense qualities to positions in physical space and time. These assignments are to be made in such a way as to fulfill, as well as possible, certain desiderata which he states, and with growth of experience the assignments are to be revised to suit. This plan, however illuminating, does not offer any key to *translating* the sentences of science into terms of observation, logic, and set theory.

We must despair of any such reduction. Carnap had despaired of it by 1936, when, in "Testability and meaning,"[2] he introduced so-called *reduction forms* of a type weaker than definition. Definitions had shown always how to translate sentences into equivalent sentences. Contextual definition of a term showed how to translate sentences containing the term into equivalent sentences lacking the term. Reduction forms of Carnap's liberalized kind, on the other hand, do not in general give equivalences; they give implications. They explain a new term, if only partially, by specifying some sentences which are implied by sentences containing the term, and other sentences which imply sentences containing the term.

It is tempting to suppose that the countenancing of reduction forms in this liberal sense is just one further step of liberalization comparable to the earlier one, taken by Bentham, of countenancing contextual definition. The former and sterner kind of rational reconstruction might have been represented as a fictitious history in which we imagined our ancestors introducing the terms of physicalistic discourse on a phenomenalistic and set-theoretic basis by a succession of contextual definitions. The new and more liberal kind of rational reconstruction is a fictitious history in which we imagine our ancestors introducing those terms by a succession rather of reduction forms of the weaker sort.

This, however, is a wrong comparison. The fact is rather that the former and sterner kind of rational reconstruction, where definition reigned, embodied no fictitious history at all. It was nothing more nor less than a set of directions—or would have been, if successful—for accomplishing everything in terms of phenomena and set theory that we now accomplish in terms of bodies. It would have been a true reduction by translation, a legitimation by elimination. *Definire est eliminare.* Rational reconstruction by Carnap's later and looser reduction forms does none of this.

To relax the demand for definition, and settle for a kind of reduction that does not eliminate, is to renounce the last remaining advantage that we supposed rational reconstruction to have over straight psychology; namely, the advantage of translational reduction. If all we hope for is a reconstruction that links science to experience in explicit ways short of translation, then it would seem more sensible to settle for psychology. Better to discover how science is in fact developed and learned than to fabricate a fictitious structure to a similar effect.

The empiricist made one major concession when he despaired of deducing the truths of nature from sensory evidence. In despairing now even of translating those truths into terms of observation and logico-mathematical auxiliaries, he makes another major concession. For suppose we hold, with the old empiricist Peirce, that the very meaning of a statement consists in the difference its truth would make to possible experience. Might we not formulate, in a chapter-length sentence in observational language, all the difference that the truth of a given statement might make to experience, and might we not then take all this as the translation? Even if the difference that the truth of the statement would make to experience ramifies indefinitely, we might still hope to embrace it all in the logical implications of our chapter-length formulation, just as we can axiomatize an infinity of theorems. In giving up hope of such translation, then, the empiricist is conceding that the empirical meanings of typical statements about the external world are inaccessible and ineffable.

How is this inaccessibility to be explained? Simply on the ground that the experiential implications of a typical statement about bodies are too complex for finite axiomatization, however lengthy? No; I have a different explanation. It is that the typical statement about bodies has no fund of experiential implications it can call its own. A substantial mass of theory, taken together, will commonly have experiential implications; this is how we make verifiable predictions. We may not be able to explain why we arrive at theories which make successful predictions, but we do arrive at such theories.

Sometimes also an experience implied by a theory fails to come off; and then, ideally, we declare the theory false. But the failure falsifies only a block of theory as a whole, a conjunction of many statements. The failure shows that one or more of those statements is false, but it does not show which. The predicted experiences, true and false, are not implied by any one of the component statements of the theory rather than another. The component statements simply do not have empirical meanings, by Peirce's standard; but a sufficiently inclusive portion of theory does. If we can aspire to a sort of *logischer Aufbau der Welt* at all, it must be to one in which the texts slated for translation into observational and logico-mathematical terms are mostly broad theories taken as wholes, rather than just terms or short sentences. The translation of a theory would be a ponderous axiomatization of all the experiential difference that the truth of the theory would make. It would be a queer translation, for it would translate the whole but none of the parts. We might better speak in such a case not of translation but simply of observational evidence for theories; and we may, following Peirce, still fairly call this the empirical meaning of the theories.

These considerations raise a philosophical question even about ordinary unphilosophical translation, such as from English into Arunta or Chinese. For, if the English sentences of a theory have their meaning only together as a body, then we can justify their translation into Arunta only together as a body. There will be no justification for pairing off the component English sentences with component Arunta sentences, except as these correlations make the translation of the theory as a whole come out right. Any translations of the English sentences into Arunta sentences will be as correct as any other, so long as the net empirical implications of the theory as a whole are preserved in translation. But it is to be expected that many different ways of translating the component sentences, essentially different individually, would deliver the same empirical implications for the theory as a whole; deviations in the translation of one component sentence could be compensated for in the translation of another component sentence. Insofar, there can be no ground for saying which of two glaringly unlike translations of individual sentences is right.[3]

For an uncritical mentalist, no such indeterminacy threatens. Every term and every sentence is a label attached to an idea, simple or complex, which is stored in the mind. When on the other hand we take a verification theory of meaning seriously, the indeterminacy would appear to be inescapable. The Vienna Circle espoused a verification theory of meaning but did not take it seriously enough. If we recognize with Peirce that the meaning of a sentence turns purely on what would count as evidence for its truth, and if we recognize with Duhem that theoretical sentences have their evidence not as single sentences but only as larger blocks of theory, then the indeterminacy of translation of theoretical sentences is the natural conclusion. And most sentences, apart from observation sentences, are theoretical. This conclusion, conversely, once it is embraced, seals the fate of any general notion of propositional meaning or, for that matter, state of affairs.

Should the unwelcomeness of the conclusion persuade us to abandon the verification theory of meaning? Certainly not. The sort of meaning that is basic to translation, and to the learning of one's own language, is necessarily empirical meaning and nothing more. A child learns his first words and sentences by hearing and using them in the presence of appropriate stimuli. These must be external stimuli, for they must act both on the child and on the speaker from whom he is learning.[4] Language is socially inculcated and controlled; the inculcation and control turn strictly on the keying of sentences to shared stimulation. Internal factors may vary *ad libitum* without prejudice to communication as long as the keying of language to external stimuli is undisturbed. Surely one has no choice but to be an empiricist so far as one's theory of linguistic meaning is concerned.

What I have said of infant learning applies equally to the linguist's learning of a new language in the field. If the linguist does not lean on related languages for which there are previously accepted translation practices, then obviously he has no data but the concomitances of native utterance and observable stimulus situation. No wonder there is indeterminacy of translation—for of course only a small fraction of our utterances report concurrent external stimulation. Granted, the linguist will end up with unequivocal translations of everything; but only by making many arbitrary choices—arbitrary even though unconscious—along the way. Arbitrary? By this I mean that different choices could still have made everything come out right that is susceptible in principle to any kind of check.

Let me link up, in a different order, some of the points I have made. The crucial consideration behind my argument for the indeterminacy of translation was that a statement about the world does not always or usually have a separable fund of empirical consequences that it can call its own. That consideration served also to account for the impossibility of an epistemological reduction of the sort where every sentence is equated to a sentence in observational and logico-mathematical terms. And the impossibility of that sort of epistemological reduction dissipated the last advantage that rational reconstruction seemed to have over psychology.

Philosophers have rightly despaired of translating everything into observational and logico-mathematical terms. They have despaired of this even when they have not recognized, as the reason for this irreducibility, that the statements largely do not have their private bundles of empirical consequences. And some philosophers have seen in this irreducibility the bankruptcy of epistemology. Carnap and the other logical positivists of the Vienna Circle had already pressed the term "metaphysics" into pejorative use, as connoting meaninglessness; and the term "epistemology" was next. Wittgenstein and his followers, mainly at Oxford, found a residual philosophical vocation in therapy: in curing philosophers of the delusion that there were epistemological problems.

But I think that at this point it may be more useful to say rather that epistemology still goes on, though in a new setting and a clarified status. Epistemology, or something like it, simply falls into place as a chapter of psychology and hence of natural science. It studies a natural phenomenon, viz., a physical human subject. This human subject is accorded a certain experimentally controlled input—certain patterns of irradiation in assorted frequencies, for instance—and in the fullness of time the subject delivers as output a description of the three-dimensional external world and its history. The relation between the meager input and the torrential output is a relation that we are prompted to study for somewhat the same reasons that always prompted epistemology; namely, in order to see how evidence relates to theory, and in what ways one's theory of nature transcends any available evidence.

Such a study could still include, even, something like the old rational reconstruction, to whatever degree such reconstruction is practicable; for imaginative constructions can afford hints of actual psychological processes, in much the way that mechanical simulations can. But a conspicuous difference between old epistemology and the epistemological enterprise in this new psychological setting is that we can now make free use of empirical psychology.

The old epistemology aspired to contain, in a sense, natural science; it would construct it somehow from sense data. Epistemology in its new setting, conversely, is contained in natural science, as a chapter of psychology. But the old containment remains valid too, in its way. We are studying how the human subject of our study posits bodies and projects his physics from his data, and we appreciate that our position in the world is just like his. Our very epistemological enterprise, therefore, and the psychology wherein it is a component chapter, and the whole of natural science wherein psychology is a component book—all this is our own construction or projection from stimulations like those we were meting out to our epistemological subject. There is thus reciprocal containment, though containment in different senses: epistemology in natural science and natural science in epistemology.

This interplay is reminiscent again of the old threat of circularity, but it is all right now that we have stopped dreaming of deducing science from sense data. We are after an understanding of science as an institution or process in the world, and we do not intend that understanding to be any better than the science which is its object. This attitude is indeed one that Neurath was already urging in Vienna Circle days, with his parable of the mariner who has to rebuild his boat while staying afloat in it.

One effect of seeing epistemology in a psychological setting is that it resolves a stubborn old enigma of epistemological priority. Our retinas are irradiated in two dimensions, yet we see things as three-dimensional without conscious inference. Which is to count as observation—the unconscious two-dimensional reception or the conscious three-dimensional apprehension. In the old epistemological context the conscious form had priority, for we were out to justify our knowledge of the external world by rational reconstruction, and that demands awareness. Awareness ceased to be demanded when we gave up trying to justify our knowledge of the external world by rational reconstruction. What to count as observation now can be settled in terms of the stimulation of sensory receptors, let consciousness fall where it may.

The Gestalt psychologists' challenge to sensory atomism, which seemed so relevant to epistemology forty years ago, is likewise deactivated. Regardless of whether sensory atoms or Gestalten are what favor the forefront of our consciousness, it is simply the stimulations of our sensory receptors that are best looked upon as the input to our cognitive mechanism. Old paradoxes about unconscious data and inference, old problems about chains of inference that would have to be completed too quickly—these no longer matter.

In the old anti-psychologistic days the question of epistemological priority was moot. What is epistemologically prior to what? Are Gestalten prior to sensory atoms because they are noticed, or should we favor sensory atoms on some more subtle ground? Now that we are permitted to appeal to physical stimulation, the problem dissolves; A is epistemologically prior to B if A is causally nearer than B to the sensory receptors. Or, what is in some ways better, just talk explicitly in terms of causal proximity to sensory receptors and drop the talk of epistemological priority.

Around 1932 there was debate in the Vienna Circle over what to count as observation sentences, or *Protokollsätze*.[5] One position was

that they had the form of reports of sense impressions. Another
was that they were statements of an elementary sort about the external world, e.g., "A red cube is standing on the table." Another,
Neurath's, was that they had the form of reports of relations between percipients and external things: "Otto now sees a red cube
on the table." The worst of it was that there seemed to be no objective way of settling the matter: no way of making real sense of the
question.

Let us now try to view the matter unreservedly in the context of
the external world. Vaguely speaking, what we want of observation
sentences is that they be the ones in closest causal proximity to the
sensory receptors. But how is such proximity to be gauged? The idea
may be rephrased this way: observation sentences are sentences
which, as we learn language, are most strongly conditioned to concurrent sensory stimulation rather than to stored collateral information. Thus let us imagine a sentence queried for our verdict as to
whether it is true or false; queried for our assent or dissent. Then the
sentence is an observation sentence if our verdict depends only on
the sensory stimulation present at the time.

But a verdict cannot depend on present stimulation to the exclusion
of stored information. The very fact of our having learned the language evinces much storing of information, and of information without which we should be in no position to give verdicts on sentences
however observational. Evidently then we must relax our definition
of observation sentence to read thus: a sentence is an observation
sentence if all verdicts on it depend on present sensory stimulation
and on no stored information beyond what goes into understanding
the sentence.

This formulation raises another problem: how are we to distinguish
between information that goes into understanding a sentence and information that goes beyond? This is the problem of distinguishing
between analytic truth, which issues from the mere meanings of
words, and synthetic truth, which depends on more than meanings.
Now I have long maintained that this distinction is illusory. There is
one step toward such a distinction, however, which does make sense:
a sentence that is true by mere meanings of words should be expected, at least if it is simple, to be subscribed to by all fluent speakers
in the community. Perhaps the controversial notion of analyticity can
be dispensed with, in our definition of observation sentence, in favor
of this straightforward attribute of community-wide acceptance.

This attribute is of course no explication of analyticity. The community would agree that there have been black dogs, yet none who talk of analyticity would call this analytic. My rejection of the analyticity notion just means drawing no line between what goes into the mere understanding of the sentences of a language and what else the community sees eye-to-eye on. I doubt that an objective distinction can be made between meaning and such collateral information as is community-wide.

Turning back then to our task of defining observation sentences, we get this: an observation sentence is one on which all speakers of the language give the same verdict when given the same concurrent stimulation. To put the point negatively, an observation sentence is one that is not sensitive to differences in past experience within the speech community.

This formulation accords perfectly with the traditional role of the observation sentence as the court of appeal of scientific theories. For by our definition the observation sentences are the sentences on which all members of the community will agree under uniform stimulation. And what is the criterion of membership in the same community? Simply general fluency of dialogue. This criterion admits of degrees, and indeed we may usefully take the community more narrowly for some studies than for others. What count as observation sentences for a community of specialists would not always so count for a larger community.

There is generally no subjectivity in the phrasing of observation sentences, as we are now conceiving them; they will usually be about bodies. Since the distinguishing trait of an observation sentence is intersubjective agreement under agreeing stimulation, a corporeal subject matter is likelier than not.

The old tendency to associate observation sentences with a subjective sensory subject matter is rather an irony when we reflect that observation sentences are also meant to be the intersubjective tribunal of scientific hypotheses. The old tendency was due to the drive to base science on something firmer and prior in the subject's experience; but we dropped that project.

The dislodging of epistemology from its old status of first philosophy loosed a wave, we saw, of epistemological nihilism. This mood is reflected somewhat in the tendency of Polányi, Kuhn, and the late Russell Hanson to belittle the role of evidence and to accentuate cultural relativism. Hanson ventured even to discredit the idea of observation, arguing that so-called observations vary from observer to observer with the amount of knowledge that the observers bring with them. The veteran physicist looks at some apparatus and sees an x-ray tube. The neophyte, looking at the same place, observes rather "a glass metal instrument replete with wires, reflectors, screws, lamps, and pushbuttons."[6] One man's observation is another man's closed book or flight of fancy. The notion of observation as the impartial and objective source of evidence for science is bankrupt. Now my answer to the x-ray example was already hinted a little while back: what counts as an observation sentence varies with the width of community considered. But we can also always get an absolute standard by taking in all speakers of the language, or most.[7] It is ironical that philosophers, finding the old epistemology untenable as a whole, should react by repudiating a part which has only now moved into clear focus.

Clarification of the notion of observation sentence is a good thing, for the notion is fundamental in two connections. These two correspond to the duality that I remarked upon early in this lecture: the duality between concept and doctrine, between knowing what a sentence means and knowing whether it is true. The observation sentence is basic to both enterprises. Its relation to doctrine, to our knowledge of what is true, is very much the traditional one: observation sentences are the repository of evidence for scientific hypotheses. Its relation to meaning is fundamental too, since observation sentences are the ones we are in a position to learn to understand first, both as children and as field linguists. For observation sentences are precisely the ones that we can correlate with observable circumstances of the occasion of utterance or assent, independently of variations in the past histories of individual informants. They afford the only entry to a language.

The observation sentence is the cornerstone of semantics. For it is, as we just saw, fundamental to the learning of meaning. Also, it is where meaning is firmest. Sentences higher up in theories have no empirical consequences they can call their own; they confront the tribunal of sensory evidence only in more or less inclusive aggregates. The observation sentence, situated at the sensory periphery of the body scientific, is the minimal verifiable aggregate; it has an empirical content all its own and wears it on its sleeve.

The predicament of the indeterminacy of translation has little bearing on observation sentences. The equating of an observation sentence of our language to an observation sentence of another language is mostly a matter of empirical generalization; it is a matter of identity between the range of stimulations that would prompt assent to the one sentence and the range of stimulations that would prompt assent to the other.[8]

It is no shock to the preconceptions of old Vienna to say that epistemology now becomes semantics. For epistemology remains centered as always on evidence, and meaning remains centered as always on verification; and evidence is verification. What is likelier to shock preconceptions is that meaning, once we get beyond observation sentences, ceases in general to have any clear applicability to single sentences; also that epistemology merges with psychology, as well as with linguistics.

This rubbing out of boundaries could contribute to progress, it seems to me, in philosophically interesting inquiries of a scientific nature. One possible area is perceptual norms. Consider, to begin with, the linguistic phenomenon of phonemes. We form the habit, in hearing the myriad variations of spoken sounds, of treating each as an approximation to one or another of a limited number of norms— around thirty altogether—constituting so to speak a spoken alphabet. All speech in our language can be treated in practice as sequences of just those thirty elements, thus rectifying small deviations. Now outside the realm of language also there is probably only a rather limited alphabet of perceptual norms altogether, toward which we tend unconsciously to rectify all perceptions. These, if experimentally identified, could be taken as epistemological building blocks, the working elements of experience. They might prove in part to be culturally variable, as phonemes are, and in part universal.

Again there is the area that the psychologist Donald T. Campbell calls evolutionary epistemology.[9] In this area there is work by Hüseyin Yilmaz, who shows how some structural traits of color perception could have been predicted from survival value.[10] And a more emphatically epistemological topic that evolution helps to clarify is induction, now that we are allowing epistemology the resources of natural science.[11]

Notes

1. Johnson 1947 [598].

2. Carnap 1936 [688].

3. See Quine 1969 [101], pp. 2 ff.

4. See Quine 1969 [101], p. 28.

5. Carnap 1932 [687]; Neurath 1932 [794].

6. N. R. Hanson 1966 [741].

7. This qualification allows for occasional deviants such as the insane or the blind. Alternatively, such cases might be excluded by adjusting the level of fluency of dialogue whereby we define sameness of language. (For prompting this note and influencing the development of this paper also in more substantial ways, I am indebted to Burton Dreben.)

8. Cf. Quine 1960 [100], pp. 31–46, 68.

9. D. T. Campbell 1959 [186].

10. Huseyin Yilmaz 1962 [855], 1967 [856].

11. See Quine 1969 [101].

2

What Is "Naturalized Epistemology"?

Jaegwon Kim

Epistemology as a Normative Inquiry

Descartes's epistemological inquiry in the *Meditations* begins with this question: What propositions are worthy of belief? In the *First Meditation* Descartes canvasses beliefs of various kinds he had formerly held as true and finds himself forced to conclude that he ought to reject them, that he ought not to accept them as true. We can view Cartesian epistemology as consisting of the following two projects: to identify the criteria by which we ought to regulate acceptance and rejection of beliefs, and to determine what we may be said to know according to those criteria. Descartes' epistemological agenda has been the agenda of Western epistemology to this day. The twin problems of identifying criteria of justified belief and coming to terms with the skeptical challenge to the possibility of knowledge have defined the central tasks of theory of knowledge since Descartes. This was as true of the empiricists, of Locke and Hume and Mill, as of those who more closely followed Descartes in the rationalist path.[1]

It is no wonder then that modern epistemology has been dominated by a single concept, that of *justification*, and two fundamental questions involving it: What conditions must a belief meet if we are justified in accepting it as true? and What beliefs are we in fact justified in accepting? Note that the first question does not ask for an "analysis" or "meaning" of the term "justified belief." And it is generally assumed, even if not always explicitly stated, that not just any statement of a necessary and sufficient condition for a belief to be justified will do. The implicit requirement has been that the stated

This chapter appeared in *Philosophical Perspectives, 2, Epistemology, 1988* edited by James E. Tomberlin (copyright by Ridgeview Publishing Co., Atascadero, CA). Reprinted by permission of Ridgeview Publishing Company.

conditions must constitute "criteria" of justified belief, and for this it is necessary that the conditions be stated *without the use of epistemic terms*. Thus, formulating conditions of justified belief in such terms as "adequate evidence," "sufficient ground," "good reason," "beyond a reasonable doubt," and so on, would be merely to issue a promissory note redeemable only when these epistemic terms are themselves explained in a way that accords with the requirement.[2]

This requirement, while it points in the right direction, does not go far enough. What is crucial is this: *the criteria of justified belief must be formulated on the basis of descriptive or naturalistic terms alone, without the use of any evaluative or normative ones, whether epistemic or of another kind.*[3] Thus, an analysis of justified belief that makes use of such terms as "intellectual requirement"[4] and "having a right to be sure"[5] would not satisfy this generalized condition; although such an analysis can be informative and enlightening about the inter-relationships of these normative concepts, it will not, on the present conception, count as a statement of *criteria* of justified belief, unless of course these terms are themselves provided with nonnormative criteria. What is problematic, therefore, about the use of epistemic terms in stating criteria of justified belief is not its possible circularity in the usual sense; rather it is the fact that these epistemic terms are themselves essentially normative. We shall later discuss the rationale of this strengthened requirement.

As many philosophers have observed,[6] the two questions we have set forth, one about the criteria of justified belief and the other about what we can be said to know according to those criteria, constrain each other. Although some philosophers have been willing to swallow skepticism just because what we regard as correct criteria of justified belief are seen to lead inexorably to the conclusion that none, or very few, of our beliefs are justified, the usual presumption is that our answer to the first question should leave our epistemic situation largely unchanged. That is to say, it is expected to turn out that according to the criteria of justified belief we come to accept, we know, or are justified in believing, pretty much what we reflectively think we know or are entitled to believe.

Whatever the exact history, it is evident that the concept of justification has come to take center stage in our reflections on the nature of knowledge. And apart from history, there is a simple reason for our preoccupation with justification: it is the only specifically epistemic component in the classic tripartite conception of knowledge. Neither belief nor truth is a specifically epistemic notion: belief is a psychological concept and truth a semantical-metaphysical one. These concepts may have an implicit epistemological dimension, but if they do, it is likely to be through their involvement with essentially normative epistemic notions like justification, evidence, and rationality. Moreover, justification is what makes knowledge itself a normative concept. On surface at least, neither truth nor belief is normative or evaluative (I shall argue below, though, that belief does have an essential normative dimension). But justification manifestly is normative. If a belief is justified for us, then it is *permissible* and *reasonable*, from the epistemic point of view, for us to hold it, and it would be *epistemically irresponsible* to hold beliefs that contradict it. If we consider believing or accepting a proposition to be an "action" in an appropriate sense, belief justification would then be a special case of justification of action, which in its broadest terms is the central concern of normative ethics. Just as it is the business of normative ethics to delineate the conditions under which acts and decisions are justified from the moral point of view, so it is the business of epistemology to identify and analyze the conditions under which beliefs, and perhaps other propositional attitudes, are justified from the epistemological point of view. It probably is only an historical accident that we standardly speak of "normative ethics" but not of "normative epistemology." Epistemology is a normative discipline as much as, and in the same sense as, normative ethics.

We can summarize our discussion thus far in the following points: that justification is a central concept of our epistemological tradition, that justification, as it is understood in this tradition, is a normative concept, and in consequence that epistemology itself is a normative inquiry whose principal aim is a systematic study of the conditions of justified belief. I take it that these points are uncontroversial, although of course there could be disagreement about the details—for example, about what it means to say a concept or theory is "normative" or "evaluative."

The Foundationalist Strategy

In order to identify the target of the naturalistic critique—in particular, Quine's—it will be useful to take a brief look at the classic response to the epistemological program set forth by Descartes. Descartes's approach to the problem of justification is a familiar story, at least as the textbook tells it: it takes the form of what is now commonly called "foundationalism." The foundationalist strategy is to divide the task of explaining justification into two stages: first, to identify a set of beliefs that are "directly" justified in that they are justified without deriving their justified status from that of any other belief, and then to explain how other beliefs may be "indirectly" or "inferentially" justified by standing in an appropriate relation to those already justified. Directly justified beliefs, or "basic beliefs," are to constitute the foundation upon which the superstructure of "nonbasic" or "derived" beliefs is to rest. What beliefs then are directly justified, according to Descartes? Subtleties aside, he claimed that beliefs about our own present conscious states are among them. In what does their justification consist? What is it about these beliefs that make them directly justified? Somewhat simplistically again, Descartes' answer is that they are justified because they are *indubitable*, that the attentive and reflective mind *cannot but assent* to them. How are nonbasic beliefs justified? By "deduction"—that is, by a series of inferential steps, or "intuitions," each of which is indubitable. If, therefore, we take Cartesian indubitability as a psychological notion, Descartes's epistemological theory can be said to meet the desideratum of providing nonepistemic, naturalistic criteria of justified belief.

Descartes's foundationalist program was inherited, in its essential outlines, by the empiricists. In particular, his "mentalism," that beliefs about one's own current mental state are epistemologically basic, went essentially unchallenged by the empiricists and positivists, until this century. Epistemologists have differed from one another chiefly in regard to two questions: first, what else belonged in our corpus of basic beliefs, and second, how the derivation of the nonbasic part of our knowledge was to proceed. Even the Logical Positivists were, by and large, foundationalists, although some of them came to renounce Cartesian mentalism in favor of a "physicalistic basis."[7] In fact, the Positivists were foundationalists twice over: for them "observation," whether phenomenological or physical, served not only as the foundation of knowledge but as the foundation of all "cognitive meaning"—that is, as both an epistemological and a semantic foundation.

Quine's Arguments

It has become customary for epistemologists who profess allegiance to a "naturalistic" conception of knowledge to pay homage to Quine as the chief contemporary provenance of their inspiration—especially to his influential paper "Epistemology Naturalized."[8] Quine's principal argument in this paper against traditional epistemology is based on the claim that the Cartesian foundationalist program has failed—that the Cartesian "quest for certainty" is "a lost cause." While this claim about the hopelessness of the Cartesian "quest for certainty" is nothing new, using it to discredit the very conception of normative epistemology is new, something that any serious student of epistemology must contend with.

Quine divides the classic epistemological program into two parts: *conceptual reduction* whereby physical terms, including those of theoretical science, are reduced, via definition, to terms referring to phenomenal features of sensory experience, and *doctrinal reduction* whereby truths about the physical world are appropriately obtained from truths about sensory experience. The "appropriateness" just alluded to refers to the requirement that the favored epistemic status ("certainty" for classic epistemologists, according to Quine) of our basic beliefs be transferred, essentially undiminished, to derived beliefs, a necessary requirement if the derivational process is to yield knowledge from knowledge. What derivational methods have this property of preserving epistemic status? Perhaps there are none, given our proneness to err in framing derivations as in anything else, not to mention the possibility of lapses of attention and memory in following lengthy proofs. But logical deduction comes as close to being one as any; it can at least be relied on to transmit truth, if not epistemic status. It could perhaps be argued that no method can preserve certainty unless it preserves (or is known to preserve) truth; and if this is so, logical deduction is the only method worth considering. I do not know whether this was the attitude of most classic epistemologists; but Quine assumes that if deduction doesn't fill their bill, nothing will.

Quine sees the project of conceptual reduction as culminating in Carnap's *Der Logische Aufbau der Welt*. As Quine sees it, Carnap "came nearest to executing" the conceptual half of the classic epistemological project. But coming close is not good enough. Because of the holistic manner in which empirical meaning is generated by experience, no reduction of the sort Carnap and others so eagerly sought could in principle be completed. For definitional reduction requires point-to-point meaning relations[9] between physical terms and phenomenal terms, something that Quine's holism tells us cannot be had. The second half of the program, doctrinal reduction, is in no better shape; in fact, it was the one to stumble first, for, according to Quine, its impossibility was decisively demonstrated long before the *Aufbau*, by Hume in his celebrated discussion of induction. The "Humean predicament" shows that theory cannot be logically deduced from observation; there simply is no way of deriving theory from observation that will transmit the latter's epistemic status intact to the former.

I don't think anyone wants to disagree with Quine in these claims. It is not possible to "validate" science on the basis of sensory experience, if "validation" means justification through logical deduction. Quine of course does not deny that our theories depend on observation for evidential support; he has said that sensory evidence is the only evidence there is. To be sure, Quine's argument against the possibility of conceptual reduction has a new twist: the application of his "holism." But his conclusion is no surprise; "translational phenomenalism" has been moribund for many years.[10] And, as Quine himself notes, his argument against the doctrinal reduction, the "quest for certainty," is only a restatement of Hume's "skeptical" conclusions concerning induction: induction after all is not deduction. Most of us are inclined, I think, to view the situation Quine describes with no great alarm, and I rather doubt that these conclusions of Quine's came as news to most epistemologists when "Epistemology Naturalized" was first published. We are tempted to respond: of course we can't define physical concepts in terms of sense-data; of course observation "underdetermines" theory. That is why observation is observation and not theory.

So it is agreed on all hands that the classical epistemological project, conceived as one of deductively validating physical knowledge from indubitable sensory data, cannot succeed. But what is the moral of this failure? What should be its philosophical lesson to us? Having noted the failure of the Cartesian program, Quine goes on:[11]

The stimulation of his sensory receptors is all the evidence anybody has had to go on, ultimately, in arriving at his picture of the world. Why not just see how this construction really proceeds? Why not settle for psychology? Such a surrender of the epistemological burden to psychology is a move that was disallowed in earlier times as circular reasoning. If the epistemologist's goal is validation of the grounds of empirical science, he defeats his purpose by using psychology or other empirical science in the validation. However, such scruples against circularity have little point once we have stopped dreaming of deducing science from observation. If we are out simply to understand the link between observation and science, we are well advised to use any available information, including that provided by the very science whose link with observation we are seeking to understand.

And Quine has the following to say about the failure of Carnap's reductive program in the *Aufbau:*[12]

To relax the demand for definition, and settle for a kind of reduction that does not eliminate, is to renounce the last remaining advantage that we supposed rational reconstruction to have over straight psychology; namely, the advantage of translational reduction. If all we hope for is a reconstruction that links science to experience in explicit ways short of translation, then it would seem more sensible to settle for psychology. Better to discover how science is in fact developed and learned than to fabricate a fictitious structure to a similar effect.

If a task is entirely hopeless, if we know it cannot be executed, no doubt it is rational to abandon it; we would be better off doing something else that has some hope of success. We can agree with Quine that the "validation"—that is, logical deduction—of science on the basis of observation cannot be had; so it is rational to abandon this particular epistemological program, if indeed it ever was a program that anyone seriously undertook. But Quine's recommendations go further. In particular, there are two aspects of Quine's proposals that are of special interest to us: first, he is not only advising us to quit the program of "validating science," but urging us to take up another specific project, an empirical psychological study of our cognitive processes; second, he is also claiming that this new program replaces the old, that both programs are part of something appropriately called "epistemology." Naturalized epistemology is to be a kind of epistemology after all, a "successor subject"[13] to classical epistemology.

How should we react to Quine's urgings? What should be our response? The Cartesian project of validating science starting from the indubitable foundation of first-person psychological reports (perhaps with the help of certain indubitable first principles) is not the whole of classical epistemology—or so it would seem at first blush. In our characterization of classical epistemology, the Cartesian program was seen as one possible response to the problem of epistemic justification, the two-part project of identifying the criteria of epistemic justification and determining what beliefs are in fact justified according to those criteria. In urging "naturalized epistemology" on us, Quine is not suggesting that we give up the Cartesian foundationalist solution and explore others within the same framework[14]—perhaps, to adopt some sort of "coherentist" strategy, or to require of our basic beliefs only some degree of "initial credibility" rather than Cartesian certainty, or to permit some sort of probabilistic derivation in addition to deductive derivation of nonbasic knowledge, or to consider the use of special rules of evidence, like Chisholm's "principles of evidence,"[15] or to give up the search for a derivational process that transmits undiminished certainty in favor of one that can transmit diminished but still useful degrees of justification. Quine's proposal is more radical than that. He is asking us to set aside the entire framework of justification-centered epistemology. That is what is new in Quine's proposals. Quine is asking us to put in its place a purely descriptive, causal-nomological science of human cognition.[16]

How should we characterize in general terms the difference between traditional epistemological programs, such as foundationalism and coherence theory, on the one hand and Quine's program of naturalized epistemology on the other? Quine's stress is on the *factual* and *descriptive* character of his program; he says, "Why not see how [the construction of theory from observation] *actually proceeds?* Why not settle for psychology?";[17] again, "Better to *discover how science is in fact developed and learned than* . . ."[18] We are given to understand that in contrast traditional epistemology is not a descriptive, factual inquiry. Rather, it is an attempt at a "validation" or "rational reconstruction" of science. Validation, according to Quine, proceeds via deduction, and rational reconstruction via definition. However, their *point* is justificatory—that is, to rationalize our sundry knowledge claims. So Quine is asking us to set aside what is "rational" in rational reconstruction.

Thus, it is normativity that Quine is asking us to repudiate. Although Quine does not explicitly characterize traditional epistemology as "normative" or "prescriptive," his meaning is unmistakable. Epistemology is to be "a chapter of psychology," a law-based predictive-explanatory theory, like any other theory within empirical science; its principal job is to see how human cognizers develop theories (their "picture of the world") from observation ("the stimulation of their sensory receptors"). Epistemology is to go out of the business of justification. We earlier characterized traditional epistemology as essentially normative; we see why Quine wants us to reject it. Quine is urging us to replace a normative theory of cognition with a descriptive science.

Losing Knowledge from Epistemology

If justification drops out of epistemology, knowledge itself drops out of epistemology. For our concept of knowledge is inseparably tied to that of justification. As earlier noted, knowledge itself is a normative notion. Quine's nonnormative, naturalized epistemology has no room for our concept of knowledge. It is not surprising that, in describing naturalized epistemology, Quine seldom talks about knowledge; instead, he talks about "science" and "theories" and "representations." Quine would have us investigate how sensory stimulation "leads" to "theories" and "representation" of the world. I take it that within the traditional scheme these "theories" and "representations" correspond to beliefs, or systems of beliefs; thus, what Quine would have us do is to investigate how sensory stimulation leads to the formation of beliefs about the world.

But in what sense of "lead"? I take it that Quine has in mind a causal or nomological sense. He is urging us to develop a theory, an empirical theory, that uncovers lawful regularities governing the processes through which organisms come to develop beliefs about their environment as a causal result of having their sensory receptors stimulated in certain ways. Quine says:[19]

[Naturalized epistemology] studies a natural phenomenon, viz., a physical human subject. This human subject is accorded experimentally controlled input—certain patterns of irradiation in assorted frequencies, for instance— and in the fullness of time the subject delivers as output a description of the three-dimensional external world and its history. *The relation between the meager input and torrential output* is a relation that we are prompted to study for somewhat the same reasons that always prompted epistemology; namely, in order to see *how evidence relates to theory*, and in what ways one's theory of nature transcends any available evidence.

The relation Quine speaks of between "meager input" and "torrential output" is a causal relation; at least it is qua causal relation that the naturalized epistemologist investigates it. It is none of the naturalized epistemologist's business to assess whether, and to what degree, the input "justifies" the output, how a given irradiation of the subject's retinas makes it "reasonable" or "rational" for the subject to emit certain representational output. His interest is strictly causal and nomological: he wants us to look for patterns of lawlike dependencies characterizing the input-output relations for this particular organism and others of a like physical structure.

If this is right, it makes Quine's attempt to relate his naturalized epistemology to traditional epistemology look at best lame. For in what sense is the study of causal relationships between physical stimulation of sensory receptors and the resulting cognitive output a way of "seeing how evidence relates to theory" in an epistemologically relevant sense? The causal relation between sensory input and cognitive output is a relation between "evidence" and "theory"; however, it is not an *evidential relation*. This can be seen from the following consideration: the nomological patterns that Quine urges us to look for are certain to vary from species to species, depending on the particular way each biological (and possibly nonbiological) species processes information, but the evidential relation in its proper normative sense must abstract from such factors and concern itself only with the degree to which evidence supports hypothesis.

In any event, the concept of evidence is inseparable from that of justification. When we talk of "evidence" in an epistemological sense we are talking about justification: one thing is "evidence" for another just in case the first tends to enhance the reasonableness or justification of the second. And such evidential relations hold in part because of the "contents" of the items involved, not merely because of the causal or nomological connections between them. A strictly nonnormative concept of evidence is not our concept of evidence; it is something that we do not understand.[20]

None of us, I think, would want to quarrel with Quine about the interest or importance of the psychological study of how our sensory input causes our epistemic output. This is only to say that the study of human (or other kinds of) cognition is of interest. That isn't our difficulty; our difficulty is whether, and in what sense, pursuing Quine's "epistemology" is a way of doing epistemology—that is, a way of studying "how evidence relates to theory." Perhaps, Quine's recommendation that we discard justification-centered epistemology is worth pondering; and his exhortation to take up the study of psychology perhaps deserves to be heeded also. What is mysterious is why this recommendation has to be coupled with the rejection of normative epistemology (if normative epistemology is not a possible inquiry, why shouldn't the would-be epistemologist turn to, say, hydrodynamics or ornithology rather than psychology?). But of course Quine is saying more; he is saying that an understandable, if misguided, motivation (that is, seeing "how evidence relates to theory") does underlie our proclivities for indulgence in normative epistemology, but that we would be better served by a scientific study of human cognition than normative epistemology.

But it is difficult to see how an "epistemology" that has been purged of normativity, one that lacks an appropriate normative concept of justification or evidence, can have anything to do with the concerns of traditional epistemology. And unless naturalized epistemology and classical epistemology share some of their central concerns, it's difficult to see how one could *replace* the other, or be a way (a better way) of doing the other.[21] To be sure, they both investigate "how evidence relates to theory." But putting the matter this way can be misleading, and has perhaps misled Quine: the two disciplines do not investigate the same relation. As lately noted, normative epistemology is concerned with the evidential relation properly so-called— that is, the relation of justification—and Quine's naturalized epistemology is meant to study the causal-nomological relation. For epistemology to go out of the business of justification is for it to go out of business.

Belief Attribution and Rationality

Perhaps we have said enough to persuade ourselves that Quine's naturalized epistemology, while it may be a legitimate scientific inquiry, is not a kind of epistemology, and, therefore, that the question whether it is a better kind of epistemology cannot arise. In reply, however, it might be said that there was a sense in which Quine's epistemology and traditional epistemology could be viewed as sharing a common subject matter, namely this: they both concern beliefs or "representations." The only difference is that the former investigates their causal histories and connections whereas the latter is concerned with their evidential or justificatory properties and relations. This difference, if Quine is right, leads to another (so continues the reply): the former is a feasible inquiry, the latter is not.

I now want to take my argument a step further: I shall argue that the concept of belief is itself an essentially normative one, and in consequence that if normativity is wholly excluded from naturalized epistemology it cannot even be thought of as being about beliefs. That is, if naturalized epistemology is to be a science of beliefs properly so called, it must presuppose a normative concept of belief.

Briefly, the argument is this. In order to implement Quine's program of naturalized epistemology, we shall need to identify, and individuate, the input and output of cognizers. The input, for Quine, consists of physical events ("the stimulation of sensory receptors") and the output is said to be a "theory" or "picture of the world"—that is, a set of "representations" of the cognizer's environment. Let us focus on the output. In order to study the sensory input-cognitive output relations for the given cognizer, therefore, we must find out what "representations" he has formed as a result of the particular stimulations that have been applied to his sensory transducers. Setting aside the jargon, what we need to be able to do is to attribute *beliefs*, and other contentful intentional states, to the cognizer. But belief attribution ultimately requires a "radical interpretation" of the cognizer, of his speech and intentional states; that is, we must construct an "interpretive theory" that simultaneously assigns meanings to his utterances and attributes to him beliefs and other propositional attitudes.[22]

Even a cursory consideration indicates that such an interpretation cannot begin—we cannot get a foothold in our subject's realm of meanings and intentional states—unless we assume his total system of beliefs and other propositional attitudes to be largely and essentially rational and coherent. As Davidson has emphasized, a given belief has the content it has in part because of its location in a network of other beliefs and propositional attitudes; and what at bottom grounds this network is the evidential relation, a relation that regulates what is reasonable to believe given other beliefs one holds. That is, unless our cognizer is a "rational being," a being whose cognitive "output" is regulated and constrained by norms of rationality—typically, these norms holistically constrain his propositional attitudes in virtue of their contents—we cannot intelligibly interpret his "output" as consisting of beliefs. Conversely, if we are unable to interpret our subject's meanings and propositional attitudes in a way that satisfies a minimal standard of rationality, there is little reason to regard him as a "cognizer," a being that forms representations and constructs theories. This means that there is a sense of "rational" in which the expression "rational belief" is redundant; every belief must be rational in certain minimal ways. It is not important for the purposes of the present argument what these minimal standards of rationality are; the only point that matters is that unless the output of our cognizer is subject to evaluation in accordance with norms of rationality, that output cannot be considered as consisting of beliefs and hence cannot be the object of an epistemological inquiry, whether plain or naturalized.

We can separate the core of these considerations from controversial issues involving the so-called "principle of charity," minimal rationality, and other matters in the theory of radical interpretation. What is crucial is this: for the interpretation and attribution of beliefs to be possible, not only must we assume the overall rationality of cognizers, but also we must continually evaluate and re-evaluate the putative beliefs of a cognizer in their evidential relationship to one another and other propositional attitudes. It is not merely that belief attribution requires the umbrella assumption about the overall rationality of cognizers. Rather, the point is that *belief attribution requires belief evaluation*, in accordance with normative standards of evidence and justification. If this is correct, rationality in its broad and fundamental sense is not an optional property of beliefs, a virtue that some beliefs may enjoy and others lack; it is a precondition of the attribution and individuation of belief—that is, a property without which the concept of belief would be unintelligible and pointless.

Two objections might be raised to counter these considerations. First, one might argue that at best they show only that the normativity of belief is an epistemological assumption—that we need to assume the rationality and coherence of belief systems when we are trying to *find out* what beliefs to attribute to a cognizer. It does not follow from this epistemological point, the objection continues, that the concept of belief is itself normative.[23] In replying to this objection, we can by-pass the entire issue of whether the rationality assumption concerns only the epistemology of belief attribution. Even if this premise (which I think is incorrect) is granted, the point has already been made. For it is an essential part of the business of naturalized epistemology, as a theory of how beliefs are formed as a result of sensory stimulation, to *find out* what particular beliefs the given cognizers have formed. But this is precisely what cannot be done, if our considerations show anything at all, unless the would-be naturalized epistemologist continually evaluates the putative beliefs of his subjects in regard to their rationality and coherence, subject to the overall constraint of the assumption that the cognizers are largely rational. The naturalized epistemologist cannot dispense with normative concepts or disengage himself from valuational activities.

Second, it might be thought that we could simply avoid these considerations stemming from belief attribution by refusing to think of cognitive output as consisting of "beliefs," namely as states having propositional contents. The "representations" Quine speaks of should be taken as appropriate neural states, and this means that all we need is to be able to discern neural states of organisms. This requires only neurophysiology and the like, not the normative theory of rational belief. My reply takes the form of a dilemma: either the "appropriate" neural states are identified by seeing how they correlate with beliefs,[24] in which case we still need to contend with the problem of radical interpretation, or beliefs are entirely bypassed. In the latter case, belief, along with justification, drops out of Quinean epistemology, and it is unclear in what sense we are left with an inquiry that has anything to do with knowledge.[25]

The "Psychologistic" Approach to Epistemology

Many philosophers now working in theory of knowledge have stressed the importance of systematic psychology to philosophical epistemology. Reasons proffered for this are various, and so are the conceptions of the proper relationship between psychology and epistemology.[26] But they are virtually unanimous in their rejection of what they take to be the epistemological tradition of Descartes and its modern embodiments in philosophers like Russell, C. I. Lewis, Roderick Chisholm, and A. J. Ayer; and they are united in their endorsement of the naturalistic approach of Quine we have been considering. Traditional epistemology is often condemned as "aprioristic," and as having lost sight of human knowledge as a product of natural causal processes and its function in the survival of the organism and the species. Sometimes, the adherents of the traditional approach are taken to task for their implicit antiscientific bias or indifference to the new developments in psychology and related disciplines. Their own approach in contrast is hailed as "naturalistic" and "scientific," better attuned to significant advances in the relevant scientific fields such as "cognitive science" and "neuroscience," promising philosophical returns far richer than what the aprioristic method of traditional epistemology has been able to deliver. We shall here briefly consider how this new naturalism in epistemology is to be understood in relation to the classic epistemological program and Quine's naturalized epistemology.

Let us see how one articulate proponent of the new approach explains the distinctiveness of his position vis-à-vis that of the traditional epistemologists. According to Philip Kitcher, the approach he rejects is characterized by an "apsychologistic" attitude that takes the difference between knowledge and true belief—that is, justification—to consist in "ways which are independent of the causal antecedents of a subject's states."[27] Kitcher writes:[28]

> . . . we can present the heart of [the apsychologistic approach] by considering the way in which it would tackle the question of whether a person's true belief that p counts as knowledge that p. The idea would be to disregard the psychological life of the subject, looking just at the various propositions she believes. If p is "connected in the right way" to other propositions which are believed, then we count the subject as knowing that p. Of course, apsychologistic epistemology will have to supply a criterion for propositions to be "connected in the right way" . . . but proponents of this view of knowledge will emphasize that the criterion is to be given in *logical* terms. We are concerned with logical relations among propositions, not with psychological relations among mental states.

On the other hand, the psychologistic approach considers the crucial difference between knowledge and true belief—that is, epistemic justification—to turn on "the factors which produced the belief," focusing on "processes which produce belief, processes which will always contain, at their latter end, psychological events."[29]

It is not entirely clear from this characterization whether a psychologistic theory of justification is to be *prohibited* from making any reference to logical relations among belief contents (it is difficult to believe how a theory of justification respecting such a blanket prohibition could succeed); nor is it clear whether, conversely, an apsychologistic theory will be permitted to refer at all to beliefs qua psychological states, or exactly what it is for a theory to do so. But such points of detail are unimportant here; it is clear enough, for example, that Goldman's proposal to explicate justified belief as belief generated by a reliable belief-forming process[30] nicely fits Kitcher's characterization of the psychologistic approach. This account, one form of the so-called "reliability theory" of justification, probably was what Kitcher had in mind when he was formulating his general characterization of epistemological naturalism. However, another influential form of the reliability theory does not qualify under Kitcher's characterization. This is Armstrong's proposal to explain the difference between knowledge and true belief, at least for noninferential knowledge, in terms of "a *law-like connection* between the state of affairs [of a subject's believing that p] and the state of affairs that makes 'p' true such that, given the state of affairs [of the subject's believing that *p*], it must be the case that *p*."[31] There is here no reference to the causal *antecedents* of beliefs, something that Kitcher requires of apsychologistic theories.

Perhaps, Kitcher's preliminary characterization needs to be broadened and sharpened. However, a salient characteristic of the naturalistic approach has already emerged, which we can put as follows: justification is to be characterized in terms of *causal* or *nomological* connections involving beliefs as *psychological states* or *processes*, and not in terms of the *logical* properties or relations pertaining to the *contents* of these beliefs.[32]

If we understand current epistemological naturalism in this way, how closely is it related to Quine's conception of naturalized epistemology? The answer, I think, is obvious: not very closely at all. In fact, it seems a good deal closer to the Cartesian tradition than to Quine. For, as we saw, the difference that matters between Quine's epistemological program and the traditional program is the former's total renouncement of the latter's normativity, its rejection of epistemology as a normative inquiry. The talk of "replacing" epistemology with psychology is irrelevant and at best misleading, though it could give us a momentary relief from a sense of deprivation. When one abandons justification and other valuational concepts, one abandons the entire framework of normative epistemology. What remains is a descriptive empirical theory of human cognition which, if Quine has his way, will be entirely devoid of the notion of justification or any other evaluative concept.

As I take it, this is not what most advocates of epistemological naturalism are aiming at. By and large they are not Quinean eliminativists in regard to justification, and justification in its full-fledged normative sense continues to play a central role in their epistemological reflections. Where they differ from their nonnaturalist adversaries is the specific way in which criteria of justification are to be formulated. Naturalists and nonnaturalists ("apsychologists") can agree that these criteria must be stated in descriptive terms—that is, without the use of epistemic or any other kind of normative terms. According to Kitcher, an apsychologistic theory of justification would state them primarily in terms of *logical* properties and relations holding for propositional contents of beliefs, whereas the psychologistic approach advocates the exclusive use of *causal* properties and relations holding for beliefs as events or states. Many traditional epistemologists may prefer criteria that confer upon a cognizer a position of special privilege and responsibility with regard to the epistemic status of his beliefs, whereas most self-avowed naturalists prefer "objective" or "externalist" criteria with no such special privileges for the cognizer. But these differences are among those that arise within the familiar normative framework, and are consistent with the exclusion of normative terms in the statement of the criteria of justification.

Normative ethics can serve as a useful model here. To claim that basic ethical terms, like "good" and "right," are *definable* on the basis of descriptive or naturalistic terms is one thing; to insist that it is the business of normative ethics to provide *conditions* or *criteria* for "good" and "right" in descriptive or naturalistic terms is another. One may properly reject the former, the so-called "ethical naturalism," as many moral philosophers have done, and hold the latter; there is no obvious inconsistency here. G. E. Moore is a philosopher who did just that. As is well known, he was a powerful critic of ethical naturalism, holding that goodness is a "simple" and "nonnatural" property. At the same time, he held that a thing's being good "follows" from its possessing certain naturalistic properties. He wrote:[33]

I should never have thought of suggesting that goodness was "non-natural," unless I had supposed that it was "derivative" in the sense that, whenever a thing is good (in the sense in question) its goodness . . . "depends on the presence of certain non-ethical characteristics" possessed by the thing in question: I have always supposed that it did so "depend," in the sense that, if a thing is good (in my sense), then that it is so *follows* from the fact that it possesses certain natural intrinsic properties . . .

It makes sense to think of these "natural intrinsic properties" from which a thing's being good is thought to follow as constituting naturalistic criteria of goodness, or at least pointing to the existence of such criteria. One can reject ethical naturalism, the doctrine that ethical concepts are definitionally eliminable in favor of naturalistic terms, and at the same time hold that ethical properties, or the ascription of ethical terms, must be governed by naturalistic criteria. It is clear, then, that we are here using "naturalism" ambiguously in "epistemological naturalism" and "ethical naturalism." In our present usage, epistemological naturalism does not include (nor does it necessarily exclude) the claim that epistemic terms are definitionally reducible to naturalistic terms. (Quine's naturalism is eliminative, though it is not a definitional eliminativism.)

If, therefore, we locate the split between Quine and traditional epistemology at the descriptive vs. normative divide, then currently influential naturalism in epistemology is not likely to fall on Quine's side. On this descriptive vs. normative issue, one can side with Quine in one of two ways: first, one rejects, with Quine, the entire justification-based epistemological program; or second, like ethical naturalists but unlike Quine, one believes that epistemic concepts are naturalistically definable. I doubt that very many epistemological naturalists will embrace either of these alternatives.[34]

Epistemic Supervenience—Or Why Normative Epistemology Is Possible

But why should we think that there *must be* naturalistic criteria of justified belief and other terms of epistemic appraisal? If we take the discovery and systematization of such criteria to be the central task of normative epistemology, is there any reason to think that this task can be fruitfully pursued, that normative epistemology is a possible field of inquiry? Quine's point is that it is not. We have already noted the limitation of Quine's negative arguments in "Epistemology Naturalized," but is there a positive reason for thinking that normative epistemology is a viable program? One could consider a similar question about the possibility of normative ethics.

I think there is a short and plausible initial answer, although a detailed defense of it would involve complex general issues about norms and values. The short answer is this: we believe in the supervenience of epistemic properties on naturalistic ones, and more generally, in the supervenience of all valuational and normative properties on naturalistic conditions. This comes out in various ways. We think, with R. M. Hare,[35] that if two persons or acts coincide in all descriptive or naturalistic details, they cannot differ in respect of being good or right, or any other valuational aspects. We also think that if something is "good"—a "good car," "good drop shot," "good argument"—then that must be so "in virtue of" its being a "certain way," that is, its having certain "factual properties." Being a good car, say, cannot be a brute and ultimate fact: a car is good *because* it has a certain contextually indicated set of properties having to do with performance, reliability, comfort, styling, economy, etc. The same goes for justified belief: if a belief is justified, that must be so *because* it has a certain factual, nonepistemic properties, such as perhaps that it is "indubitable," that it is seen to be entailed by another belief that is independently justified, that it is appropriately caused by perceptual experience, or whatever. That it is a justified belief cannot be a brute fundamental fact unrelated to the kind of belief it is. There must be a *reason* for it, and this reason must be grounded in the factual descriptive properties of that particular belief. Something like this, I think, is what we believe.

Two important themes underlie these convictions: first, values, though perhaps not reducible to facts, must be "consistent" with them in that objects that are indiscernible in regard to fact must be indiscernible in regard to value; second, there must be nonvaluational "reasons" or "grounds" for the attribution of values, and these "reasons" or "grounds" must be *generalizable*—that is, they are covered by *rules* or *norms*. These two ideas correspond to "weak supervenience" and "strong supervenience" that I have discussed elsewhere.[36] Belief in the supervenience of value upon fact, arguably, is fundamental to the very concepts of value and valuation.[37] Any valuational concept, to be significant, must be governed by a set of criteria, and these criteria must ultimately rest on factual characteristics and relationships of objects and events being evaluated. There is something deeply incoherent about the idea of an infinitely descending series of valuational concepts, each depending on the one below it as its criterion of application.[38]

It seems to me, therefore, that epistemological supervenience is what underlies our belief in the possibility of normative epistemology, and that we do not need new inspirations from the sciences to acknowledge the existence of naturalistic criteria for epistemic and other valuational concepts. The case of normative ethics is entirely parallel: belief in the possibility of normative ethics is rooted in the belief that moral properties and relations are supervenient upon nonmoral ones. Unless we are prepared to disown normative ethics as a viable philosophical inquiry, we had better recognize normative epistemology as one, too.[39] We should note, too, that epistemology is likely to parallel normative ethics in regard to the degree to which scientific results are relevant or useful to its development.[40] Saying this of course leaves large room for disagreement concerning how relevant and useful, if at all, empirical psychology of human motivation and action can be to the development and confirmation of normative ethical theories.[41] In any event, once the normativity of epistemology is clearly taken note of, it is no surprise that epistemology and normative ethics share the same metaphilosophical fate. Naturalized epistemology makes no more, and no less, sense than naturalized normative ethics.[42]

Notes

1. In making these remarks I am only repeating the familiar textbook history of philosophy; however, what *our* textbooks say about the history of a philosophical concept has much to do with *our* understanding of that concept.

2. Goldman 1979 [397] explicitly states this requirement as a desideratum of his own analysis of justified belief. Chisholm's 1977 [555] definition of "being evident" does not satisfy this requirement as it rests ultimately on an unanalyzed epistemic concept of one belief being *more reasonable than* another. What does the real "criteriological" work for Chisholm is his "principles of evidence." See especially (A) on p. 73 of his 1977 [555], which can usefully be regarded as an attempt to provide nonnormative, descriptive conditions for certain types of justified beliefs.

3. The basic idea of this stronger requirement seems implicit in Furth's notion of "warrant-increasing property" in his 1964 [719]. It seems that Alston 1976 [673] has something similar in mind when he says, ". . . like any evaluative property, epistemic justification is a supervenient property, the application of which is based on more fundamental properties" (at this point Alston refers to Firth's paper cited above) (the quoted remark occurs on p. 170). Although Alston doesn't further explain what he means by "more fundamental properties," the context makes it plausible to suppose that he has in mind nonnormative, descriptive properties. See section 7 below for further discussion.

4. See Chisholm 1977 [555] p. 14. Here Chisholm refers to a "person's responsibility or duty *qua* intellectual being."

5. This term was used by Ayer 1956 [539] to characterize the difference between lucky guessing and knowing, p. 33.

6. Notably by Chisholm in 1977 [555] 1st ed., ch. 4.

7. See Carnap, 1936 [688]. We should also note the presence of a strong coherentist streak among some positivists; see, e.g., Hempel 1935 [743].

8. In Quine 1969 [101]. Also see his 1960 [100]; 1973 [103]; 1970 [102]; and especially 1975 [165]. See Schmitt's excellent bibliography on naturalistic epistemology in Kornblith 1985 [73].

9. Or conformational relations, given the Positivists' verificationist theory of meaning.

10. I know of no serious defense of it since Ayer's 1940 [538].

11. See this volume, pp. 19–20.

12. Ibid., p. 21.

13. To use an expression of Rorty's 1979 [114], p. 11.

14. Sober 1978 [246] makes a similar point: "And on the question of whether the failure of a foundationalist programme shows that questions of justification cannot be answered, it is worth noting that Quine's advice 'Since Carnap's foundationalism failed, why not settle for psychology' carries weight only to the degree that Carnapian epistemology exhausts the possibilities of epistemology."

15. See Chisholm 1977 [555], ch. 4.

16. "If we are seeking only the causal mechanism of our knowledge of the external world, and not a justification of that knowledge in terms prior to science . . . ," Quine 1970 [102], p. 2.

17. Quine 1970 [102], p. 75. Emphasis added.

18. Quine 1970 [102], p. 78. Emphasis added.

19. Quine 1970 [102], p. 83. Emphasis added.

20. But aren't there those who advocate a "causal theory" of evidence or justification? I want to make two brief points about this. First, the nomological or causal input-output relations are not in themselves evidential relations, whether these latter are understood causally or otherwise. Second, a causal theory of evidence attempts to state *criteria* for "e is evidence for h" in causal terms; even if this is successful, it does not necessarily give us a causal "definition" or "reduction" of the concept of evidence. For more details see section 6 below.

21. I am not saying that Quine is under any illusion on this point. My remarks are directed rather at those who endorse Quine without, it seems, a clear appreciation of what is involved.

22. Here I am drawing chiefly on Davidson's writings on radical interpretation. See Essays 9, 10, and 11 in his 1984 [558]. See also Lewis 1974 [774].

23. Robert Audi suggested this as a possible objection.

24. For some considerations tending to show that these correlations cannot be lawlike, see my 1985 [760].

25. For a more sympathetic account of Quine than mine, see Kornblith's introductory essay in his 1985 [73].

26. See, for more details, Goldman 1986 [49].

27. Kitcher 1983 [71], p. 14.

28. Kitcher 1983 [71].

29. Kitcher 1983 [71], p. 13. I should note that Kitcher considers the apsychologistic approach to be an aberration of the twentieth-century epistemology,

as represented by philosophers like Russell, Moore, C. I. Lewis, and Chisholm, rather than an historical characteristic of the Cartesian tradition. Kornblith 1982 [218] gives an analogous characterization of the two approaches to justification; he associates "justification-conferring processes" with the psychologistic approach and "epistemic rules" with the apsychologistic approach.

30. See Goldman 1979 [397].

31. Armstrong 1973 [3], p. 166.

32. The aptness of this characterization of the "apsychologistic" approach for philosophers like Russell, Chisholm, Lehrer, Pollock, etc. can be debated. Also, there is the issue of "internalism" vs. "externalism" concerning justification, which I believe must be distinguished from the psychologistic vs. apsychologistic division.

33. Moore, 1942 [792], p. 588.

34. Rorty's claim, which plays a prominent role in his arguments against traditional epistemology, that Locke and other modern epistemologists conflated the normative concept of justification with causal-mechanical concepts is itself based, I believe, on a conflation of just the kind I am describing here. See Rorty, 1979 [114], pp. 139ff. Again, the critical conflation consists in not seeing that the view, which I believe is correct, that epistemic justification, like any other normative concept, must have factual, naturalistic criteria, is entirely consistent with the rejection of the doctrine, which I think is incorrect, that justification *is*, or is *reducible* to, a naturalistic-nonnormative concept.

35. Hare 1952 [589], p. 145.

36. See Kim 1984 [759].

37. Sosa, too, considers epistemological supervenience as a special case of the supervenience of valuational properties on naturalistic conditions in his 1980 [833], especially p. 551. See also Van Cleve's instructive discussion in his 1985 [851], especially, pp. 97–99.

38. Perhaps one could avoid this kind of criteriological regress by embracing directly apprehended valuational properties (as in ethical intuitionism) on the basis of which criteria for other valuational properties could be formulated. The denial of the supervenience of valuational concepts on factual characteristics, however, would sever the essential connection between value and fact on which, it seems, the whole point of our valuational activities depends. In the absence of such supervenience, the very notion of valuation would lose its significance and relevance. The elaboration of these points, however, would have to wait for another occasion; but see Van Cleve's paper cited in the preceding note for more details.

39. Quine will not disagree with this: he will "naturalize" them both. For his views on values see 1978 [808]. For a discussion of the relationship between epistemic and ethical concepts see Firth 1978 [720].

40. For discussions of this and related issues see Goldman 1986 [49].

41. For a detailed development of a normative ethical theory that exemplifies the view that it is crucially relevant, see Brandt 1979 [551].

42. An earlier version of this paper was read at a meeting of the Korean Society for Analytic Philosophy in 1984 in Seoul. An expanded version was presented at a symposium at the Western Division meetings of the American Philosophical Association in April, 1985, and at the epistemology conference at Brown University in honor of Roderick Chisholm in 1986. I am grateful to Richard Foley and Robert Audi who presented helpful comments at the APA session and the Chisholm Conference respectively. I am also indebted to Terence Horgan and Robert Meyers for helpful comments and suggestions.

3

Natural Kinds

W. V. O. Quine

What tends to confirm an induction? This question has been aggravated on the one hand by Hempel's puzzle of the non-black non-ravens,[1] and exacerbated on the other by Goodman's puzzle of the grue emeralds.[2] I shall begin my remarks by relating the one puzzle to the other, and the other to an innate flair that we have for natural kinds. Then I shall devote the rest of the paper to reflections on the nature of this notion of natural kinds and its relation to science.

Hempel's puzzle is that just as each black raven tends to confirm the law that all ravens are black, so each green leaf, being a non-black non-raven, should tend to confirm the law that all non-black things are non-ravens, that is, again, that all ravens are black. What is paradoxical is that a green leaf should count toward the law that all ravens are black.

Goodman propounds his puzzle by requiring us to imagine that emeralds, having been identified by some criterion other than color, are now being examined one after another and all up to now are found to be green. Then he proposes to call anything *grue* that is examined today or earlier and found to be green or is not examined before tomorrow and is blue. Should we expect the first one examined tomorrow to be green, because all examined up to now were green? But all examined up to now were also grue; so why not expect the first one tomorrow to be grue, and therefore blue?

The predicate "green," Goodman says,[3] is *projectible*; "grue" is not. He says this by way of putting a name to the problem. His step toward solution is his doctrine of what he calls entrenchment,[4] which I shall touch on later. Meanwhile the terminological point is simply that projectible predicates are predicates ζ and η whose shared instances all do count, for whatever reason, toward confirmation of ⌜All ζ are η⌝.

Now I propose assimilating Hempel's puzzle to Goodman's by inferring from Hempel's that the complement of a projectible predicate need not be projectible. "Raven" and "black" are projectible; a black raven does count toward "All ravens are black." Hence a black raven counts also, indirectly, toward "No non-black things are non-ravens," since this says the same thing. But a green leaf does not count toward "All non-black things are non-ravens," nor, therefore, toward "All ravens are black"; "non-black" and "non-raven" are not projectible. "Green" and "leaf" are projectible, and the green leaf counts toward "All leaves are green" and "All green things are leaves"; but only a black raven can confirm "All ravens are black," the complements not being projectible.

If we see the matter in this way, we must guard against saying that a statement ⌜All ζ are η⌝ is lawlike only if ζ and η are projectible. "All non-black things are non-ravens" is a law despite its non-projectible terms, since it is equivalent to "All ravens are black." Any statement is lawlike that is logically equivalent to ⌜All ζ are η⌝ for some projectible ζ and η.[5]

Having concluded that the complement of a projectible predicate need not be projectible, we may ask further whether there is *any* projectible predicate whose complement is projectible. I can conceive that there is not, when complements are taken strictly. We must not be misled by limited or relative complementation; "male human" and "non-male human" are indeed both projectible.

To get back now to the emeralds, why do we expect the next one to be green rather than grue? The intuitive answer lies in similarity, however subjective. Two green emeralds are more similar than two grue ones would be if only one of the grue ones were green. Green things, or at least green emeralds, are a kind.[6] A projectible predicate is one that is true of all and only the things of a kind. What makes Goodman's example a puzzle, however, is the dubious scientific standing of a general notion of similarity, or of kind.

The dubiousness of this notion is itself a remarkable fact. For surely there is nothing more basic to thought and language than our sense of similarity; our sorting of things into kinds. The usual general term, whether a common noun or a verb or an adjective, owes its generality to some resemblance among the things referred to. Indeed, learning to use a word depends on a double resemblance: first, a resemblance between the present circumstances and past circumstances in which the word was used, and second, a phonetic resemblance between the present utterance of the word and past utterances of it. And every reasonable expectation depends on resemblance of circumstances, together with our tendency to expect similar causes to have similar effects.

The notion of a kind and the notion of similarity or resemblance seem to be variants or adaptations of a single notion. Similarity is immediately definable in terms of kind; for, things are similar when they are two of a kind. The very words for "kind" and "similar" tend to run in etymologically cognate pairs. Cognate with "kind" we have "akin" and "kindred." Cognate with "like" we have "ilk." Cognate with "similar" and "same" and "resemble" there are "sammeln" and "assemble," suggesting a gathering into kinds.

We cannot easily imagine a more familiar or fundamental notion than this, or a notion more ubiquitous in its applications. On this score it is like the notions of logic: like identity, negation, alternation, and the rest. And yet, strangely, there is something logically repugnant about it. For we are baffled when we try to relate the general notion of similarity significantly to logical terms. One's first hasty suggestion might be to say that things are similar when they have all or most or many properties in common. Or, trying to be less vague, one might try defining comparative similarity—"a is more similar to b than to c"—as meaning that a shares more properties with b than with c. But any such course only reduces our problem to the unpromising task of settling what to count as a property.

The nature of the problem of what to count as a property can be seen by turning for a moment to set theory. Things are viewed as going together into sets in any and every combination, describable and indescribable. Any two things are joint members of any number of sets. Certainly then we cannot define "a is more similar to b than to c" to mean that a and b belong jointly to more sets than a and c do. If properties are to support this line of definition where sets do not, it must be because properties do not, like sets, take things in every random combination. It must be that properties are shared only by things that are significantly similar. But properties in such a sense are no clearer than kinds. To start with such a notion of property, and define similarity on that basis, is no better than accepting similarity as undefined.

The contrast between properties and sets which I suggested just now must not be confused with the more basic and familiar contrast between properties, as intensional, and sets as extensional. Properties are intensional in that they may be counted as distinct properties even though wholly coinciding in respect of the things that have them. There is no call to reckon kinds as intensional. Kinds can be seen as sets, determined by their members. It is just that not all sets are kinds.

If similarity is taken simple-mindedly as a yes-or-no affair, with no degrees, then there is no containing of kinds within broader kinds. For, as remarked, similarity now simply means belonging to some one same kind. If all colored things comprise a kind, then all colored things count as similar, and the set of all red things is too narrow to count as a kind. If on the other hand the set of all red things counts as a kind, then colored things do not all count as similar, and the set of all colored things is too broad to count as a kind. We cannot have it both ways. Kinds can, however, overlap; the red things can comprise one kind, the round another.

When we move up from the simple dyadic relation of similarity to the more serious and useful triadic relation of comparative similarity, a correlative change takes place in the notion of kind. Kinds come to admit now not only of overlapping but also of containment one in another. The set of all red things and the set of all colored things can now both count as kinds; for all colored things can now be counted as resembling one another more than some things do, even though less, on the whole, than red ones do.

At this point, of course, our trivial definition of similarity as sameness of kind breaks down; for almost any two things could count now as common members of some broad kind or other, and anyway we now want to define comparative or triadic similarity. A definition that suggests itself is this: a is more similar to b than to c when a and b belong jointly to more kinds than a and c do. But even this works only for finite systems of kinds.

The notion of kind and the notion of similarity seemed to be substantially one notion. We observed further that they resist reduction to less dubious notions, as of logic or set theory. That they at any rate be definable each in terms of the other seems little enough to ask. We just saw a somewhat limping definition of comparative similarity in terms of kinds. What now of the converse project, definition of kind in terms of similarity?

One may be tempted to picture a kind, suitable to a comparative similarity relation, as any set which is "qualitatively spherical" in this sense: it takes in exactly the things that differ less than so-and-so much from some central norm. If without serious loss of accuracy we can assume that there are one or more actual things *(paradigm cases)* that nicely exemplify the desired norm, and one or more actual things *(foils)* that deviate just barely too much to be counted into the desired kind at all, then our definition is easy: *the kind with paradigm a and foil b is the set of all the things to which a is more similar than a is to b*. More generally, then, a set may be said to be a *kind* if and only if there are *a* and *b*, known or unknown, such that the set is the kind with paradigm *a* and foil *b*.

If we consider examples, however, we see that this definition does not give us what we want as kinds. Thus take red. Let us grant that a central shade of red can be picked as norm. The trouble is that the paradigm cases, objects in just that shade of red, can come in all sorts of shapes, weights, sizes, and smells. Mere degree of overall similarity to any one such paradigm case will afford little evidence of degree of redness, since it will depend also on shape, weight, and the rest. If our assumed relation of comparative similarity were just comparative chromatic similarity, then our paradigm-and-foil definition of kind would indeed accommodate redkind. What the definition will not do is distill purely chromatic kinds from mixed similarity.

A different attempt, adapted from Carnap, is this: a set is a kind if all its members are more similar to one another than they all are to any one thing outside the set. In other words, each non-member differs more from some member than that member differs from any member. However, as Goodman showed in a criticism of Carnap,[7] this construction succumbs to what Goodman calls the difficulty of imperfect community. Thus consider the set of all red round things, red wooden things, and round wooden things. Each member of this set resembles each other member somehow: at least in being red, or in being round, or in being wooden, and perhaps in two or all three of these respects or others. Conceivably, moreover, there is no one thing outside the set that resembles every member of the set to even the least of these degrees. The set then meets the proposed definition of kind. Yet surely it is not what anyone means by a kind. It admits yellow croquet balls and red rubber balls while excluding yellow rubber balls.

The relation between similarity and kind, then, is less clear and neat than could be wished. Definition of similarity in terms of kind is halting, and definition of kind in terms of similarity is unknown. Still the two notions are in an important sense correlative. They vary together. If we reassess something *a* as less similar to *b* than to *c*, where it had counted as more similar to *b* than *c*, surely we will correspondingly permute *a*, *b*, and *c* in respect of their assignment to kinds; and conversely.

I have stressed how fundamental the notion of similarity or of kind is to our thinking, and how alien to logic and set theory. I want to go on now to say more about how fundamental these notions are to our thinking, and something also about their non-logical roots. Afterward I want to bring out how the notion of similarity or of kind changes as science progresses. I shall suggest that it is a mark of maturity of a branch of science that the notion of similarity or kind finally dissolves, so far as it is relevant to that branch of science. That is, it ultimately submits to analysis in the special terms of that branch of science and logic.

For deeper appreciation of how fundamental similarity is, let us observe more closely how it figures in the learning of language. One learns by *ostension* what presentations to call yellow; that is, one learns by hearing the word applied to samples. All he has to go on, of course, is the similarity of further cases to the samples. Similarity being a matter of degree, one has to learn by trial and error how reddish or brownish or greenish a thing can be and still be counted yellow. When he finds he has applied the word too far out, he can use the false cases as samples to the contrary; and then he can proceed to guess whether further cases are yellow or not by considering whether they are more similar to the in-group or the out-group. What one thus uses, even at this primitive stage of learning, is a fully functioning sense of similarity, and relative similarity at that: *a* is more similar to *b* than to *c*.

All these delicate comparisons and shrewd inferences about what to call yellow are, in Sherlock Holmes's terminology, elementary. Mostly the process is unconscious. It is the same process by which an animal learns to respond in distinctive ways to his master's commands or other discriminated stimulations.

The primitive sense of similarity that underlies such learning has, we saw, a certain complexity of structure: *a* is more similar to *b* than to *c*. Some people have thought that it has to be much more complex still: that it depends irreducibly on *respects*, thus similarity in color, similarity in shape, and so on. According to this view, our learning of yellow by ostension would have depended on our first having been told or somehow apprised that it was going to be a question of color. Now hints of this kind are a great help, and in our learning we often do depend on them. Still one would like to be able to show that a single general standard of similarity, but of course comparative similarity, is all we need, and that respects can be abstracted afterward. For instance, suppose the child has learned of a yellow ball and block that they count as yellow, and of a red ball and block that they do not, and now he has to decide about a yellow cloth. Presumably he will find the cloth more similar to the yellow ball and to the yellow block than to the red ball or red block; and he will not have needed any prior schooling in colors and respects. Carnap undertook to show long ago how some respects, such as color, could by an ingenious construction be derived from a general similarity notion;[8] however, this development is challenged, again, by Goodman's difficulty of imperfect community.

A standard of similarity is in some sense innate. This point is not against empiricism; it is a commonplace of behavioral psychology. A response to a red circle, if it is rewarded, will be elicited again by a pink ellipse more readily than by a blue triangle; the red circle resembles the pink ellipse more than the blue triangle. Without some such prior spacing of qualities, we could never acquire a habit; all stimuli would be equally alike and equally different. These spacings of qualities, on the part of men and other animals, can be explored and mapped in the laboratory by experiments in conditioning and extinction.[9] Needed as they are for all learning, these distinctive spacings cannot themselves all be learned; some must be innate.

If then I say that there is an innate standard of similarity, I am making a condensed statement that can be interpreted, and truly interpreted, in behavioral terms. Moreover, in this behavioral sense it can be said equally of other animals that they have an innate standard of similarity too. It is part of our animal birthright. And, interestingly enough, it is characteristically animal in its lack of intellectual status. At any rate we noticed earlier how alien the notion is to mathematics and logic.

This innate qualitative spacing of stimulations was seen to have one of its human uses in the ostensive learning of words like "yellow." I should add as a cautionary remark that this is not the only way of learning words, nor the commonest; it is merely the most rudimentary way. It works when the question of the reference of a word is a simple question of spread: how much of our surroundings counts as yellow, how much counts as water, and so on. Learning a word like "apple" or "square" is more complicated, because here we have to learn also where to say that one apple or square leaves off and another begins. The complication is that apples do not add up to an apple, nor squares, generally, to a square. "Yellow" and "water" are mass terms, concerned only with spread; "apple" and "square" are terms of divided reference, concerned with both spread and individuation. Ostension figures in the learning of terms of this latter kind too, but the process is more complex.[10] And then there are all the other sorts of words, all those abstract and neutral connectives and adverbs and all the recondite terms of scientific theory; and there are also the grammatical constructions themselves to be mastered. The learning of these things is less direct and more complex still. There are deep problems in this domain, but they lie aside from the present topic.

Our way of learning "yellow," then, gives less than a full picture of how we learn language. yet more emphatically, it gives less than a full picture of the human use of an innate standard of similarity, or innate spacing of qualities. For, as remarked, every reasonable expectation depends on similarity. Again on this score, other animals are like man. Their expectations, if we choose so to conceptualize their avoidance movements and salivation and pressing of levers and the like, are clearly dependent on their appreciation of similarity. Or, to put matters in their methodological order, these avoidance movements and salivation and pressing of levers and the like are typical of what we have to go on in mapping the animals' appreciation of similarity, their spacing of qualities.

Induction itself is essentially only more of the same: animal expectation or habit formation. And the ostensive learning of words is an implicit case of induction. Implicitly the learner of "yellow" is working inductively toward a general law of English verbal behavior, though a law that he will never try to state; he is working up to where he can in general judge when an English speaker would assent to "yellow" and when not.

Not only is ostensive learning a case of induction; it is a curiously comfortable case of induction, a game of chance with loaded dice. At

any rate this is so if, as seems plausible, each man's spacing of qualities is enough like his neighbor's. For the learner is generalizing on
his yellow samples by similarity considerations, and his neighbors
have themselves acquired the use of the word "yellow," in their day,
by the same similarity considerations. The learner of "yellow" is thus
making his induction in a friendly world. Always, induction expresses our hope that similar causes will have similar effects; but
when the induction is the ostensive learning of a word, that pious
hope blossoms into a forgone conclusion. The uniformity of people's
quality spaces virtually assures that similar presentations will elicit
similar verdicts.

It makes one wonder the more about other inductions, where what
is sought is a generalization not about our neighbor's verbal behavior
but about the harsh impersonal world. It is reasonable that our quality space should match our neighbor's, we being birds of a feather;
and so the general trustworthiness of induction in the ostensive
learning of words was a put-up job. To trust induction as a way of
access to the truths of nature, on the other hand, is to suppose, more
nearly, that our quality spaces matches that of the cosmos. The brute
irrationality of our sense of similarity, its irrelevance to anything in
logic and mathematics, offers little reason to expect that this sense is
somehow in tune with the world—a world which, unlike language,
we never made. Why induction should be trusted, apart from special
cases such as the ostensive learning of words, is the perennial philosophical problem of induction.

One part of the problem of induction, the part that asks why there
should be regularities in nature at all, can, I think, be dismissed. *That*
there are or have been regularities, for whatever reason, is an established fact of science; and we cannot ask better than that. *Why* there
have been regularities is an obscure question, for it is hard to see
what would count as an answer. What does make clear sense is this
other part of the problem of induction: why does our innate subjective spacing of qualities accord so well with the functionally relevant
groupings in nature as to make our inductions tend to come out right?
Why should our subjective spacing of qualities have a special pur-
chase on nature and a lien on the future?

There is some encouragement in Darwin. If people's innate spacing
of qualities is a gene-linked trait, then the spacing that has made for
the most successful inductions will have tended to predominate

through natural selection.[11] Creatures inveterately wrong in their inductions have a pathetic but praiseworthy tendency to die before reproducing their kind.

At this point let me say that I shall not be impressed by protests that I am using inductive generalizations, Darwin's and others, to justify induction, and thus reasoning in a circle. The reason I shall not be impressed by this is that my position is a naturalistic one; I see philosophy not as an *a priori* propaedeutic or groundwork for science, but as continuous with science. I see philosophy and science as in the same boat—a boat which, to revert to Neurath's figure as I so often do, we can rebuild only at sea while staying afloat in it. There is no external vantage point, no first philosophy. All scientific findings, all scientific conjectures that are at present plausible, are therefore in my view as welcome for use in philosophy as elsewhere. For me then the problem of induction is a problem about the world: a problem of how we, as we now are (by our present scientific lights), in a world we never made, should stand better than random or coin-tossing chances of coming out right when we predict by inductions which are based on our innate, scientifically unjustified similarity standard. Darwin's natural selection is a plausible partial explanation.

It may, in view of a consideration to which I next turn, be almost explanation enough. This consideration is that induction, after all, has its conspicuous failures. Thus take color. Nothing in experience, surely, is more vivid and conspicuous than color and its contrasts. And the remarkable fact, which has impressed scientists and philosophers as far back at least as Galileo and Descartes, is that the distinctions that matter for basic physical theory are mostly independent of color contrasts. Color impresses man; raven black impresses Hempel; emerald green impresses Goodman. But color is cosmically secondary. Even slight differences in sensory mechanisms from species to species, Smart remarks,[12] can make overwhelming differences in the grouping of things by color. Color is king in our innate quality space, but undistinguished in cosmic circles. Cosmically, colors would not qualify as kinds.

Color is helpful at the food-gathering level. Here it behaves well under induction, and here, no doubt, has been the survival value of our color-slanted quality space. It is just that contrasts that are crucial for such activities can be insignificant for broader and more theoretical science. If man were to live by basic science alone, natural selection would shift its support to the color-blind mutation.

Living as he does by bread and basic science both, man is torn. Things about his innate similarity sense that are helpful in the one sphere can be a hindrance in the other. Credit is due man's inveterate ingenuity, or human sapience, for having worked around the blinding dazzle of color vision and found the more significant regularities elsewhere. Evidently natural selection has dealt with the conflict by endowing man doubly: with both a color-slanted quality space and the ingenuity to rise above it.

He has risen above it by developing modified systems of kinds, hence modified similarity standards for scientific purposes. By the trial-and-error process of theorizing he has regrouped things into new kinds which prove to lend themselves to many inductions better than the old.

A crude example is the modification of the notion of fish by excluding whales and porpoises. Another taxonomic example is the grouping of kangaroos, opossums, and marsupial mice in a single kind, marsupials, while excluding ordinary mice. By primitive standards the marsupial mouse is more similar to the ordinary mouse than to the kangaroo; by theoretical standards the reverse is true.

A theoretical kind need not be a modification of an intuitive one. It may issue from theory full-blown, without antecedents; for instance the kind which comprises positively charged particles.

We revise our standards of similarity or of natural kinds on the strength, as Goodman remarks,[13] of second-order inductions. New groupings, hypothetically adopted at the suggestion of a growing theory, prove favorable to inductions and so become "entrenched." We newly establish the projectibility of some predicate, to our satisfaction, by successfully trying to project it. In induction nothing succeeds like success.

Between an innate similarity notion or spacing of qualities and a scientifically sophisticated one, there are all gradations. Science, after all, differs from common sense only in degree of methodological sophistication. Our experiences from earliest infancy are bound to have overlaid our innate spacing of qualities by modifying and supplementing our grouping habits little by little, inclining us more and more to an appreciation of theoretical kinds and similarities, long before we reach the point of studying science systematically as such. Moreover, the later phases do not wholly supersede the earlier; we retain different similarity standards, different systems of kinds, for use in different contexts. We all still say that a marsupial mouse is more like an ordinary mouse than a kangaroo, except when we are concerned with genetic matters. Something like our innate quality space continues to function alongside the more sophisticated regroupings that have been found by scientific experience to facilitate induction.

We have seen that a sense of similarity or of kinds is fundamental to learning in the widest sense—to language learning, to induction, to expectation. Toward a further appreciation of how utterly this notion permeates our thought, I want now to point out a number of other very familiar and central notions which seem to depend squarely on this one. They are notions that are definable in terms of similarity, or kinds, and further irreducible.

A notable domain of examples is the domain of dispositions, such as Carnap's example of solubility in water. To say of some individual object that it is soluble in water is not to say merely that it always dissolves when in water, because this would be true by default of any object, however insoluble, if it merely happened to be destined never to get into water. It is to say rather that it *would* dissolve if it were in water; but this account brings small comfort, since the device of a subjunctive conditional involves all the perplexities of disposition terms and more. Thus far I simply repeat Carnap.[14] But now I want to point out what could be done in this connection with the notion of kind. Intuitively, what qualifies a thing as soluble though it never gets into water is that it is of the same kind as the things that actually did or will dissolve; it is similar to them. Strictly we can't simply say "*the* same kind," nor simply "similar," when we have wider and narrower kinds, less and more similarity. Let us then mend our definition by saying that the soluble things are the common members of *all* such kinds. A thing is soluble if *each* kind that is broad enough to embrace all actual victims of solution embraces it too.

Graphically the idea is this: we make a set of all the sometime victims, all the things that actually did or will dissolve in water, and then we add just enough other things to round the set out into a kind. This is the water-soluble kind.

If this definition covers just the desired things, the things that are really soluble in water, it owes its success to a circumstance that could be otherwise. The needed circumstance is that a sufficient variety of things actually get dissolved in water to assure their not all falling under any one kind narrower than the desired water-soluble kind itself. But it is a plausible circumstance, and I am not sure that its accidental character is a drawback. If the trend of events had bee otherwise, perhaps the solubility concept would not have been wanted.

However, if I seem to be defending this definition, I must now hasten to add that of course it has much the same fault as the definition which used the subjunctive conditional. This definition uses the unreduced notion of kind, which is certainly not a notion we want to rest with either; neither theoretical kind nor intuitive kind. My purpose in giving the definition is only to show the link between the problem of dispositions and the problem of kinds.

As between theoretical and intuitive kinds, certainly the theoretical ones are the ones wanted for purposes of defining solubility and other dispositions of scientific concern. Perhaps "amiable" and "reprehensible" are disposition terms whose definitions should draw rather on intuitive kinds.

In considering the disposition of solubility we observed a link first with the subjunctive conditional and then with the notion of kind. This suggests comparing also the two end terms, so as to see the connection between the subjunctive conditional and the notion of kind. We had then, on the one side, the subjunctive conditional "If x were in water it would dissolve"; and on the other side, in terms of kinds, we had "Each kind that embraces all things that ever get into water and dissolve, embraces x." Here we have equated a sample subjunctive conditional to a sentence about kinds. We can easily enough generalize the equivalence to cover a significant class of subjunctive conditionals: the form "If x were an F then x would be a G" gets equated to "Each kind that embraces all Fs that are Gs embraces x." Notice that the Fs themselves, here, would not be expected to constitute a kind; nor the Gs; nor the Fs which are Gs. But you take the fewest things you can which, added to the Fs which are Gs, suffice to round the set out to a kind. Then x is one of these few additional things; this is the interpretation we get of the subjunctive conditional "If x were an F then x would be a G."

One might try this formula out on other examples, and study it for possible light on subjunctive conditionals more generally. Some further insight into this queer idiom might thus be gained. But let us remember that we are still making uncritical use of the unreduced notion of kind. My purpose, again, is only to show the link between these matters.

Another dim notion, which has intimate connections with dispositions and subjunctive conditionals, is the notion of cause; and we shall see that it too turns on the notion of kinds. Hume explained cause as invariable succession, and this makes sense as long as the cause and effect are referred to by general terms. We can say that fire causes heat, and we can mean thereby, as Hume would have it, that each event classifiable under the head of fire is followed by an event classifiable under the head of heat, or heating up. But this account, whatever its virtues for these general causal statements, leaves singular causal statements unexplained.

What does it mean to say that the kicking over of a lamp in Mrs. Leary's barn caused the Chicago fire? It cannot mean merely that the event at Mrs. Leary's belongs to a set, and the Chicago fire belongs to a set, such that there is invariable succession between the two sets: every member of the one set is followed by a member of the other. This paraphrase is trivially true and too weak. Always, if one event happens to be followed by another, the two belong to *certain* sets between which there is invariable succession. We can rig the sets arbitrarily. Just put any arbitrary events in the first set, including the first of the two events we are interested in; and then in the other set put the second of those two events, together with other events that happen to have occurred just after the other members of the first set.

Because of this way of trivialization, a singular causal statement says no more than that the one event was followed by the other. That is, it says no more if we use the definition just now contemplated; which, therefore, we must not. The trouble with that definition is clear enough: it is the familiar old trouble of the promiscuity of sets. Here, as usual, kinds, being more discriminate, enable us to draw distinctions where sets do not. To say that one event caused another is to say that the two events are of *kinds* between which there is invariable succession. If this correction does not yet take care of Mrs. Leary's cow, the fault is only with invariable succession itself, as affording too simple a definition of general causal statements; we need to hedge it around with provisions for partial or contributing causes and a good deal else. That aspect of the causality problem is not my concern. What I wanted to bring out is just the relevance of the notion of kinds, as the needed link between singular and general causal statements.

We have noticed that the notion of kind, or similarity, is crucially relevant to the notion of disposition, to the subjunctive conditional, and to singular causal statements. From a scientific point of view these are a pretty disreputable lot. The notion of kind, or similarity, is equally disreputable. Yet some such notion, some similarity sense, was seen to be crucial to all learning, and central in particular to the processes of inductive generalization and prediction which are the very life of science. It appears that science is rotten to the core.

Yet there may be claimed for this rot a certain undeniable fecundity. Science reveals hidden mysteries, predicts successfully, and works technological wonders. If this is the way of rot, then rot is rather to be prized and praised than patronized.

Rot, actually, is not the best model here. A better model is human progress. A sense of comparative similarity, I remarked earlier, is one of man's animal endowments. Insofar as it fits in with regularities of nature, so as to afford us reasonable success in our primitive inductions and expectations, it is presumably an evolutionary product of natural selection. Secondly, as remarked, one's sense of similarity or one's system of kinds develops and changes and even turns multiple as one matures, making perhaps for increasingly dependable prediction. And at length standards of similarity set in which are geared to theoretical science. This development is a development away from the immediate, subjective, animal sense of similarity to the remoter objectivity of a similarity determined by scientific hypotheses and posits and constructs. Things are similar in the later or theoretical sense to the degree that they are interchangeable parts of the cosmic machine revealed by science.

This progress of similarity standards, in the course of each individual's maturing years, is a sort of recapitulation in the individual of the race's progress from muddy savagery. But the similarity notion even in its theoretical phase is itself a muddy notion still. We have offered no definition of it in satisfactory scientific terms. We of course have a behavioral definition of what counts, for a given individual, as similar to what, or as more similar to what than to what; we have this for similarity old and new, human and animal. But it is no definition of what it means really for a to be more similar to b than to c; really, and quite apart from this or that psychological subject.

Did I already suggest a definition to this purpose, metaphorically, when I said that things are similar to the extent that they are interchangeable parts of the cosmic machine? More literally, could things be said to be similar in proportion to how much of scientific theory would remain true on interchanging those things as objects of reference in the theory? This only hints a direction; consider for instance the dimness of "how much theory." Anyway the direction itself is not a good one; for it would make similarity depend in the wrong way on theory. A man's judgments of similarity do and should depend on his theory, on his beliefs; but similarity itself, what the man's judgments purport to be judgments of, purports to be an objective relation in the world. It belongs in the subject matter not of our theory of theorizing about the world, but of our theory of the world itself. Such would be the acceptable and reputable sort of similarity concept, if it could be defined.

It does get defined in bits: bits suited to special branches of science. In this way, on many limited fronts, man continues his rise from savagery, sloughing off the muddy old notion of kind or similarity piecemeal, a vestige here and a vestige there. Chemistry, the home science of water-solubility itself, is one branch that has reached this stage. Comparative similarity of the sort that matters for chemistry can be stated outright in chemical terms, that is, in terms of chemical composition. Molecules will be said to *match* if they contain atoms of the same elements in the same topological combinations. Then, in principle, we might get at the comparative similarity of objects a and b by considering how many pairs of matching molecules there are, one molecule from a and one from b each time, and how many unmatching pairs. The ratio gives even a theoretical measure of relative similarity, and thus abundantly explains what it is for a to be more similar to b than to c. Or we might prefer to complicate our definition by allowing also for degrees in the matching of molecules; molecules having almost equally many atoms, or having atoms whose atomic numbers or atomic weights are almost equal, could be reckoned as matching better than others. At any rate a lusty chemical similarity concept is assured.

From it, moreover, an equally acceptable concept of kinds is derivable, by the paradigm-and foil definition noted early in this paper. For it is a question now only of distilling purely chemical kinds from purely chemical similarity; no admixture of other respects of similarity interferes. We thus exonerate water-solubility, which, the last time around, we had reduced no further than to an unexplained notion of kind. Therewith also the associated subjunctive conditional, "If this were in water it would dissolve," gets its bill of health.

The same scientific advances that have thus provided a solid underpinning for the definition of solubility in terms of kinds, have also, ironically enough, made that line of definition pointless by providing a full understanding of the mechanism of solution. One can redefine water-solubility by simply describing the structural conditions of that mechanism. This embarrassment of riches is, I suspect, a characteristic outcome. That is, once we can legitimize a disposition term by defining the relevant similarity standard, we are apt to know the mechanism of the disposition, and so bypass the similarity. Not but that the similarity standard is worth clarifying too, for its own sake or for other purposes.

Philosophical or broadly scientific motives can impel us to seek still a basic and absolute concept of similarity, along with such fragmentary similarity concepts as suit special branches of science. This drive for a cosmic similarity concept is perhaps identifiable with the age-old drive to reduce things to their elements. It epitomizes the scientific spirit, though dating back to the pre-Socratics: to Empedocles with his theory of four elements, and above all to Democritus with his atoms. The modern physics of elementary particles, or of hills in space-time, is a more notable effort in this direction.

This idea of rationalizing a single notion of relative similarity, throughout its cosmic sweep, has its metaphysical attractions. But there would remain still need also to rationalize the similarity notion more locally and superficially, so as to capture only such similarity as is relevant to some special science. Our chemistry example is already a case of this, since it stops short of full analysis into neutrons, electrons, and the other elementary particles.

A more striking example of superficiality, in this good sense, is afforded by taxonomy, say in zoology. Since learning about the evolution of species, we are in a position to define comparative similarity suitably for this science by consideration of family trees. For a theoretical measure of the degree of similarity of two individual animals we can devise some suitable function that depends on proximity and frequency of their common ancestors. Or a more significant concept of degree of similarity might be devised in terms of genes. When kind is construed in terms of any such similarity concept, fishes in the corrected, whale-free sense of the word qualify as a kind while fishes in the more inclusive sense do not.

Different similarity measures, or relative similarity notions, best suit different branches of science; for there are wasteful complications in providing for finer gradations of relative similarity than matter for the phenomena with which the particular science is concerned. Perhaps the branches of science could be revealingly classified by looking to the relative similarity notion that is appropriate to each. Such a plan is reminiscent of Felix Klein's so-called *Erlangerprogramm* in geometry, which involved characterizing the various branches of geometry by what transformations were irrelevant to each. But a branch of science would only qualify for recognition and classification under such a plan when it had matured to the point of clearing up its similarity notion. Such branches of science would qualify further as unified, or integrated into our inclusive systematization of nature, only insofar as their several similarity concepts were *compatible;* capable of meshing, that is, and differing only in the fineness of their discriminations.

Disposition terms and subjunctive conditionals in these areas, where suitable senses of similarity and kind are forthcoming, suddenly turn respectable; respectable and, in principle, superfluous. In other domains they remain disreputable and practically indispensable. They may be seen perhaps as unredeemed notes; the theory that would clear up the unanalyzed underlying similarity notion in such cases is still to come. An example is the disposition called intelligence—the ability, vaguely speaking, to learn quickly and to solve problems. Sometime, whether in terms of proteins or colloids or nerve nets or overt behavior, the relevant branch of science may reach the stage where a similarity notion can be constructed capable of making even the notion of intelligence respectable. And superfluous.

In general we can take it as a very special mark of the maturity of a branch of science that it no longer needs an irreducible notion of similarity and kind. It is that final stage where the animal vestige is wholly absorbed into the theory. In this career of the similarity notion, starting in its innate phase, developing over the years in the light of accumulated experience, passing then from the intuitive phase into theoretical similarity, and finally disappearing altogether, we have a paradigm of the evolution of unreason into science.

Notes

1. C. G. Hempel 1965 [744], p. 15.

2. Nelson Goodman 1955 [53], p. 74. I am indebted to Goodman and to Burton Dreben for helpful criticisms of earlier drafts of the present paper.

3. Goodman 1955 [53], pp. 82 ff.

4. Ibid., pp. 95 ff.

5. I mean this only as a sufficient condition of lawlikeness. See Donald Davidson 1966.

6. The relevance of kind is noted by Goodman 1955 [53], 1st edition, pp. 119 ff; 2d edition, pp. 121 f.

7. Nelson Goodman 1966 [584], pp. 163 ff.

8. Rudolf Carnap 1967 [688], pp. 141–147.

9. See Quine 1960 [100], pp. 83 ff, for further discussion and references.

10. See Quine 1960 [100], pp. 90–95.

11. This was noted by S. Watanabe on the second page of his 1965 [853].

12. J. J. C. Smart 1963 [656], pp. 68–72.

13. Goodman 1955 [53], pp. 95 ff.

14. Carnap 1936 [688].

4

Natural Kinds

Ellen Markman

In this chapter about natural kind terms I pursue the suggestion that children might expect categories, or at least categories of a special status, to have a correlated structure.

Recent arguments in philosophy about natural kind terms provide another challenge to traditional theories of concepts (Kripke 1971 [766], 1972 [767]; Putnam 1970 [634]). According to these analyses, natural kind terms do not have meaning in the traditional sense.

The term "natural kind" has various uses in philosophy and psychology, but to begin with some clear cases, natural kinds are categories that are found in nature, such as various categories of plants and animals. For example, the categories "mammal," "gold," and "water" are all natural kinds.

One of the most distinctive characteristics of natural kinds is the remarkable richness of their correlated structure. According to Mill (1843) [616],

Some classes have little or nothing in common to characterize them by, except precisely what is connoted by the name. (p. 135)

Consider the category of white things.

White things are not distinguished by any common properties except whiteness or if they are—it is only by such as are in some way dependent upon or connected with whiteness. . . . But hundreds of generations have not exhausted the common properties of animal or plants. . . . If anyone were to propose for the investigation the common properties of all things which are of the same color, the same shape, or the same specific gravity, the absurdity would be palpable. . . . Of these two classifications, the one answers to a much more radical distinction in the things themselves than the other does. One classification is made by *nature*, the other by us. (p. 136)

Reprinted from *Categorization and Naming in Children*, by Ellen Markman (Cambridge, Mass.: MIT Press, 1989, by permission of the publisher. Copyright © 1989, MIT Press.

Thus, some categories allow us to infer a great deal about their members. A related point has been made about basic level categories, which also have a correlated structure (Rosch et al. 1976 [818]); for example, if we know that something is a bird, we know that it has feathers and wings, that it is quite likely to have a beak and to fly, and so on. Mill's claim is that some categories have such an extraordinarily rich correlated structure that even after extensive study of the category, we have not exhausted all there is to learn about it. We have sciences devoted to discovering and understanding different animal species such as mammals. Although a category such as "mammal" may have originally been delimited by a few superficial features, such as having fur or hair, members of the category have unforeseen properties in common. We have continued to discover properties that are characteristic of mammals, so much so that separate scientific disciplines are needed to account for the accumulation of knowledge. The properties of mammals figure in scientific laws or generalizations from various sciences, including physiology, anatomy, genetics, and ethology. The fact that several scientific disciplines continue to discover new facts about this category is testimony to how richly structured it is.

Now, to take Mill's contrasting example, consider a category defined as "white things." If it seemed important or useful, we could certainly define such a category; yet we could not have a science devoted to determining what these diverse objects that happen to be white have in common. This category has a minimal correlated structure. It includes a white cloud but excludes a grey one. It includes a white car but excludes cars of any other color. It includes white paper but excludes yellow paper, and so on. Being white does not tell us very much about an object beyond the fact that it is white. Whiteness does not correlate with or predict much else.

The Causal Theory of Reference

The new theory of reference for natural kinds poses several problems for traditional theories of meaning. According to the traditional view, each category term has both an intension (the set of necessary and sufficient properties that define the concept) and an extension (the set of objects to which the term applies). The intension specifies the criteria that determine which objects will make up the extension. That is, in order for an object to be in the extension of the term, it must satisfy the relevant criteria. To take a concrete example, consider the concept "square." The intension of the term "square" is an equilateral quadrangle with four right angles. In order for an object to be a square, it must fulfill these criteria; that is, it must have four sides, four right angles, and so on. The extension of the word "square" is the set of objects that meet these criteria. That is, the extension of the word "square" is composed of the objects that are squares.

One view of category terms that contrasts with this traditional view [makes use of the notion of] family resemblances. On this view, there may be no features that are necessary and sufficient; instead, the intension of the term consists of a set of features some number of which must apply to an object for it to qualify as an instance of the category. As long as an object has enough of the relevant features, it will qualify; it is not required to fulfill all of them.

What these two views have in common, however, is that they are both criterial accounts of category terms; that is, both claim that the meaning of a category term derives in some way or another from a set of criteria associated with that category. In this regard, the causal theory of reference contrasts with both the classical view and the family resemblance view of categories. In a major departure from the typical way of looking at category terms, Kripke (1971 [766], 1972 [777]) and Putnam (1977) [806] suggest that category terms be treated on analogy with proper names. This is a radical view, because on their treatment, at least, proper names do not have criterial meaning in the ordinary sense. (For a good summary of the issues, see Schwartz 1977 [651].) As an example, consider the proper name "Shakespeare." We know a fair amount about Shakespeare—for example, that he was the author of *Hamlet, Romeo and Juliet,* and so on. Imagine a list of such facts about Shakespeare that we would use to identify him or describe him to someone who does not yet know who he is. It is possible, however, that we are mistaken about these facts. It could turn out that Shakespeare never really wrote those plays and that our beliefs about him were therefore erroneous. Nevertheless, the name "Shakespeare" would still apply to the same person. We wouldn't decide that we were wrong and that that person isn't really Shakespeare. We would conclude instead that Shakespeare did not write those plays. Thus, the facts or descriptions that we might use to identify Shakespeare do not function as *criteria.* They are not necessary and sufficient features of what it takes to be Shakespeare. They are beliefs about Shakespeare that are helpful in *identifying* him, but they do not constitute criteria in the traditional sense.

Kripke argues that instead of being based on criteria, the "meaning" of a proper name derives from the causal history of its use, going back to its first introduction, on analogy with a baptismal ceremony. Moreover, he claims, proper names refer to the same individual, even in counterfactual situations. When we ask, "If Johnson had not declined to run again, would Nixon have been elected president?" there is no question that we are still referring to Nixon, even though he might not have been president. We would still be using the proper name "Nixon" to refer to Nixon. The name refers to the same individual even when used in hypothetical discussions where important facts about the world and about the individual in question are changed.

Analysis of Natural Kind Terms

According to Kripke and Putnam, there are important analogies in the way that natural kind terms and proper names function. First, Kripke and Putnam argue that many of the properties that we may have taken to define a category term do not really do so. The claim is that the superficial properties that we use to identify natural kind categories do not function as necessary and sufficient criteria and that in fact each such property could be violated and yet we would still agree on the classification of the object. Putnam uses the existence of abnormal members of categories to demonstrate this point. As a way of describing the natural kind term "lemon," one might specify that lemons have an oval shape, yellow skin, and a sour taste. Yet one could imagine a change in some chemical in the atmosphere that would modify the pigment in the skin, causing lemons to become green. Similarly, a change in the nutrients in the soil could effect a change in the taste of lemons, causing them to be bitter, and so on. Yet, Putnam argues, despite all of these changes in the properties we have listed, we would still agree that these (green, bitter) objects are lemons. That is, the word "lemon" would still refer to lemons despite the changes that we would need to make in the description of the properties. To further illustrate this point, Putnam notes that what we currently take to be normal members of the category might, in fact, be abnormal members. Perhaps lemons were originally green and bitter but alterations in the chemical composition of the atmosphere and land have caused them to be yellow and sour.

On this causal theory of reference, the descriptions that we give for natural kinds function just like the descriptions we might give for a proper name. They are useful in identifying the objects in question, and they may effectively describe the stereotype we have of the object, but they do not qualify as criteria for the category. Even if the superficial properties change, the natural kind term will continue to refer to the same category.

Given this rejection of the traditional account of meaning, two questions naturally arise: How is the referent for a term established? and How can we tell whether or not the term is being used correctly—for example, how do we know that an object we call a "lemon" is in fact a lemon?

According to this theory, the reference of a term may be established by a causal chain, by analogy to the way the reference for proper names is established. While the object is present, someone labels the object, and that provides the first link in a causal chain in which subsequent speakers continue to use the label to refer to the same kind of object. For natural kind terms, speakers will typically select a prototypical exemplar to label at first, and they may provide a description of the natural kind to identify the relevant category. The description does not define the category, however, but serves as a way of helping speakers to fix the referent, that is, to identify what is being labeled. Tigers might be described as large, striped, ferocious, wild cats to enable someone to identify what objects are being referred to as "tigers." Yet under some circumstances we might readily agree that a small, albino, tame cat was, nevertheless, a tiger. First, Putnam points out that there is a "division of linguistic labor." Not everyone need acquire the methods for determining whether or not something is gold, for example. Instead, we may often rely on experts to make the final determination. But what do the experts rely on? Experts base their judgments on the best scientific knowledge that is available at the time—on the most well established empirical theory. In the case of gold, its atomic number will be the deciding factor; in the case of water, its molecular formula (H_2O); and in the case of lemons, their chromosomal structure. Here Putnam embraces a kind of essentialism. The assumption is that there are some "deep" properties, or hidden structural properties, that account for or determine what the more superficial properties will be. These structural properties establish the "essential nature which the thing shares with other members of the natural kind. What the essential nature is is not a matter of language analysis but of scientific theory construction" (Putnam 1977 [806], 104).

Contrast this analysis of natural kind terms with a standard analysis of more arbitrary "one-criterion" terms, such as Mill's example of "white things." Here the properties we would give to describe the meaning of the term would function as a definition and not just as a useful aid to identifying the category. If the properties changed—for example, if pollution turned all white things a dingy grey—they would no longer be white things. We do not have a scientific theory of white things to rely on, nor do we expect there to be some deep, hidden structure that is common to all white things.

Each of these points—the unlimited richness of the categories, the search for more theory-relevant explanatory properties, the reliance on authority to distinguish exemplars of a category from nonexemplars, the acceptance of abnormal members, and the corrigibility of beliefs about categories—distinguishes natural kinds from other types of categories.

Natural Kinds and Induction

Susan Gelman and I (Gelman and Markman 1986 [732], 1987 [733]) have argued that this analysis of natural kinds, especially the emphasis on the richness of the structure and the belief that unobservable properties are common to members of a natural kind, predicts that natural kinds will often be used to support inductive inferences from one category member to another. That is, if categories are structured so as to capture indefinitely rich clusters of information, then new features learned about one category member will often be projected onto other category members as well. In this way, natural kind categories should promote inductive inferences. Moreover, there are two ways in which the inductions are made without perceptual support. First, even if an object does not look much like other members of a given natural kind, knowing what kind it belongs to should lead people to assume that it will share relevant properties with other members of the category. Second, these properties, such as internal organs or chemical structure, are often unobservable by the average person.

Certainly, only some types of inferences within a kind are justified. Whether the inference is reasonable or not depends in part on what type of property is attributed to what type of natural kind. Among animal species, for example, we expect members of the same species to share methods of reproduction, respiration, and locomotion. We do not expect other kinds of properties to be common even to members of the same species. For example, if one poodle is 2 years old, we should not expect another poodle also to be 2 years old. Thus, at least implicitly, people have embedded natural kind categories in scientific or prescientific theories that limit what classes of properties are expected to be common to a given natural kind category.

Little is known about how expectations about natural kinds originate. How much exploration of categories or even explicit scientific training is needed before children come to expect that categories reflect more than superficial perceptual similarities? There is a large developmental literature suggesting that young children rely on superficial perceptual properties on cognitive tasks, including those involving classification, free recall, free association, and word definitions (see Flavell 1963 [571], 1977 [572]; Mansfield 1977 [785]). Young children have often been characterized as "concrete" and as "perceptually bound," meaning that their cognition is captured by the appearances of things. A well-known example is the Piagetian conservation problems. In a task involving conservation of number, for example, two equal rows of objects—say, pennies—are lined up in one-to-one correspondence. Children judge that both rows have the same number of pennies. Then, while the child watches, one of the rows is spread out. Children now judge that the lengthened row has more pennies. One interpretation of this is that the children are unable to overlook the misleading perceptual cue of the length of the row. Their judgment of equality or inequality is presumably based on the available perceptual information rather than on the actual quantity. To take an example concerning categorization, Tversky (1985) [850] has found that young children prefer to group objects together on the basis of color or shape rather than on the basis of common category membership. On one of her tasks, for example, a 4-year-old typically groups a fire engine with an apple because both are red rather than grouping a fire engine with a car because both are vehicles. In this task and others, children seem unable to override what are sometimes misleading perceptual cues.

Based on these findings, one might expect that young children would rely heavily on perceptual characteristics of objects for judgments of category membership. Young children may have no means of appreciating the rationale for grouping perceptually dissimilar objects together. Even for natural kinds, children might represent category members as sharing superficial properties and only later come to realize that they have deeper properties in common. Thus, according to this view, children, with their reliance on perceptual features and their limited scientific knowledge, should not rely on natural kind categories to support inductive inferences about objects.

On the other hand, given the importance of natural kind categories for human cognition, children might quite early on expect categories to have a richly correlated structure. Even with only rudimentary scientific knowledge, children might believe that natural kind categories are united by many unobservable properties. Children could be biased from the start to expect that categories they learn will share clusters of features, or such an expectation could be derived from experience. Even with only limited scientific knowledge, children could notice that natural kinds have many observable features in common. They could then extend this belief and expect natural kinds to be united by many unobservable properties as well. Any appreciation of natural kinds at this early age would probably reflect an unsophisticated, undifferentiated belief in the richness of categories. Children would lack the requisite scientific knowledge that could limit their inductions to categories and attributes that are appropriate.

One piece of evidence that children are not solely dependent on perceptual similarity for drawing inferences comes from work by Carey (1985) [552]. In one study she showed several groups of children between ages 4 and 10 a mechanical monkey, one that could move its arms to bang cymbals together. The mechanical monkey looked much like a real monkey. Children, who knew that real monkeys breathe, eat, and have baby monkeys, were asked whether the mechanical monkey could breathe, eat, and have babies too. All but one group of 4-year-old children denied that the mechanical monkey possessed these animate properties. In other words, despite the striking perceptual similarity of these two types of objects—mechanical and real monkeys—children did not generalize facts about one to the other. These children had differentiated living things from nonliving things and therefore refused to impute properties that characterize living things to nonliving things. It could be, however, that it is only at the level of such basic ontological distinctions (Keil 1979 [600]) such as living versus nonliving that children treat categories as natural kinds.

Gelman and I (Gelman and Markman 1986 [732]) questioned children about much more specific natural kind categories, from both biological (e.g., squirrel and snake) and nonbiological (e.g., gold and salt) domains. To determine whether children would induce new information from natural kind categories, rather than from perceptual appearances, we pitted category membership against perceptual similarity. Children were shown two objects and told a new fact abut each. They then had to infer which of the facts applied to a third object that looked very much like one of the first two objects but was given the same category label as the other one. These experiments test whether very young children are sensitive to the richness of natural kind categories and whether they use these categories, in the absence of perceptual support, to justify inductive inferences.

One of the main assumptions about natural kind categories that motivated our developmental work is that adults expect members of a natural kind to share many properties and will therefore use the natural kind category to support inductive inferences. In particular, adults should rely on the natural kind membership of an object more than on its superficial perceptual appearance to make inferences about its internal structure, behavior, and other theoretically relevant properties. Gelman and I conducted a preliminary study (reported in Gelman and Markman 1986 [732]) to establish that adults would use the natural kind category to support inductions for those categories that would later be used with children.

Undergraduates were presented with 20 problems. Each problem consisted of a set of three pictures. New information was given about two of the pictures, then a question was asked about the third picture. The correct answer could not be determined from the picture. The subject could arrive at one of two answers: either by making an inference based on category membership or by making a different inference based on perceptual similarity.

The three pictures for each problem were arranged on a card. Two pictures were at the top of the card, and the third (the target) was directly underneath, centered below the first two. Directly below each of the two topmost pictures was a sentence that labeled the picture and provided some new factual information about it. Directly below the target picture was a question asking which of two new

attributes applied. For example, on one problem subjects saw a flamingo and a bat at the top of the card. Underneath the flamingo was
written, "This bird's heart has a right aortic arch only." Underneath
the bat was written, "This bat's heart has a left aortic arch only."
Below these two pictures was a picture of a blackbird (which looked
more like the bat than the flamingo). Underneath the blackbird was
written, "What does this bird's heart have?" For each item, subjects
were to choose one of the two answers. After each choice they were
asked to justify their selection by responding to the question, "Why
is this the best answer?" Finally they were asked to rate their confidence in their answer on a scale from "1" (very unsure) to "7" (very
sure).

As predicted, adults based their inferences on the common natural
kind membership of the objects. Overall, they concluded that the target picture had the same property as the other similarly labeled object
an average of 86% of the time. Apparently subjects expected slightly
more variation within a category for the biological categories than for
the nonbiological categories. They inferred properties on the basis of
common category 92% of the time for the nonbiological categories
and 80% of the time for the biological categories. In addition, subjects
were highly confident that their choices were correct (the mean rating
was 5.8 on the 7-point scale). However, they were significantly more
confident about their judgments for the nonbiological categories
(mean = 6.0) than biological categories (mean = 5.5).

Young children might, like the adults, infer a new property of an
object from its category, or they might instead be governed by the
perceptual appearances of the objects. In study 1 from Gelman and
Markman 1986 [732] children were tested on the same categories as
the adult subjects in the preliminary study. They were asked about
different attributes, however, because they would not understand
most of the ones that adults were questioned about.

Preschool children ranging in age from 4:0 to 4:11 (with a mean age
of 4:5) participated in the study.

There were three conditions in this study. In the experimental condition children were taught information about each of two objects.
They were then shown a third object that looked like one of the two
training objects but was given the same category label as the other.
Children were asked to infer which piece of information applied to
the third object. This condition was designed to reveal whether children's influences are influenced by their knowledge of an object's
category or by perceptual similarity.

A second condition, the no-conflict control, was designed to demonstrate that when perceptual similarity and category membership coincide, children readily draw the correct inferences. In this condition, like the first, children were taught properties of two objects. However, the third object not only looked like one of the training objects but also was given the same label as that object. This task provides a baseline measure for how often children will draw the correct inference when both perceptual similarity and category membership lead to the same conclusion.

A final condition, the attributes control, was designed to make certain that children did not already know the information we would be teaching them. Children saw only one picture at a time—the third item in the other two conditions—and were asked which of the two properties applied. Children were expected to perform at about chance level in this condition.

Since the experiment proper involved teaching children new properties about two objects and asking them to judge which of the properties applied to a third object, it was important to ensure that children did not already know the information to be presented. A preliminary study was conducted to select questions about various animals, plants, and substances to which children would not yet know the answers.

An item was selected for inclusion in the experiment proper only if children were unable to answer the question significantly above or below chance. Table 4.1 shows examples of items that were selected. Half of the items concerned biological natural kinds and half concerned nonbiological natural kinds.

In the experimental condition, children saw 20 sets of three pictures each. Information was given concerning two of the pictures in each set, and children were asked a question about the third picture. The third picture looked like one of the first two pictures but was given the same category label as the other. Children could answer on the basis of either perceptual similarity or category membership. For example, children were shown a tropical fish, a dolphin, and a shark. In this case the shark was perceptually similar to the dolphin but was given the same label as the tropical fish. The experimenter labeled the three pictures, "fish" for the tropical fish, "dolphin" for the dolphin, and "fish" for the shark. Children were asked to repeat the names until they could name all three pictures correctly. (On 88% of the trials, children repeated all three names correctly on their first try.)

Table 4.1
Sample Items and Attributes Used in Gelman and Markman 1986 [732]

Biological items
This squirrel eats bugs. (gray squirrel)*
This rabbit eats grass. (brown rabbit)
(Target:) squirrel (Kaibab, looks like rabbit)

This dinosaur has cold blood. (brontosaurus)
This rhinoceros has warm blood. (gray rhinoceros)
(Target:) dinosaur (triceratops, looks like rhinoceros)

Nonbiological items
If you put this gold in a hot oven, it melts. (gold bar)
If you put this clay in a hot oven, it burns. (reddish blob)
(Target:) gold (brown blob; looks like clay)

This pearl comes from inside a sea animal. (seed pearl)
This marble comes from a big piece of rock. (round, pink)
(Target:) pearl (round, pink; looks like marble)

---

*Descriptions of the objects used are given in parentheses. These descriptions were *not* mentioned to subjects.

The experimenter then pointed to the tropical fish and said, "This fish stays underwater to breathe." She pointed to the dolphin and said, "This dolphin pops above the water to breathe." Finally she pointed to the shark and said, "See this fish. Does it breathe underwater, like this fish, or does it pop above the water to breathe, like this dolphin?" Comparable questions were asked for each item in table 4.1. Figure 4.1 presents an example of another triad: bird, bat, bird.

In the no-conflict control condition, the picture triads and procedure used were identical to those used in the experimental condition, with one exception. In this case the labels of the two similar objects were made to agree rather than conflict. For example, children heard the tropical fish labeled "fish," the dolphin labeled "dolphin," and the third picture (shark) labeled "dolphin" (instead of "fish" as in the previous condition). The children in this condition were provided with the same information about the two initial pictures—that is, that the fish breathes underwater and the dolphin pops above the water to breathe. The experimenter then pointed to the third picture and said, "See this dolphin. Does it breathe underwater, like this fish, or does it pop above the water to breathe, like this dolphin?"

In the attributes control condition children viewed only one picture at a time—the third item from each of the triads in the experimental condition. Without hearing any prior information, children were

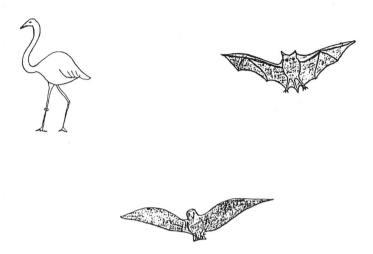

Figure 4.1
The bird, bat, bird triad from Gelman and Markman 1986 [732].

asked to judge which of the two properties applied. For example, children were shown the picture of the shark and asked, "See this fish. Does this fish breathe underwater or does it pop above the water to breathe?"

The main question that this study was designed to address is whether preschool children are willing to infer properties of an object based on its natural kind category. In particular, when category membership and perceptual similarity are in conflict, will children show any sensitivity to category membership, or will their inferences be based on the appearance of the objects? If children do use category membership as a basis for induction even in the absence of perceptual support, it is likely that they will do so for some conceptual domains before others. Therefore, we included both biological and nonbiological natural kinds, to test for generality. Table 4.2 presents the data according to condition and item type.

To address these questions, we first needed to establish that children's inferences in the experimental condition were based on the information provided to them in the experiment rather than on preexisting knowledge. The results of the attributes control condition indicate that children were in fact unaware of the correct answers. When simply given the test question, with no extra information to guide their answer, children performed at chance level, answering a mean of 53% of the questions correctly.

Table 4.2
Percent Correct (Category Choices) from Gelman and Markman 1986 [732]

	Experimental Condition	Non-conflict Control Condition	Attributes Control Condition
Biological	67	89	59
Nonbiological	69	87	48

On the other hand, when the perceptual similarity and category label coincided in the no-conflict control condition, children were capable of drawing the correct inference. When both the label and the appearance of the object led to the same conclusion, children were correct on 88% of the items.

In the experimental condition, where perceptual similarity and category membership were opposed, children preferred to use the category information 68% of the time, which is significantly better than chance, $p < .001$. Thirty-seven percent of the children consistently based their judgments on common category membership; that is, they inferred the property of the new object based on category membership on at least 15 out of 20 items. In contrast, no child showed a consistent preference for basing inferences on the perceptual similarity of the objects.

Thus, the children in the experimental condition were taking account of the training information in deciding about the properties of the new objects, as performance in that condition was better than in the attributes control condition. Although children in the experimental condition often based their judgments on the natural kind category of the object, they were in some conflict because of the divergence between category membership and perceptual appearances. Also, giving the category name may not be a perfect way of establishing category membership. That is, this procedure tests the power of the category in governing inductive inferences only insofar as the label successfully conveys the natural kind category. Some failure to respond to the category may reflect some degree of weakness in this for children, and not necessarily weakness in natural kind inductions per se. When category labels and perceptual similarity coincided (the no-conflict control condition), children answered more questions correctly.

Children were able to use category membership as often for the biological as for the nonbiological categories. Overall the mean correct was 67% for the biological and 69% for the nonbiological categories. However, there was a sex difference in the experimental condition. Boys performed better on the biological categories than on the nonbiological categories, whereas girls showed the reverse pattern. We could not explain this difference, although it is possible that boys and girls differ in which categories they find more familiar. Boys may be more familiar with such things as snakes, worms, bugs, and leaves (that is, the biological categories we tested), whereas girls may be more familiar with such things as sugar, salt, diamonds, and pearls (the nonbiological categories we tested).

In summary, even 4-year-olds realize that natural kind categories such as "squirrel" and "diamond" promote a rich set of inductive inferences. These young children have already come to expect new knowledge to be organized in accord with the categories named by their language, even in the stringent test case where the label conflicts with perceptual appearances. Using a simplified procedure, Gelman and Markman (1987) [733] determined that this conclusion extends to 3-year-olds as well. For these young children, the procedure used in Gelman and Markman 1986 was too demanding. Instead of pitting objects against each other, we taught children a new fact about an object (as before) and then determined which objects it would generalize to: an object that (a) looked like the original, (b) had the same label as the original, (c) looked like the original and had the same label, or (d) differed from the original in both respects. The findings were that children drew more inferences based on category membership than inferences based on perceptual appearances. Thus, even 3-year-olds assume that categories named by their language will include more than superficial features.

Study 3 of Gelman and Markman 1986 [732] addressed two questions raised by this finding. One question was whether identity of the linguistic information is necessary for children to use the common category as a basis for inductive inferences, or whether other means of indicating common category membership would be sufficient. To address this question, we designed a synonyms condition in which category membership was conveyed by means of synonyms rather than identical labels. For example, one triplet consisted of a target rabbit, another rabbit with a different appearance, and a squirrel that had long ears and looked like the target rabbit. The two rabbits in the synonyms condition were called "rabbit" and "bunny." If children infer that objects named by synonyms share the same properties, then their inferences cannot be based simply on identity of the labels.

Another question that was addressed in study 3 of Gelman and Markman 1986 [732] was whether children would use the common category to make arbitrary decisions for which common category membership is not relevant. To test this, we designed an arbitrary decision condition in which children were asked to decide what color chip should go on a picture after witnessing the experimenter place a chip of one color on a perceptually similar picture and a chip of another color on a dissimilar picture with the same category label. For example, the experimenter placed a red dot on the picture of one rabbit (called "rabbit") and a yellow dot on the picture of the squirrel (called "squirrel"). The child then had to pick which color dot to put on the third picture, the other rabbit (called "rabbit") that looked like the squirrel. If children are distinguishing between the induction task, where category labels are relevant, and this arbitrary task, where they are not, then they should be at chance in this condition, having no real basis on which to make a decision.

The third condition in this study was the standard condition that replicated the procedure of the experimental condition in the first study using the items that appeared in the synonyms and arbitrary decision conditions.

In the standard condition children once again drew inferences to category members at an above-chance level (68%). As before, even when the category conflicted with perceptual appearances, children tended to base their inductive inferences on the common category membership. Moreover, as the results from the synonyms condition indicated, children do not need to hear common labels to use common category membership to draw inferences. When children heard synonyms to indicate common category membership, they still based their inferences on category membership at a level greater than chance (63% of the time). The results of this study further indicate that children have begun to differentiate between inferences where category membership is relevant and arbitrary decisions where it is not. When children were asked about arbitrary decisions such as what color chip should go on a given picture, they were no more likely to base that decision on the color chip they had seen placed on a common category member than to base it on a chip placed on a perceptually similar picture.

In summary, children's inferences were based on the category membership of the objects and not simply on how the pictures were labeled. Children drew inferences based on common category membership even when category members were not given identical labels. Moreover, when category members were given identical labels, children relied on these labels only when the task required them to draw inferences.

From these studies, we know that young children will infer that an object shares properties with another object from the same category, even when these inferences do not have perceptual support. With the exception of the completely arbitrary property, the properties that were examined were ones that in fact would be largely determined by the natural kind category of the objects. That is, we asked about the internal organs, method of respiration, feeding habits, behavior, and so on, of animals—all properties that typically are common to a species. Similarly, we asked about the internal structure and chemical and physical properties of the nonbiological categories—again, all properties that typically are common to a mineral, metal, or other substance.

There are cases, however, where inductive inferences based on category membership would be unwarranted. For some properties, the perceptual similarity of objects should be used as the basis for induction rather than the common category membership. The size of an object, for example, is a better predictor of its weight than is its category.

Study 4 of Gelman and Markman 1986 [732] examined whether young children are selective in the kinds of inferences that they make based on category judgments. Preschool children have impoverished scientific knowledge, yet they believe that category members share unobservable properties. This implies that their beliefs about categories may be fairly general ones, not modulated by specific knowledge. In other words, such young children may not have sorted out which properties legitimately do and do not promote inferences within natural kind categories. They might, then, erroneously infer information on the basis of common category membership, even when asked about attributes that are more likely to be consequences of superficial perceptual properties. If attention to category membership dominates their judgments regardless of type of property, then children should assert, for example, that a rocklike chunk of salt will blow away in the wind as does fine-grained salt, and not remain in place as does a rock.

In this experiment children were taught a fact about each of two objects and then asked which of the properties applied to a third object. The third object was from the same category as one of the objects but was more similar in appearance to the other object. Unlike the previous studies, however, the properties were predicted more by perceptual similarity than by common category membership.

This study had two conditions, an experimental condition and a control condition. Children in the control condition were given the final test questions without any extra information. For example, they were shown a shark and were asked, "This is a fish. Do you think it weighs 20 pounds or 100 pounds?"

The procedure for the experimental condition was identical to that of the earlier studies, except that different attributes were being taught. Children viewed three objects, two placed side by side and one centered beneath them. Each object was labeled. A property was attributed to each of the two topmost pictures, and the children were then asked which of the properties applied to the third (target) picture. For example, after the pictures were labeled, children were told about a tropical fish, "This fish weighs 20 pounds." They were told about an object from a different category, in this case a dolphin, that, "This dolphin weighs 100 pounds." They were then asked about the target picture, a shark that looked more like the dolphin than the tropical fish, "See this fish. Does it weigh 20 pounds, like this fish, or 100 pounds, like this dolphin?"

In this study children were asked questions about perceptually based attributes: weight, visibility at night, and so forth. With no prior information on which to make inferences, children in the control condition selected the category choice no more often than expected by chance (48% of the time). In contrast to what happened in the earlier studies, fewer children in the experimental condition based their inferences on common category membership. They selected on the basis of common category an average of 49% of the time, which is not significantly different from chance or from the control group. However, the experimental condition, unlike the control condition, was markedly trimodal. Four of the 20 children consistently selected on the basis of perceptual similarity (that is, they chose the attribute of the perceptually similar picture on at least 15 out of 20 items); and 4 children consistently selected on the basis of common

gory of the object to support inductive inferences, even when this conflicted with the appearance of the objects.

Children drew these inferences when asked about properties that were reasonable to project from one category member to another. We asked about the eating habits, means of respiration, and internal organs of the biological categories and about chemical and physical properties of the nonbiological categories. Young children, able to answer these questions correctly, might overgeneralize the importance of the natural kind category. That is, even when it is unwarranted to do so, they may use categories more than appearances to support inductions. The results of subsequent studies indicate ways in which children have begun to limit the importance of the category. First, when the task involves making an arbitrary decision, children are not biased to infer on the basis of category membership. Second, children have at least begun to distinguish some kinds of properties from others as a basis for induction. To test this, we asked children about properties that should generalize on the basis of superficial perceptual similarity rather than on category membership. In answering such questions, children did not reliably use the category to support the inductions. Across several studies, those children who were asked about perceptually based properties were the only ones to reliably use the perceptual appearances of objects to support their inductions.

By age 3 and 4 children expect natural kinds to have a richly correlated structure that goes beyond superficial appearances. They use category membership to support inductions, even in the stringent test case where perceptual appearance and category label lead to different conclusions. Moreover, children have begun to differentiate between the kinds of properties that can justifiably be projected to other category members and those that cannot. Despite all these accomplishments, however, there is much left for children to learn about natural kind categories.

The Problem of Determining Which Properties Support Inductive Inferences

First, children must sort out which properties are likely to be common to members of different types of natural kinds. Although they have begun to work out this problem by age 4, their distinctions on even a crude level are imperfect. Even with properties that for adults are blatantly determined by superficial perceptual features (such as weight), some children based their inductions on the category—claiming, for example, that a large fish weighs the same amount as a little fish, because both are fish. Furthermore, there are constraints on inferences that no one has yet been able to characterize (Goodman 1955 [53]). Even for adults, we do not have good theories to explain how inferences are constrained.[1] A predicate may or may not promote inductions, depending on the level of abstraction of a category (all dogs bark, but not all animals bark) or the scientific domain (density at room temperature is important for metals but not animals). Nisbett, Krantz, and Kunda (1983) [471] have shown that adults are quite willing to infer new information from one category member to other members of the same category, but they do so selectively, depending on the property involved. Our studies have not tested the limits of children's abilities, but even so it is clear that children must develop more finely tuned distinctions among predicates and learn not to overgeneralize to obviously inappropriate predicates.

The Problem of Determining Which Categories Support Inductive Inferences

A related issue is how to constrain which kinds of categories support inductions. Some categories, such as "artifacts," do not pick out objects in nature that have indefinitely many properties in common. We do not assume, for example, that all forks or all saws will have unlimited numbers of properties in common. It is possible that children could very early on notice the natural kind-artifact distinction and use categories to support inductions mainly for natural kinds. It is also possible that children would begin by expecting most categories named by language to promote inductive inferences. That is, they would assume for a variety of conceptual domains that category members share many features with each other. Only after learning more about various domains would they restrict their inferences.

To address this question, Gelman (1984) [578] draws several distinctions between types of concepts. Natural kinds are expected to share many features besides the obvious ones, whereas artifacts are not. This is not a strict dichotomy, however, as some complex artifacts (computers and cars, for example) are probably similar to natural kinds. Building on findings from Rips (1975) [813] and Nisbett, Krantz, and Kunda (1983) [471], Gelman argues that in addition to the complexity of the category, assumptions about its homogeneity also may well affect how likely it is to support inductive inferences. For example, adults will infer that other samples of a metal conduct electricity, given that one sample of the metal does, but they will not infer that other people within a geographical region are obese, given that one person in that region is (Nisbett, Krantz, and Kunda 1983) [471]. Adults rely on their conception of how variable the property is within the domain being questioned (for instance, conductivity for metals) to make their inferences. Gelman suggests that natural kinds tend to be more homogeneous than artifacts and therefore support more inferences. Another possibility, however, is that it is homogeneity of the category per se, rather than its natural kind status, that predicts which categories are more likely to support certain inductions.

In a series of studies Gelman had adults rate categories in various ways to determine whether they perceive natural kinds and artifacts as differing in homogeneity. One procedure was to ask subjects to predict what percentage of the category members would be expected to have a given characteristic. Another was to ask subjects directly to rate on a scale from 1 to 9 how similar the members of a given category were to each other. The results using both of these procedures were comparable, indicating that natural kinds on the whole tend to be seen as more homogeneous than artifacts. Although on some of the measures minerals were seen as less homogeneous, natural kinds were in general thought of as homogeneous, regardless of complexity. This difference held up for superordinate level categories, as well as for basic level categories. The main exception was that, as expected, complex artifacts such as machines were perceived as being more like natural kinds.

Gelman then went on to determine what kinds of distinctions children have made between categories. Four- and seven-year-old children were taught a new fact—for example, that a rabbit has a spleen—and then had to decide whether the fact applied to a similar object (a similar rabbit), a different object from the same category (another rabbit), an object from the same superordinate category (a dog), and an unrelated object (a telephone). As evidence that the children were taking the task seriously, Gelman found that children virtually always drew inferences to a similar looking object and rarely drew inferences to an unrelated object. Only for the two intermediate levels of generality does it make sense to ask whether there is a natural kind-artifact distinction. Seven-year-olds clearly distinguish between natural kinds and artifacts. They drew more inferences from natural kinds than from artifacts at both basic and superordinate levels of categorization. The results from 4-year-olds are not so clear. These children may have begun to draw such a distinction, but it is unstable. They are more likely to draw inferences from categories that adults perceive as homogeneous. Thus, Gelman argues that the natural kind-artifact distinction is not used by preschool children but that it may evolve from an earlier distinction based on homogeneity.

Another way in which young children are likely to be limited is that they may not be able to look much beyond perceptual features of objects when they form categories on their own. In the studies reported here children were told the category labels and then asked to infer information from one member to another. This task is simpler than the converse problem of having to form the category in the first place, without knowing beforehand which properties are relevant. When initially forming a category, children are likely to be much more susceptible to perceptual appearances. Most standard classification procedures (see Inhelder and Piaget 1964 [596]) require children to divide objects into categories where many bases of classification are possible. Given the complexity of this problem (see Gelman and Baillargeon 1983 [596]; Markman and Callanan 1983 [785a]), children often find the superficial perceptual appearances of objects to be an easier basis on which to organize the material.

As for natural kinds, Keil (in press [755]) found young children to be more dependent on perceptual similarity than on deeper biological properties when they are asked to classify anomalous objects. he asked children to classify artifacts and natural kind objects, given conflicting information. For example, one object looked exactly like a skunk but its biological structures (heart, bones) and lineage (parents) were supposed to be that of a raccoon. The youngest children believed for both natural kinds and artifacts that appearance determined category membership. For example, they would say that the animal that looked like a skunk was in fact a skunk, even though they had been told it had a raccoon heart, gave birth to raccoon babies, and so forth. Not until about second to fourth grade were children willing to say that internal structure was an important criterion for categorizing natural kind objects. But these children probably have no way of knowing whether internal structure or external structure is more important. Another way of stating the difference between Keil's task and ours is that children were asked to make different sorts of comparisons in the two studies. On Keil's task children had to compare two different kinds of attributes: perceptual appearance versus biological properties. On our task children had to compare attributes (perceptual appearance) to membership in a category. The category label may be considered a more powerful source of information than a few biological properties such as having a particular heart or set of parents. Gelman, Collman, and Maccoby (1986) [734] found that inferring properties on the basis of categories was easier than inferring category membership on the basis of properties for one category: namely, gender.

Primitive Theories as Possible Constraints on Induction

Finally, as Carey (1985) [552] has argued, children must learn how natural kind categories are related to one another in a system of theory-based knowledge. Carey has found that children initially organize biological knowledge around humans as a prototype. Inferences about the biological properties of other species are based both on what children believe about humans and on how similar the other species is to humans. For example, children in Carey's study were taught that humans have an omentum and were asked whether various animals and artifacts also have an omentum. Children generalized in accord with a rough similarity gradient from most to least similar to humans. What is most striking about Carey's findings, however, is how dependent children are on the category of humans to organize new biological knowledge and to trigger inferences. Children draw inferences about biological categories primarily when the property is known to be true of humans. They are more likely to infer that a biological property of *humans* will generalize to bugs than they are to infer that a property of *bees* will generalize to bugs, despite the far greater similarity of bugs to bees than to humans. This marked dependence on humans as the prototype changes with age: adults generalize from one species to another based on how similar the two species are to each other (Rips 1975 [813]).

Carey discusses this work in terms of developmental changes in the scientific theories in which these natural kind terms are embedded. One of the roles of scientific theory is to constrain the kinds of inductive inferences that are made. The marked asymmetries in projection found at age 4 (that 4-year-olds generalize more from human to bug than from bug to bee, for example) disappear by about age 10. This change reflects a major restructuring in the organization of children's biological knowledge. The biological knowledge of 4-year-olds is focused on humans. Biological properties are fundamentally properties of humans and only secondarily properties of animals. New biological knowledge must be related to humans in order for 4-year-olds to project the properties to other animals. By age 10 the special status of humans as biological creatures has diminished. Now humans are only one of many mammals as far as biological properties are concerned.

Conclusions

At age 4, then, children still have much to learn about natural kind categories. Yet, at an age when children are known to find perceptual appearances compelling, they nevertheless expect rich similarities among natural kind objects with the same name. Perhaps 4-year-olds have learned enough information about natural kinds for them to have reached this conclusion about the structure of categories. It is also possible that children are initially biased to interpret category terms this way, independent of experience. Other expectations about the structure of natural language categories appear quite early. When children as young as 18 to 24 months hear an object labeled with a common noun, they assume the term refers to the object as a whole rather than to one of its properties (Macnamara 1982 [782]). By the age of 3 or 4 and possibly earlier, children expect a noun to refer to objects that are taxonomically related (e.g., a dog and a cat) even though in the absence of a label they are likely to group objects on the basis of thematic relations (e.g., a dog and a bone) (Markman and Hutchinson 1984 [786]). The assumption that categories will be structured as are natural kinds could be another early bias, one that helps children acquire category terms rapidly, organize knowledge efficiently, and induce information to novel exemplars of familiar categories. By expecting unforeseen nonperceptual properties to be common to members of a kind, children could go beyond the original basis for grouping objects into a category and discover more about the category members than they knew before. Children might start out assuming that categories will have the structure of natural kinds. With development, they would then refine these expectations, limiting them to properties, domains, and category types that are appropriate.

Note

1. Sternberg (1982) [835] has found that familiarity and complexity of a predicate affect how quickly adults can process it. However, familiarity and complexity alone cannot characterize the sorts of inferences we draw. Certainly, some simple and familiar predicates (say, "has a fever" or "is 3 days old") are not projectable. For example, just because one poodle is 3 days old, we do not expect the next poodle we see also to be 3 days old. Hence it is not clear how to extend Sternberg's findings to the problem of what confirms some inductions and not others.

5   What Is Justified Belief?

Alvin I. Goldman

The aim of this chapter is to sketch a theory of justified belief. What I
have in mind is an explanatory theory, one that explains in a general
way why certain beliefs are counted as justified and others as unjustified. Unlike some traditional approaches, I do not try to prescribe
standards for justification that differ from, or improve upon, our ordinary standards. I merely try to explicate the ordinary standards,
which are, I believe, quite different from those of many classical, e.g.,
'Cartesian', accounts.

Many epistemologists have been interested in justification because
of its presumed close relationship to knowledge. This relationship is
intended to be preserved in the conception of justified belief presented here. In previous papers on knowledge,[1] I have denied that
justification is necessary for knowing, but there I had in mind
'Cartesian' accounts of justification. On the account of justified belief
suggested here, it *is* necessary for knowing, and closely related to it.

The term 'justified', I presume, is an evaluative term, a term of
appraisal. Any correct definition or synonym of it would also feature
evaluative terms. I assume that such definitions or synonyms might
be given, but I am not interested in them. I want a set of *substantive*
conditions that specify when a belief is justified. Compare the moral
term 'right'. This might be defined in other ethical terms or phrases,
a task appropriate to meta-ethics. The task of normative ethics, by
contrast, is to state substantive conditions for the rightness of actions.
Normative ethics tries to specify non-ethical conditions that determine when an action is right. A familiar example is act-utilitarianism,
which says an action is right if and only if it produces, or would pro-

Reprinted from *Justification and Knowledge*, ed. George Pappas (Dordrecht: Reidel,
1979), pp. 1–23, by permission of the publisher. Copyright © 1979, Reidel.

duce, at least as much net happiness as any alternative/open to the agent. These necessary and sufficient conditions clearly involve no ethical notions. Analogously, I want a theory of justified belief to specify in non-epistemic terms when a belief is justified. This is not the only kind of theory of justifiedness one might seek, but it is one important kind of theory and the kind sought here.

In order to avoid epistemic terms in our theory, we must know which terms are epistemic. Obviously, an exhaustive list cannot be given, but here are some examples: 'justified', 'warranted', 'has (good) grounds', 'has reason (to believe)', 'knows that', 'sees that', 'apprehends that', 'is probable' (in an epistemic or inductive sense), 'shows that', 'establishes that', and 'ascertains that'. By contrast, here are some sample non-epistemic expressions: 'believes that', 'is true', 'causes', 'it is necessary that', 'implies', 'is deducible from', and 'is probable' (either in the frequency sense or the propensity sense). In general, (purely) doxastic, metaphysical, modal, semantic, or syntactic expressions are not epistemic.

There is another constraint I wish to place on a theory of justified belief, in addition to the constraint that it be couched in non-epistemic language. Since I seek an explanatory theory, i.e., one that clarifies the underlying source of justificational status, it is not enough for a theory to state 'correct' necessary and sufficient conditions. Its conditions must also be appropriately deep or revelatory. Suppose, for example, that the following sufficient condition of justified belief is offered: 'If S senses redly at t and S believes at t that he is sensing redly, then S's belief at t that he is sensing redly is justified.' This is not the kind of principle I seek; for, even if it is correct, it leaves unexplained *why* a person who senses redly and believes that he does, believes this justifiably. Not every state is such that if one is in it and believes one is in it, this belief is justified. What is distinctive about the state of sensing redly, or 'phenomenal' states in general? A theory of justified belief of the kind I seek must answer this question, and hence it must be couched at a suitably deep, general, or abstract level.

A few introductory words about my *explicandum* are appropriate at this juncture. It is often assumed that whenever a person has a justified belief, he knows that it is justified and knows what the justification is. It is further assumed that the person can state or explain what his justification is. On this view, a justification is an argument, defense, or set of reasons that can be given in support of a belief. Thus, one studies the nature of justified belief by considering what a person might *say* if asked to defend, or justify, his belief. I make none of these sorts of assumptions here. I leave it an open question whether, when a belief *is* justified, the believer *knows* it is justified. I also leave it an open question whether, when a belief is justified, the believer can *state* or *give* a justification for it. I do not even assume that when a belief is justified there is something 'possessed' by the believer which can be called a 'justification'. I do assume that a justified belief gets its status of being justified from some processes or properties that make it justified. In short, there must be some justification-conferring processes or properties. But this does not imply that there must be an argument, or reason, or anything else, 'possessed' at the time of belief by the believer.

I

A theory of justified belief will be a set of principles that specify truth-conditions for the schema ⌜S's belief in p at time t is justified⌝, i.e., conditions for the satisfaction of this schema in all possible cases. It will be convenient to formulate candidate theories in a recursive or inductive format, which would include (A) one or more base clauses, (B) a set of recursive clauses (possibly null), and (C) a closure clause. In such a format, it is permissible for the predicate 'is a justified belief' to appear in recursive clauses. But neither this predicate, nor any other epistemic predicate, may appear in (the antecedent of) any base clause.[2]

Before turning to my own theory, I want to survey some other possible approaches to justified belief. Identification of problems associated with other attempts will provide some motivation for the theory I shall offer. Obviously, I cannot examine all, or even very many, alternative attempts. But a few sample attempts will be instructive.

Let us concentrate on the attempt to formulate one or more adequate base-clause principles.[3] Here is a classical candidate:

(1) If S believes p at t, and p is indubitable for S (at t), then S's belief in p at t is justified.

To evaluate this principle, we need to know what 'indubitable' means. It can be understood in at least two ways. First, 'p is indubitable for S' might mean: 'S has no *grounds* for doubting p'. Since 'ground' is an epistemic term, however, principle (1) would be inadmissible on this reading, for epistemic terms may not legitimately appear in the antecedent of a base-clause. A second interpretation would avoid this difficulty. One might interpret 'p is indubitable for S' psychologically, i.e., as meaning 'S is psychologically incapable of doubting p'. This would make principle (1) admissible, but would it be correct? Surely not. A religious fanatic may be psychologically incapable of doubting the tenets of his faith, but that doesn't make his belief in them justified. Similarly, during the Watergate affair, someone may have been so blinded by the aura of the Presidency that even after the most damaging evidence against Nixon had emerged he was still incapable of doubting Nixon's veracity. It doesn't follow that his belief in Nixon's veracity was justified.

A second candidate base-clause principle is this:

(2)   If S believes p at t, and p is self-evident, then S's belief in p at t is justified.

To evaluate this principle, we again need an interpretation of its crucial term, in this case 'self-evident'. On one standard reading, 'evident' is a synonym for 'justified'. '*Self*-evident' would therefore mean something like 'directly justified', 'intuitively justified', or 'nonderivatively justified'. On this reading 'self-evident' is an epistemic phrase, and principle (2) would be disqualified as a base-clause principle.

However, there are other possible readings of 'p is self-evident' on which it isn't an epistemic phrase. One such reading is: 'It is impossible to understand p without believing it'.[4] According to this interpretation, trivial analytic and logical truths might turn out to be self-evident. Hence, any belief in such a truth would be a justified belief, according to (2).

What does 'it is *impossible* to understand p without believing it' mean? Does it mean '*humanly* impossible'? That reading would probably make (2) an unacceptable principle. There may well be propositions which humans have an innate and irrepressible disposition to believe, e.g., 'Some events have causes'. But it seems unlikely that people's inability to refrain from believing such a proposition makes every belief in it justified.

Should we then understand 'impossible' to mean 'impossible in principle', or 'logically impossible'? If that is the reading given, I suspect that (2) is a vacuous principle. I doubt that even trivial logical or analytic truths will satisfy this definition of 'self-evident'. Any proposition, we may assume, has two or more components that are somehow organized or juxtaposed. To understand the proposition one must 'grasp' the components and their juxtaposition. Now in the case of *complex* logical truths, there are (human) psychological operations that suffice to grasp the components and their juxtaposition but do not suffice to produce a belief that the proposition is true. But can't we at least *conceive* of an analogous set of psychological operations even for simple logical truths, operations which perhaps are not in the repertoire of human cognizers but which might be in the repertoire of some conceivable beings? That is, can't we conceive of psychological operations that would suffice to grasp the components and componential-juxtaposition of these simple propositions but do not suffice to produce *belief* in the propositions? I think we can conceive of such operations. Hence, for any proposition you choose, it will be possible for it to be understood without being believed.

Finally, even if we set these two objections aside, we must note that self-evidence can at best confer justificational status on relatively few beliefs, and the only plausible group are beliefs in necessary truths. Thus, other base-clause principles will be needed to explain the justificational status of beliefs in contingent propositions.

The notion of a base-clause principle is naturally associated with the idea of 'direct' justifiedness, and in the realm of contingent propositions first-person-current-mental-state propositions have often been assigned this role. In Chisholm's terminology, this conception is expressed by the notion of a *'self-presenting'* state or proposition. The sentence 'I am thinking', for example, expresses a self-presenting proposition. (At least I shall *call* this sort of content a 'proposition', though it only has a truth value given some assignment of a subject who utters or entertains the content and a time of entertaining.) When such a proposition is true for person S at time t, S is justified in believing it at t: in Chisholm's terminology, the proposition is 'evident' for S at t. This suggests the following base-clause principle.

(3) If p is a self-presenting proposition, and p is true for S at t, and S believes p at t, then S's belief in p at t is justified.

What, exactly, does 'self-presenting' mean? In the second edition of *Theory of Knowledge,* Chisholm offers this definition: "h is self-presenting for S at $t =_{df}$ h is true at t; and necessarily, if h is true at t, then h is evident for S at t."[5] Unfortunately, since 'evident' is an epistemic term, 'self-presenting' also becomes an epistemic term on this definition, thereby disqualifying (3) as a legitimate base-clause. Some other definition of self-presentingness must be offered if (3) is to be a suitable base-clause principle.

Another definition of self-presentation readily comes to mind. 'Self-presentation' is an approximate synonym of 'self-intimation', and a proposition may be said to be self-intimating if and only if whenever it is true of a person that person believes it. More precisely, we may give the following definition.

(SP) Proposition p is self-presenting if and only if: necessarily, for any S and any t, if p is true for S at t, then S believes p at t.

On this definition, 'self-presenting' is clearly not an epistemic predicate, so (3) would be an admissible principle. Moreover, there is initial plausibility in the suggestion that it is *this* feature of first-person-current-mental-state proposition—viz., their truth guarantees their being believed—that makes beliefs in them justified.

Employing this definition of self-presentation, is principle (3) correct? This cannot be decided until we define self-presentation more precisely. Since the operator 'necessarily' can be read in different ways, there are different forms of self-presentation and correspondingly different versions of principle (3). Let us focus on two of these readings: a *'nomological'* reading and a *'logical'* reading. Consider first the nomological reading. On this definition a proposition is self-presenting just in case it is nomologically necessary that if p is true for S at t, then S believes p at t.[6]

Is the nomological version of principle (3)—call it '(3_N)'—correct? Not at all. We can imagine cases in which the antecedent of (3_N) is satisfied but we would not say that the belief is justified. Suppose, for example, that p is the proposition expressed by the sentence 'I am in brain-state B', where 'B' is shorthand for a certain highly specific neural state description. Further suppose it is a nomological truth that anyone in brain-state B will ipso facto *believe* he is in brain-state B. In other words, imagine that an occurrent belief with the content 'I am in brain-state B' is realized whenever one is in brain-state B.[7] According to (3_N), any such belief is justified. But that is clearly false. We can readily imagine circumstances in which a person goes into brain-state B and therefore has the belief in question, though this belief is by no means justified. For example, we can imagine that a brain-surgeon operating on S artifically induces brain-state B. This results, phenomenologically, in S's suddenly believing—out of the blue—that he is in brain-state B, without any relevant antecedent beliefs. We would hardly say, in such a case, that S's belief that he is in brain-state B is justified.

Let us turn next to the logical version of (3)—call it '(3_L)'—in which a proposition is defined as self-presenting just in case it is logically necessary that if p is true for S at t, then S believes p at t. This stronger version of principle (3) might seem more promising. In fact, however, it is no more successful than (3_N). Let p be the proposition 'I am awake' and assume that it is logically necessary that if this proposition is true for some person S and time t, then S believes p at t. This assumption is consistent with the further assumption that S frequently believes p when it is false, e.g., when he is dreaming. Under these circumstances, we would hardly accept the contention that S's belief in this proposition is always justified. But nor should we accept the contention that the belief is justified when it is *true*. The truth of the proposition logically guarantees that the belief is *held*, but why should it guarantee that the belief is *justified?*

The foregoing criticism suggests that we have things backwards. The idea of self-presentations is that truth guarantees belief. This fails to confer justification because it is compatible with there being belief without truth. So what seems necessary—or at least sufficient—for justification is that belief should guarantee truth. Such a notion has usually gone under the label of '*infallibility*', or '*incorrigibility*'. It may be defined as follows.

(INC)   Proposition p is incorrigible if and only if: necessarily, for any S and any t, if S believes p at t, then p is true for S at t.

Using the notion of incorrigibility, we may propose principle (4).

(4)   If p is an incorrigible proposition, and S believes p at t, then S's belief in p at t is justified.

As was true of self-presentation, there are different varieties of incorrigibility, corresponding to different interpretations of 'necessarily'. Accordingly, we have different versions of principle (4). Once again, let us concentrate on a nomological and a logical version, (4_N) and (4_L) respectively.

We can easily construct a counterexample to (4_N) along the lines of the belief-state/brain-state counterexample that refuted (3_N). Suppose it is nomologically necessary that if anyone believes he is in brain-state B then it is true that he is in brain-state B, for the only way this belief-state is realized is through brain-state B itself. It follows that 'I am in brain-state B' is a nomologically incorrigible proposition. Therefore, according to (4_N), whenever anyone believes this proposition at any time, that belief is justified. But we may again construct a brain-surgeon example in which someone comes to have such a belief but the belief isn't justified.

Apart from this counterexample, the general point is this. Why should the fact that S's believing p guarantees the truth of p imply that S's belief is justified? The nature of the guarantee might be wholly fortuitous, as the belief-state/brain-state example is intended to illustrate. To appreciate the point, consider the following related possibility. A person's mental structure might be such that whenever he believes that p will be true (of him) a split second later, then p is true (of him) a split second later. This is because, we may suppose, his believing it brings it about. But surely we would not be compelled in such a circumstance to say that a belief of this sort is justified. So why should the fact that S's believing p guarantees the truth of p *precisely at the time of belief* imply that the belief is justified? There is no intuitive plausibility in this supposition.

The notion of *logical* incorrigibility has a more honored place in the history of conceptions of justification. But even principle (4_L), I believe, suffers from defects similar to those of (4_N). The mere fact that belief in p logically guarantees its truth does not confer justificational status on such a belief.

The first difficulty with (4_L) arises from logical or mathematical truths. Any true proposition of logic or mathematics is logically necessary. Hence, any such proposition p is logically incorrigible, since it is logically necessary that, for any S and any t, if S believes p at t then p is true (for S at t). Now assume that Nelson believes a certain very complex mathematical truth at time t. Since such a proposition is logically incorrigible, (4_L) implies that Nelson's belief in this truth at t is justified. But we may easily suppose that this belief of Nelson is not at all the result of proper mathematical reasoning, or even the result of appeal to trustworthy authority. Perhaps Nelson believes this complex truth because of utterly confused reasoning, or because of hasty and ill-founded conjecture. Then his belief is not justified, contrary to what (4_L) implies.

The case of logical or mathematical truths is admittedly peculiar, since the truth of these propositions is assured independently of any beliefs. It might seem, therefore, that we can better capture the idea of 'belief logically guaranteeing truth' in cases where the propositions in question are *contingent*. With this in mind, we might restrict (4_L) to *contingent* incorrigible propositions. Even this amendment cannot save (4_L), however, since there are counterexamples to it involving purely contingent propositions.

Suppose that Humperdink has been studying logic—or, rather, pseudologic—from Elmer Fraud, whom Humperdink has no reason to trust as a logician. Fraud has enunciated the principle that any disjunctive proposition consisting of at least 40 distinct disjuncts is very probably true. Humperdink now encounters the proposition p, a contingent proposition with 40 disjuncts, the 7th disjunct being 'I exist'. Although Humperdink grasps the proposition fully, he doesn't notice that it is entailed by 'I exist'. Rather, he is struck by the fact that it falls under the disjunction rule Fraud has enunciated (a rule I assume Humperdink is not *justified* in believing). Bearing this rule in mind, Humperdink forms a belief in p. Now notice that p is logically incorrigible. It is logically necessary that if anyone believes p, then p is true (of him at that time). This simply follows from the fact that, first, a person's believing anything entails that he exists, and second, 'I exist' entails p. Since p is logically incorrigible, principle (4_L) implies that Humperdink's belief in p is justified. But surely, given our example, that conclusion is false. Humperdink's belief in p is not at all justified.

One thing that goes wrong in this example is that while Humperdink's belief in p logically implies its truth, Humperdink doesn't *recognize* that his believing it implies its truth. This might move a theorist to revise (4_L) by adding the requirement that S 'recognize' that p is logically incorrigible. But this, of course, won't do. The term 'recognize' is obviously an epistemic term, so the suggested revision of (4_L) would result in an inadmissible base-clause.

II

Let us try to diagnose what has gone wrong with these attempts to produce an acceptable base-clause principle. Notice that each of the foregoing attempts confers the status of 'justified' on a belief without restriction on *why* the belief is held, i.e., on what *causally initiates* the belief or *causally sustains* it. The logical versions of principles (3) and (4), for example, clearly place no restriction on causes of belief. The same is true of the nomological versions of (3) and (4), since nomological requirements can be satisfied by simultaneity or cross-sectional laws, as illustrated by our brain-state/belief-state examples. I suggest that the absence of causal requirements accounts for the failure of the foregoing principles. Many of our counterexamples are ones in which the belief is caused in some strange or unacceptable way, e.g., by the accidental movement of a brain-surgeon's hand, by reliance on an illicit, pseudo-logical principle, or by the blinding aura of the Presidency. In general, a strategy for defeating a noncausal principle of justifiedness is to find a case in which the principle's antecedent is satisfied but the belief is caused by some faulty belief-forming process. The faultiness of the belief-forming process will incline us, intuitively, to regard the belief as unjustified. Thus, correct principles of justified belief must be principles that make causal requirements, where 'cause' is construed broadly to include sustainers as well as initiators of belief (i.e., processes that determine, or help to overdetermine, a belief's continuing to be held.)[8]

The need for causal requirements is not restricted to base-clause principles. Recursive principles will also need a causal component. One might initially suppose that the following is a good recursive principle: 'If S justifiably believes q at t, and q entails p, and S believes p at t, then S's belief in p at t is justified'. But this principle is unacceptable. S's belief in p doesn't receive justificational status simply from the fact that p is entailed by q and S justifiably believes q. If what causes S to believe p at t is entirely different, S's belief in p may well not be justified. Nor can the situation be remedied by adding to the antecedent the condition that S justifiably believes that q entails p. Even if he believes this, and believes q as well, he might not put these beliefs together. He might believe p as a result of some other wholly extraneous, considerations. So once again, conditions that fail to require appropriate causes of a belief don't guarantee justifiedness.

Granted that principles of justified belief must make reference to causes of belief, what kinds of causes confer justifiedness? We can gain insight into this problem by reviewing some faulty processes of belief-formation, i.e., processes whose belief-outputs would be classed as unjustified. Here are some examples: confused reasoning, wishful thinking, reliance on emotional attachment, mere hunch or guesswork, and hasty generalization. What do these faulty processes have in common? They share the feature of *unreliability:* they tend to produce *error* a large proportion of the time. By contrast, which species of belief-forming (or belief-sustaining) processes are intuitively justification-conferring? They include standard perceptual processes, remembering, good reasoning, and introspection. What these processes seem to have in common is *reliability*: the beliefs they produce are generally true. My positive proposal, then, is this. The justificational status of a belief is a function of the reliability of the process or processes that cause it, where (as a first approximation) reliability consists in the tendency of a process to produce beliefs that are true rather than false.

To test this thesis further, notice that justifiedness is not a purely categorical concept, although I treat it here as categorical in the interest of simplicity. We can and do regard certain beliefs as more justified than others. Furthermore, our intuitions of comparative justifiedness go along with our beliefs about the comparative reliability of the belief-causing processes.

Consider perceptual beliefs. Suppose Jones believes he has just seen a mountain-goat. Our assessment of the belief's justifiedness is determined by whether he caught a brief glimpse of the creature at a great distance, or whether he had a good look at the thing only 30 yards away. His belief in the latter sort of case is *(ceteris paribus)* more justified than in the former sort of case. And, if his belief is true, we are more prepared to say he *knows* in the latter case than in the former. The difference between the two cases seems to be this. Visual beliefs formed from brief and hasty scanning, or where the perceptual object is a long distance off, tend to be wrong more often than visual beliefs formed from detailed and leisurely scanning, or where the object is in reasonable proximity. In short, the visual processes in the former category are less reliable than those in the latter category. A similar point holds for memory beliefs. A belief that results from a hazy and indistinct memory impression is counted as less justified than a belief that arises from a distinct memory impression, and our inclination to classify those beliefs as 'knowledge' varies in the same way. Again, the reason is associated with the comparative reliability of the processes. Hazy and indistinct memory impressions are generally less reliable indicators of what actually happened; so beliefs formed from such impressions are less likely to be true than beliefs formed from distinct impressions. Further, consider beliefs based on inference from observed samples. A belief about a population that is based on random sampling, or on instances that exhibit great variety, is intuitively more justified than a belief based on biased sampling, or on instances from a narrow sector of the population. Again, the degree of justifiedness seems to be a function of reliability. Inferences based on random or varied samples will tend to produce less error or inaccuracy than inferences based on non-random or non-varied samples.

Returning to a categorical concept of justifiedness, we might ask just *how* reliable a belief-forming process must be in order that its resultant beliefs be justified. A precise answer to this question should not be expected. Our conception of justification is *vague* in this respect. It does seem clear, however, that *perfect* reliability isn't required. Belief-forming processes that *sometimes* produce error still confer justification. It follows that there can be justified beliefs that are false.

I have characterized justification-conferring processes as ones that have a 'tendency' to produce beliefs that are true rather than false. The term 'tendency' could refer either to *actual* long-run frequency, or to a 'propensity', i.e., outcomes that would occur in merely *possible* realizations of the process. Which of these is intended? Unfortunately, I think our ordinary conception of justifiedness is vague on this dimension too. For the most part, we simply assume that the 'observed' frequency of truth versus error would be approximately replicated in the actual long-run, and also in relevant counterfactual situations, i.e., ones that are highly 'realistic', or conform closely to the circumstances of the actual world. Since we ordinarily assume these frequencies to be roughly the same, we make no concerted effort to distinguish them. Since the purpose of my present theorizing is to capture our ordinary conception of justifiedness, and since our ordinary conception is vague on this matter, it is appropriate to leave the theory vague in the same respect.

We need to say more about the notion of a belief-forming *'process'*. Let us mean by a 'process' a *functional operation* or procedure, i.e., something that generates a *mapping* from certain states—'inputs'—into other states—'outputs'. The outputs in the present case are states of believing this or that proposition at a given moment. On this interpretation, a process is a *type* as opposed to a *token*. This is fully appropriate, since it is only types that have statistical properties such as producing truth 80% of the time; and it is precisely such statistical properties that determine the reliability of a process. Of course, we also want to speak of a process as *causing* a belief, and it looks as if types are incapable of being causes. But when we say that a belief is caused by a given process, understood as a functional procedure, we may interpret this to mean that it is caused by the particular *inputs* to the process (and by the intervening events 'through which' the functional procedure carries the inputs into the output) on the occasion in question.

What are some examples of belief-forming 'processes' construed as functional operations? One example is reasoning processes, where the inputs include antecedent beliefs and entertained hypotheses. Another example is functional procedures whose inputs include desires, hopes, or emotional states of various sorts (together with antecedent beliefs). A third example is a memory process, which takes as input beliefs or experiences at an earlier time and generates as output beliefs at a later time. For example, a memory process might take as input a belief *at* t_1 that Lincoln was born in 1809 and generate as output a belief *at* t_n that Lincoln was born in 1809. A fourth example is perceptual processes. Here it isn't clear whether inputs should include states of the environment, such as the distance of the stimulus from the cognizer, or only events within or on the surface of the organism, e.g., receptor stimulations. I shall return to this point in a moment.

A critical problem concerning our analysis is the degree of generality of the process-types in question. Input-output relations can be specified very broadly or very narrowly, and the degree of generality will partly determine the degree of reliability. A process-type might be selected so narrowly that only one instance of it ever occurs, and hence the type is either completely reliable or completely unreliable. (This assumes that reliability is a function of *actual* frequency only.) If such narrow process-types were selected, beliefs that are intuitively unjustified might be said to result from perfectly reliable processes; and beliefs that are intuitively justified might be said to result from perfectly unreliable processes.

It is clear that our ordinary thought about process-types slices them broadly, but I cannot at present give a precise explication of our intuitive principles. One plausible suggestion, though, is that the relevant processes are *content-neutral*. It might be argued, for example, that the process of *inferring p whenever the Pope asserts p* could pose problems for our theory. If the Pope is infallible, this process will be perfectly reliable; yet we would not regard the belief-outputs of this process as justified. The content-neutral restriction would avert this difficulty. If relevant processes are required to admit as input beliefs (or other states) with *any* content, the aforementioned process will not count, for its input beliefs have a restricted propositioned content, viz., 'the *Pope* assert *p*'.

In addition to the problem of 'generality' or 'abstractness' there is the previously mentioned problem of the *'extent'* of belief-forming processes. Clearly, the causal ancestry of beliefs often includes events outside the organism. Are such events to be included among the 'inputs' of belief-forming processes? Or should we restrict the extent of belief-forming processes to *'cognitive'* events, i.e., events within the organism's nervous system? I shall choose the latter course, though with some hesitation. My general grounds for this decision are roughly as follows. Justifiedness seems to be a function of how a cognizer deals with his environmental input, i.e., with the goodness or badness of the operations that register and transform the stimulation that reaches him. ('Deal with', of course, does not mean *purposeful* action; nor is it restricted to *conscious* activity.) A justified belief is, roughly speaking, one that results from cognitive operations that are, generally speaking, good or successful. But *'cognitive'* operations are most plausibly construed as operations of the cognitive faculties, i.e., 'information-processing' equipment *internal* to the organism.

With these points in mind, we may now advance the following base-clause principle for justified belief.

(5) If S's believing p at t results from a reliable cognitive belief-forming process (or set of processes), then S's belief in p at t is justified.

Since 'reliable belief-forming process' has been defined in terms of such notions as belief, truth, statistical frequency, and the like, it is not an epistemic term. Hence, (5) is an admissible base-clause.

It might seem as if (5) promises to be not only a successful base clause, but the only principle needed whatever, apart from a closure clause. In other words, it might seem as if it is a necessary as well as a sufficient condition of justifiedness that a belief be produced by reliable cognitive belief-forming processes. But this is not quite correct, give our provisional definition of 'reliability'.

Our provisional definition implies that a reasoning process is reliable only if it generally produces beliefs that are true, and similarly, that a memory process is reliable only if it generally yields beliefs that are true. But these requirements are too strong. A reasoning procedure cannot be expected to produce true belief if it is applied to false premisses. And memory cannot be expected to yield a true belief if the original belief it attempts to retain is false. What we need for reasoning and memory, then, is a notion of *'conditional reliability'*. A process is conditionally reliable when a sufficient proportion of its output-beliefs are true *given that its input-beliefs are true*.

With this point in mind, let us distinguish *belief-dependent* and *belief-independent* cognitive processes. The former are processes *some* of whose inputs are belief-states.[9] The latter are processes *none* of whose inputs are belief-states. We may then replace principle (5) with the following two principles, the first a base-clause principle and the second a recursive-clause principle.

(6_A)   If S's belief in p at t results ('immediately') from a belief-independent process that is (unconditionally) reliable, then S's belief in p at t is justified.

(6_B)   If S's belief in p at t results ("immediately") from a belief-dependent process that is (at least) conditionally reliable, and if the beliefs (if any) on which this process operates in producing S's belief in p at t are themselves justified, then S's belief in p at t is justified.[10]

If we add to (6_A) and (6_B) the standard closure clause, we have a complete theory of justified belief. The theory says, in effect, that a belief is justified if and only it is *'well-formed'*, i.e., it has an ancestry of reliable and/or conditionally reliable cognitive operations. (Since a dated belief may be over-determined, it may have a number of distinct ancestral trees. These need not all be full of reliable or conditionally reliable processes. But at least one ancestral tree must have reliable or conditionally reliable processes throughout.)

The theory of justified belief proposed here, then, is an *Historical* or *Genetic* theory. It contrasts with the dominant approach to justified belief, an approach that generates what we may call (borrowing a phrase from Robert Nozick) *'Current Time-Slice'* theories. A Current Time-Slice theory makes the justificational status of a belief wholly a function of what is true of the cognizer *at the time* of belief. An Historical theory makes the justificational status of a belief depend on its prior history. Since my Historical theory emphasizes the reliability of the belief-generating processes, it may be called *'Historical Reliabilism'*.

The most obvious examples of Current Time-Slice theories are 'Cartesian' Foundationalist theories, which trace all justificational status (at least of contingent propositions) to current mental states. The usual varieties of Coherence theories, however, are equally Current Time-Slice views, since they too make the justificational status of a belief wholly a function of *current* states of affairs. For Coherence theories, however, these current states include all other beliefs of the cognizer, which would not be considered relevant by Cartesian Foundationalism. Have there been other Historical theories of justified belief? Among contemporary writers, Quine and Popper have Historical epistemologies, though the notion of 'justification' is not their avowed *explicandum*. Among historical writers, it might seem that Locke and Hume had Genetic theories of sorts. But I think that their Genetic theories were only theories of ideas, not of knowledge or justification. Plato's theory of recollection, however, is a good example of a Genetic theory of knowing.[11] And it might be argued that Hegel and Dewey had Genetic epistemologies (if Hegel can be said to have had a clear epistemology at all).

The theory articulated by (6_A) and (6_B) might be viewed as a kind of 'Foundationalism,' because of its recursive structure. I have no objection to this label, as long as one keeps in mind how different this 'diachronic' form of Foundationalism is from Cartesian, or other 'synchronic' varieties of, Foundationalism.

Current Time-Slice theories characteristically assume that the justificational status of a belief is something which the cognizer is able to know or determine at the time of belief. This is made explicit, for example, by Chisholm.[12] The Historical theory I endorse makes no such assumption. There are many facts about a cognizer to which he lacks 'privileged access', and I regard the justificational status of his beliefs as one of those things. This is not to say that a cognizer is necessarily ignorant, at any given moment, of the justificational status of his current beliefs. It is only to deny that he necessarily has, or can get, knowledge or true belief about this status. Just as a person can know without knowing that he knows, so he can have justified belief without knowing that it is justified (or believing justifiably that it is justified.)

A characteristic case in which a belief is justified though the cognizer doesn't know that it's justified is where the original evidence for the belief has long since been forgotten. If the original evidence was compelling, the cognizer's original belief may have been justified; and this justificational status may have been preserved through memory. But since the cognizer no longer remembers how or why he came to believe, he may not know that the belief is justified. If asked now to justify his belief, he may be at a loss. Still, the belief *is* justified, though the cognizer can't demonstrate or establish this.

The Historical theory of justified belief I advocate is connected in spirit with the causal theory of knowing I have presented elsewhere.[13] I had this in mind when I remarked near the outset of the paper that my theory of justified belief makes justifiedness come out closely related to knowledge. Justified beliefs, like pieces of knowledge, have appropriate histories; but they may fail to be knowledge either because they are false or because they founder on some other requirement for knowing of the kind discussed in the post-Gettier knowledge-trade.

There is a variant of the Historical conception of justified belief that is worth mentioning in this context. It may be introduced as follows. Suppose S has a set B of beliefs at time t_0, and some of these beliefs are *un*justified. Between t_0 and t_1 he reasons from the entire set B to the conclusion p, which he then accepts at t_1. The reasoning procedure he uses is a very sound one, i.e., one that is conditionally reliable. There is a sense or respect in which we are tempted to say that S's belief in p at t_1 is 'justified'. At any rate, it is tempting to say that the *person* is justified in believing p at t. Relative to his antecedent cognitive state, he did as well as could be expected: the *transition* from his cognitive state at t_1 to his cognitive state at t_1 was entirely sound. Although we may acknowledge this brand of justifiedness—it might be called *'Terminal-Phase Reliabilism'*—it is not a kind of justifiedness so closely related to knowing. For a person to know proposition p, it is not enough that the *final phase* of the process that leads to his belief in p be sound. It is also necessary that some entire history of the process be sound (i.e., reliable or conditionally reliable).

Let us return now to the Historical theory. In the next section of this chapter, I shall adduce reasons for strengthening it a bit. Before looking at these reasons, however, I wish to review two quite different objections to the theory.

First, a critic might argue that *some* justified beliefs do not derive their justificational status from their causal ancestry. In particular, it might be argued that beliefs about one's current phenomenal states and intuitive beliefs about elementary logical or conceptual relationships do not derive their justificational status in this way. I am not persuaded by either of these examples. Introspection, I believe, should be regarded as a form of retrospection. Thus, a justified belief that I am 'now' in pain gets its justificational status from a relevant, though brief, causal history.[14] The apprehension of logical or conceptual relationships is also a cognitive process that occupies time. The psychological process of 'seeing' or 'intuiting' a simple logical truth is very fast, and we cannot introspectively dissect it into constituent parts. Nonetheless, there are mental operations going on, just as there are mental operations that occur in *idiots savants*, who are unable to report the computational processes they in fact employ.

A second objection to Historical Reliabilism focuses on the reliability element rather than the causal or historical element. Since the theory is intended to cover all possible cases, it seems to imply that for any cognitive process C, if C is reliable in possible world W, then any belief in W that results from C is justified. But doesn't this permit easy counterexamples? Surely we can imagine a possible world in which wishful thinking is reliable. We can imagine a possible world where a benevolent demon so arranges things that beliefs formed by wishful thinking usually come true. This would make wishful thinking a reliable process in that possible world, but surely we don't want to regard beliefs that result from wishful thinking as justified.

There are several possible ways to respond to this case and I am unsure which response is best, partly because my own intuitions (and those of other people I have consulted) are not entirely clear. One possibility is to say that in the possible world imagined, beliefs that result from wishful thinking *are* justified. In other words we reject the claim that wishful thinking could never, intuitively, confer justifiedness.[15]

However, for those who feel that wishful thinking couldn't confer justifiedness, even in the world imagined, there are two ways out. First, it may be suggested that the proper criterion of justifiedness is the propensity of a process to generate beliefs that are true *in a non-manipulated environment*, i.e., an environment in which there is no purposeful arrangement of the world either to accord or conflict with the beliefs that are formed. In other words, the suitability of a belief-forming process is only a function of its success in '*natural*' situations, not situations of the sort involving benevolent or malevolent demons, or any other such manipulative creatures. If we reformulate the theory to include this qualification, the counterexample in question will be averted.

Alternatively, we may reformulate our theory, or reinterpret it, as follows. Instead of construing the theory as saying that a belief in possible world W is justified if and only if it results from a cognitive process that is reliable in W, we may construe it as saying that a belief in possible world W is justified if and only if it results from a cognitive process that is reliable *in our world*. In short, our conception of justifiedness is derived as follows. We note certain cognitive processes in the actual world, and form beliefs about which of these are reliable. The ones we believe to be reliable are then regarded as justification-conferring processes. In reflecting on hypothetical beliefs, we deem them justified if and only if they result from processes already picked out as justification-conferring, or processes very similar to those. Since wishful thinking is not among these processes, a belief formed in a possible world W by wishful thinking would not be deemed justified, even if wishful thinking is reliable *in W*. I am not sure that this is a correct reconstruction of our intuitive conceptual scheme, but it would accommodate the benevolent demon case, at least if the proper thing to say in that case is that the wishful-thinking-caused beliefs are unjustified.

Even if we adopt this strategy, however, a problem still remains. Suppose that wishful thinking turns out to be reliable *in the actual world!*[16] This might be because, unbeknownst to us at present, there is a benevolent demon who, lazy until now, will shortly start arranging things so that our wishes come true. The long-run performance of wishful thinking will be very good, and hence even the new construal of the theory will imply that beliefs resulting from wishful thinking (in *our* world) are justified. Yet this surely contravenes our intuitive judgment on the matter.

Perhaps the moral of the case is that the standard format of a 'conceptual analysis' has its shortcomings. Let me depart from that format and try to give a better rendering of our aims and the theory that tries to achieve that aim. What we really want is an *explanation* of why we count, or would count, certain beliefs as justified and others as unjustified. Such an explanation must refer to our *beliefs* about

reliability, not to the actual *facts*. The reason we *count* beliefs as justified is that they are formed by what we *believe* to be reliable belief-
forming processes. Our beliefs about which belief-forming processes
are reliable may be erroneous, but that does not affect the adequacy
of the explanation. Since we *believe* that wishful thinking is an unreliable belief-forming process, we regard beliefs formed by wishful thinking as unjustified. What matters, then, is what we *believe* about
wishful thinking, not what is *true* (in the long run) about wishful
thinking. I am not sure how to express this point in the standard
format of conceptual analysis, but it identifies an important point in
understanding our theory.

III

Let us return, however, to the standard format of conceptual analysis, and let us consider a new objection that will require some revisions in the theory advanced until now. According to our theory, a
belief is justified in case it is caused by a process that is in fact reliable,
or by one we generally believe to be reliable. But suppose that although one of S's beliefs satisfies this condition, S has no reason to
believe that it does. Worse yet, suppose S has reason to believe that
his belief is caused by an *un*reliable process (although *in fact* its causal
ancestry is fully reliable). Wouldn't we deny in such circumstances
that S's belief is justified? This seems to show that our analysis, as
presently formulated, is mistaken.

Suppose that Jones is told on fully reliable authority that a certain
class of his memory beliefs is almost all mistaken. His parents fabricate a wholly false story that Jones suffered from amnesia when he
was seven but later developed *pseudo*-memories of that period.
Though Jones listens to what his parents say and has excellent reason
to trust them, he persists in believing the ostensible memories from
his seven-year-old past. Are these memory beliefs justified? Intuitively, they are not justified. But since these beliefs result from genuine memory and original perceptions, which are adequately reliable
processes, our theory says that these beliefs are justified.

Can the theory be revised to meet this difficulty? One natural suggestion is that the actual reliability of a belief's ancestry is not enough
for justifiedness; in addition, the cognizer must be *justified in believing*
that the ancestry of his belief is reliable. Thus one might think of

replacing (6$_A$), for example, with (7). (For simplicity, I neglect some of the details of the earlier analysis.)

(7)   If S's belief in p at t is caused by a reliable cognitive process, and S justifiably believes at t that his p-belief is so caused, then S's belief in p at t is justified.

It is evident, however, that (7) will not do as a base clause, for it contains the epistemic term 'justifiably' in its antecedent.

A slightly weaker revision, without this problematic feature, might next be suggested, viz.,

(8)   If S's belief in p at t is caused by a reliable cognitive process, and S believes at t that his p-belief is so caused, then S's belief in p at t is justified.

But this won't do the job. Suppose that Jones believes that his memory beliefs are reliably caused despite all the (trustworthy) contrary testimony of his parents. Principle (8) would be satisfied, yet we wouldn't say that these beliefs are justified.

Next, we might try (9), which is stronger than (8) and, unlike (7), formally admissible as a base clause.

(9)   If S's belief in p at t is caused by a reliable cognitive process, and S believes at t that his p-belief is so caused, and this meta-belief is caused by a reliable cognitive process, than S's belief in p at t is justified.

A first objection to (9) is that it wrongly precludes unreflective creatures—creatures like animals or young children, who have no beliefs about the genesis of their beliefs—from having justified beliefs. If one shares my view that justified belief is, at least roughly, *well-formed* belief, surely animals and young children can have justified beliefs.

A second problem with (9) concerns its underlying rationale. Since (9) is proposed as a substitute for (6$_A$), it is implied that the reliability of a belief's own cognitive ancestry does not make it justified. But, the suggestion seems to be, the reliability of a *meta-belief*'s ancestry confers justifiedness on the first-order belief. Why should that be so? Perhaps one is attracted by the idea of a 'trickle-down' effect: if an $n+1$-level belief is justified, its justification trickles down to an n-level belief. But even if the trickle-down theory is correct, it doesn't help here. There is no assurance from the satisfaction of (9)'s antecedent that the meta-belief itself is *justified*.

To obtain a better revision of our theory, let us re-examine the Jones case. Jones has strong evidence against certain propositions concerning his past. He doesn't *use* this evidence, but if he *were* to use it properly, he would stop believing these propositions. Now the proper use of evidence would be an instance of a (conditionally) reliable process. So what we can say about Jones is that he *fails* to use a certain (conditionally) reliable process that he could and should have used. Admittedly, had he used this process, he would have 'worsened' his doxastic states: he would have replaced some true beliefs with suspension of judgment. Still, he couldn't have known this in the case in question. So, he failed to do something which, epistemically, he should have done. This diagnosis suggests a fundamental change in our theory. The justificational status of a belief is not only a function of the cognitive processes *actually* employed in producing it; it is also a function of processes that could and should be employed.

With these points in mind, we may tentatively propose the following revision of our theory, where we again focus on a base-clause principle but omit certain details in the interest of clarity.

(10)   If S's belief in *p* at *t* results from a reliable cognitive process, and there is no reliable or conditionally reliable process available to S which, had it been used by S in addition to the process actually used, would have resulted in S's not believing *p* at *t*, then S's belief in *p* at *t* is justified.

There are several problems with this proposal. First, there is a technical problem. One cannot use an additional belief-forming (or doxastic-state-forming) process *as well as* the original process if the additional one would result in a different doxastic state. One wouldn't be using the original process at all. So we need a slightly different formulation of the relevant counter-factual. Since the basic idea is reasonably clear, however, I won't try to improve on the formulation here. A second problem concerns the notion of *'available'* belief-forming (or doxastic-state-forming) processes. What is it for a process to be 'available' to a cognizer? Were scientific procedures 'available' to people who lived in pre-scientific ages? Furthermore, it seems implausible to say that all 'available' processes ought to be used, at least if we include such processes as gathering *new* evidence. Surely a belief can sometimes be justified even if additional evidence-gathering would yield a different doxastic attitude. What I think we should have in mind here are such additional processes as calling previously acquired evidence to mind, assessing the implications of that evidence, etc. This is admittedly somewhat vague, but here again our ordinary notion of justifiedness is vague, so it is appropriate for our analysans to display the same sort of vagueness.

This completes the sketch of my account of justified belief. Before concluding, however, it is essential to point out that there is an important use of 'justified' which is not captured by this account but can be captured by a closely related one.

There is a use of 'justified' in which it is not implied or presupposed that there is a *belief* that is justified. For example, if S is trying to decide whether to believe p and asks our advice, we may tell him that he is 'justified' in believing it. We do not thereby imply that he *has* a justified *belief*, since we know he is still suspending judgement. What we mean, roughly, is that he *would* or *could* be justified if he were to believe p. The justificational status we ascribe here cannot be a function of the causes of S's believing p, for there is no belief by S in p. Thus, the account of justifiedness we have given thus far cannot explicate *this* use of 'justified'. (It doesn't follow that this use of 'justified' has no connection with causal ancestries. Its proper use may depend on the causal ancestry of the cognizer's cognitive state, though not on the causal ancestry of his believing p.)

Let us distinguish two uses of 'justified': an *ex post* use and an *ex ante* use. The *ex post* use occurs when there exists a belief, and we say *of that belief* that it is (or isn't) justified. The *ex ante* use occurs when no such belief exists, or when we wish to ignore the question of whether such a belief exists. Here we say of the *person*, independent of his doxastic state vis-à-vis p, that p is (or isn't) suitable for him to believe.[17]

Since we have given an account of *ex post* justifiedness, it will suffice if we can analyze *ex ante* justifiedness in terms of it. Such an analysis, I believe, is ready at hand. S is *ex ante* justified in believing p at t just in case his total cognitive state at t is such that from that state he could come to believe p in such a way that this belief would be *ex post* justified. More precisely, he is *ex ante* justified in believing p at t just in case a reliable belief-forming operation is available to him such that the application of that operation to his total cognitive state at t would result, more or less immediately, in his believing p and this belief would be *ex post* justified. Stated formally, we have the following:

(11)   Person S is *ex ante* justified in believing p at t if and only if there is a reliable belief-forming operation available to S which is such that if S applied that operation to his total cognitive state at t, S would believe p at t-plus-delta (for a suitably small delta) and that belief would be *ex post* justified.

For the analysans of (11) to be satisfied, the total cognitive state at t must have a suitable causal ancestry. Hence, (11) is implicitly an Historical account of *ex ante* justifiedness.

As indicated, the bulk of this paper was addressed to *ex post* justifiedness. This is the appropriate analysandum if one is interested in the connection between justifiedness and knowledge, since what is crucial to whether a person *knows* a proposition is whether he has an actual *belief* in the proposition that is justified. However, since many epistemologists are interested in *ex ante* justifiedness, it is proper for a general theory of justification to try to provide an account of that concept as well. Our theory does this quite naturally, for the account of *ex ante* justifiedness falls out directly from our account of *ex post* justifiedness.[18]

Notes

1. Goldman 1967 [266], 1975 [365], 1976 [339].

2. Notice that the choice of a recursive format does not prejudice the case for or against any particular theory. A recursive format is perfectly general. Specifically, an explicit set of necessary and sufficient conditions is just a special case of a recursive format, i.e., one in which there is no recursive clause.

3. Many of the attempts I shall consider are suggested by material in William Alston 1971 [347].

4. Such a definition (though without the modal term) is given, for example, by W. V. Quine and J. S. Ullian 1970 [106], p. 21. Statements are said to be self-evident just in case "to understand them is to believe them".

5. Chisholm 1977 [555], p. 22.

6. I assume, of course, that 'nomologically necessary' is *de re* with respect to 'S' and 't' in this construction. I shall not focus on problems that may arise in this regard, since my primary concerns are with different issues.

7. This assumption violates the thesis that Davidson calls 'The Anomalism of the Mental'. Cf. Davidson 1970 [702]. But it is unclear that this thesis is a necessary truth. Thus, it seems fair to assume its falsity in order to produce a counterexample. The example neither entails nor precludes the mental-physical identity theory.

8. Keith Lehrer's example of the gypsy lawyer is intended to show the inappropriateness of a causal requirement. (See Lehrer 1974 [77], pp. 124–125.) But I find this example unconvincing. To the extent that I clearly imagine that the lawyer fixes his belief solely as a result of the cards, it seems intuitively wrong to say that he *knows*—or has a *justified belief*—that his client is innocent.

9. This definition is not exactly what we need for the purposes at hand. As Ernest Sosa points out, introspection will turn out to be a belief-dependent process since sometimes the input into the process will be a belief (when the introspected content is a belief). Intuitively, however, introspection is not the sort of process which may be merely conditionally reliable. I do not know how to refine the definition so as to avoid this difficulty, but it is a small and isolated point.

10. It may be objected that principles (6_A) and (6_B) are jointly open to analogues of the lottery paradox. A series of processes composed of reliable but less-than-perfectly-reliable processes may be extremely unreliable. Yet applications of (6_A) and (6_B) would confer justifiedness on a belief that is caused by such a series. In reply to this objection, we might simply indicate that the theory is intended to capture our ordinary notion of justifiedness, and this ordinary notion has been formed without recognition of this kind of problem. The theory is not wrong *as* a theory of the ordinary (naive) conception of justifiedness. On the other hand, if we want a theory to do more than capture the ordinary conception of justifiedness, it might be possible to strengthen the principles to avoid lottery-paradox analogues.

11. I am indebted to Mark Pastin for this point.

12. Cf. Chisholm 1977 [555], pp. 17, 114–116.

13. Cf. Goldman 1967 [266]. The reliability aspect of my theory also has its precursors in earlier papers of mine on knowing: Goldman 1975 [365], 1976 [339].

14. The view that introspection is retrospection was taken by Ryle, and before him (as Charles Hartshorne points out to me) by Hobbes, Whitehead, and possibly Husserl.

15. Of course, if people in world W learn *inductively* that wishful thinking is reliable, and regularly base their beliefs on this inductive inference, it is quite unproblematic and straightforward that their beliefs are justified. The only interesting case is where their beliefs are formed *purely* by wishful thinking, without using inductive inference. The suggestion contemplated in this paragraph of the text is that, in the world imagined, even pure wishful thinking would confer justifiedness.

16. I am indebted here to Mark Kaplan.

17. The distinction between *ex post* and *ex ante* justifiedness is similar to Roderick Firth's distinction between *doxastic* and *propositional* warrant. See Firth 1978 [720].

18. Research on this paper was begun while the author was a fellow of the John Simon Guggenheim Memorial Foundation and of the Center for Advanced Study in the Behavioral Sciences. I am grateful for their support. I have received helpful comments and criticism from Holly S. Goldman, Mark Kaplan, Fred Schmitt, Stephen P. Stich, and many others at several universities where earlier drafts of the paper were read.

6

Beyond Foundationalism
and the Coherence Theory

Hilary Kornblith

One of the legacies of positivist epistemology is a tendency to divorce epistemological questions from psychological questions. Epistemology is a normative discipline; it is concerned, among other things, with questions about how reasoning ought to proceed. Such questions can be answered, we are told, independently of investigation into the processes that in fact occur when reasoning takes place. Questions about justified belief are thus "translated" from the mental realm—'What kinds of transitions between mental states make for justified belief?'—to the logical realm—'What kinds of arguments are "good" arguments?' This approach to epistemological questions pervades much of contemporary philosophy.

I believe that this approach is mistaken. The approach I favor, a psychological approach to questions about knowledge and justification, is the naturalized epistemology of W. V. Quine and Alvin Goldman.[1] In this chapter, I will explore the implications of this approach for questions about justification, and, in particular, for the debate between foundationalists and coherence theorists.

Foundationalism and the coherence theory of justification may be viewed as two sides of a Kantian antinomy. Arguments for each view are predominantly negative; they are arguments for the claim that the opposing view is untenable. When the best available argument for a view is that competing views are untenable, one is left with the suspicion that a different conclusion would have been reached had one only considered the competing positions in a different order. More important, this suggests that the competing views may rest on a common false presupposition.

Reprinted from *The Journal of Philosophy* LXXII (October 1980): 597–612, by permission of the publisher. Copyright © 1980, *The Journal of Philosophy*.

I do not believe that the standard objections to either foundation-alism or the coherence theory have been adequately addressed. If I am correct in this, then it is worth considering whether there are other possible views about the nature of justification. I will argue that foundationalism and the coherence theory share a common false pre-supposition and that this lies in their antipsychological approach to epistemological questions. Once this false presupposition is rejected, the insights of both foundationalism and the coherence theory may be joined in a single unified theory of justification.

Knowledge and Justified Belief

The standard account of knowledge is that knowledge is some sort of justified, true belief. This account is often presented as a rival to causal theories of knowledge. Causal theorists of knowledge believe that knowledge is reliably produced true belief. This, we are told, leaves justification out of the picture.

I do not believe that this way of presenting the causal theory of knowledge is correct. Causal theorists of knowledge do not deny that knowledge is some sort of justified true belief; they merely give a nonstandard account of what it is for a belief to be justified. They claim that a belief is justified just in case it is caused by a reliable process. Self-styled justified-true-belief theorists of knowledge typi-cally give a quite different account of justification.

This may sound like a merely terminological dispute, but I do not believe that it is. The notion of justification was not invented by phi-losophers. Answers to questions about justification play an important action-guiding role. It is thus important to develop a theory that tells us what justification is. Causal theorists of knowledge are not exempt from this task. I do not believe, however, that they have tried to avoid dealing with it.

The claim that knowledge requires justified true belief is a mere truism. What is controversial is the proper analysis of the notion of justification. There are two ways in which one might try to go about giving an analysis of justification. One is to tackle this problem di-rectly; the other is to try to give an account of knowledge. A proper account of knowledge will include an account of justification. This must be true, unless the truism that knowledge requires justified be-lief is false. In claiming that knowledge is reliably produced true belief, causal theorists of knowledge are thus not abandoning the notion of justification, but rather committing themselves to a reliabilist account of justification.[2]

It is thus worth pointing out that there is room for dispute about what justification consists in. This is important because there is a standard account of justification which is so widely accepted—indeed, so widely taken for granted—that its merits as a theory of justification are rarely examined. This is especially unfortunate, I believe, because the standard account is false.

The Arguments-on-Paper Thesis

The standard account of what it is to be justified in believing a proposition is an apsychological account. If such an account is correct, questions about justification amount to nothing more than questions about the quality of various sorts of arguments. I will thus call the view that underlies the standard account the *arguments-on-paper thesis.*

Let us suppose that, for any person, it is possible, at least in principle, to list all the propositions that person believes. The arguments-on-paper thesis is just the view that a person has a justified belief that a particular proposition is true just in case that proposition appears on the list of propositions that person believes, and either it requires no argument, or a good argument can be given for it which takes as premises certain other propositions on the list.[3] Crucial to this explanation of the arguments-on-paper thesis is the notion of a "good argument." Foundationalism and the coherence theory of justification provide us with rival accounts of what it is to be a "good argument."

On the foundationalist version of the thesis, some of the propositions on the list of propositions one believes will have a special epistemic status: these propositions will be such that, if a person believes one of them, that person is justified in that belief. It has been widely held that some propositions are incorrigible; they are known if they are believed. If there are any incorrigible propositions, these propositions have the required epistemic status. There may be some propositions, however, that are not incorrigible and yet have the required status. Let us suppose that all propositions that have the required special epistemic status are starred whenever they occur on the list of propositions a person believes. The foundationalist will now provide us with a list of rules of inference. It is then claimed that a proposition requires no argument if and only if it is starred, and that an argument for a proposition is a good one just in case all its premises are starred and all the rules that must be applied to get from the premises to the conclusion are on the appropriate list. Various claims are often made for the epistemic status of the rules of inference, but we need not be concerned with these here.

Coherence theorists suppose that there are no starred propositions. The coherentist thus makes different claims about what makes for a good argument. It is claimed that there is a relation, call it C, which a proposition might bear to a set of propositions and which is such that, if a proposition appears on the list of propositions a person believes and bears C to the set of all the remaining propositions on that list, this provides a good argument for that proposition. In keeping with the spirit of the arguments-on-paper thesis, C must of course be definable solely in terms of relations among propositions.

The Psychological Turn

There are familiar objections against both foundationalism and the coherence theory, as presented above. Against foundationalism, it has been argued that there are no propositions the content of which guarantees that anyone who believes them is justified in believing them; in short, there are no starred propositions.[4] Against the coherence theory, it has been argued that the mere fact that a set of propositions cohere with one another is no evidence of their truth; in short, there is no such relation as C.[5] In response to these objections, various epicycles have been added to both foundationalist and coherentist accounts, but I do not believe that these objections have ever been answered.

I would therefore like to propose an account alternative to both foundationalism and the coherence theory, and here I have in mind not just a rival account of what it is to be a good argument, but rather an account that rejects the framework common to both of these theories. In this section, I will argue that the arguments-on-paper thesis is false;[6] in the following sections, I will develop an account that avoids the standard objections to both foundationalism and the coherence theory.

Consider Alfred. Alfred justifiably believes that p and justifiably believes that if p then q; he also believes that q. Is Alfred justified in believing that q?

Notice, first, that if the arguments-on-paper thesis is true, then, on any reasonable foundationalist or coherentist account, Alfred is justified in believing q. Foundationalists must allow that Alfred is justified in believing q, for it must surely be allowed that modus ponens is on the list of rules available for constructing good arguments.[7] Since Alfred is justified in believing p and if p then q, there are "good" arguments available for each of these propositions, and, given that modus ponens is an available rule, an acceptable argument for q is easily constructed. Similarly, coherence theorists will surely grant that a proposition that follows from others by modus ponens coheres with them, and thus, they too must insist that Alfred is justified in believing q.

It is clear, however, that Alfred need not be justified in believing q. Alfred may well be aware that he believes that p and that if p then q, and yet fail to believe that q on these grounds. If Alfred has a strong distrust of modus ponens, and yet believes q because he likes the sound of some sentence that expresses the proposition that q, then surely Alfred is not justified in believing that q. Nor will it do to suggest that this problem can be cleared up if we merely stipulate that Alfred must also believe that if p and if p and q, then q; for the same problem arises all over again.

Alfred is justified in believing that q only if his belief that q *depends* on his beliefs that p, and if p then q. The notion of belief dependence cannot be accounted for in terms of the contents of the various beliefs held. The arguments-on-paper thesis is thus false.

In rejecting the arguments-on-paper thesis, we must take a psychological turn.[8] The notion of belief dependence must be accounted for by looking at the belief states of persons and, in particular, at the relations among them. Questions about the justification of beliefs are thus intimately tied to questions about the sorts of processes responsible for the presence of those beliefs. This is the first step toward a naturalized epistemology, and the failure of the arguments-on-paper thesis shows that it is a step we must take.

I will not attempt to give an account of what it is for one belief to depend on another. I will, however, adopt the following working hypothesis: if one belief depends on another, the former must be *causally* dependent on the latter· one belief cannot depend on another when the two are causally independent. This suggestion, I believe, allows us to recognize an important insight of foundationalism.

The Hierarchical Structure of Justification

That causal dependence is a necessary condition of belief dependence leads immediately to the conclusion that the structure of belief dependence is hierarchical. The argument for this conclusion is nothing more than the familiar *regress argument*, an argument frequently advanced by foundationalists.

Consider some person's justified belief that p. What might make a person justified in having such a belief? Either that belief is not justified, even in part, by its dependence on other beliefs, or there is a set of beliefs B such that p is justified in virtue of its dependence on the members of B. We may now ask of each of the members of B whether that belief is justified in virtue of its dependence on other beliefs, and so on. A tree structure results.

Clearly, it is not possible, in tracing the source of a belief's justification in this way, that one should come across an unjustified belief; a belief cannot be justified in virtue of its dependence on an unjustified belief. There are then three possibilities. Either (1) at least one branch of the tree will be made up of infinitely many distinct justified beliefs; (2) there will be no branches made up of infinitely many distinct beliefs, but at least one branch, in effect, will turn back on itself; that is, there will be some branch that forms a closed circle; or (3) all branches will be finite in length and contain no circles; all branches will terminate with what we shall call a *terminal belief*—a belief that is not justified in virtue of its dependence on other beliefs.

The fact that belief dependence requires causal dependence guarantees that justificatory trees fall into the last of these three categories. Consider the causal chain of events that accounts for a person's holding a particular belief. A complete explanation of the presence of a belief will include a complete description of this chain of events. There must be a first belief on this causal chain; thus, there must be a belief on any such chain which is justified, though not justified in virtue of its dependence on any other beliefs. It therefore follows that each justified belief is either such that, though justified, it is not justified in virtue of its dependence on any other beliefs, or such that it is justified, ultimately, in virtue of its dependence on beliefs which, though justified, are not justified in virtue of their dependence on other beliefs.[9]

I have said nothing about the content of terminal beliefs, for I am interested not so much in their content as in their existence. If the view championed by J. J. Gibson,[10] that perception is detection, is correct, terminal beliefs are perceptual beliefs. On the other hand, the view that perception is hypothesis, favored by R. L. Gregory,[11] would suggest that perceptual beliefs are not typically terminal. I will briefly sketch each of these two views.

Gibson's view gives foundationalists a good part of what they have always wanted. If Gibson is correct, the causal chain of events that leads to the production of a perceptual belief typically does not itself include any believings. Perceptual beliefs, when justified, are thus typically not justified in virtue of their dependence on other beliefs.

Gregory, on the other hand, claims that if we examine the etiology of a perceptual belief we will typical find that it is dependent on other previously acquired beliefs, many of which are also perceptual. These, in turn, will also typically depend on other previously held beliefs; and so on. Of course the position that all beliefs are causally dependent on previously held beliefs is incoherent, and this is not the position that Gregory holds. If Gregory is right, however, then if we trace the etiology of a typical perceptual belief we will find that it is dependent on many beliefs that were acquired in the past, and perhaps as long ago as early childhood.

There is no need for me to enter this psychological controversy. I wish only to argue that some beliefs must be terminal, and each justified belief must either be terminal or be dependent on terminal beliefs. Although this conclusion sounds very much like foundationalism, it is important to emphasize the contrast between foundationalism and the view I am defending here. The argument just given demonstrates the existence of terminal beliefs; it does not demonstrate the existence of what foundationalists have called "self-justifying beliefs." First, it should be noted that this argument does not in any way suggest that terminal beliefs are justified in virtue of their content, nor does it suggest that a belief that is terminal at one time must be terminal at another. Moreover, it does not show that a belief might not depend on itself; this argument in no way precludes the possibility that, in tracing the etiology of a belief, it should be discovered that an agent's holding the belief that p at time t is dependent, in part, on his holding the belief that p at some time earlier than t. Most importantly, however, the justificatory trees that have been described are nothing more than trees of belief dependence. Although justification is clearly in part a matter of belief dependence, this is not to say that there is nothing more to justification than belief dependence.[12] Indeed I will argue that relations among beliefs other than those captured by the justificatory trees just described play a crucial role in making beliefs justified.

The Role of Background Beliefs

I have argued thus far that part of what determines whether a particular person is justified in holding a particular belief at a particular time is the process responsible for the presence of that belief in that person at that time.[13] Such processes, however, are not the sole determinants of justification.

Consider the following example. Joe and Moe are both looking at a bowl of fruit, and this causes both Joe and Moe to believe that there is an apple in front of them. Let us suppose that the psychological processes responsible for the presence of these beliefs in Joe and Moe are the same, and thus the tree diagram illustrating the beliefs (if any) upon which Moe's belief that there is an apple in front of him depends is the same as the corresponding diagram for Joe. Let us suppose further that Joe also believes that he is myopic and, thus, that if the basket of fruit in front of him were artificial fruit, he would not be able to tell at this distance; Moe has no such belief. In spite of Joe's belief that he cannot distinguish what is in front of him from artificial fruit, Joe still believes that he is looking at a genuine apple.[14]

In this circumstance, Moe is justified in believing that there is an apple in front of him, but Joe is not. Since the processes that produced their beliefs are the same, something other than the process responsible for the presence of their beliefs must be involved in determining whether they are justified. In this case, it is quite clear what this additional factor is. Although the process responsible for the presence of Joe's belief would ordinarily be adequate for justification, it is not adequate for justification given Joe's background beliefs— beliefs which do not appear on the justificatory tree tracing the etiology of the belief in question. In determining whether a process is adequate for justification, we must examine not only features intrinsic to the process itself, but also background beliefs which may play no part at all in the process. A belief's justificatory status is thus a function of (at least) the process responsible for its presence, as well as the background beliefs had by the agent at the time in question.

The importance of background beliefs should not be underestimated. It has sometimes been suggested that some beliefs, though not incorrigible, are justified independently of their relations to other beliefs.[15] This cannot, however, be true. As long as a belief is not incorrigible, its justificatory status will vary not only with changes in the process responsible for its presence but also with changes in background beliefs. Thus, for any given belief-forming process, there will always be background beliefs that would make that process inadequate for justification. *All nonincorrigible beliefs are thus justified, in part, in virtue of their relations to other beliefs.* The qualification is unnecessary, of course, if there are no incorrigible beliefs. I have nothing to add to the arguments available against the existence of incorrigible beliefs, and since there is a growing consensus that such beliefs do not exist, I will take for granted in what follows that the justificatory status of all beliefs has been shown to depend, in part, on other beliefs.

Beyond Foundationalism and the Coherence Theory

Foundationalists have argued that the structure of belief dependence is hierarchical; that some beliefs, though justified, are not dependent on others; and that all other justified beliefs must ultimately be dependent on these. If the argument I have given [previously] is correct, foundationalists are correct about all these points.

Coherence theorists have argued that no belief is justified independently of its relations to other beliefs. This claim too is vindicated by the account I offer. Although there must be some beliefs such that an account of the process responsible for their presence does not involve other beliefs, an account of what makes these processes adequate for justification must involve other beliefs. A complete account of what makes a particular belief justified will always involve beliefs other than the one in question.

Foundationalists have argued that the coherence theory of justification "cuts justification off from the world." Justified beliefs are beliefs that, in some sense or other, are likely to be true. A proper theory of justification must therefore explain in what sense it is that justified beliefs are likely to be true. Since it is the way the world is which makes beliefs true or false, a proper theory of justification must explain what it is about justified beliefs which makes it likely that they should "match up" with the way the world is. The outline of a theory of justification which I have offered explicitly makes room for such an account. Any adequate account of the features of belief-producing processes that make for justified belief must surely indicate the relation between these processes and the world. The fact that the account offered is a causal account requires that, in filling in the outline offered, the connection between justified beliefs and the world must be included.

Coherence theorists have argued that foundationalism is not plausible unless foundationalists can come up with some plausible candidates for foundational (or "starred," as I have called them) beliefs, and that no such plausible candidates have ever been offered. Though I have not made any suggestions about which beliefs might be terminal, this does not leave me vulnerable to the coherence theorist's objection. Foundationalists have made quite elaborate claims for the epistemic status of foundational beliefs; I make no such claims for the superficially similar terminal beliefs of my account. What makes a belief terminal at a particular time is simply that the chain of events responsible for its presence does not include any believings. There can be little doubt that there are such beliefs, though nothing short of a psychological theory of the mechanisms involved in belief acquisition will tell us what they are. Needless to say, I am not prepared to offer such a theory.

I thus hope that the outline of a theory of justified belief which I have offered incorporates those features of foundationalism and the coherence theory which have made each of these views attractive and yet avoids those features which have made each of these views unacceptable. Let me close this section with a brief discussion of the notion of *epistemic priority*.

Some philosophers have suggested that there is a special class of beliefs that are "epistemically prior" to other beliefs; it has sometimes been claimed that this special class might consist of beliefs about one's present state of mind, or, alternatively, about medium-sized physical objects. I believe that claims about epistemic priority are to be understood as claims about the relative position of beliefs on the justificatory trees described above. In these terms, we may distinguish among a number of different theses about epistemic priority.

The following is a very weak claim about epistemic priority. There is some class of beliefs that tend to be epistemically prior—i.e., lower in justificatory trees—than some other class of beliefs. This claim is clearly true. Consider the class of beliefs about medium-sized physical objects and the class of beliefs about subatomic particles. Beliefs in the former class tend to occur lower in justificatory trees than beliefs in the latter class; beliefs about subatomic particles tend to depend on beliefs about medium-sized physical objects, rather than vice versa. This is of course compatible with the claim that, for example, if the structure of human sense organs were different, the epistemic ordering of these two classes might have been different. It is also compatible with the claim that some beliefs about subatomic particles are epistemically prior to some beliefs about medium-sized physical objects.

Foundationalists have argued for a stronger claim about epistemic priority: the class of beliefs that are in fact terminal must be terminal; the class of beliefs that are in fact epistemically prior to other beliefs must be epistemically prior to other beliefs. I think this view is plausible only if the terminal beliefs are incorrigible. Let us suppose that there is a terminal belief t that is not incorrigible. Since t is not incorrigible, there is some evidence e which one might obtain that t is false. Let us suppose that one comes to believe e, and on this basis one gives up one's belief that t. Let us further suppose that e is later discovered to be misleading evidence and that one thus comes to believe t again, this time on the basis of one's belief that e is misleading. Thus, although t was once a terminal belief, it now no longer is. Since such a chain of events might occur, no (nonincorrigible) terminal belief is necessarily terminal. The fact that one belief is epistemically prior to another at a particular time does not in any way guarantee that the order of epistemic priority will not shift at a later time.

Most importantly, it should be pointed out again that the fact that a certain class of beliefs is terminal at a particular time, and thus epistemically prior to all other beliefs at that time, does not show that what makes these beliefs justified has nothing to do with other beliefs higher up in the tree. In spite of the "foundational" structure of justificatory trees, no beliefs are justified independently of their relations to other beliefs.

Reliabilism

The outline of a theory of justification which I have presented is neutral on the question of what makes a belief-forming process adequate for justification. For the purposes of this paper, namely, to extract the elements of truth from foundationalism and the coherence theory and combine them in a unified theory of justification, it is unnecessary to take a stand on this question. Nevertheless, there is only one theory currently in the field which addresses this question, *reliabilism,* and it will thus be worth while to see how my outline looks in reliabilist dress.[16]

Reliabilism is the view that knowledge is reliably produced true belief, and thus that justified belief is reliably produced belief. This view is presented in what is now a *locus classicus* of reliabilism, Alvin Goldman's "Discrimination and Perceptual Knowledge"[17]:

> What kinds of causal processes or mechanisms must be responsible for a belief if that belief is to count as knowledge? They must be mechanisms that are, in an appropriate sense, "reliable." Roughly, a cognitive mechanism or process is reliable if it not only produces true beliefs in actual situations, but would also produce true beliefs, or at least inhibit false beliefs, in relevant counterfactual situations (771).

In presenting my account of justification in reliabilist terms, I will follow Goldman's analysis closely.

A belief-producing process is reliable just in case it tends to produce true beliefs in actual situations as well as in counterfactual situations that are relevant alternatives to the actual situation. A belief is justified just in case the process responsible for its presence is reliable.

Given an epistemic agent, a proposition, and a time at which that agent believes that proposition, the determinants of the relevant alternatives to that proposition, for that agent, at that time, fall into two categories: the way the world is, and the way the agent believes the world to be. Goldman does not offer an account of how relevant alternatives are determined, nor is such an account available in the literature. In spite of this, it will be useful to see how, in particular cases, relevant alternatives are determined.

Let us bring Joe and Moe back to center stage. Joe, it will be remembered, believes that there is an apple in front of him in spite of the fact that he believes that if he were looking at artificial fruit he would be unable to tell the difference. Joe's belief that he is looking at an apple is thus clearly unjustified. How do we account for this within the Goldman framework?

The process that produces Joe's belief, we have supposed, is a standard perceptual process. This is a perfectly respectable belief-forming process, but it is not adequate for justification unless it tends to produce true beliefs in both actual and relevant counterfactual situations. Joe's belief that he cannot tell the difference between genuine and artificial fruit at this distance makes a certain counterfactual situation relevant that would otherwise not be relevant: namely the situation in which he is actually looking at artificial fruit. The process that produced Joe's belief in the actual situation would tend to produce false beliefs in this relevant counterfactual situation, and thus Joe is unjustified in believing that he sees an apple. Since what makes this counterfactual situation relevant is Joe's belief about his myopia and since Moe does not have a similar belief, this counterfactual situation is not relevant for Moe. The process that produced Moe's belief, namely, the very same process that produced Joe's, is reliable because it tends to produce true beliefs in actual situations as well as in those which are relevant for Moe. Moe thus has a justified belief.

It might seem, in light of this example, that the relevant alternatives for justification should be determined only by the way the agent believes the world to be, and not also by the way the world is. Nevertheless, situations outside the agent's doxastic realm may serve to determine relevant alternatives. Just as there are cases of morally culpable ignorance, there are cases of epistemically culpable ignorance. Had Moe been frequently fooled by artificial fruit before, he would be no more justified than Joe. The way the world is thus enters in determining relevant alternatives.

Alternatively, it might be argued that one needn't take into account the way the world is believed to be in order to determine relevant alternatives. It might be argued that all the facts about justification which can be accounted for by allowing an agent's beliefs to determine some of the relevant alternatives can equally well be accounted for by by-passing the agent's beliefs and looking only at certain facts about the way the world is. Beliefs thus play no role in the determination of relevant alternatives.

This argument is a non sequitur. Consider a particular belief that seems to determine a particular relevant alternative, e.g., Joe's belief that he is myopic. Now consider the causal chain that leads to the production of Joe's belief. This chain of events surely determines that the situation in which Joe is looking at artificial fruit is a relevant alternative to the actual situation. The only reason that this chain of events determines the relevant alternative, however, is that it also determines that Joe will come to believe he is unable to tell the difference between artificial fruit and genuine fruit from this distance. Chains of events that do not thus determine Joe's belief will not determine relevant alternatives.

Relevant alternative situations are thus determined, in part, by an agent's beliefs, and questions of justification are determined by the tendency of the process responsible for the presence of a belief to produce true beliefs in relevant alternative situations. I have urged that all justified beliefs must either be or depend on beliefs that do not depend on others, simply because there must be some first belief involved in any belief-forming process. Nevertheless, no belief is justified independently of its relations to other beliefs; for in order to be justified a belief must be produced by a process that tends to produce true beliefs in relevant counterfactual situations, and relevance is always determined, in part, by an agent's beliefs. Concessions are thus made to both foundationalism and the coherence theory.

It is a short step from a reliabilist account of justified belief to a reliabilist account of knowledge, for knowledge is merely reliably produced true belief. Here, however, we "up the ante" in setting the standards of reliability adequate for knowledge. A process must tend to produce true beliefs in a wider range of counterfactual circumstances if it is to be sufficiently reliable for knowledge than if it is to be merely reliable enough for justified belief. A single example should make this point clear.

Alphonse is looking at a bowl of fruit and, as a consequence, comes to believe that there is an apple in front of him. Alphonse is terribly myopic, although he's never had any reason to believe this, and if the apple in front of him were made of wax, Alphonse wouldn't notice the difference. In this situation, Alphonse's belief that there is an apple in front of him is surely justified—he does not realize that he is myopic, and his ignorance is not culpable—but he does not have knowledge. Here it seems that the fact that Alphonse is myopic determines a relevant alternative as regards knowledge, but not as regards justification.

The determinants of the relevant alternatives as regards justification are thus the class of the agent's beliefs, as well as a subclass of the true propositions about the world apart from the agent's beliefs. The determinants of the relevant alternatives as regards knowledge are the class of the agent's beliefs as well as a larger subclass of the true propositions about the world.

This concludes my outline of a theory of justification. Many questions remain open. Most obviously, it remains to be shown how relevant alternatives are determined, and a great deal remains to be said about terminal beliefs. Nevertheless I hope this sketch serves to focus questions about the nature of justification in a more productive way than the endless battle between foundationalists and coherence theorists might have suggested was possible.

Notes

An earlier version of this paper was presented to colloquia at the universities of Pittsburgh, Michigan, Cornell, and UCLA; versions more like the present one were read at the University of Delaware and the University of Vermont. I have received helpful comments from Kristin Guyot, Harold Hodes, Patricia Kitcher, George Sher, Nicholas Sturgeon, and William Wilcox, Jr. Sydney Shoemaker, Carl Ginet, and Richard Boyd have given me extensive comments on numerous drafts. I am especially indebted to Philip Kitcher.

1. See especially Quine 1969 [100], and Goldman 1976 [339], 1979 [397].

2. In Goldman 1975 [365], Goldman suggested that the causal theory of knowledge amounts to an account of knowledge without justification. In his more recent Goldman 1979 [397], he insists that a causal theory of knowledge brings with it a causal theory of justification.

3. The following is a representative sampling of those who have held the arguments-on-paper thesis in this century, with references: Ayer 1974 [541], p. 63; Chisholm 1957 [553], p. 16; Chisholm 1977 [555], p. 109; Chisholm 1976 [554], pp. 182–3; Cornman 1978 [698], p. 230; Firth 1965 [718] passim; Firth 1969 [719] passim; Ginet 1975 [582], p. 52; Lehrer 1974 [77], p. 17; Lewis 1946 [609], pp. 265–314; Neurath 1959 [794], p. 203; Pastin 1976 [798], p. 575; Pastin 1976 [799], passim; Pollock 1974 [631], pp. 33–39; Popper 1979 [632], p. 6; Russell 1912 [644], p. 134; Russell 1948 [645], p. 155; Sellars 1963 [122], p. 169; Sosa 1978 [832], p. 188.

4. See, e.g., Sellars 1963 [122], pp. 127–196; Williams 1977 [142], pp. 25–59.

5. Lewis 1969 [772], p. 128.

6. Similar arguments have been offered by Harman 1973 [59], pp. 24–33; Stroud 1979 [177]; Goldman 1979 [397].

7. This assumption is used only for purposes of illustration. Foundationalists must accept some rules of inference, and, if modus ponens is not among these, an analogous example can be constructed making use of one of the accepted rules. Similarly, for coherence theorists, the assumption is unnecessary.

8. Lehrer 1974 [77], pp. 124–5, has resisted this move. He presents an example that purports to show that the psychological turn should not be taken. In

their simplest form, examples of the type Lehrer offers presuppose that a person's reason for holding a certain belief must always be tied to the reason for which the belief was acquired; this presupposition is false. When this presupposition is not made, it is not obvious that Lehrer's intuitions about the example are correct.

9. One might try to escape this conclusion by arguing that the notion of belief, like that of baldness, is vague. If the notion of belief were vague in this way, this would undermine my argument. I know of no reason for thinking, however, that this is so. We make use of the notion of belief in explaining action. If such explanations were to break down with further investigation of the etiology of action, we might have to conclude that the notion of belief is as vague as that of baldness. There is no reason yet, however, to draw this conclusion.

10. Gibson 1966 [580].

11. Gregory 1970 [586].

12. Sydney Shoemaker and Richard Boyd argued with me relentlessly to get me to see this point. I would never have come to see it if not for discussions with Philip Kitcher.

13. I am very much indebted in this section, as I am throughout the paper, to Goldman 1979 [397].

14. Joe is, of course, being irrational; but this is surely possible.

15. This view has come to be known as "modest foundationalism." See, e.g., Firth 1969 [719]; Pastin 1976 [799].

16. This is not quite true. There is also the account offered in Harman 1973 [59].

17. Reliabilism is also defended in Armstrong 1973 [3].

7 — A Priori Knowledge

Philip Kitcher

I

"A priori" has been a popular term with philosophers at least since
Kant distinguished between a priori and a posteriori knowledge. Yet,
despite the frequency with which it has been used in twentieth-century philosophy, there has been little discussion of the concept of
apriority.[1] Some writers seem to take it for granted that there are
propositions, such as the truths of logic and mathematics, which are
a priori; others deny that there are any a priori propositions. In the
absence of a clear characterization of the a priori/a posteriori distinction, it is by no means obvious what is being asserted or what is being denied.

"A priori" is an epistemological predicate. What is *primarily* a priori
is an item of knowledge.[2] Of course, we can introduce a derivative
use of "a priori" as a predicate of propositions:[3] a priori propositions
are those which we could know a priori. Somebody might protest
that current practice is to define the notion of an a priori proposition
outright, by taking the class of a priori propositions to consist of the
truths of logic and mathematics (for example). But when philosophers allege that truths of logic and mathematics are a priori, they do
not intend merely to recapitulate the definition of a priori propositions. Their aim is to advance a thesis about the epistemological status
of logic and mathematics.

To understand the nature of such epistemological claims, we
should return to Kant, who provided the most explicit characterization of a priori knowledge: "we shall understand by a priori knowledge, not knowledge which is independent of this or that experience,

Reprinted from *The Philosophical Review* LXXXVI (1980): 3–23, by permission of the author and the publisher. Copyright © 1980, *The Philosophical Review*.

but knowledge absolutely independent of all experience."[4] While acknowledging that Kant's formulation sums up the classical notion of apriority, several recent writers who have discussed the topic have despaired of making sense of it.[5] I shall try to show that Kant's definition can be clarified, and that the concept of a priori knowledge can be embedded in a naturalistic epistemology.

II

Two questions naturally arise. What are we to understand by "experience"? And what is to be made of the idea of independence from experience? Apparently, there are easy answers. Count as a person's experience the stream of her sensory encounters with the world, where this includes both "outer experience," that is, sensory states caused by stimuli external to the body, and "inner experience," that is, those sensory states brought about by internal stimuli. Now we might propose that someone's knowledge is independent of her experience just in case she could have had that knowledge whatever experience she had had. To this obvious suggestion there is an equally obvious objection. The apriorist is not ipso facto a believer in innate knowledge: indeed, Kant emphasized the difference between the two types of knowledge. So we cannot accept an analysis which implies that a priori knowledge could have been obtained given minimal experiences.[6]

Many philosophers (Kant included) contend both that analytic truths can be known a priori and that some analytic truths involve concepts which could only be acquired if we were to have particular kinds of experience. If we are to defend their doctrines from immediate rejection, we must allow a minimal role to experience, even in a priori knowledge. Experience may be needed to provide some concepts. So we might modify our proposal: knowledge is independent of experience if any experience which would enable us to acquire the concepts involved would enable us to have the knowledge.

It is worth noting explicitly that we are concerned here with the *total* experience of the knower. Suppose that you acquire some knowledge empirically. Later you deduce some consequences of this empirical knowledge. We should reject the suggestion that your knowledge of those consequences is independent of experience because, at the time you perform the deduction, you are engaging in a process of reasoning which is independent of the sensations you are then having.[7] As Kant recognized,[8] your knowledge, in cases like this, is dependent on your total experience: different total sequences of sensations would not have given you the premises for your deductions.

Let us put together the points which have been made so far. A person's experience at a particular time will be identified with his sensory state at the time. (Such states are best regarded physicalistically in terms of stimulation of sensory receptors, but we should recognize that there are both "outer" and "inner" receptors.) The total sequence of experiences X has had up to time t is *X's life at t*. A life will be said to be *sufficient for X for p* just in case X could have had that life and gained sufficient understanding to believe that p. (I postpone, for the moment, questions about the nature of the modality involved here.) Our discussion above suggests the use of these notions in the analysis of a priori knowledge: X knows a priori that p if and only if X knows that p and, given any life sufficient for X for p, X could have had that life and still have known that p. Making temporal references explicit: at time t X knows a priori that p just in case, at time t, X knows that p and, given any life sufficient for X for p, X could have had that life at t and still have known, at t, that p. In subsequent discussions I shall usually leave the temporal references implicit.

Unfortunately, the proposed analysis will not do. A clear-headed apriorist should admit that people can have empirical knowledge of propositions which can be known a priori. However, on the account I have given, if somebody knows that p and if it is possible for her to know a priori that p, then, apparently, given any sufficiently rich life she could know that p, so that she would meet the conditions for a priori knowledge that p. (This presupposes that modalities "collapse," but I don't think the problem can be solved simply by denying the presupposition.) Hence it seems that my account will not allow for empirical knowledge of propositions that can be known a priori.

We need to amend the analysis. We must differentiate situations in which a person knows something empirically which could have been known a priori from situations of actual a priori knowledge. The remedy is obvious. What sets apart corresponding situations of the two types is a difference in the ways in which what is known is known. An analysis of a priori knowledge must probe the notion of knowledge more deeply than we have done so far.

III

We do not need a general analysis of knowledge, but we do need the *form* of such an analysis. I shall adopt an approach which extracts what is common to much recent work on knowledge, an approach which may appropriately be called "the psychologistic account of knowledge."[9] The root idea is that the question of whether a person's true belief counts as knowledge depends on whether the presence of that true belief can be explained in an appropriate fashion. The difference between an item of knowledge and mere true belief turns on the factors which produced the belief; thus the issue revolves around the way in which a particular mental state was generated. It is important to emphasize that, at different times, a person may have states of belief with the same content, and these states may be produced by different processes. The claim that a process produces a belief is to be understood as the assertion that the presence of the current state of belief is to be explained through a description of that process. Hence the account is not committed to supposing that the original formation of a belief is relevant to the epistemological status of later states of belief in the same proposition.[10]

The question of what conditions must be met if a belief is to be explained in an appropriate fashion is central to epistemology, but it need not concern us here. My thesis is that the distinction between knowledge and true belief depends on the characteristics of the process which generates the belief, and this thesis is independent of specific proposals about what characteristics are crucial. Introducing a useful term, let us say that some processes *warrant* the beliefs they produce, and that these processes are *warrants* for such beliefs. The general view of knowledge I have adopted can be recast as the thesis that X knows that *p* just in case X correctly believes that *p* and X's belief was produced by a process which is a warrant for it. Leaving the task of specifying the conditions on warrants to general epistemology, my aim is to distinguish a priori knowledge from a posteriori knowledge. We discovered above that the distinction requires us to consider the ways in which what is known is known. Hence I propose to reformulate the problem: let us say that X knows a priori that *p* just in case X has a true belief that *p* and that belief was produced by a process which is an *a priori warrant* for it. Now the crucial notion is that of an a priori warrant, and our task becomes that of specifying the conditions which distinguish a priori warrants from other warrants.

At this stage, some examples may help us to see how to draw the distinction. Perception is an obvious type of process which philosophers have supposed *not* to engender a priori knowledge. Putative a priori warrants are more controversial. I shall use Kant's notion of pure intuition as an example. This is not to endorse the claim that processes of pure intuition are a priori warrants, but only to see what features of such processes have prompted Kant (and others) to differentiate them from perceptual processes.

On Kant's theory, processes of pure intuition are supposed to yield a priori mathematical knowledge. Let us focus on a simple geometrical example. We are supposed to gain a priori knowledge of the elementary properties of triangles by using our grasp on the concept of triangle to construct a mental picture of a triangle and by inspecting this picture with the mind's eye.[11] What are the characteristics of this kind of process which make Kant want to say that it produces knowledge which is independent of experience? I believe that Kant's account implies that three conditions should be met. The same type of process must be *available* independently of experience. It must produce *warranted* belief independently of experience. And it must produce *true* belief independently of experience. Let us consider these conditions in turn.

According to the Kantian story, if our life were to enable us to acquire the appropriate concepts (the concept of a triangle and the other geometrical concepts involved) then the appropriate kind of pure intuition would be available to us. We could represent a triangle to ourselves, inspect it, and so reach the same beliefs. But, if the process is to generate *knowledge* independently of experience, Kant must require more of it. Given any sufficiently rich life, if we were to undergo the same type of process and gain the same beliefs, then those beliefs would be warranted by the process. Let us dramatize the point by imagining that experience is unkind. Suppose that we are presented with experiments which are cunningly contrived so as to make it appear that some of our basic geometrical beliefs are false. Kant's theory of geometrical knowledge presupposes that if, in the circumstances envisaged, a process of pure intuition were to produce geometrical belief then it would produce warranted belief, despite the background of misleading experience.

So far I have considered how a Kantian process of pure intuition might produce warranted belief independently of experience. But to generate *knowledge* independently of experience, a priori warrants must produce warranted *true* belief in counterfactual situations where experiences are different. This point does not emerge clearly in the Kantian case because the propositions which are alleged to be known a priori are taken to be necessary, so that the question of whether it would be possible to have an a priori warrant for a false belief does not arise. Plainly, we could ensure that a priori warrants produce warranted *true* belief independently of experience by declaring that a priori warrants only warrant necessary truths. But this proposal is unnecessarily strong. Our goal is to construe a priori knowledge as knowledge which is independent of experience, and this can be achieved, without closing the case against the contingent a priori, by supposing that, in a counterfactual situation in which an a priori warrant produces belief that p then p. On this account, a priori warrants are ultra-reliable; they never lead us astray.[12]

Summarizing the conditions that have been uncovered, I propose the following analysis of a priori knowledge.

1. X knows a priori that p if and only if X knows that p and X's belief that p was produced by a process which is an a priori warrant for it.

2. α is an a priori warrant for X's belief that p if and only if α is a process such that, given any life e, sufficient for X for p, then
a. some process of the same type could produce in X a belief that p
b. if a process of the same type were to produce in X a belief that p then it would warrant X in believing that p
c. if a process of the same type were to produce in X a belief that p then p.

It should be clear that this analysis yields the desired result that, if a person knows a priori that p then she could know that p whatever (sufficiently rich) experience she had had. But it goes beyond the proposal of section II in spelling out the idea that the knowledge be obtainable in the same way. Hence we can distinguish cases of empirical knowledge of propositions which could be known a priori from cases of actual a priori knowledge.

IV

In this section, I want to be more explicit about the notion of "types of processes" which I have employed, and about the modal and conditional notions which figure in my analysis. To specify a process which produces a belief is to pick out some terminal segment of the causal ancestry of the belief. I think that, without loss of generality, we can restrict our attention to those segments which consist solely of states and events internal to the believer.[13] Tracing the causal ancestry of a belief beyond the believer would identify processes which would not be available independently of experience, so that they would violate our conditions on a priori warrants.

Given that we need only consider psychological processes, the next question which arises is how we divide processes into types. It may seem that the problem can be sidestepped: can't we simply propose that to defend the apriority of an item of knowledge is to claim that that knowledge was produced by a psychological process and that *that very process* would be available and would produce warranted true belief in counterfactual situations where experience is different? I think it is easy to see how to use this proposal to rewrite (2) in a way which avoids reference to "types of processes." I have not adopted this approach because I think that it shortcuts important questions about what makes a process the same in different counterfactual situations.

Our talk of processes which produce belief was originally introduced to articulate the idea that some items of knowledge are obtained in the same way while others are obtained in different ways. To return to our example, knowing a theorem on the basis of hearing a lecture and knowing the same theorem by following a proof count, intuitively, as different ways of knowing the theorem. Our intuitions about this example, and others, involve a number of different principles of classification, with different principles appearing in different cases. We seem to divide belief-forming processes into types by considering content of beliefs, inferential connections, causal connections, use of perceptual mechanisms and so forth. I suggest that these principles of classification probably do not give rise to one definite taxonomy, but that, by using them singly, or in combination, we obtain a number of different taxonomies which we can and do employ. Moreover, within each taxonomy, we can specify types of processes more or less narrowly.[14] Faced with such variety, what characterization should we pick?

There is probably no privileged way of dividing processes into types. This is not to say that our standard principles of classification will allow *anything* to count as a type. Somebody who proposed that the process of listening to a lecture (or the terminal segment of it which consists of psychological states and events) belongs to a type which consists of itself and instances of following a proof, would flout *all* our principles for dividing processes into types. Hence, while we may have many admissible notions of types of belief-forming processes, corresponding to different principles of classification, some collections of processes contravene all such principles, and these cannot be admitted as genuine types.[15]

My analysis can be read as issuing a challenge to the apriorist. If someone wishes to claim that a particular belief is an item of a priori knowledge then he must specify a segment of the causal ancestry of the belief, consisting of states and events internal to the believer, and type-identity conditions which conform to some principle (or set of principles) of classification which are standardly employed in our divisions of belief-forming processes (of which the principles I have indicated above furnish the most obvious examples). If he succeeds in doing this so that the requirements in (2) are met, his claim is sustained; if he cannot, then his claim is defeated.

The final issue which requires discussion in this section is that of explaining the modal and conditional notions I have used. There are all kinds of possibility, and claims about what is possible bear an implicit relativization to a set of facts which are held constant.[16] When we say, in (2), that, given any sufficiently rich life, X could have had a belief which was the product of a particular type of process, should we conceive of this as merely logical possibility or are there some features of the actual world which are tacitly regarded as fixed? I suggest that we are not just envisaging any logically possible world. We imagine a world in which X has similar mental powers to those he has in the actual world. By hypothesis, X's experience is different. Yet the capacities for thinking, reasoning, and acquiring knowledge which X possesses as a member of *homo sapiens* are to remain unaffected: we want to say that X, *with the kinds of cognitive capacities distinctive of humans*, could have undergone processes of the appropriate type, even if his experiences had been different.[17]

Humans might have had more faculties for acquiring knowledge than they actually have. For example, we might have had some strange ability to "see" what happens on the other side of the Earth. When we consider the status of a particular type of process as an a priori warrant, the existence of worlds in which such extra faculties come into play is entirely irrelevant. Our investigation focuses on the question of whether a particular type of process would be available to a person with the kinds of faculties people actually have, not on whether such processes would be available to creatures whose capacities for acquiring knowledge are augmented or diminished. Conditions (2(b)) and (2(c)) are to be read in similar fashion. Rewriting (2(b)) to make the form of the conditional explicit, we obtain: for any life e sufficient for X for p and for any world in which X has e, in which he believes that p, in which his belief is the product of a process of the appropriate kind, and *in which X has the cognitive capacities distinctive of humans*, X is warranted in believing that p. Similarly, (2(c)) becomes: for any life e sufficient for X for p and for any world in which X has e, in which he believes that p, in which his belief is the product of a process of the appropriate kind, *and in which X has the cognitive capacities distinctive of humans*, p. Finally, the notion of a life's being sufficient for X for p also bears an implicit reference to X's native powers. To say that a particular life enables X to form certain concepts is to maintain that, given the genetic programming with which X is endowed, that life allows for the formation of the concepts.

The account I have offered can be presented more graphically in the following way. Consider a human as a cognitive device, endowed initially with a particular kind of structure. Sensory experience is fed into the device and, as a result, the device forms certain concepts. For any proposition p, the class of experiences which are sufficiently rich for p consists of those experiences which would enable the device, with the kind of structure it actually has, to acquire the concepts to believe that p. To decide whether or not a particular item of knowledge that p is an item of a priori knowledge we consider whether the type of process which produced the belief that p is a process which would have been available to the device, with the kind of structure it actually has, if different sufficiently rich experiences had been fed into it, whether, under such circumstances, processes of the type would warrant belief that p, and would produce true belief that p.

Seen in this way, claims about apriority are implicitly indexical, in that they inherit the indexical features of "actual."[18] If this is not recognized, use of "a priori" in modal contexts can engender confusion. The truth value of "Possibly, X knows a priori that p" can be determined in one of two ways: we may consider the proposition expressed by the sentence at our world, and inquire whether there is a world at which that proposition is true; or we may ask whether there is a world at which the sentence expresses a true proposition. Because of the covert indexicality of "a priori," these lines of investigation may yield different answers. I suspect that failure to appreciate this point has caused trouble in assessing theses about the limits of the a priori. However, I shall not pursue the point here.[19]

V

At this point, I want to address worries that my analysis is too liberal, because it allows some of our knowledge of ourselves and our states to count as a priori. Given its Kantian psychologistic underpinnings, the theory appears to favor claims that some of our self-knowledge is a priori. However, two points should be kept in mind. First, the analysis I have proposed can only be applied to cases in which we know enough about the ways in which our beliefs are warranted to decide whether or not the conditions of (2) are met. In some cases, our lack of a detailed account of how our beliefs are generated may mean that no firm decision about the apriority of an item of knowledge can be reached. Second, there may be cases, including cases of self-knowledge, in which we have no clear pre-analytic intuitions about whether a piece of knowledge is a priori.

Nevertheless, there are some clear cases. Obviously, any theory which implied that I can know a priori that I am seeing red (when, in fact, I am) would be suspect. But, when we apply my analysis, the unwanted conclusion does not follow. For, if the process which leads me to believe that I am seeing red (when I am) can be triggered in the absence of red, then (2(c)) would be violated. If the process cannot be triggered in the absence of red, then, given some sufficiently rich experiences, the process will not be available, so that (2(a)) will be violated. In general, knowledge of any involuntary mental state— such as pains, itches or hallucinations—will work in the same way. Either the process which leads from the occurrence of pain to the belief that I am in pain can be triggered in the absence of pain, or not: if it can, (2(c)) would be violated, if it cannot, then (2(a)) would be violated.

This line of argument can be sidestepped when we turn to cases in which we have the power, independently of experience, to put ourselves into the appropriate states. For, in such cases, one can propose that the processes which give us knowledge of the states cannot be triggered in the absence of the states themselves *and* that the processes are always available because we can always put ourselves into the states.[20] On this basis, we might try to conclude that we have a priori knowledge that we are imagining red (when we are) or thinking of Ann Arbor (when we are). However, the fact that such cases do not fall victim to the argument of the last paragraph does not mean that we are compelled to view them as cases of a priori knowledge. In the first place, the thesis that the processes through which we come to know our imaginative feats and our voluntary thoughts cannot be triggered in the absence of the states themselves requires evaluation—and, lacking detailed knowledge of those processes, we cannot arrive at a firm judgment here. Secondly, the processes in question will be required to meet (2(b)) if they are to be certified as a priori warrants. This means that, whatever experience hurls at us, beliefs produced by such processes will be warranted. We can cast doubt on this idea by imagining that our experience consists of a lengthy, and apparently reliable, training in neurophysiology, concluding with a presentation to ourselves of our own neurophysiological organization which appears to show that our detection of our imaginative states (say) is slightly defective, that we always make mistakes about the contents of our imaginings. If this type of story can be developed, then (2(b)) will be violated, and the knowledge in question will not count as a priori. But, even if it cannot be coherently extended, and even if my analysis does judge our knowledge of states of imagination (and other "voluntary" states) to be a priori, it is not clear to me that this consequence is counterintuitive.

In fact, I think that one can make a powerful case for supposing that *some* self-knowledge is a priori. At most, if not all, of our waking moments, each of us knows of herself that she exists.[21] Although traditional ideas to the effect that self-knowledge is produced by some "non-optical inner look" are clearly inadequate, I think it is plausible to maintain that there are processes which do warrant us in believing that we exist—processes of reflective thought, for example—and which belong to a general type whose members would be available to us independently of experience.[22] Trivially, when any such process produces in a person a belief that she exists that belief is true. All that remains, therefore, is to ask if the processes of the type in question inevitably warrant belief in our own existence, or whether they would fail to do so, given a suitably exotic background experience. It is difficult to settle this issue conclusively without a thorough survey of the ways in which reflective belief in one's existence can be challenged by experience, but perhaps there are Cartesian grounds for holding that, so long as the belief is the product of reflective thought, the believer is warranted, no matter how wild his experience may have been. If this is correct, then at least some of our self-knowledge will be a priori. However, in cases like this, attributions of apriority seem even less vulnerable to the criticism that they are obviously incorrect.

At this point we must consider a doctrinaire objection. If the conclusion of the last paragraph is upheld then we can know some contingent propositions a priori.[23] Frequently, however, it is maintained that only necessary truths can be known a priori. Behind this contention stands a popular argument.[24] Assume that a person knows a priori that p. His knowledge is independent of his experience. Hence he can know that p without any information about the kind of world he inhabits. So, necessarily p.

This hazy line of reasoning rests on an intuition which is captured in the analysis given above. The intuition is that a priori warrants must be ultrareliable: if a person is entitled to ignore empirical information about the type of world she inhabits then that must be because she has at her disposal a method of arriving at belief which guarantees *true* belief. (This intuition can be defended by pointing out that if a method which could produce false belief were allowed to override experience, then we might be blocked from obtaining knowledge which we might otherwise have gained.) In my analysis, the intuition appears as (2(c)).[25]

However, when we try to clarify the popular argument we see that it contains an invalid step. Presenting it as a *reductio*, we obtain the following line of reasoning. Assume that a person knows a priori that p but that it is not necessary that p. Because p is contingent there are worlds at which p is false. Suppose that the person had inhabited such a world and behaved as she does at the actual world. Then she would have had an a priori warrant for a false belief. This is debarred by (2(c)). So we must conclude that the initial supposition is erroneous: if someone really does know a priori that p then p is necessary.

Spelled out in this way, the argument fails. We are not entitled to conclude from the premise that there are worlds at which p is false the thesis that there are worlds at which p is false *and* at which the person behaves as she does at the actual world. There are a number of propositions which, although they could be false, could not both be false and also believed by us. More generally, there are propositions which could not both be false and also believed by us in particular, definite ways. Obvious examples are propositions about ourselves and their logical consequences: such propositions as those expressed by tokens of the sentences "I exist," "I have some beliefs," "There are thoughts," and so forth. Hence the attempted *reductio* breaks down and allows for the possibility of a priori knowledge of some contingent propositions.

I conclude that my analysis is innocent of the charge of being too liberal in ascribing to us a priori knowledge of propositions about ourselves. Although it is plausible to hold that my account construes some of our self-knowledge as a priori, none of the self-knowledge it takes to be a priori is clearly empirical. Moreover, it shows how a popular argument against the contingent a priori is flawed, and how certain types of contingent propositions—most notably propositions about ourselves—escape that argument. Thus I suggest that the analysis illuminates an area of traditional dispute.

VI

I now want to consider two different objections to my analysis. My replies to these objections will show how the approach I have developed can be further refined and extended.

The first objection, like those considered above, charges that the analysis is too liberal. My account apparently allows for the possibility that a priori knowledge could be gained through perception. We can imagine that some propositions are true at any world of which we can have experience, and that, given sufficient experience to entertain those propositions, we could always come to know them on the basis of perception. Promising examples are the proposition that there are objects, the proposition that some objects have shapes, and other, similar propositions. In these cases, one can argue that we cannot experience worlds at which they are false and that any (sufficiently rich) experience would provide perceptual warrant for belief in the propositions, regardless of the specific content of our perceptions. If these points are correct (and I shall concede them both, for the sake of argument), then perceptual processes would qualify as a priori warrants. Given any sufficiently rich experience, some perceptual process would be available to us, would produce warranted belief and, *ex hypothesi*, would produce warranted *true* belief.

Let us call cases of the type envisaged cases of *universally empirical* knowledge. The objection to my account is that it incorrectly classifies universally empirical knowledge as a priori knowledge. My response is that the classical notion of apriority is too vague to decide such cases: rather, this type of knowledge only becomes apparent when the classical notion is articulated. One could defend the classification of universally empirical knowledge as a priori by pointing out that such knowledge requires no particular type of experience (beyond that needed to obtain the concepts, of course). One could oppose that classification by pointing out that, even though the content of the experience is immaterial, the knowledge is still gained by perceiving, so that it should count as a posteriori.

If the second response should seem attractive, it can easily be accommodated by recognizing a stronger and a weaker notion of apriority. The weaker notion is captured in (1) and (2). The stronger adds an extra requirement: no process which involves the operation of a perceptual mechanism is to count as an a priori warrant.

At this point, it is natural to protest that the new condition makes the prior analysis irrelevant. Why not define a priori knowledge outright as knowledge which is produced by processes which do not involve perceptual mechanisms? The answer is that the prior conditions are not redundant: knowledge which is produced by a process which does not involve perceptual mechanisms need not be independent of experience. For the process may fail to generate warranted belief against a backdrop of misleading experience. (Nor may it generate true belief in all relevant counterfactual situations.) So, for example, certain kinds of thought-experiments may generate items of knowledge given a particular type of experience, but may not be able to sustain that knowledge against misleading experiences. Hence, if we choose to exclude universally empirical knowledge from the realm of the a priori in the way suggested, we are building on the analysis given in (1) and (2), rather than replacing it.

A different kind of criticism of my analysis is to accuse it of revealing the emptiness of the classical notion of apriority. Someone may suggest that, in exposing the constraints on a priori knowledge, I have shown that there could be very little a priori knowledge. Although I believe that this suggestion is incorrect, it is worth pointing out that, even if it is granted, my approach allows for the development of weaker notions which may prove epistemologically useful.

Let me first note that we can introduce approximations to a priori knowledge. Suppose that A is any type of process all of whose instances culminate in belief that p. Define the *supporting class* of A to be that class of lives, *e*, such that, (a) given *e*, some process in *A* could occur (and so produce belief that *p*), (b) given *e*, any process in *A* which occurred would produce warranted true belief that *p*. (Intuitively, the supporting class consists of those lives which enable processes of the type in question to produce knowledge.) The *defeating class* of *A* is the complement of the supporting class of *A* within the class of lives which are sufficient for *p*. A priori warrants are those processes which belong to a type whose defeating class is null. But we can be more liberal, and allow approximations to a priori knowledge by considering the size and/or nature of the defeating class. We might, for example, permit the defeating class to contain those radically disruptive experiences beloved of sceptics. Or we can define a notion of *contextual* apriority by allowing the defeating class to include experiences which undermine "framework principles."[26] Or we may employ a concept of *comparative* apriority by ordering defeating classes according to inclusion relations. Each of these notions can serve a useful function in delineating the structure of our knowledge.

VII

Finally, I want to address a systematic objection to my analysis. The approach I have taken is blatantly psychologistic. Some philosophers may regard these psychological complications as objectionable intrusions into epistemology. So I shall consider the possibility of rival apsychologistic approaches.

Is there an acceptable view of a priori knowledge which rivals the Kantian conception? The logical positivists hoped to understand a priori knowledge without dabbling in psychology. The simplest of their proposals was the suggestion that X knows a priori that *p* if and only if X believes that *p* and *p* is analytically true.[27]

Gilbert Harman has argued cogently that, in cases of factual belief, the nature of the reasons for which a person believes is relevant to the question of whether he has knowledge.[28] Similar considerations arise with respect to propositions which the positivists took to be a priori. Analytic propositions, like synthetic propositions, can be believed for bad reasons, or for no reasons at all, and, when this occurs, we should deny that the believer knows the propositions in question. Assume, as the positivists did, that mathematics is analytic, and imagine a mathematician who comes to believe that some unobvious theorem is true. This belief is exhibited in her continued efforts to prove the theorem. Finally, she succeeds. We naturally describe her progress by saying that she has come to know something she only believed before. The positivistic proposal forces us to attribute knowledge from the beginning. Worse still, we can imagine that the mathematician has many colleagues who believe the theorem because of dreams, trances, fits of Pythagorean ecstasy, and so forth. Not only does the positivistic approach fail to separate the mathematician after she has found the proof from her younger self, but it also gives her the same status as her colleagues.

A natural modification suggests itself: distinguish among the class of analytic truths those which are elementary (basic laws of logic, immediate consequences of definitions, and, perhaps, a few others), and propose that elementary analytic truths can be known merely by being believed, while the rest are known, when they are known a priori, by inference from such truths. Even this restricted version of the original claim is vulnerable. If you believe the basic laws of logic because you have learned them from an eminent mathematician who has deluded himself into believing that the system of *Grundgesetze* is consistent and true, then you do not have a priori knowledge of those laws. Your belief in the laws of logic is undermined by evidence which you do not currently possess, namely the evidence which would expose your teacher as a misguided fanatic. The moral is obvious: apsychologistic approaches to a priori knowledge fail because, for a priori knowledge as for factual knowledge, the reasons for which a person believes are relevant to the question of whether he knows.

Although horror of psychologizing prevented the positivists from offering a defensible account of a priori knowledge, I think that my analysis can be used to articulate most of the doctrines that they wished to defend. Indeed, I believe that many classical theses, arguments and debates can be illuminated by applying the analysis presented here. My aim has been to prepare the way for investigations of traditional claims and disputes by developing in some detail Kant's conception of a priori knowledge. "A priori" has too often been a label which philosophers could attach to propositions they favored, without any clear criterion for doing so. I hope to have shown how a more systematic practice is possible.

Notes

I am grateful to several members of the Department of Philosophy at the University of Michigan for their helpful comments on a previous version of this paper, and especially to Alvin Goldman and Jaegwon Kim for their constructive suggestions. I would also like to thank Paul Benacerraf, who first interested me in the problem of characterizing a priori knowledge, and prevented many errors in early analyses. Above all, I am indebted to Patricia Kitcher and George Sher, who have helped me to clarify my ideas on this topic. Patricia Kitcher's advice on issues in the philosophy of mind relevant to section V was particularly valuable.

1. There are some exceptions. Passing attention to the problem of defining apriority is given in Pollock 1974 [631], chapter 10; Swinburne 1975 [842], esp. pp. 238–241; Erwin 1974 [714], especially pp. 593–597. The inadequacy of much traditional thinking about apriority is forcefully presented in Kripke 1971 [766], especially pp. 149–151, and Kripke 1972 [767], especially pp. 260–264.

2. See Kripke 1971 [766], 1972 [767].

3. For ease of reference, I take propositions to be the objects of belief and knowledge, and to be what declarative sentences express. I trust that my conclusions would survive any successful elimination of propositions in favor of some alternative approach to the objects of belief and knowledge.

4. Kant 1787, B2–3.

5. See Pollock 1974 [631]; Swinburne 1975 [842]; Erwin 1974 [714].

6. Someone might be tempted to propose, conversely, that all innate knowledge is a priori (cf. Swinburne 1975 [842], p. 239). In Kitcher 1978 [762], I have argued that there may well be no innate knowledge and that, if there were any such knowledge, it would not have to be a priori.

7. Pollock 1974 [631], p. 301, claims that we can only resist the suggestion that this knowledge is independent of experience by complicating the notion of experience. For the reason given in the text, such desperate measures seem to me to be unnecessary.

8. See the example of the man who undermines the foundations of his house, Kant 1787, B3.

9. Prominent exponents of this approach are Alvin Goldman, Gilbert Harman and David Armstrong. See Goldman 1967 [266], 1975 [365], 1976 [339], 1979 [397]; Harman 1973 [59]; Armstrong 1973 [3].

10. Psychologistic epistemologies are often accused of confusing the context of discovery with the context of justification. For a recent formulation of this type of objection, see Lehrer 1974 [77], pp. 123 ff. I have tried to show that psychologistic epistemology is not committed to mistakes with which it is frequently associated in Kitcher 1979 [763]. I shall consider

the possibility of an apsychologistic approach to apriority in section VII below.

11. More details about Kant's theory of pure intuition can be found in my paper Kitcher 1975 [761], especially pp. 28–33.

12. For further discussion of this requirement and the possibility of the contingent a priori, see §V below.

13. For different reasons, Goldman proposes that an analysis of the general notion of warrant (or, in his terms, justification) can focus on psychological processes. See section 2 of Goldman 1979 [397].

14. Consider, for example, a Kantian process of pure intuition which begins with the construction of a triangle. Should we say that a process of the same type must begin with the construction of a triangle of the same size and shape, a triangle of the same shape, any triangle, or something even more general? Obviously there are many natural classifications here, and I think the best strategy is to suppose that an apriorist is entitled to pick any of them. Strictly, the sets which do not constitute types are those which violate correct taxonomies. In making present decisions about types, we assume that our current principles of classification are correct. If it should turn out that those principles require revision then our judgments about types will have to be revised accordingly.

15. Strictly, the sets which do not constitute types are those which violate correct taxonomics. In making present decisions about types, we assume that our current principles of classification are correct. If it should turn out that those principles require revision, then our judgments about types will have to be revised accordingly.

16. For a lucid and entertaining presentation of this point, see Lewis 1976 [775], pp. 149–151.

17. Of course, X might have been more intelligent, that is, he might have had better versions of the faculties he has. We allow for this type of change. But we are not interested in worlds where X has extra faculties.

18. The idea that "actual" is indexical is defended by David Lewis in Lewis 1970 [773]. In van Fraassen 1977 [852], Bas van Fraassen puts Lewis' ideas about "actual" in a general context. The machinery which van Fraassen presents in that paper can be used to elaborate the ideas of the present paragraph.

19. Jaegwon Kim has pointed out to me that, besides the "species-relative" notion of apriority presented in the text, there might be an absolute notion. Perhaps there is a class of propositions which would be knowable a priori by any being whom we would count as a rational being. Absolute a priori knowledge would thus be that a priori knowledge which is available to all possible knowers.

20. In characterizing pain as an involuntary state one paragraph back I may seem to have underestimated our powers of self-torture. But even a masochist could be defeated by unkind experience: as he goes to pinch himself his skin is anesthetized.

21. I shall ignore the tricky issue of trying to say exactly what is known when we know this and kindred things. For interesting explorations of this area, see Casteneda 1967 [689], 1968 [690]; Perry 1977 [800], 1979 [801]. The issue of how to represent the content of items of self-knowledge may force revision of the position taken in footnote 3 above: it may not be possible to identify objects of belief with meanings of sentences. Although such a revision would complicate my analysis, I don't think it would necessitate any fundamental modifications.

22. This presupposes that our knowledge of our existence does not result from some special kind of "inner sensation." For, if it did, different lives would deprive us of the warrant.

23. Kripke 1971 [766], 1972 [767], has attempted to construct examples of contingent propositions which can be known a priori. I have not tried to decide here whether his examples are successful, since full treatment of this question would lead into issues about the analysis of the propositions in question which are well beyond the scope of the present paper. For a discussion of some of the difficulties involved in Kripke's examples, see Donnellan 1977 [710].

24. Kripke seems to take this to be the main argument against the contingent a priori. See Kripke 1972 [767], p. 263.

25. As the discussion of this paragraph suggests, there is an intimate relation between my requirements (2(b)) and (2(c)). Indeed, one might argue that (2(b)) would not be met unless (2(c)) were also satisfied—on the grounds that one cannot allow a process to override experience unless it guarantees truth. The subsequent discussion will show that this type of reasoning is more complicated than appears. Hence, although I believe that the idea that a priori warrants function independently of experience does have implications for the reliability of these processes, I have chosen to add (2(c)) as a separate condition.

26. This notion of contextual apriority has been used by Hilary Putnam. See, for example, Putnam 1975 [633], 1978 [635], especially p. 154.

27. See Ayer 1936 [537], chapter IV and Schlick 1959 [825], especially p. 224.

28. Harman 1973 [59], chapter 2; see also Goldman 1979 [397], section 1.

8 Truth and Confirmation

Michael Friedman

Ideally, there is a close connection between confirmation and truth. Theories that are well confirmed tend to be true, or at least *approximately* true. Theories that are disconfirmed tend to be false. It would seem that some such nice connection between confirmation and truth must exist if scientific method is to be justified as a rational activity. For one of the important ends of scientific method is the construction of theories that are true, or at least approximately true. Obviously, then, scientific method will be an effective means to this end only if it does indeed tend to produce true, or at least approximately true, theories. Of course, this is not sufficient to justify scientific method as a rational activity, if only because scientific method has other important ends besides the construction of true theories: for example, to produce theories that have a lot of explanatory power. However, assuming (as I will here) that the construction of true theories is *one* important end of scientific method, such a connection between confirmation and truth is clearly necessary.

Now I don't know whether there really is this kind of relationship between confirmation and truth, whether scientific method really does tend to produce true theories (from now on I will omit the qualification about *approximate* truth). What I hope to do in this chapter is to see what must be the case *if* such a connection between confirmation and truth is to exist. In particular, what must theories of confirmation and theories of truth look like, and how must they fit together, if we are to have such a desirable connection? Balancing the demands of theories of confirmation and theories of truth against one another in this way produces some, to my mind, interesting results: first, that a theory of confirmation must itself be an empirical science,

Reprinted from *The Journal of Philosophy* LXXVI (July 1979): 361–382, by permission of the author and the publisher. Copyright © 1979, *The Journal of Philosophy*.

that it must appeal to facts about the actual world; second, that a theory of truth must go beyond the usual Tarskian format, that it must contain in addition something like a causal theory of reference.

I

What does traditional philosophy of science have to say about the connection between confirmation and truth? According to one view, which I will call the *positivist* view, the connection is remarkably simple: (i) theories are confirmed by their true observational consequences; (ii) theories are true if all their observational consequences are true. This view explains the notion of truth for theories in terms of the relatively unproblematic notion of truth for observation sentences. Further, it promises to give us the desired relationship between confirmation and truth: the better a theory is confirmed—that is, the larger the set of its true observational consequences—the closer it is to being true.

Unfortunately, this kind of view is faced with two immediate, and devastating, objections. First, although it tells us what it is for an entire theory to be true, it cannot supply a workable notion of truth for individual sentences of a theory. Given that our theories contain nonobservational sentences,[1] there can be two theories, T and T', both of which have all true observational consequences, even though, for some nonobservational sentence S, S belongs to T and the negation of S belongs to T'. Consequently, we cannot extend our definition of truth to individual sentences by requiring that a sentence be true just in case it is an element of a true theory; for this would result in both S and its negation being true.

Hence, the positivist view fails to define an even minimally adequate notion of truth. However, even if its definition of truth were formally satisfactory, it would still fail to deliver the promised connection between truth and confirmation. The positivist definition tells us that if *all* the observational consequences of a theory are true then the theory itself is true. Does it follow that theories that are confirmed— that is, *some* of whose observational consequences are true—tend to be true? Not at all. Most theories that have some true observational consequences do *not* have all true observational consequences. So the mere fact that a theory is confirmed does not make it probable or likely that it is true; it shows simply that its truth is still possible. The positivist view tells us that when all the evidence is in, when all the observational consequences of our theory have been checked, we will know whether the theory is true or false. It tells us absolutely nothing about the likelihood of our theory being true when less than all the evidence is in. Therefore, it really tells us nothing useful about confirmation at all, since *our* situation is always that all the evidence is not yet in.

A second type of view, which I will call the *Peircean* view, also tries to ensure a connection between scientific method and truth by giving a special *definition* of truth. According to this view, a sentence is true just in case it belongs to the unique theory that scientific method will arrive at "in the limit" when all the evidence is in. Waiving questions about the existence and uniqueness of its "limiting" theory, the Peircean view avoids some of the problems that beset the positivist view. That is, assuming existence and uniqueness, there can be only one true theory. Consequently, we are not faced with the possibility of a sentence and its negation both being true. Note, however, that unless the "limiting" theory is complete, it will not be the case that each sentence *or* its negation is true.

Thus, the Peircean notion of truth is more satisfactory from a formal point of view than the positivist notion. Nevertheless, the connection between truth and confirmation which it establishes is just as useless. We know, again by definition, that the theory produced by scientific method when all the evidence is in is true. What about the theories that scientific method produces when less than all the evidence is in? We are told nothing at all about the relation between *these* theories (which are all the theories *we* will ever know) and the ideal "limiting" theory. For all we know, all these theories are arbitrarily far from the "limiting" theory and are arbitrarily far, therefore, from the truth. Once one has defined truth as what scientific method arrives at "in the limit," it is easy to start picturing scientific method as gradually and steadily climbing closer and closer to the truth. However, just as on the positivist view, no gradual and steady *convergence* toward truth is guaranteed by the Peircean definition; it guarantees, merely, that truth is there waiting at the end.

The basic problem facing both the positivist view and the Peircean view can be brought out most clearly, I think, by examining the more sophisticated account of confirmation offered by Hans Reichenbach. By giving a highly idealized and specific model of confirmation, Reichenbach was able to achieve the same type of connection between truth and confirmation—a guarantee of truth in the "long run"—

without having to give a special definition of truth. On both the positivist view and the Peircean view, on the other hand, we are given only the vaguest description of confirmation. A guarantee of truth in the "long run" is achieved only by redefining the word 'true'.

According to Reichenbach, we should think of scientific method in the following idealized way. The hypotheses we are trying to confirm are all about the relative frequencies of kinds of events in particular sequences of events. We are interested in hypotheses like 'The relative frequency of heads in a given sequence of tosses of a coin is $1/2$', 'The relative frequency of black ravens in a given sequence of ravens is 1', etc. Now, in general, the sequence in question will be infinite; so what we are really interested in are *limits* of relative frequencies. Given a sequence of events (for example, coin tossings), e_1, e_2, e_3, . . . , and a property F of interest (for example, the property of coming up heads), form the sequence of relative frequencies, s_1, s_2, s_3, . . . , where s_n is the relative frequency of Fs among the first n es, that is, the number of Fs in the set $\{e_1, e_2, \ldots, e_n\}$ divided by n. What we are interested in knowing, on Reichenbach's model, is the number

$$p = \lim_{n \to \infty} s_n$$

if it exists. (If the sequence of events is finite, p is just the ordinary relative frequency of Fs in the sequence.)

Such, according to Reichenbach, is the object of scientific method. The method itself proceeds as follows: Given a sequence of events and a property F of interest, we assume that our *evidence* consists of the relative frequency of Fs in an initial segment of the sequence. For example, we've observed ten tosses of a coin and noted that half of them so far have come up heads. Our problem is to say what the relative frequency will be if we continue the sequence. How do we infer this from the given evidence? First, we arbitrarily pick a small positive number ϵ. It doesn't matter what number we pick, as long as we use the same number for every inference we make about this particular sequence. Given an initial segment e_1, e_2, . . . , e_n of our sequence and the relative frequency s_n of Fs so far, we infer that $s_n - \epsilon < p < s_n + \epsilon$; that is, we infer that p—the eventual limiting relative frequency—lies within ϵ of s_n—the observed relative frequency.

What can we say about the tendency of this method of inference to lead to true beliefs? On Reichenbach's view we can say something limit of the relative frequency of Fs actually exists, our method will eventually find it. More precisely, there is a number N such that the inferences we make after observing N or more elements of the sequence all have true conclusions. This follows directly from the definition of 'limit'. For recall that

$$p = \lim_{n \to \infty} s_n \text{ iff } \quad \text{for every positive } \epsilon, \text{ there exists an } N, \text{ such that,}$$
$$\text{for all } m \geq N, \ s_n - \epsilon < p < s_m + \epsilon.$$

That is, if p really is the limit, then, for every positive ϵ no matter how small, there comes a point in the sequence of relative frequencies such that all later relative frequencies lie within ϵ of p. Thus, no matter which ϵ we pick to begin with, there will be a point N such that all inferences made after observing N or more elements (all of which have conclusions of the form $'s_m - \epsilon < p < s_m + \epsilon'$ with $m \geq N$) are correct.

Reichenbach's account of the connection between truth and confirmation, like the accounts given by the positivist view and the Peircean view, establishes a connection in the "long run": scientific method is guaranteed to produce true hypotheses if we wait long enough. Reichenbach's account, however, has several advantages over the other two views. First, as noted above, it is not necessary to give any special redefinition of the notion of truth. Reichenbach can simply rely on our intuitive understanding that a statement of the form $'s_m - \epsilon < p < s_m + \epsilon'$ is true just in case p really does lie within ϵ of s_m. Second, we don't have to wait until *all* the evidence is in. We know that there is a *finite* number N—which may, of course, be very large—such that the inferences based on the evidence of the first N members of our sequence are guaranteed of true conclusions. We are guaranteed of true conclusions, provided a limit exists at all, at some point considerably before we have examined all the elements of our sequence. Thus, unlike the positivist view and the Peircean view, Reichenbach's account gives us genuine *convergence* toward truth.

Nevertheless, it seems to me that Reichenbach's view does not really overcome the basic problem—which is a problem for all "long run" justifications, whether the "long run" is infinite or finite. We know that scientific method will produce truth at some point, but (i) we have no idea where the happy point, the point of convergence, occurs, and (ii) we have no idea what the connection between scientific method and truth is before the point of convergence; before the point of convergence our hypotheses may be arbitrarily far from the truth. In particular, we don't know whether the inferences we actually do make, or even whether the inferences that are physically possible for us to make, occur before or after the point of convergence. So, for all we know, all the inferences we ever actually make, and even all physically possible inferences, may have no likelihood whatever of having true conclusions. In other words, although Reichenbach's method converges, it doesn't necessarily converge in the class of actual (or even physically possible) inferences. This difficulty is highlighted if we notice, as Reichenbach himself immediately points out, that there are infinitely many different methods of inference which all lead to truth in the "long run" in the very same sense. To see this, observe that if $c_1, c_2, c_3, \ldots$ is any sequence of positive numbers such that

$$\lim_{n \to \infty} c_n = 0$$

then the method that concludes that p lies within ϵ of $s_n + c_n$ on evidence s_n will eventually find the true limit p (if it exists) in exactly the same sense as the method that concludes that p lies within ϵ of s_n. This, of course, is because

$$\lim_{n \to \infty} (s_n + c_n) = \lim_{n \to \infty} s_n$$

Reichenbach's method is just a special case in this more general class of *convergent* methods, the special case when $c_n = 0$.

Now all these convergent methods—methods that conclude that p lies within ϵ of $s_n + c_n$ (with $\lim_{n \to \infty} c_n = 0$) on evidence s_n—agree in the "long run," and this fact may lead one to conclude that the choice of one method from among them does not really matter. This, however, would be to underestimate drastically the severity of the problem. For, given any particular piece of evidence—that a coin has come up heads 95% of the time in 1000 tosses, say—the different convergent methods yield arbitrarily divergent conclusions. One method will say that the eventual limiting relative frequency of heads is about .95; another will say that it is .05; a third will say that it is .50, etc. In short, any inference from any evidence is licensed by some convergent method. And we are given no reason to think that any one convergent method is better than any of the others.

Reichenbach himself thought there was a reason to prefer the value $c_n = 0$:

Now it is obvious that a system of wagers of the more general type may have advantages. The "correction" c_n may be determined in such a way that the resulting wager furnishes even at an early stage of the series a good approximation of the limit p. The prophesies of a good clairvoyant would be of this type. On the other hand, it may happen also that c_n is badly determined, i.e., the convergence is delayed by the correction. If the term c_n is arbitrarily formulated, we know nothing about the two possibilities. The value $c_n = 0$—i.e., the inductive method—is therefore the value of the smallest risk; any other determination may worsen the convergence. This is a practical reason for preferring the inductive principle.[2]

But it is clear that the situation with respect to the relative riskiness of the value $c_n = 0$ and any other value is perfectly symmetrical. Granted, any other value may worsen the convergence, may lead to true conclusions at a later point, when compared to $c_n = 0$. Equally, however, the value $c_n = 0$ may worsen the convergence when compared to any other value. A priori, there is no way of knowing which value, including the value $c_n = 0$, will lead to convergence soonest. A priori, all values of c_n are equally risky.

How, then, can one value of c_n, one particular convergent method, be superior to the others? I think the answer is obvious: a method is superior if, when it is used in the inferences we actually do make, it leads to true conclusions sooner and more often than the other methods. And which method actually enjoys this kind of superiority depends on empirical facts: facts about the distribution of observed and unobserved relative frequencies. To take an absurdly simple example, suppose we are living in a world containing a single sequence of eight coin tossings. Suppose we never actually observe more than the first four tossings (the coin is tossed by a machine), and the distribution of heads looks like this in the entire sequence:

H T H T H H H H

The relative frequency of heads in the observed portion of the sequence is $1/2$, but the true relative frequency is $3/4$. In this simple world, the method that takes $c_n = 1/n$ does better than the method $c_n = 0$. $c_n = 1/n$ yields the true value $1/2 + 1/4 = 3/4$ on the evidence we actually observe; $c_n = 0$ yields the incorrect value $1/2$. In general, the value $c_n = 0$ works better in worlds in which the distribution of relative frequencies is uniform as between the observed and the unobserved parts; other values of c_n work better in worlds that are not so uniform.[3]

If this is correct, if the superiority of an inductive method consists in its propensity to produce true conclusions in the class of actual or physically possible inferences, it follows that "long run" justifications are completely beside the point. If a method does not tend to produce true conclusions in the inferences we actually make, or even in the inferences we (physically) could make, why should its properties in the "long run" be of any interest to us? Conversely, if a method does tend to produce true conclusions when used in actual inferences, we should prefer it, regardless of its behavior "in the limit"—which may, after all, be physically impossible for us to reach. Conclusion: "long run" justifications, whether of the simple definitional type characteristic of the positivist and Peircean views or of the more sophisticated Reichenbachian type, do not provide us with the kind of connection that we want between confirmation and truth. They do not and cannot show that scientific method tends to produce true theories in actual practice.

II

The moral that I would like to draw from the failure of "long run" justifications, then, is this: What needs to be shown is that scientific method tends to produce true hypotheses not "in the limit" or when all the evidence is in, but in the class of actual and physically possible inferences. Further, I would like to suggest that we explain what it is for a method to tend toward truth in the class of actual and physically possible inferences, in terms of the existence of *statistical laws* of the form:

For all S, the probability that S is true, given that S is accepted (rejected) by method M is r.

Thus, we can say that a method M is *reliable* if

For all S and R, if M rejects R in favor of S, then the probability that S is true is greater than the probability that R is true.

(If M attaches a numerical degree of belief p to S, we can say that M is reliable just in case the probability that S is true, given that M assigns value p to S, is p.) In other words, although a reliable method does not necessarily produce true conclusions, or even conclusions with a high probability of truth, it does *tend* toward truth: as time goes on, the conclusions that it accepts acquire ever increasing probabilities of truth. My suggestion is that it is the task of confirmation theory to show that the methods scientists actually use are reliable in this sense.

This suggestion calls for a few words of explanation. First, since we are concerned with statistical laws, the kind of probability at issue is objective or physical probability, not epistemic probability. We are requiring that there be a lawlike statistical correlation between the property of being reached by M and the property of being true, in the very same sense in which there is a lawlike statistical correlation between being a radium atom in a particular state and emitting radiation during a given interval of time, between tosses of a fair coin and the property of coming up heads, between smoking and lung cancer, etc. Such lawlike statistical correlations hold independently of our knowledge that they hold; just as lawlike *universal* correlations hold independently of our knowledge that they hold. Second, such a statistical law should not be confused with the statement

$r\%$ of the sentences accepted (rejected) by actual applications of M are true.

In a sense, the corresponding statistical law is both stronger and weaker than a statement about actual relative frequencies. It is stronger because the statement about actual relative frequencies may be merely accidental and not hold as a matter of law. It is weaker because the statistical law can be true even if the actual relative frequency is arbitrarily far from r. Thus, for example, a method can be reliable in my sense even if all its actual applications lead to false conclusions. It seems to me, however, that this is as it should be. What we are interested in is the lawlike correlation between our method and truth, not in the—perhaps merely accidental—distribution of actual true and false conclusions. This is just to say that we are interested in the class of actual and physically possible inferences, not merely in the class of actual inferences.

How is confirmation theory to arrive at such statistical laws connecting our inductive methods and truth? How are we to establish the reliability of scientific method? The way to proceed, I think, is to try to *derive* the reliability of our inductive methods from our psychological and physical theories, our theories about how the human mind arrives at beliefs through interaction with its environment. For the reliability of our inductive methods, if indeed they are reliable, depends on general facts relating the process of belief acquisition to events in the world. Thus, for example, the reliability of the regularities we follow in coming to hold simple perceptual beliefs depends on two factors: (i) general connections between perceptual beliefs and sensory stimulation; (ii) general connections between sensory stimulation and physical objects. Very roughly, I am usually right when I assent to 'There is a table in front of me' as a result of sensory stimulation, because such stimulation is usually due to the presence of a table. Since the reliability of an inductive method depends in this way on general connections between the mind and the world, the way to establish the reliability of an inductive method is to appeal to our best theories of the mind and the world, our best psychological and physical theories.

Now, of course, on this type of view the justification that confirmation theory provides for scientific method is in an important sense circular. For we derive the reliability of scientific method from theories that are themselves the product of scientific method. In appealing to general facts about the actual world, confirmation theory has to depend on the very methods it is attempting to justify. And, of course, it is the desire to avoid precisely this kind of circularity that motivates philosophers to look for an a priori justification of scientific method: a connection between scientific method and truth which does not depend on facts about the actual world. Such is the nature of the connection between scientific method and truth provided by the positivist view, the Peircean view, and Reichenbach's view. In looking for a connection between scientific method and truth only "in the limit" or in the "long run" we avoid the appeal to empirical facts about the reliability of scientific method in actual practice. However, if I am right, this kind of circularity is both necessary and inevitable. Can we say anything to make it more palatable?

First, one should appreciate just how hopeless the idea of an a priori justification of scientific method is. The impossibility of such a justification follows, it seems to me, from two simple and fundamental truths: (i) there has to be some kind of link between justification and truth; a justification of scientific method must say something about its propensity to lead to truth; (ii) scientific method is not logically guaranteed of reaching true conclusions; it is an incurably nondeductive method. There is no inductive method that is more reliable in every logically possible world than every other method; consequently, there is no method that is a priori best, there is no method that is a priori the most reliable. We have to know facts about the actual world if we are to know which method is best; and we have to know facts about the actual world to know even that any given method has any chance at all of leading to truth. This is why attempts to justify induction by appealing to the *meaning* of 'justified' or of 'rational' or of 'inference' are so unsatisfying. No such facts about meaning (if indeed they exist) can guarantee that there is any connection at all between inductive inference and truth. It is not very comforting to be told that scientific method is justified or rational in virtue of the meaning of 'justified' or the meaning of 'rational', if, for all we know, we inhabit a world in which scientific method has no chance whatever of producing true conclusions.

Second, although the justification we obtain by deriving the reliability of scientific method from general facts about the actual world is undoubtedly circular, it is not necessarily *viciously* circular. That is, the procedure I envision is certainly not *guaranteed* of success. Just because the facts about the world that we appeal to in attempting to justify scientific method are themselves obtained by scientific method, it by no means follows that these facts will actually justify scientific method, that they will entail its reliability. For all we know, the theories produced by our inductive methods will eventually undermine the reliability of those very methods. And, in fact, some skeptically minded philosophers have argued that this is the situation in which we find ourselves. Some philosophers, for example, have claimed that science shows that material objects never, or almost never, have the properties that they seem to have in ordinary perceptual contexts. According to these philosophers, then, the regularities we follow in coming to hold ordinary perceptual beliefs are completely unreliable. As Russell puts it: "Naive realism leads to physics, and physics, if true, shows that naive realism is false. Therefore, naive realism, if true, is false; therefore, it is false."[4] Russell neglects to point out that this kind of situation would cast doubt on physics as well as naive realism, since physics is itself inferred from naive-realist perceptual beliefs. As I see it, an important task of scientific epistemology is to show that science does not undermine its own evidential base in this way. Our task, in Quine's words, is to "defend science from within, against its self-doubts."[5]

Finally, it is helpful to compare the problem of justifying inductive methods of inference with the problem of justifying deductive methods of inference. How do we justify our deductive methods? In particular, how do we establish a connection between deductive inference and truth? Ideally, we proceed as follows. First, we give a syntactic description of the class of deductive arguments: a definition of a syntactic consequence relation that, we hope, holds between two sentences of our language just in case the second is deductively inferable from the first. Second, we define a semantic consequence relation that holds between two sentences just in case every interpretation of the nonlogical vocabulary of the language that makes the first sentence true also makes the second sentence true. Third, we try to prove a completeness theorem that establishes the equivalence of the syntactic and the semantic consequence relations. This procedure furnishes a justification of our deductive methods of inference in the following sense. It shows that every deductive inference that is captured by our syntactic description is in fact truth-preserving, that if the premises of such an argument are true, the conclusion is also. And it gives us a reason to think that our syntactic description does indeed capture all deductive inferences—or, at any rate, that it captures all deductive inferences that we are willing to call correct.

It is obvious that this procedure is also in an important sense circular. In proving the desired completeness theorem, we have to use the very methods of deductive inference that we are attempting to justify. In proving the soundness of *modus ponens,* for example, we have to use an argument that is, in effect, itself just an instance of *modus ponens.* However, it is just as obvious, I think, that our procedure does nonetheless provide an important kind of justification for deductive methods of inference. It shows that there is a desirable harmony between the methods we use in practice and our conception of what the point of those methods is, namely, preservation of truth from premises to conclusion. And, just as in the case of inductive methods, we have no guarantee in advance that this kind of harmony exists. The completeness theorem, therefore, accomplishes something significant despite its circularity.

Moreover, following an extremely illuminating discussion by Michael Dummett,[6] we should observe that the purpose of justifying deductive inference in this way is not to persuade someone who rejects our deductive methods to adopt them. Rather, it is to explain to ourselves why our deductive methods are good methods to use. The kind of circularity exhibited by the completeness theorem detracts from its usefulness in the former case but not in the latter. I think the situation with inductive inference is similar. The aim of confirmation theory is not to persuade someone who rejects our inductive methods to adopt them. Rather, it is to explain to ourselves what is so good about the methods we actually employ. And, again, the circularity exhibited by the kind of empirical approach to confirmation theory that I am suggesting presents no obstacle to *this* goal. On the contrary, if I am right, this approach represents the only possible way to achieve it.

III

We saw above that formal demands coming from the side of semantics or the theory of truth place constraints on the possible connections between scientific method and truth which confirmation theory can hope to establish. Thus, for example, the positivist view is unsatisfactory, because it relies on a notion of truth according to which a sentence and its negation can both be true. Similarly, the Peircean view is unsatisfactory, because, unless we have some guarantee that the ideal "limiting" theory is complete, it will not be the case that each sentence or its negation is true. In this section I would like to see whether the demands of confirmation theory place any analogous constraints on the theory of truth. In particular, does asking confirmation theory to derive *reliability statements:* statements of the form

For all *S*, the probability that *S* is true, given that *S* is accepted (rejected) by method *M*, is *r*.

from our psychological and physical theories, have any implications for the theory of truth? I will argue that this requirement on confirmation theory does indeed have such implications, that it can be satisfied only if the theory of truth includes something like a causal theory of reference.

Before proceeding with the argument, it will be helpful to have before us examples of the two kinds of semantic theories we will be discussing: a theory of truth without a theory of reference (this, of course, is the kind that Tarski himself actually constructed) and a theory of truth that includes a theory of reference. For simplicity, let us suppose that the language we are giving a theory of has the structure of a first-order quantificational language; that it has a finite number of primitive one-place predicates $'P_1'$, $'P_2'$, . . . , $'P_n'$; a finite number of individual constants $'a_1'$, $'a_2'$, . . . , $'a_m'$; an infinite number of variables $'x_1'$, $'x_2'$, $'x_3'$, . . . ; and that the well-formed formulas of the language are built up from these and the primitive logical symbols '$\sim$', 'V', '$\exists$' '(',')' in the usual way. Call this language L. We will give our two theories of truth in a metalanguage M^L for L which consists of English, plus corner quotes, plus L *itself*. In addition, α will be an assignment of objects to the terms—the variables and individual constants—of L; and α *(v/d)* will be the assignment that assigns the object d to the variable v and agrees with α on all other terms of L.

T1 will be a theory of truth without a theory of reference. We construct T1 by adding a two-place predicate 'sat' to M^L which relates assignments to formulas of L. The axioms of T1 are:

1.1 $\alpha('a_1') = a_1$

1.2 $\alpha('a_2') = a_2$

$\vdots$ $\vdots$

1.m $\alpha('a_m') = a_m$

2.1 α sat $\ulcorner P_1 t \urcorner$ iff $P_1 \alpha(t)$

2.2 α sat $\ulcorner P_2 t \urcorner$ iff $P_2 \alpha(t)$

$\vdots$ $\vdots$

2.n α sat $\ulcorner P_n t \urcorner$ iff $P_n \alpha(t)$

3. α sat $\ulcorner \sim f \urcorner$ iff α does not sat f

4. α sat $\ulcorner f$ V $g \urcorner$ iff α sat f or α sat g

5. α sat $\ulcorner \exists v f \urcorner$ iff for some object d, $\alpha(v/d)$ sat f

where f, g are formulas of L, t is a term of L, and v is a variable of L. Finally, we define a one-place predicate 'Tr' in M^L by

6.   Tr (f) iff every α sat f

T2 will be a theory of truth that includes a theory of reference. It consists of two parts. First, we add a two-place predicate 'sat' as above, plus two additional two-place predicates from the theory of reference: 'Den', which relates individual constants of L to the objects they denote; and 'Ap', which relates predicates of L to the objects in their extensions. As axioms we take:

1. $\alpha(c) = d$ iff Den (c, d)

2. α sat $\ulcorner Ft \urcorner$ iff Ap $(F\alpha(t))$

where c is an individual constant and F a predicate; and 3–6 exactly as in T1. Second, we add a body of general truths about the relations Den and Ap: a theory of reference.[7] Of course, neither I nor anyone else actually has such a theory, and that is one reason the idea of settling for T1 is attractive. Nevertheless, I will try to show that patience would be a better strategy.

What does the difference between T1 and T2 amount to? Let us call axioms 3–6, which are common to the two theories, the *induction axioms;* the remaining axioms, on which T1 and T2 differ, the *basis axioms.* The basis axioms of T1 are all singular assertions, one for each particular individual constant of L and each particular primitive predicate of L. The basic axioms of T2, on the other hand, generalize over all individual constants of L and all primitive predicates of L, respectively. The significance of this kind of distinction is clarified if we compare T1 and T2 to an even simpler theory of truth, T3. T3 is constructed by adding a single one-place predicate 'Tr' to M^L, and for each sentence (formula with no free variables) S of L an axiom of the form:[8]

Tr('S') iff S

Thus, T3, unlike T1 and T2, has an infinite number of axioms.

The difference between T2 and T1 is analogous to the difference between T1 and T3. T3 contains no general assertions involving Tr, just an infinite number of singular assertions about particular sentences of L; whereas T1 allows us to make general assertions involving Tr and the logical vocabulary of L. Thus, in T1 (plus a bit of concatenation theory) we can prove:

For all sentences S and R Tr ($\ulcorner S \vee R \urcorner$) iff Tr ($S$) or Tr ($R$)

but in T3 we can prove only, for each particular S and R,

Tr ('$S \vee R$') iff Tr ('S') or Tr ('R')

Similarly, T1 contains no general assertions involving the primitive predicates of L and sat; just n singular assertions, one for each particular predicate. T2, on the other hand, in virtue of the general truths in its (as yet unknown) theory of reference, can contain such general assertions about the primitive predicates of L.

The advantage that T1 enjoys over T3—the fact that T1 contains generalizations where T3 contains just the instances of such generalizations—allows us to derive desirable general laws about truth in T1 which are not derivable in T3. We can prove in T1 such general laws as

For all S, either Tr (S) or Tr ($\ulcorner \sim S \urcorner$)

and

For all S, Tr ($\ulcorner S \vee \sim S \urcorner$).

Most important, in T1 plus concatenation theory, we can prove a general soundness theorem:

For all S and R, if $S \vdash R$ and Tr (S), then Tr (R).

where $\vdash$ is the usual syntactic consequence relation. In T3, on the other hand, even together with concatenation theory, there is no hope of deriving a general soundness theorem. We can derive at most particular instances of the theorem. This, then, is one clear virtue of inductive Tarski-style theories of truth as compared to *purely* disquotational theories like T3. A Tarski-style theory is necessary if we wish to justify deductive inference by appealing to the fact that it preserves truth.

I suggest that T2 enjoys an analogous advantage over T1 with respect to the justification of inductive inference. If one wishes to justify inductive inference in the way I sketched above—by deriving reliability statements about our inductive methods—then a Tarski-style theory of truth is insufficient: a theory of reference is needed. For note first that a reliability statement is a general assertion, a statement of a statistical law. But the only general assertions contained in T1 concern the interaction of 'Tr' and 'sat' with the logical vocabulary of L; T1 makes no general claims about the nonlogical vocabulary of L. Reliability statements, however, if true at all, are not true simply in virtue of general facts about the logical vocabulary of L; they depend on general facts about the nonlogical vocabulary of L as well. Furthermore, reliability statements, if true at all, depend largely on facts of physics and psychology, on how the world is and how the human mind interacts with the world. To derive reliability statements, therefore, we need some way of connecting up our physical and psychological theories with our semantic theories. We need general laws connecting physics and psychology with the theory of truth; and it is precisely this kind of generality that a theory of reference attempts to provide. On the other hand, it is difficult to see how a Tarski-style theory of truth can be connected up with physics and psychology in any general way, since it contains only a list of singular assertions in its basis, one for each individual constant and one for each predicate. It provides no mechanism, therefore, by which general laws from other disciplines can have implications for semantics.

Now this point about generality is important; but, by itself, it is not very informative unless we know what *kind* of general laws are supposed to be contained in our theory of reference. For mere generality is far too easy to come by. To see this, observe that we can even transform T1 into a theory that generalizes over primitive expressions by the following trivial expedient:

1.   Den (c,d) iff $c = 'a_1'$ and $d = a_1$ or $c = 'a_2'$ and $d = a_2$ or . . . or
     $c = 'a_m'$ and $d = a_m$

2.   Ap(F,d) iff $F = 'P_1'$ and $P_1 d$ or $F = 'P_2'$ and $P_2 d$ or . . . or
     $F = 'P_n'$ and $P_n d$

These two axioms are indeed *general* assertions about the nonlogical vocabulary of L. Nevertheless, they clearly do not take us beyond the disquotational spirit of T1, and they are not the sort of assertions one has in mind when one speaks of a genuine *theory* of reference. We are faced, therefore, with two large questions: What sort of assertions do make up a genuine theory of reference? Why should one prefer such assertions to trivial disquotational theories?[9]

Unfortunately, I have relatively little to say about the first question. What I have in mind is the kind of causal theory of reference that has been sketched, for example, by Hilary Putnam.[10] This kind of theory looks for physical and psychological mechanisms that relate the acquisition and use of expressions of L to features in the environment of speakers of L. The hope is to explain reference in terms of such physical and psychological mechanisms: a predicate of a certain general type (for example, a natural-kind word) has an object in its extension if that object bears the "right sort" of causal relation to the history of the predicate's acquisition and use. The obvious model here is the causal theory of perception. Just as the causal theory of perception determines the objects of perception by causal relations between those objects and perceptual activities, the causal theory of reference hopes to determine the objects of belief generally by similar (?) relations between those objects and linguistic activities.

What is important for our present purposes is that this kind of theory is historical or genetic. To determine the referent of an expression it looks "backward" to features of the environment that bear the "right sort" of causal relation to the use of the expression. As such, this kind of theory is to be distinguished not only from trivial disquotational theories, but also from what one might call *charity-based* theories of reference. Charity-based theories are teleological rather than genetic; instead of looking "backward" for causal mechanisms, they look "forward" to the theory of the world that speakers of L eventually construct. The idea is to assign referents in such a way that we maximize (roughly) the number of *true* sentences of this theory.[11] Of course, there is a very close relationship between charity-based theories and disquotational theories. A disquotational theory is the optimal charity-based theory for one's *own* language: it maximizes the number of sentences of one's own theory that are true (according to that very theory).

Why should one prefer causal or genetic theories of reference to both disquotational and charity-based theories? The above point about generality is insufficient to explain such a preference, because all three kinds of theory can be formulated in general terms. However, if we recall our earlier discussion of circularity, an interesting explanation emerges: a causal theory of reference is the only kind of theory that can figure in a justification of inductive inference which is not *viciously* circular. The "justification" provided by a charity-based theory, for example, is obviously viciously circular. Given that it is possible to assign referents in accordance with the principle of charity, we can easily prove in our semantics that most of the theory to be "justified" is in fact true. But this procedure puts no significant constraints on that theory; indeed, it can be carried out completely and optimally for any theory that is merely consistent. The "justification" provided by disquotational theories is similarly defective. On the basis of such a theory, together with the rest of our theory of the world, we can easily prove that each sentence of our theory of the world is true. (If this theory is finitely axiomatizable, we can even prove the general claim that all sentences in our theory of the world are true.) But again, this procedure puts no constraints at all on what our theory of the world must be like; it can be carried out for any theory whatsoever.

By contrast, the requirement that we derive reliability statements from our general theory of the world plus a causal theory of reference does put a significant constraint on our theory. It requires our theory to contain a detailed general description of how the mind interacts with its environment, on the basis of which our processes of belief acquisition can be shown to tend toward truth. There is no guarantee in advance that we can find any interesting general relations between the mind and its environment, nor, even if we can, that it will turn out that our theories are true or even tend toward truth. This is because a causal theory of reference, unlike the other two theories, specifies the referents of terms by considerations that are independent of the truth or falsehood of the sentences we happen to accept. The great virtue of this kind of theory is that it leaves open the *possibility* that most (or all) of our beliefs are false. For, if we can show nonetheless that our beliefs are true or at least tend toward truth, we will have accomplished something significant. Unlike the other two theories, a causal theory of reference allows our over-all theory of the world to have genuine self-critical power and, therefore, genuine potential for self-justification as well.

IV

To illustrate these points, let us consider the problem of saying when a generalization is confirmed by its instances. Under what conditions is a sentence of the form $\ulcorner \forall v(Fv \rightarrow Gv) \urcorner$ confirmed by the observed truth of a conjunction of instances of the form $\ulcorner(Fc \ \& \ Gc) \urcorner$? From the present point of view, the problem is to find a relation between sentences $C(S,R)$ such that if S is a generalization and R is a conjunction of its instances, we can derive a statistical law of the form:

(*) For all S and R, the probability that S is true given that R is observed to be true and $C(S,R)$, is p.

We can then say that S is confirmed by R if p is sufficiently large, large compared with competing generalizations, for example.

It was the hope of philosophers of science in the logical positivist tradition to characterize C in a purely syntactic or logical way, to describe the confirmation relation by appealing only to the logical forms of the sentences involved.[12] For example, on the simplest possible model, we just say that S and R have the required forms:

$C(S,R)$ iff there are predicates F, G such that $S = \ulcorner \forall v(Fv \rightarrow Gv) \urcorner$
and R is a conjunction of sentences of the form $\ulcorner(Fc \ \& \ Gc) \urcorner$.

However, a purely syntactic approach was shown to be inadequate by the work of Nelson Goodman. Goodman shows that, for every generalization of the form $\ulcorner \forall v(Fv \rightarrow Gv) \urcorner$ that has true observed instances of the form $\ulcorner(Fc \ \& \ Gc) \urcorner$, there is a second generalization $\ulcorner \forall v(F'v \rightarrow G'v) \urcorner$—containing grue-like predicates—which is incompatible with the first and which also has true observed instances of the form $\ulcorner(F'c \ \& \ G'c)\urcorner$. The two generalizations bear exactly the same logical and syntactic relations to their observed instances, but they are not both confirmed by their instances. From the present point of view, this is not at all surprising, because, as I noted above, there is no hope of deriving reliability statements on the basis of logical and syntactic information alone. Accordingly, Goodman's examples show that the method of inference on which $C(S,R)$ is defined purely syntactically is simply not reliable.

What we need to add to the characterization of the confirmation relation is some information about the *predicates* occurring in our generalization. Goodman's work suggests that there is a class of predicates, the *projectible* predicates, such that generalizations in which only projectible predicates occur are confirmed by their instances, whereas generalizations in which nonprojectible predicates occur are not.[13] In other words, we want to modify the above syntactic characterization of confirmation to:

> $C(S,R)$ iff there are *projectible* predicates F, G such that $S = \ulcorner \forall v (Fv \rightarrow Gv) \urcorner$
> and R is a conjunction of sentences of the form $\ulcorner(Fc \ \& \ Gc)\urcorner$.

But which predicates are projectible? On Goodman's view they are the entrenched predicates, the predicates that have been frequently used in actual inductive inferences. This account, however, although it may be correct, leaves too much unexplained. By itself, it gives us no hint of why it is *better* to make inferences with projectible predicates rather than nonprojectible predicates.[14]

From the present point of view, Goodman's definition of 'projectible' is a good example of a charity-based strategy. The projectible predicates are just those which appear in *our* inductive inferences and, therefore, in the generalizations that *we* accept. Following out this kind of strategy, we can define 'projectible' by

> (P) Proj (F) iff $F = 'P_1'$ or $F = 'P_2'$ or $\ldots$ or $F = 'P_k'$.

where $'P_1'$, $'P_2'$, $\ldots$, $'P_k'$ are the predicates occurring in our accepted generalizations. We can then use (P), together with those same generalizations, to derive something very like (*) from T1. The trouble with this strategy, of course, is that it makes it far too easy to establish reliability. Since we have given no *independent* specification of the class of projectible predicates, all the generalizations we actually accept are automatically justified. A justification of scientific method based on (P) and T1 *is* viciously circular: the requirement that we derive reliability statements of the form (*) from $T + (P) + T1$, where T is the rest of our theory of the world, puts no significant constraints on T.

The alternative suggestion is that we try to define 'projectible' in a manner independent of the generalizations we actually accept; we specify the projectible predicates in terms of the history of their acquisition, for example. We then use a causal theory of reference—a general theory of how physical and psychological mechanisms relate predicates with such-and-such a history of acquisition to features of the environment of such-and-such a kind—together with the rest of our theory of the world, to show that inductive inferences to generalizations whose vocabulary is limited to projectible predicates are in fact reliable. This strategy, unlike the above charity-based strategy, is circular but not viciously so. The requirement that we derive reliability statements of the form (*) from $T + T2$, where T2 contains a causal theory of reference, does put a significant constraint on T. Furthermore, I can think of no plausible way of achieving this result without something like a causal theory of reference. Conclusion: if one wants a nontrivial naturalistic justification of inductive inference one needs a nontrivial naturalistic semantics.

V

The upshot of my discussion is that both semantic theories and theories of confirmation have to be much more empirical than most philosophers have supposed. Confirmation theory has to appeal to statistical correlations between the methods of inference scientists actually employ and the physical environment. Semantic theory has to appeal to causal relations between the learning and use of words and their referential properties. Neither kind of theory can be purely formal in the way that the study of deductive logic is formal, and neither kind of theory, therefore, can be developed exclusively by philosophers or by philosopher-logicians. It seems to me that this is one important reason many philosophers have been so reluctant to pursue the point of view outlined here. This is one reason theories of confirmation that do not appeal to the actual probability of success or failure and semantic theories that don't involve a naturalistic notion of reference have been so popular. If my diagnosis is correct, however, these kinds of theories prevent us from establishing precisely the connection between confirmation theory and semantics that is necessary for the justification of scientific method. By jealously guarding the purity of our subject matter we rob our theories of explanatory power; we leave ourselves unable to explain why scientific method is a rational activity.

Notes

An earlier version of this paper was presented at a Tufts University philosophy of science colloquium in April 1976. I am indebted to Hartry Field and Hilary Putnam for helpful conversations and general inspiration. I am also grateful to the editors of the *Journal of Philosophy* for forcing me to clarify and (I hope) improve my argument.

1. This is the heart of the problem, of course. It is the failure of attempts to define theoretical vocabulary explicitly in observational terms (à la Carnap's *Aufbau*) that leads to the collapse of this kind of positivism.

2. Reichenbach 1938 [637], p. 355.

3. A similar point can be made with respect to more sophisticated classes of inductive methods: e.g., Carnap's λ-continuum. The λ-continuum is characterized as follows: Let h_F be the hypothesis that the next observed object will have property F, where F is an element of a partition of the universe (a class of mutually exclusive and jointly exhaustive properties). Let e be the statement that s_F out of s already observed objects have property F. The different confirmation functions c_λ satisfy

$$c_\lambda(h_F e) = \frac{s_F + \lambda/K}{s + \lambda}$$

where K is the size of our partition. (i) For every finite λ, c_λ *is convergent in* (almost) Reichenbach's sense: as $s \to \infty$, $c_\lambda(h_F e) \to \lim_{s \to \infty} S_F/S$. (ii) For small (compared with s) λ, $c_\lambda(h_F e) \approx S_F/S \approx 1/K$. Thus, the larger λ we choose, the more reluctant we are to extrapolate from our observed samples. Smaller values of λ work better in worlds in which observed samples (of almost any size) tend to be representative of the entire universe. Larger values of λ work better in worlds in which observed samples (unless they are very big) tend not to be so representative.

4. Russell 1965 [646], p. 13.

5. Quine 1974 [165], p. 3.

6. Dummett 1973 [713].

7. Note that it is really such a body of *general truths* about Den and Ap that distinguishes T2 from T1. If we like, we can add the *predicates* Den and Ap to T1 by the definitions T2: 1–2. I will have a bit more to say below about the *kind* of general truths that belong in such a theory of reference.

8. In this schema " 'S' " is not a name for the letter 'S'; rather, it is the result of enclosing the sentence S of L in quotation marks. Instead of " 'S' " I could have more accurately, but less perspicuously, written " '"∩S∩"'."

9. It is not enough to complain that the disquotational theories *are* trivial—cf. Field 1972 [715], where the distinction between T1 and T2 is first clearly set out (note that my T2 is Field's T1, and vice versa)—for the notion of reference might just be a trivial notion; it might have no serious explanatory role. In this paper I am trying to suggest that there *is* an important explanatory role for the notion of reference.

10. Cf. Putnam 1975 [634].

11. Cf. Donald Davidson's use of the principle of charity, e.g., in Davidson 1973 [704]. I am indebted to the editors of the *Journal of Philosophy* for suggesting that such charity-based theories be considered and for the basic idea of the criticism to follow.

12. The classical treatments are Carnap 1936 [688]; and Hempel 1945 [744] . A recent contribution to this tradition is Glymour 1975 [737].

13. Here, and in what follows, I ignore various technical niceties: that, for Goodman, 'projectible' ' applies to generalizations not predicates; that we should consider *pairs* of predicates rather than *single* predicates; *etc.* These complications do not affect my main point.

14. Of course, Goodman explicitly rejects the demand for this kind of explanations; cf. Goodman 1965 [53], pp. 98–9. This is because he is too quick to assume that a circular explanation of the kind suggested here is as good as no explanation at all.

9

The Dogma that Didn't Bark (A Fragment of a Naturalized Epistemology)

Jerry A. Fodor

As an empiricist I continue to think of the conceptual scheme of science as a tool, ultimately, for predicting future experience in the light of past experience.
W. V. Quine in "Two Dogmas of Empiricism"

Introduction

Observation seems to be a process of special epistemological interest. In the sequence of events that issues in empirical knowledge, observation seems to be the precise point where the world impinges on the mind. So let's start with observation.

There is a famous story about the acquisition of empirical knowledge that goes like this: First, things happen in the world (light is reflected off the surfaces of objects, soundwaves are propagated through the atmosphere); then there are interactions between these things in the world and the sensitive surfaces of organisms (light stimulates the retina; soundwaves cause the tympanic membrane to vibrate); then mental things start to happen: there are some observations. And then some more mental things happen—there are inferences drawn from these observations. And when all of this goes right, empirical knowledge is the upshot.

That, roughly, is supposed to be the story about how you get empirical knowledge from perception; and science is supposed to be much the same sort of thing, only writ larger. There are the happenings in the world that we want to know about; there is the impacting of these happenings (or of effects of these happenings, or of effects of effects of these happenings . . .) upon our instruments of observa-

Reprinted from *Mind*, vol. 100 (Oxford: Oxford University Press, 1991), pp. 201–220, by permission of the publisher. Copyright © 1991, Oxford University Press.

tion; there are the observations that we make when we deploy these instruments; and finally, there is the body of theoretical elaborations and interpretations of these observations which constitutes our empirical science.

If you take this sort of story seriously, you are likely to think that, somehow or other, our observations must make up the real content of what we know about the world (hence, a fortiori, of our scientific theories). Because, after all, our observations are the only place where our mental processes come into contact with the world. Everything else is either things that happen in the world (light being reflected, soundwaves being emitted, and so on) in which we have no part; or things that happen in us (inferences being drawn, theories being revised, and so on) in which the world has no part. It's only at the interface—only where observation happens—that the world molds our thoughts to its shape. "The totality of our so-called knowledge . . . impinges on experience only along the edges. . . . total science is like a field of force whose boundary conditions are experience" (Quine, 1953, pp. 42–43). In another essay, Quine (1969, p. 427) says of observation sentences that they are ". . . the channel through which empirical content is imbibed". No wonder, then, that philosophers have cared so much about the epistemology of observation. If observation is not objective, what can be? If observation is not reliable, whom can we trust? If observation is not informative, what can we ever know?

This picture, according to which observation (or "experience") is at the interface between the mind and the world, comports with an instrumental understanding of theories, which may be viewed as devices whose essential function is to predict, or otherwise accommodate, the observations. "Saving the appearances," this is sometimes called. Quine, again: "As an empiricist I continue to think of the conceptual scheme of science as a tool, ultimately, for predicting future experience in the light of past experience" (1953, p. 44). Or: "Each man is given a scientific heritage plus a continuing barrage of sensory stimulation; and the considerations which guide him in warping his scientific heritage to fit his continuing sensory promptings are, where rational, pragmatic" (1953, p. 46). Speaking of the ontological commitments of science at large, Quine says they are ". . . myths . . . neither better nor worse except for differences in the degree to which they expedite our dealings with sense experiences" (1953, p. 45).

Now, I know that this story about science being about saving the appearances or dealing with one's sense experiences or whatever has a terrific grip on the imagination. It's such a familiar story that we hardly hear what we are saying when we tell it to each other. But, if you do actually stop to listen, isn't it, in fact, quite preposterous? I'm prepared to believe there is something importantly right about instrumentalism—theories and the rest of the scientific armamentarium are *(inter alia)* instruments for doing *something*—but what's so good about predicting experiences? Could the goal of scientific activity really just be to make up stories that accommodate one's sensory promptings? Would that be a way for a grown man to spend his time? Isn't it, on the contrary, pretty plausible that the goal of the scientific enterprise is to increase our knowledge of the world? And that we value the predictive successes of our theories mostly as a warrant that they are true? I mean, if all you want is to be able to predict your experiences, the rational strategy is clear: Don't revise your theories, just *arrange to have fewer experiences;* close your eyes, put your fingers in your ears, and don't move. Now, why didn't Newton think of that?

Surely this stuff about the business of science being to save the appearances gets the priorities backward, and the tail has commenced to wag the dog. What goes on in science is not that we try to have theories that accommodate our experiences; it's closer that we try to have experiences that adjudicate among our theories. (Though, as we're about to see, that's not *very* close either.) But if there is something wrong with the story that science is about saving the appearances, maybe there is also something wrong with the story about the world being on one side, the mind on the other side, and observation in the middle, which is what spawns the story about science being about saving the appearances.

And, indeed, both stories have recently come under a lot of philosophical pressure; for, however, what seem to me entirely the wrong reasons. If what we observe is substantively to constrain our empirical theories—to constitute a (to say nothing of *the*) "boundary condition" to which our science is required to be responsive—then it had better be that what we observe is substantially independent of what scientific theories we hold. And, for reasons the details of which we needn't go into here (a farrago, in my view, of relativism, holism and bad psychological experiments) it is often claimed that because perception is continuous with cognition, observation fails to exhibit the required theory neutrality. More about this at the very end; suffice it for now that, though I'm worried about the traditional epistemological story about how observation fits into the scientific enterprise, it's not for fear that maybe observation isn't theory neutral.

I'm worried because I'm increasingly dubious that there *is* a specifiable place where empirical information crosses the world-mind interface. My worry isn't that there is *more* than one such place (that, for example, maybe there are two, or seven); and it's not that the mind/world boundary is vague or unprincipled, so that it's like a region rather than a line. No, my worry is that the whole picture is radically wrong; and that, because it is radically wrong, it has lead us to much overestimate the significance of observation as an epistemological category; to grotesquely misconstrue the goals of the scientific enterprise (see above); to overlook some very interesting, general and important features of our epistemic practices; to miss what's right about the instrumentalist account of scientific theories, while wholeheartedly endorsing what's wrong about it; to misunderstand such basic scientific tactics as experimentation and the cultivation of expertise; and quite likely to do many other bad things too, though I suppose the preceding will suffice to be getting on with.

What follows is, in about this order: How it began to occur to me that there is something terribly wrong with the standard epistemological story about observation; what I think the right epistemological story about observation might look like; and what the implications of changing stories might be for some philosophical issues that aren't usually thought to be closely connected with the epistemology of observation; for example, issues about the semantics of deferential concepts. I'm afraid—no, I *know*—that this is all going to be irritatingly, frustratingly, gallingly loose and impressionistic. But, as I say, the standard story has a terrific grip on the imagination, and I propose in this paper to try to loosen it. Details deferred till later.

Part I: How It Began to Occur to Me that There Is Something Terribly Wrong with the Standard Epistemological Story about Observation

The standard story about observation cohabits with a certain understanding of experimentation: Experiments are episodes in which scientists make experimental observations. Making experimental observations involves having certain experiences. Experimental laboratories are environments designed to make the having of these experiences by scientists possible.

Now, I don't doubt that this picture does fit some of the cases. For example, one's theory might say that a certain liquid is an acid, and one might test the theory by doing an experiment: You put some litmus paper in the fluid, and the upshot is that the you see the litmus paper turn pink (if the fluid is an acid) or you see it not turn pink (if the fluid isn't). This fits the standard picture very nicely; there are "hidden" interactions in the world—between the fluid and the litmus paper; there are observations made, the character of which is contingently determined by these interactions; and inferences are drawn from the observations the gist of which is that the theory is refuted or confirmed. In this kind of case, it really is quite natural to think of observation as the boundary where the world impinges on the theory. And, no doubt, you can think of lots and lots of other kinds of experiments that are like this. So I'm certainly not arguing that experiments are never plausibly described as designed to make certain observations possible. I am, however, prepared to argue that experiments aren't *always* plausibly so described; that providing opportunities for making observations isn't the *essence* of experiments.

For example, when I try to match the story about "first the world, then observation, then inference" to what goes on in my laboratory, it doesn't seem to fit very well. In particular, I can't figure out what the observations are supposed to be. Nothing happens that seems naturally analogized to seeing the litmus paper turn pink.

Let me give you a brief sketch of what *does* go on in my laboratory; just enough for you to understand what the epistemological problem is.

Most of the experiments we do are studies of the effects of materials variables (for example, syntactic or contextual variables) on the ease with which speaker/hearers understand spoken or written tokens of sentences in their native language. The usual strategy is to require the subject to perform some subsidiary task while listening to an utterance. The relative facility—typically, the relative speed—with which the subsidiary task is performed by the subject is taken to measure the relative complexity of the sentence he is listening to.

For example, a typical experiment might investigate the hypothesis that *(ceteris paribus)* passive sentences are more difficult than otherwise matched active sentences. The experimental environment might be like this: The subject hears active and passive sentences through earphones while attending to a display presented on a computer screen. He is instructed to pronounce aloud any word that is exhibited on the screen. The reaction time (called a "naming" time in this sort of experiment) for a word that's simultaneous with an active sentence is compared with the naming time for the same word when it's simultaneous with the corresponding passive. If the finding is that the second naming time is longer than the first, that will be taken to support the theory that passives are harder to understand than actives *(ceteris paribus)*.[1]

Now, what actually happens when the subject "names" a stimulus word is this: His utterance triggers a voice-activated relay, which turns off a millisecond timer that was turned on by the presentation of the word. The elapsed time is then stored on the hard disk of the computer that runs the experiment. Nobody but a computer *could* run the experiment because, as it turns out, the reaction time asymmetries that are caused by the sorts of materials variables that we are examining, though often quite reliable, are nevertheless very small. In a naming task of the kind I've been describing, overall reaction times should fall in the vicinity of 600 msec, and a mean difference of 15 or 20 msec may constitute a statistically significant effect of the materials manipulation.

One consequence is that the chronometrics of the experimental environment must be very precisely controlled; for example, there has to be a precise determination of the interval between the presentation of the stimulus and the subject's initiation of his response. And often the precise interval between the presentation of the visual stimulus and some feature of the sentence that the subject is listening to will also be crucial to the bearing of the data on the theory. The required precision could not be reliably achieved except by computerizing the entire environment, including both the scheduling of the stimulus display and the measurement of the response times.

So, then, in an experiment of this sort, the registration of a data point typically consists in a reaction time being stored by a computer. It is worth remarking that, at this epistemically crucial juncture in the experimental episode, *nobody is observing anything*. The subject is sitting in an acoustically controlled, partially darkened cubicle, doing his best to comply with the experimental instruction to "respond as fast and as accurately as possible." The guy who designed the experiment is, likely as not, half a mile away lecturing to his introductory course in psycholinguistics. The graduate research assistant who is in charge of the experimental session is drinking coffee and reading *The World According to Garp*. (His job will be to reboot the computer at the end of the session and start it up again when the next batch of subjects arrives.) Nothing, in short, plausibly analogous to watching the litmus turn pink is, or needs to be, going on.

There are, of course, things happening that you could observe if you wanted to. For example, you could stand in the cubicle with the subject and watch while he names the stimulus word that's flashed on the computer screen. This would, however, be distracting to the subject and of no earthly use to you. For you can't tell, by watching, the difference between a subject who is responding at about 600 msec latencies and one who is responding at about 615 msec; though, as remarked above, that is the likely magnitude of a significant materials effect.

Or we could set things up so that the computer running the experiment displays the reaction times as they come in, and you could observe those. That wouldn't do you the slightest good either, however, because the asymmetries of performance that are being examined emerge only after data from, say, fifty or sixty subjects has been pooled and analyzed. So watching the reaction times roll in wouldn't buy you anything epistemic; *not even if the experiment is successful and the pooled data do exhibit the predicted asymmetries.*

Or, if you like, we could have the computer "dump" the raw scores, and you could observe a data matrix with, perhaps, 1,800 cells (60 subjects × 30 sentences per subject). This, again, wouldn't do you any good epistemically speaking since you can't see, by just looking, whether 1,800 cells of data exhibit the sort of asymmetries that a successful experimental hypothesis would predict. Significant raw data look quite remarkably like nonsignificant raw data. In my experience, psychologists look at raw scores primarily when they're worried that the machine in control of the experiment has done something crazy; a quick look (what they call "eyeballing the data") can tell you whether the numbers are falling in the right ball park. But it usually can't tell you anything about whether the experiment has worked.

So nobody observes anything. What happens, instead, is that the raw data are run through an ANOVA program (or the like), which delivers news about whether the behaviours of the subject groups has, indeed, been asymmetric in the way that the experimental hypothesis predicts. At this point in the proceedings, something that it's not unreasonable to call an interaction between the theory and the world does indeed take place; and you can, if you like, say that what the psychologist "observes" is the F scores (or p-values or whatever) that the statistical analysis of the data produces. But this is, surely, just a way of talking; and not, perhaps, a very good way. It insists on an analogy between the sort of experiment I've been describing and the sort of experiment in which one watches the litmus paper turn pink. And as I hope the preceding has convinced you, it's a serious question whether the analogy is actually there.

If, however, you're *not* convinced, consider the following: In the litmus sort of case, we can specify the class of confirming observations independent of the beliefs in which they eventuate; viz., by reference to *how things will look to the experimenter* if the predictions his theory makes are sustained. There is, as one says, "something it's like" to see litmus paper turn pink, and what confirms the theory is the experimenter's having an experience that is *like that*. But there's nothing it's like to "observe" a p-value; to a first approximation, "observing that p is less than .05" is just having some or other experience that *causes one to believe* that p is less than .05. To put it another way: There is such a thing as *an experience as of litmus paper turning pink*; but there is no such thing as *an experience as of p being less than .05*. So, it's true about the litmus case that what the theory (together with the appropriate ancillary assumptions) predicts is that the experimenter will have a certain kind of experience; and what confirms the prediction is that he *does* have that kind of experience. But to say that about the p-value case is, as previously remarked, just to insist upon a way of talking.[2]

There is, to put the point in still another way, a usage according to which "experimental observations" and "experimental data" are understood as simply synonyms. Since we do, of course, collect experimental data in my laboratory, I suppose it follows, according to this way of talking, that we are making experimental observations when we do so. But if you propose to use "observations" so that it just *means* "data", you must not also take for granted the Empiricist thesis that there is any specially interesting connection between *making observations* and *having experiences*. It is, for example, just not true that the experimental data that my lab produces typically consist in the having of experiences by the experimenter. Yet we are, I suppose, doing experimental science? Aren't we?

A lot of the philosophy of science since Hanson's *Patterns of Discovery* is enthusiastic for including among observables not just the usual middle sized paradigms (tables, chairs, the cat's being on the mat, and the like), but also a range of entities and events that an earlier epistemological tradition would have taken to be pretty clearly inferred. ". . . the physicist sees the X-ray tube's anode overheating" Hanson says, and the context makes it clear that the stress is on "sees" (Hanson, 1958, p. 17).[3] Various arguments are alleged in aid of this revisionism, including fidelity to the way scientists actually talk about observations, and the need to take seriously what modern psychology is said to tell us about the theory laden character of perception. The epistemological issue about observation thus presents itself as a border dispute, requiring for its solution some principled (presumably a posteriori, since the context is *naturalized* epistemology) criterion for drawing a perception/inference distinction.

But in philosophy—as, indeed, in larger affairs—border disputes are often the visible signs of hidden agendas. I suggest that, if observation is coming under pressure, that's because Empiricists wanted it to do two jobs which are increasingly to be seen as not compatible. On the one hand, observation was to be what the confirmation of theories depends on, insofar as it doesn't depend on systematic considerations of conservatism, simplicity, plausibility and the like; *the observations* and *the data* were thus to be the very same thing. And, on the other hand, observation was to maintain its traditional internal connection to experience: theories get confirmed by confirming the observation sentences that they entail, and observation sentences get confirmed by the experiences that scientists have. That observation mediates the relation between experience and confirmation vindicates the Empiricist doctrine that the empirical content of theories is experiential.

But this doesn't work. Because, while observation is supposed to be constrained by a conceptual connection between what one can observe and how one can see things, the *data* for a theory are just *whatever confirms its predictions*, and can thus be *practically anything at all* (including, by the way, bits and pieces of other theories). So, the data for big bang cosmology include "observations" of the cosmic microwave radiation background;[4] the data for Mendelian genetics include the "observed" ratios of traits in the offspring of heterozygotes; the data for the gene theory include Mendel's "observation" (i.e., they include the Mendelian *law*) that heterozygotes breed true; the data for parsing theories include "observed" asymmetries of reaction times between subjects listening to sentences of related syntactic types. And so on. These uses of "observe" and its cognates have pretty clearly come unstuck from "seeing as" or, indeed, from *anything* that's psychological; *pace* Hanson, Churchland, Kuhn, Feyerabend, Goodman and the rest. So, then: It's fine to let psychology settle what an observation is. And it's equally fine to forget about psychology and just let the observations be the data. But it's sheer Empiricist dogmatism to take it for granted that you can do both at once. In fact, there is no good reason to suppose that the psychological notion of perception—or, indeed, *any* psychological notion—will reconstruct the epistemological notion of a datum.

The observability of data is thus the third dogma of Empiricism.[5] Attempts to defend it have now run through two distinguishable phases. According to the old Empiricist story, data have to be observable because it's true a priori that only *sense* data can *be* data. According to the new Empiricist story, data have to be observable because it's true a posteriori that scientists learn to see confirming instances as having the properties that make them confirmatory. The trendy idea that practically anyone can learn to see practically anything under practically any description is really in much the same line of work as the discredited idea that the language of confirmation is sense datum language: If you can't shrink the epistemology to fit the psychology by being restrictive about data, maybe you can stretch the psychology to fit the epistemology by being permissive about "seeing as". But this is all quite futile if, as I have been suggesting, *datum* just isn't a psychological category. What God has put asunder, let no man join together.

Two remarks to end this section: First, though I'm pretty sure about what goes on in my laboratory, I don't actually know what happens in other sciences. Still, I'm prepared to bet that it's often quite a lot like what I've been reporting. As the predictions that distinguish theories become increasingly precise, it becomes correspondingly inadvisable to let the burden of experimental confirmation rest on the observational capacities of the scientist. It makes sense to get experiences, sensory bombardments, and the like, out of the circuit if you can. What you want, if you can get it, is data that *don't* consist of observations; observations aren't all that reliable.

The second point is this: Imagine a really hi-tech, capital intensive sort of future science, in which you just plug the experimenter's cortex into the computer that collects the experimental data. So now there aren't any sensory bombardments at all, and nobody ever looks at anything. All that happens is that the subject's responses determine what's in the computer's data files, and what's in the computer's data files determines the outcome of the statistical analyses that the computer performs, and the outcome of the statistical analyses determines the pattern of stimulation of the experimenter's cortex, and the pattern of stimulation of the experimenter's cortex determines that the experimenter comes to believe, say, that the subjects in materials condition A respond, on average, 18 msec slower than the subjects in materials condition B, and that this asymmetry is statistically significant. And let us suppose that this whole hook up, starting with the subject's response and ending with the experimenter's coming to have this belief, is well understood and, in fact, thoroughly reliable. We're now about as far as you can get from the sort of experiment where confirmation consists of seeing the litmus paper turn pink. But have we, therefore, stopped doing science? Have our experiments therefore ceased to provide rational constraints on our theories? Has, in fact, anything gone wrong at all?[6]

Here's what I think: The story that experience is the interface between the world and the mind spawns a view of scientific theories as instruments for saving the observations (/appearances/experiences/ sensory bombardments). And this view of scientific theories spawns a view of experiments as environments designed to provide the observations that the theories are supposed to save. And this view of experiments as providing occasions for observations spawns a conflation between the truism that scientific theories are typically constrained by experimental data, and the falsism that they are typically constrained by observational data. *Some* experimental environments are reasonably described as providing opportunities for scientists to make observations, and some aren't. It isn't, therefore, of the essence of experiments to provide such opportunities.

But, then, what are experiments for? And, how, if not by shaping our observations, does the world contrive to constrain our theories?

Part II: On Cognitive Management

Here's an old idea about what experiments are for: Experiments are a way that we have of putting questions to Nature. I think this suggestion is actually quite good; much better than the Empiricist suggestion that experiments are a way that we have of providing opportunities for scientists to have experiences. But though "putting questions to Nature" is an idea I like a lot, I do admit that it wants some analysis. I suppose that to understand what it is to put questions to Nature, we must first have some view about what it is to put questions *tout court*. So let's look at a simple case of that. Let's consider what goes on when you ask someone the time.

To ask someone the time (I mean, to ask someone the time not frivolously; to ask someone the time actually wanting to know the time) is, *inter alia*, to compose one's mind to a certain state of receptivity. To ask Jones the time, for example, is to so dispose yourself that, all else equal, if Jones say that it is X o'clock, then you will thereupon come to believe that it is X o'clock. Indeed, it is to so dispose yourself that Jones' saying that it is X o'clock will *cause* you to believe that it is X o'clock. Moreover, it is to put yourself in this condition with, as it were, malice afore-thought. Part of *what you had in mind* in asking Jones the time was precisely that Jones should say that it is something-or-other o'clock, and that, *ceteris paribus*, you should thereupon be caused to believe that it is whatever o'clock Jones says it is. (Notice, however, that the *ceteris paribus* condition is essential. Jones' saying that it is 13 o'clock on the 31st of February, 545 bc would very likely *not* cause you to believe that it is. To unfrivolously ask someone the time is thus to compose one's mind to a state of *judicious* receptivity.)

But why should you wish your mind to be in this receptive state? Presumably because you are convinced that Jones is an authority about what time it is to the extent that, if Jones says that it's X o'clock, then, in all likelihood, it is in fact X o'clock. Jones has a watch, after all; and you don't. So probably Jones knows what the time is better, anyhow, than you do. And probably Jones will tell you what he knows about what the time is if you ask him nicely. All this being so, by asking Jones what the time is you contrive to put yourself in a position where, likely enough, you will be caused to believe that it's X o'clock just in case it *is* X o'clock. Since you wanted to know what o'clock it is, that is a reasonable position for you to contrive to put yourself in.

Epistemologists often remark that there is no such thing as deciding to believe that P; and, since it's arguable that you can't be obliged to do anything that you can't decide to do, there's maybe something wrong with the idea that you are sometimes obliged to believe that P given the state of the evidence. Well, maybe so. But here's something that you *can* do about what you believe: You can put yourself in a situation where, depending on how things turn out in that situation, you may be caused to believe that P. And, if you're sufficiently clever, you can construct this situation that you put yourself in so that the-outcome-that-would-be-sufficient-to-cause-you-to-believe-that-P[7] will occur if and only if it's the case that P. Putting a question to someone who is compliant and in the know is one species of this kind of behaviour. Putting a question to Nature is another. The latter, I think, is what it is to do an experiment.

An experiment to test the hypothesis that P is an environment designed to have the property that *being in that environment will cause the scientist* (and/or his chums; see below) *to believe P if (but only if) P is true.*[8] An experiment is a sort of trick that you play on yourself; an exercise in cognitive self-management. You set things up so that, given what you know about the way that the experimental environment works, and given what you know about the way that your mind works, you can be confident that the consequence of running the experiment will be that you will come to believe your hypothesis if and only if your hypothesis is true. To put it slightly otherwise: An experiment is a gadget that's designed (not to cause you to have certain experiences but) to cause the state of your mind to correspond to the state of the world.

What you do when you design an experiment is: You ask yourself "what outcome would make me believe that P; and what outcome would make me believe that not-P" and then you try to set things up so that you will get the first kind of outcome if and only if P is the case and the second kind of outcome if and only if not-P is the case. I want to emphasize that it is not an objection to this account that, instead of asking yourself what outcome would *make you believe* (cause you to believe) that P, you might instead ask yourself what outcome would *convince you* that P.[9] To the contrary, one way of making it very likely that you will come to believe-that-P just in case it's the case that

P, is *precisely* to think of an outcome that you are convinced would transpire if and only if *P*; and then run the experiment and see if you get that outcome. You've designed the best experiment that you can when you're as convinced as you can be that you will get the predicted outcome just when *P* obtains; when you're perfectly convinced, that is to say, that getting that outcome would mean that *P*.[10] But, of course, if you're perfectly convinced that you would get the predicted outcome just in the case that *P*, then if you do get that outcome, then that will cause you to believe that *P*. To be perfectly convinced that if *O* then *P* *is* to be in a state of mind in which you would come to believe that *P* if something caused you to believe that *O*. (Unless, however, you happen to change your mind about if *O* then *P* in the meantime; see below.)

In fact, it's part of the cognitive management strategy that we're only interested in experimental outcomes that would make us believe that *P* where we *are* convinced that what would make us believe that *P* means that *P*. (We're interested in the outcome where the litmus turns pink because we're convinced that if the litmus turns pink, that means that the fluid is an acid.) Experiments that consist in swallowing a believe-that-*P* pill, for example, are of no use to us. That's because we're not interested in being caused to believe that *P simpliciter*, or come what may. What we're interested in is being caused to believe that *P* if and only if *P* is true. Whereas, to imagine oneself as caused to believe that *P* by an experimental outcome that one *isn't* convinced would mean that *P* is to imagine oneself in a situation where it may well be that one would be caused to believe that *P* *whether or not P* is true. It is therefore to imagine oneself as not getting from the experimental outcome what one wanted (or as getting what one wanted only by chance).

All of which is to say that experimentation is a species of *rational* cognitive management: in an experiment, you use what you are convinced would mean that *P* to cause you to believe that *P*. There is nothing wrong with undertaking, with malice afore-thought, to bring it about that you will be caused to believe that *P* on certain contingencies; at least, there's nothing wrong with it so long as you also arrange that, if those contingencies obtain, then *P* is, according to your best lights, what you *ought* to believe.[11]

Perhaps it goes without saying that even a rational strategy can fail. It may be that the outcome that would mean that *P* according to your best lights, doesn't mean that P after all. In that case, by running your experiment you will have managed to manage yourself into a false belief. Tant pis. Or it may be that the outcome that you are convinced would mean that P actually *would* mean that P, but your execution of the experiment is slovenly (or the equipment goes down, or you do the statistics wrong, or whatever) so you fail to get the outcome that would have caused you to-believe-truly-that-P if only the experiment had worked. Or, it may be that you were wrong about what would cause you to believe that P: You get the outcome that you were convinced would mean that P, but nevertheless you don't believe that P; perhaps because you are bull-headed, or because you've failed to notice that you got the predicted outcome, or because, in the course of post hoc analysis, you've changed your mind about whether the outcome really does mean that P. These are all species of ills that flesh is heir to. A good epistemic strategy (and experimentation is about the best epistemic strategy that we've got) offers no guarantees against them. This is not a paper about scepticism; it's a paper about *how science works*.

Notice that having experiences in the experimental environment plays no essential role in any of what I've been describing; though, no doubt, there are kinds of experimental environments that are set up so that part of what's required to cause the experimenter to believe that such and such is that he has an experience which (assuming the design of the experiment is good) he will have only if such and such is indeed the case. You might say that, on the present analysis, your experiences play an *instrumental* role in the experiment (when they play any role at all). Having contrived that you will be caused to believe P iff you have a certain experience, having the experience then comes in as a link in a causal chain that the experimental outcome initiates and that eventuates in your having the belief.

But, of course, the belief that the experience causes you to have doesn't have to be about the experience that causes you to have it; or, indeed, about any experience at all. Seeing the litmus turn pink—having that experience—causes you to come to believe that the fluid is an acid. You wouldn't have performed the litmus test but that you knew that seeing the litmus turn pink *would* cause you to come to believe that the fluid is an acid. But your belief that the fluid is an acid isn't a belief about your experience; and the point of running the experiment wasn't to provide you with an opportunity to see the litmus change colour. The point of running the experiment was to put yourself in an environment where you would come-to-have-the-belief-that-the-liquid-is-an-acid iff it's the case that the liquid is an acid. Cognitive management is management of cognition in aid of forming true beliefs.

There are several senses in which theories, too, have an instrumental role to play in the acquisition of empirical knowledge, assuming that the cognitive management story has the stick by the right end. For one thing, theories, like experiences, function as links in the causal chain that runs from experimental outcomes to the fixation of beliefs.[12] You have it in mind that a certain experimental outcome would cause you to believe that P. Well, how do you know that it would? Answer: you know (introspectively, or something) that you believe a theory from which it follows that getting that outcome would mean that P. And you are therefore confident that, short of an unaccountable excess of stupidity, if you get the outcome when you run the experiment, you will draw this inference from the theory you believe, and therefore come to believe that P. Or you will remember that when you designed the experiment you had it in mind that this outcome would mean that P, and *that*, together with the outcome, will cause you to believe that P. Either way, the theories with which you enter the experimental environment, like the experiences you have in the experimental environment, and like, for that matter, the complex of paraphernalia by which the experimental environment is physically constituted, form part of a complex causal network that is calculated to cause you to have true beliefs. The Instrumentalists were right about their epistemology: Our scientific armamentarium, our theories very much included, is a machine designed so that it has, as is might be, acids on one end and true beliefs about acids on the other.[13] Where the Instrumentalists went wrong was in supposing that this epistemological insight somehow implies a verificationist semantics. Or—worse yet—an Irrealist ontology.

Implicit in all this is an important sense in which our theories are devices we use to calculate our future psychological states; the Instrumentalists were right about that, too. It's not, however, that what we use theories for is to predict our future experiences; if theories were instruments in that sense, it would be hard to understand why their being good instruments would have anything much to do with their being *true*. No, what we use our theories for is to design environments in which, if all goes well, we will be caused-to-believe-that-P

iff *P*. Here's how we do it: If you believe what a theory says about what experimental outcome would mean that *P*, then you know what you would be caused to believe by an experiment that has that outcome; viz., you know that you would be caused to believe that *P*. So the theory licenses, on the one hand, your conviction that you would come to believe that *P* if you got the predicted outcome and, on the other hand, your conviction that in coming to believe that *P* contingent on the predicted outcome you would come to believe something true. Clearly, however, to be good tools for *this* sort of purpose, our theories will themselves have to be true. If what a theory says an outcome means *isn't* true, then if an experiment that has that outcome nevertheless causes you to believe something that *is* true, then that's just sheer blind luck. It is, I suppose, rational of us not to wish to leave the management of our cognition to sheer blind luck.

The Empiricist story about your theories being instruments for predicting your experiences makes it seem surprising that so many scientific theories are, prima facie, not about experiences at all, but about the world. Why, if Geology is really a device for predicting my experiences, should it go on and on the way it does about mountains and glaciers and what happened in the Pleistocene. Why doesn't it keep its eye on the target and just talk about my experiences? Whereas, according to the present view, theories-qua-instruments are calculating devices that we use to help design experimental environments in which the state of our beliefs will depend, causally, upon the state of the world.[14] It's hardly surprising that, if that's what we use them for, then we want our theories to tell us quite a lot about what the state of the world *is;* specifically, about what the various outcomes that the experiment might have would mean that the state of the world is. And it's also not surprising, if that's what we use them for, that we should place a premium on what our theories tell us about what the experimental outcomes would mean being *true*.

Viewing experiments as exercises in cognitive management is thus a key to understanding our ability to bootstrap our science. Because we have a lot of beliefs that are by and large true, including, importantly, lots of true beliefs about what outcomes would be convincing that *P*, we are able to design environments in which we will be caused to have still more beliefs that are by and large true. To recognize the phenomenon of cognitive management is thus to understand what is, surely, the most egregious feature of our epistemic situation: the fact that our science is cumulative and progressive. Given that we have a start—which is to say, given that we have some true beliefs—cognitive management predicts the accelerating development of our empirical knowledge. It's not at all clear to me why one would predict this on the Empiricist picture, according to which science consists of reflecting upon one's sensations.

By the way, it's a corollary of what I've been saying that experiments are designed with an audience—a peer group—in mind. Since the causal route from the experimental outcome to the fixation of beliefs about the experimental hypothesis is typically theory mediated, only people who believe the theory on which the experimental design is predicated are likely to be caused by the outcome to believe that P *even if it's true that the outcome does mean that P*. It's not true that experiments can only preach to the converted; to believe what a theory says about what an experimental outcome would *mean* isn't, of course, to believe what it says about what the experimental outcome will *be*. But what *is* true is that, if we're going to use litmus to test for acid, then it has to be common ground that if the litmus turns pink that means that pretty likely it's an acid, and if it doesn't turn pink that means that pretty likely it isn't.

An experiment isn't a gadget that's intended to cause-the-belief-that-P just in case its the case that P in just *anybody*, or even in just *anybody rational*; it probably wouldn't be possible to design a gadget that would do *that*. No, an experiment is at best a gadget which will induce-the-belief-that-P just in case it's the case that P in anybody rational who is au courant with the currently accepted theoretical framework; anybody who is in the club. So there really is something intrinsically social about the scientific enterprise: The only way to say who an experiment is designed to induce the belief that P in, is to refer to a community defined by a (more or less comprehensive) sophistication about theory. And one counts the experiment *a failure* if one gets the result that was supposed to cause people in the club to believe that P *and it doesn't*. Typically, you get this sort of failure when someone in the club is able to argue that you would have gotten the result that was designed-to-cause-you-to-believe-that-P even if it *hadn't* been the case that P; hence that the experiment was ill designed; for instance, that it was inadequately controlled.

A good experiment is *(inter alia)* one where the outcome that means that P would cause the club to believe that P; an experiment is no good unless it's *convincing*. Conversely, good clubs are *(inter alia)* clubs that are convinced that P by experimental outcomes that do in fact mean that *P*. It's a goal of scientific education to make our club as good as we can. Partly this is a matter of inculcating theories which, according to our best lights, predict-experimental-outcomes-that-would-mean-that-*P* iff *P*; for to believe such a theory is to be disposed to be caused to believe *P* by experimental outcomes which, according to our best lights, are convincing that *P*. So we design our experiments to convince the club; and we design the club to be convinced by our experiments. If you think that this is circular and can't work, look about you.

Well, enough about experiments. I use experiments as my main example of managed cognition because the Empiricist account of them is so achingly, obviously in want of replacement. But it ought now to be clear that cognitive management—putting oneself in a position where one will be caused to believe that *P* just in case it's the case that *P*—is a pervasive feature of cognitive activity. You find it not just in our intentional behaviour, but also in our reflexes; and not just in us but also throughout quite a lot of the animal kingdom.

If there are noises off, many organisms will orient reflexively to foveate the noise source. (And if a light goes on at the edge of the visual field, the eye moves reflexively to foveate the light.) Not because these organisms are designed to like their sensations to come in a certain order (sounds followed by sights, as it might be); but because they are designed to so position themselves that if, for example, it was a Heffalump that made the noise, then they will come (and promptly too) to *believe* that it was a Heffalump that made the noise. They achieve this by turning so that if it was a Heffalump that made the noise, then a foveated retinal image as of a Heffalump will be formed. And the reason *that* works is that, on the one hand, the world is so constructed that almost nothing but a Heffalump ever causes a retinally foveated image to be as-of-a-Heffalump; and, on the other hand, the minds of these animals are so constructed that, if an image as-of-a-Heffalump is foveated on their retinas, a Heffalump belief is thereby caused in them.

It's instructive to contrast this arrangement with the famous, but apocryphal, ethology of the ostrich which, according to the story, would *rather not know* if there's a Heffalump, and which buries its head in the sand to avoid finding out. Or consider Piglet: " 'It's the Heffalump!' thought Piglet nervously. . . . But he didn't look round because if you look round and see a Very Fierce Heffalump looking down at you, sometimes you forget what you were going to say."

Piglet and the ostrich prefer to manage themselves out of believing that P, even if it is, in fact, the case that P, when it's being the case that P doesn't bear thinking about. One sympathizes with their point of view, of course, but it's probably not viable outside fiction.

The moral, anyhow, is that the epistemology of the orienting reflex is unlike the epistemology of experimental design only in that the former illustrates cognitive management by Mother Nature rather than cognitive *self*-management. The orienting reflex is one of the little tricks Mother N. employs to assure that (in a variety of ecologically salient cases) organisms will be caused to believe that P by things that mean that P.[15]

Other examples: One wants one's feet not to get wet, so one wants to know whether it will rain. So one reads the *Times* because if the *Times* says that it will rain, then if you read the *Times*, that will cause you to believe that it will rain. You know that reading the *Times* will cause you to believe that it will rain if the *Times* says that it will rain because you know (by introspection, or something) that you are convinced that what the *Times* says about the weather is reliable. (The worse fool you, by the way.)

And since you *are* convinced that what the *Times* says about the weather is reliable, you are convinced that arranging to be caused to believe that it will rain by reading in the *Times* that it will rain will eventuate in your being caused to believe that it will rain just in case it's true that it will rain. Which is what you wanted.

Or, for a last example, you could just ask the weatherman. A lot of what seems to me to be rather unedifying stuff has recently been written about the significance for epistemology, and even for semantics, of our practice of deferring to experts. But, in my view, there's nothing much in it. We use experts, instrumentally, as a means to get our beliefs correlated with the world. But if that's what deferring to experts comes to, then in the sense in which I defer to the experts so as to get my elm-thoughts correlated with the elms, I likewise defer to my wrist watch so as to get my time thoughts correlated with the time. Both kinds of deference are techniques of cognitive management; beside that, nothing epistemologically interesting would seem to follow.[16] And, as far as I can see, nothing semantically interesting follows at all.

In "The Meaning of 'Meaning,'" Hilary Putnam (1975) emphasizes the division of labour according to which our experts keep track of the elms so the rest of us don't have to bother. Fair enough, but not different in epistemological import from the division of labour according to which our clocks keep track of the time so the rest of us don't have to bother. In *Representation and Reality* Putnam argues that since appeals to experts mediate the coordination of one's tokens of "elm" with instances of elmhood, it follows that "reference is a social phenomenon" (Putnam 1988). *Prima facie,* this seems about as sensible as arguing that since one uses telescopes to coordinate one's tokens of "star" with instances of starhood, it follows that reference is an optical phenomenon.

That Putnam, of all people, should make this mistake is heavy with irony. For, it is Putnam who is always—and rightly—reminding us that ". . . 'meanings' are preserved under the usual procedures of belief fixation . . ." (1988, p. 14). I take this to say that the ways we have of telling what our terms and concepts apply to are *not*, in general, germane to their semantics. Why, I wonder, does Putnam make an exception in the case where our ways of telling involve exploiting experts?

Cognitive management is, I think, such a pervasive feature of our way of life that if you get it wrong, you're likely to go wrong about quite a lot else too. Maybe the old philosophers were right after all when they advised: "Do the epistemology first."

Conclusion: Granny Reconsidered

I suppose the bottom line is that Granny missed the point about observation too. I remember her remarking, several years ago, that there are two routes to the fixation of empirical belief (Fodor 1985), these being observation and inference. She thereby bought into the Empiricist picture, according to which observation—hence perception—supplies whatever underived contingent premises thought has access to. This identification of what confirms our theories with what we can observe makes the objectivity of our science hostage to the theory neutrality of our perception. So Granny had to face the question whether perception is in fact sufficiently encapsulated from cognition (sufficiently "modular," as one says) to provide an objective, theory neutral, data base for science.

This question is, of course, interesting for epistemology on anybody's story, since nobody could doubt that *some* empirical data are observational. And it's fascinating for psychologists, since they care about cognitive architecture for its own sweet sake. But the epistemological urgency of the modularity thesis is much reduced if, as I've argued, providing opportunities for making observations is just one tactic among many that scientists can use to achieve cognitive management; one way among many for scientists to design environments in which they will be caused to believe their experimental hypotheses just in case their experimental hypotheses are true.

For what it's worth, however, I do think Granny was right about the facts. Recent psychology suggests pretty much what common sense has always supposed: that perception is sufficiently encapsulated so that experimental environments can be designed in which what a scientist observes will be largely independent of his theoretical commitments. So, observation is vindicated as a means to the fixation of empirical belief; and Granny is vindicated too. But for all that, it seems to me she missed the really interesting point: It wouldn't have mattered all that much, epistemologically speaking, if it had turned out that perception *isn't* encapsulated. Because the data that constrain our science don't have to be perceptual, and often enough aren't. The only way to make it true (to say nothing of true a priori) that the fixation of empirical belief depends exhaustively on inference and observation is to read "observation" to mean not "perception" but "perception and whatever other means we can devise to cause ourselves to have true beliefs."

The cleverer we get at experimental design, the more new methods of cognitive management we'll think of; the more new environments, that is to say, in which the outcome that would mean that P would cause us to believe that P. The existence of such environments does not *essentially* depend on our capacity for having experiences, or making observations, or being bombarded by sensory stimulations. What it depends on *essentially* is our capacity to be caused to have beliefs that are true. Empiricism is the philosopher's philosophy of science; but Realism is the experimentalist's. (As, indeed, Ian Hacking has also recently observed; though for somewhat different reasons.)

I remarked above that one finds devices for cognitive management (orienting reflexes, for example) built-in over a wide spectrum of the phylogenetic continuum. No doubt all the vertebrates have them. But it is, perhaps, the supreme achievement of *our* species that we have made cognitive management a project. We have learned to manage cognition with malice afore-thought. This has worked brilliantly: So well that we know more than anybody else. So well that we alone in all Creation are in danger of knowing more than is good for us.

Notes

1. Psycholinguists have more interesting questions to worry about these days than whether actives or passives are harder to understand, so the simple experiment in the text is just expository. But the description of the experimental environment is perfectly realistic. For example, David Swinney's (1979) [843] "cross modal priming" paradigm uses precisely this sort of set-up.

2. Gabe Segal has suggested to me that perhaps the datum that's "observed" in this sort of experiment is the inscription ("$p<.05$" as is might be) on the computer printout. But what if I did the statistics in my head?.

3. The context also makes clear that Hanson isn't just trading on the transparency of "see" to substitution of identicals. "The visitor [to the laboratory] must learn some physics before he can see what the physicist sees. . . . The infant and the layman can see: they are not blind. But they cannot see what the physicist sees; they are blind to what he sees" (1958 [58], p. 17). Nor is this a willful confusion of seeing with seeing as, though no doubt it's that inter alia. The point is that it's what the scientist sees in the nontransparent sense—what he sees things as—that his observation sentences report.

4. And, concurrently, the "observed" proportions of elements in the universe are part of the data for the theory that the "observed" background radiation is really left over from the big bang. Cf. ". . . from the observed abundance of hydrogen we can infer that the universe must in the first few minutes have been filled with an enormous amount of radiation which could prevent the formation of the heavier elements; the expansion of the universe would then have lowered its equivalent temperature to a few degrees Kelvin, so that it would now appear as a background of radio noise . . ." (Weinberg 1977 [664], p. 51).

5. That the doctrine of the observability of data is merely dogmatic is, no doubt, a minority view; but it's by no means unprecedented. See, for a recent example, Bogen and Woodward 1988 [681]. Modulo some differences of terminology, most of what I say in Part I of this paper is in close agreement with things that they say in Part I of theirs.

I'm not, however, entirely clear how their distinction between "data" (i.e., what experiments seek to provide) and "phenomena" (i.e., what theories seek to explain) applies to the sort of experiments with which I'm most familiar. Perhaps the most natural thing to say about these experiments is that the data they yield are asymmetries of reaction times, and that it's these asymmetries for which theoretical explanation is required. Or perhaps one should say that the data are the rt assymetries, and the phenomenon is the correlation of task complexity with the materials variables. However, according to Bogen and Woodward, phenomena, unlike data, abstract from the details of the experimental set-up. This suggests that the *real* phenomenon must be the correlation of task complexity with linguistic structure, of which the experimentally observed correlations are merely instances. On the other hand, phenomena are supposed to be what theories explain, and the correlation of linguistic structure with task complexity is plausibly less an explanandum than an explanans. This begins to seem a little thankless. In these cases, there appears to be no principled reason to talk one way or the other, hence nothing to suggest a principled data/phenomena distinction.

6. In a paper called "Science without Experience," Paul Feyerabend imagines much the same sort of thought experiment as I suggest in the text and concludes, correctly in my view, that ". . . a natural science without experience is *conceivable* [sic]," hence that "Empiricism, insofar as it goes beyond the invitation not to forget considering observations, is therefore an unreasonable doctrine, not in agreement with scientific practice" (1981 [570], pp. 134–135).

7. In what follows, there will be a fair number of cases where biconditionals appear to the right of a verb like "believe" or "predict" or "mean" (as in ". . . you will come to believe that P just in case it's the case that P"). In most (but not all) such cases, the verb has the shorter of the two possible scopes; viz., the intended bracketing will be "(believe that P) iff P" rather than "believe that (P iff P)." From time to time, I'll use hyphens to indicate what goes with what.

8. This is actually stronger than what the spirit of the story I want to tell requires, which is just that experimental environments are designed to cause the experimenter's beliefs to change in the direction of increased correspondence to the world. Possible weakenings would include: They're designed to cause the subjective probability that the experimenter assigns to P to increase if it's the case that P, and to cause the subjective probability that he assigns to P to decrease if it's not the case that P. Or: they're designed to cause the experimenter's degree of belief in P to increase if it's the case that P and to cause his degree of belief in not P to increase if it's not the case that P.

The sorts of issues involved here are familiar from discussions of degrees of belief; and, since they are orthogonal to my main concerns, I propose to ignore them.

9. It's a subtext of this paper—never explicitly announced, but always at work below the surface—that the present epistemological views comport quite nicely with an informational approach to belief content. (See, for example, Fodor 1990 [727]). It's a consequence of informational semantic theories that beliefs that have the right sort of etiology are ipso facto true. It follows that if you work things properly, you can bring it about that what you believe is true *by* bringing it about that your believing it is caused in the right sort of way. The present view of experiments is that they are environments devised to cause one to have true beliefs about the hypothesis under investigation.

In passing: I am, of course, discussing the sort of experiments that is intended to choose among theories, not the kind that is supposed merely to collect data for later explanation. Still, people do sometimes run experiments that don't have experimental hypotheses, or that aren't designed to affect the epistemic relation that the scientific community bears to the experimental hypothesis. The latter are called *demonstration* experiments; the former, *fishing expeditions*. From the point of view of the present discussion, both are the sorts of exceptions that prove a rule.

10. This is the "means that" that's dear to informational semanticists; the one that means "indicates that"; the one you get in "all those clouds mean that it's going to rain." Bogen and Woodward argue, very convincingly in my view, that ". . . [experimental] data typically cannot be predicted or systematically explained by theory" (1988 [681], pp. 305–306) and that nothing in the epistemology of experimentation demands that such predictions/explanations should be forthcoming. Experimentation *does*, however, presuppose a background of theoretical claims about what the experimental outcomes (would) mean. The point of running experiments is to get results that are *interpretable*.

Perhaps it doesn't need saying that it's an empirical issue (not a matter of convention or stipulation or anything of that sort) whether it's true that an experimental outcome means what someone thinks it does.

11. "But why is it required that getting the predicted outcome should *cause* you to believe that P; why wouldn't it be good enough if getting the outcome *convinced* you that *P*?" I take it that to be convinced by an outcome that P is at least to be caused to believe that *P* by an outcome that one is convinced means that *P*. (Maybe that's all it is.)

12. In this sentence, "theories" refers, of course, to things-in-your-head, not to the abstract objects that the things-in-your-head express. It is another subtext of this paper that the epistemology I'm selling here comports nicely with an account of belief-states as relations to token mental representations, and with an account of belief fixation as a process which causes mental representations to be tokened. This is the so-called "Representational Theory of the Mind," which I've had on sale elsewhere for some years now. See, for example, Fodor 1975 [574].

13. I.e., acids on one end and tokens of the mental representation type "acid" in the scientist's belief box on the other, assuming RTM. (See the preceding footnote.)

14. The reader is urged to bear in mind that the present issues are epistemological, not semantic or ontological. The question is "how do our theories function to further the pursuit of knowledge?" and the answer is "instrumentally," as per the text. It is not implied thereby that their instrumental success constitutes the truth of our theories; to the contrary, what constitutes the truth of our theories is, of course, their correspondence with the world.

15. The preceding several paragraphs were written for people who—unlike Auntie, for example—are prepared to concede beliefs to organisms other than ourselves. For people who aren't, the point would be not that *cognitive* management is phylogenetically widespread, but that a sort of *behavioral*

management is which has much the same utility for animals that cognitive management has for us. Thus, the animal's orienting to foveate the noise source brings it about that, with some likelihood, the noise source will elicit Heffalump-appropriate behavior if and only if it is a Heffalump.

Putting it that way loses a generalization, but it makes Auntie much happier. Silly old Auntie.

16. However, a lot does follow that's *sociologically* interesting; keeping a stable of experts to exploit for purposes of cognitive management costs a mint, and the structure of our society undoubtedly reflects our ways of distributing the burden.

For example, the audience and the expert have to work out an arrangement according to which the audience must compose itself into a state of mental receptivity, to use the language of the text. Notice that the audience, as well as the expert, has an interest in this. There's no use consulting an oracle if you're not going to believe what it tells you. Why pay for advice if you're not going to take it, lawyers always ask.

Hence, I suppose, the cloud of ceremony in which our experts contrive to cloak themselves in order that we should be caused to believe that P when they tell us that P (and in which we conspire that they should cloak themselves in order that we should be caused to believe that P when they tell us that P). Think of the Pentagon and the AMA. Think of presidential inaugurations and academic processions. That the experts often don't know *much* more than the audience, does, of course, makes all this seem a little comic. (There's a cartoon that shows a medicine man in full ceremonial regalia making his apologies to the widow beside the corpse of his just expired client: "There's so much we still don't know," he explains.) But the arrangement is nevertheless rational on the assumption that the experts know at least a little more than the audience in the cases where it matters most that one act on true beliefs. Which, I suppose, some of them probably do.

10

Précis of *Knowledge and the Flow of Information*

Fred I. Dretske

Knowledge and the Flow of Information (Dretske 1981 [32]; henceforth *Knowledge*) is an attempt to develop a philosophically useful theory of information. To be philosophically useful the theory should: (1) preserve enough of our common understanding of information to justify calling it a theory *of* information; (2) make sense of (or explain its failure to make sense of) the theoretically central role information plays in the descriptive and explanatory efforts of cognitive scientists; and (3) deepen our understanding of the baffling place of mind, the chief consumer of information, in the natural order of things.

A secondary motive in writing this book, and in organizing its approach to philosophical problems around the notion of information, was to build a bridge, if only a terminological one, to cognitive science. Even if we don't have the same problems (psychologists are no more interested in Descartes's Demon than philosophers are in Purkinje's twilight shift), we have the same subject, and both sides could profit from improved communication.

In pursuit of these ends, it was found necessary to think of information as an *objective* commodity, as something whose existence (as information) is (largely) independent of the interpretative activities of conscious agents. It is common among cognitive scientists to regard information as a creation of the mind, as something we conscious agents assign to, or impose on, otherwise meaningless events. Information, like beauty, is in the eye of the beholder. For philosophical purposes though, this puts things exactly backward. It assumes what is to be explained. For we want to know what this interpretative ability amounts to, why some physical systems (typically, those with brains) have this capacity and others do not. What makes *some*

Reprinted from *The Behavioral and Brain Sciences* 6 (1983): 55–63, by permission of the publisher. Copyright © 1983, Cambridge University Press.

processors of information (persons, but not television sets) sources of meaning? If we *begin* our study by populating the world with fully developed cognitive systems, systems that can transform "meaning-less" stimuli into thoughts, beliefs, and knowledge (or whatever is involved in interpretation), we make the analysis of information more tractable, perhaps, but only by abandoning it as a tool in our quest to understand the nature of cognitive phenomena. We merely postpone the philosophical questions.

Part I of *Knowledge* develops a semantic theory of information, a theory of the propositional *content* of a signal (events, structure, or state of affairs). It begins by rehearsing some of the elementary ideas of the mathematical theory of communication (Shannon and Weaver 1949 [654]). This theory, though developed for quite different pur-poses, and though having (as a result) only the remotest connection (some would say *none*) with the kinds of cognitive issues of concern to this study, does, nonetheless, provide a key that can be used to articulate a semantical theory of information. Chapters 2 and 3 are devoted to *adapting* and *extending* this theory's account of an informa-tion source and channel into an account of how much information a *particular* signal carries about a source and what (if any) information this is.

Part II applies this theory of information to some traditional prob-lems in epistemology: knowledge, skepticism, and perception. Knowledge is characterized as information-produced belief. Percep-tion is a process in which incoming information is coded in analog form in preparation for further selective processing by cognitive (con-ceptual) centers. The difference between seeing a duck and recogniz-ing it *as* a duck (seeing *that* it is a duck) is to be found in the different way information about the duck is coded (analog vs. digital).

Part III is devoted to an information—theoretic analysis of what has come to be called our propositional attitudes—in particular, the belief that something is so. Belief, the *thinking* that something is so, is char-acterized in terms of the instantiation of structures (presumably neural) that have, through learning, acquired a certain information-carrying role. Instances of these structures (the types of which are identified as concepts) sometimes fail to perform satisfactorily. This is false belief.

Information

The mathematical theory of communication (Cherry 1951 [694]; Shan-non and Weaver 1949 [654]) is concerned with certain statistical quantities associated with "sources" and "channels." When a certain condition is realized at a source, and there are other possible conditions that might have been realized (each with its associated probability of occurring), the source can be thought of as a generator of information. The ensemble of possibilities has been reduced to a single reality, and the amount of information generated is a function of these possibilities and their associated probabilities. The die is cast. Any one of six faces might appear uppermost. A "3" appears. Six possibilities, all (let us say) equally likely, have been reduced to one. The source, in this case the throw of the die, generates 2.6 bits of information ($\log_2 6 = 2.6$).

But more important (for my purposes and for the purpose of understanding *communication*) is the measure of how much information is transmitted from one point to another, how much information there is at point r (receiver) about what is transpiring at s (source). Once again, communication theory is concerned with the statistical properties of the "channel" connecting r and s, because, for most engineering purposes, it is this channel whose characteristics must be exploited in designing effective coding strategies. The theory looks at a statistical quantity that is a certain weighted average of the conditional probabilities of all signals that can be transmitted from s to r. It does not concern itself with the individual events (the particular signals) except as a basis for computing the statistical functions that define the quantities of interest.

I skip over these matters rather lightly here, because it should be obvious that, insofar as communication theory deals with quantities that are statistical *averages* (sometimes called *entropy* to distinguish them from real information), it is *not* dealing with information as it is ordinarily understood. For information as it is ordinarily understood, and as it must figure in semantic and cognitive studies, is something associated with, and *only* with, individual events (signals, structures, conditions). It is only the particular signal (utterance, track, print, gesture, sequence of neural discharges) that has a content that can be given propositional expression (the content, message, or information carried by the signal). *This* is the relevant commodity in semantic and cognitive studies, and content—*what* information a signal carries— cannot be averaged. All one can do is average *how much* information is carried. There is no meaningful average for the information that my grandmother had a stroke and that my daughter is getting married. If we can say *how much* information these messages represent, then we can speak about their average. But this tells us nothing about *what* information is being communicated. Hence, the quantities of interest in engineering—and, of course, some psychophysical contexts (Attneave 1959 [536a]; Garner 1962 [577a]; Miller 1953 [789a])—are not the quantities of interest to someone, like myself, concerned to develop an account of *what* information travels from source to receiver (object to receptor, receptor to brain, brain to brain) during communication.

Nevertheless, though communication theory has its attention elsewhere, it does, as Sayre (1965 [646a]) and others have noted, highlight the relevant objective relations on which the communication of genuine information depends. For what this theory tells us is that the amount of information at r about s is a function of the *degree of lawful (nomic) dependence* between conditions at these two points. If two conditions are statistically independent (the way the ringing of *your* telephone is independent of the ringing of *mine*), then the one event carries no information about the other. When there is a lawful regularity between two events, statistical or otherwise, as there is between your dialing my number and my phone's ringing, then we can speak of one event's carrying information about the other. And, of course, this is the way we *do* speak. The ring *tells me* (informs me) that someone is calling my number, just as fingerprints carry information about the identity of the person who handled the gun, tracks in the snow about the animals in the woods, the honeybee's dance about the location of nectar, and light from a distant star about the chemical constitution of that body. Such events are pregnant with information, because they depend, in some lawfully regular way, on the conditions about which they are said to carry information.

If things are working properly, the ringing of my phone *tells* me that someone has dialed my number. It delivers this piece of information. It does *not* tell me that your phone is ringing, even if (coincidentally) your phone happens to be ringing at the same time. Even if A dials B's number whenever C dials D's number (so that D's phone rings *whenever* A dials B's number), we cannot say that the ringing of D's phone carries information about A's dialing activities—*not* if this "correlation" is a mere coincidence. We cannot say this, because the correlation, being (by hypothesis) completely fortuitous, does not affect the conditional *probability* of A's dialing B's number, given that D's phone is ringing. Of course, if we *know* about this (coincidental) correlation (though *how* one could know about its *persistence* is beyond me), we can predict one event from a knowledge of the other, but this doesn't change the fact that they are statistically independent. If

I correctly describe your future by consulting tea leaves, this is not genuine communication *unless* the arrangement of tea leaves somehow depends on what you are going to do, in the way a barometer depends on meteorological conditions and, therefore, indirectly on the impending weather. To deny the existence of mental telepathy is not to deny the possibility of improbable cooccurrences (between what *A* thinks and what *B* thinks *A* is thinking); it is, rather, to deny that they are manifestations of *lawful* regularities.

Communication theory only makes sense if it makes sense to talk about the probability of certain specific conditions given certain specific signals. This is so because the quantities of interest to communication theory are statistical functions of these probabilities. It is this *presupposed* idea that I exploit to develop an account of a signal's content. These conditional probabilities determine how much, and indirectly *what*, information a particular signal carries about a remote source. One needs only to stipulate that the content of the signal, the information it carries, be expressed by a sentence describing the condition (at the source) on which the signal depends in some regular, lawful way. I express this theoretical definition of a signal's (structure's) informational content in the following way:

A signal *r* carries the information that *s* is *F* = The conditional probability of *s*'s being *F*, given *r* (and *k*), is 1 (but, given *k* alone, less than 1)

My gas gauge carries the information that I still have some gas left, if and only if the conditional probability of my having some gas left, given the reading on the gauge, is 1. For the same reason, the discharge of a photoreceptor carries the information that a photon has arrived (perhaps a photon of a certain wavelength), and the pattern of discharge of a cluster of ganglion cells carries the information that there is a sharp energy gradient (a line) in the optic array (Lindsay and Norman 1972 [610a]; Rumelhart 1977 [643a]). The following comments explain the main features of this definition.

1. There are, essentially, three reasons for insisting that the value of the conditional probability in this definition be 1—nothing less. They are:

a. If a signal could carry the information that *s* was *F* while the conditional probability (of the latter, given the former) was less than 1 (.9 say), then the signal could carry the information that *s* was *F* (probability = .91), the information that *s* was *G* (probability = .91), but *not* the information that s was *F and G* (because the probability of their *joint* occurrence might be less than .9). I take this to be an unacceptable result.

b. I accept something I call the xerox principle: If C carries the information that *B*, and B's occurrence carries the information that *A*, then C carries the information that A. You don't *lose* information about the original (*A*) by perfectly reproduced copies (*B* of *A and* C of *B*). Without the transitivity this principle describes, the *flow* of information would be impossible. If we put the threshold of information at anything less than 1, though, the principle is violated. For (using the same numbers) the conditional probability of B, given C, could be .91, the conditional probability of A, given B, also .91, but the conditional probability of A, given C, less than .9. The noise (equivocation, degree of nomic *in*dependence, or nonlawful relation) between the end points of this communication channel is enough to break communication, even though every link in the chain passes along the information to its successor. Somehow the information fails to get through, despite the fact that it is nowhere lost.

c. Finally, there is no nonarbitrary place to put a threshold that will retain the intimate tie we all intuitively feel between knowledge and information. For, if information about s's being *F* can be obtained from a signal that makes the conditional probability of this situation only (say) .94, then information loses its cognitive punch. Think of a bag with 94 red balls and 6 white balls. If one is pulled at random (probability of red = .94), can you *know* (just from the fact that it was drawn from a bag with that composition of colored marbles) that it was red? Clearly not. Then why suppose you have the information that it is red?

The only reason I know for *not* setting the required probability this high is worries (basically skeptical in character) that there are no (or precious few) conditional probabilities of 1—hence, that no information is ever communicated. I address these worries in chapter 5. They raise issues (e.g., the idea of a "relevant alternative") that have received some attention in recent epistemology.

2. The definition captures the element that makes information (in contrast, say, to meaning) an important *epistemic* commodity. No structure can carry the information that s is *F* unless, in fact, s is *F*. False information, misinformation, and (grimace!) disinformation are not varieties of information—any more than a decoy duck is a kind of duck. A glance at the dictionary reveals that information is related to

intelligence, news, instruction, and knowledge—things that have an important connection to *truth*. And so it should be with any theoretical approximation to this notion. Information *is* an important commodity: We buy it, sell it, torture people to get it, and erect booths to dispense it. It should not be confused with meaning, despite some people's willingness to speak of anything (true, false, or meaningless) stored on a magnetic disk as information.

3. Information, as defined above, is an objective commodity, the sort of thing that can be delivered to, processed by, and transmitted from instruments, gauges, computers, and neurons. It is something that can be *in* the optic array,[1] on the printed page, carried by a temporal configuration of electrical pulses, and stored on a magnetic disk, and it exists there *whether or not anyone appreciates this fact or knows how to extract it*. It is something that was in this world before we got here. It was, I submit, the raw material out of which minds were manufactured.

The parenthetical *k* occurring in the definition above (and explained below) relativizes information to what the receiver already knows (if anything) about the possibilities at the source, but this relativization does not undermine the essential objectivity of the commodity so relativized (MacKay 1969 [612]). We still have the flow of information (perhaps not so much) without conscious agents who know things, but without a lawfully regular universe (no matter how much knowledge we assign the occupants), no information is ever communicated.

4. A signal's informational content is not unique. There is, generally speaking, no *single* piece of information in a signal or structure. For anything that carries the information that *s* is a square, say, also carries the information that it is a rectangle, a parallelogram, *not* a circle, a circle *or* a square, and so on. If the acoustic pattern reaching my ears carries the information that the doorbell is ringing, and the ringing of the bell carries the information that the doorbell button is being pressed, then the acoustic pattern also carries the information that the doorbell button is being pressed (xerox principle). The one piece of information is *nested* in the other. This, once again, is as it should be. The linguistic meaning of an utterance may be unique (distinguishable, for instance, from what it implies), but not the information carried by that utterance. Herman's statement that he won't come to my party means, simply, that he won't come to my party. It doesn't mean (certainly not in any linguistically relevant sense of "meaning")

that he doesn't like me or that he can speak English, although his utterance may well carry these pieces of information.

5. The definition of a signal's informational content has been relativized to k, what the receiver (in the event that we are talking about a communication system in which the receiver—organism or computer—already has knowledge about the possible conditions existing at the source) already knows. This is a minor concession to the way we think and talk about information. The k is dischargeable by recursive applications of the definition. So, for instance, if I receive the information that your knight is *not* on KB-3 (by some signal), this carries the information that it *is* on KB-5, *if* I already know that the other possible positions to which your knight could have moved are already occupied by your pieces. To someone lacking such knowledge, the same signal does not carry this information (though it still carries the information that your knight is not on KB-3). The less we know, the more pregnant with information must be the signals we receive if we are to learn.

6. There is, finally, the important fact, already mentioned, that the informational content of a signal is a function of the *nomic* (or law-governed) relations it bears to other conditions. Unless these relations are what philosophers like to call "counterfactual supporting" relations (a symptom of a background, lawful regularity), the relations in question are not such as to support an assignment of informational content (Dretske 1977 [712]). The reason my thermometer carries information about the temperature of *my* room (the information *that* it is 72°F. in the room), but not about your room though both rooms are at the same temperature, is that (given its location) the registration of my thermometer is such that it *would not* read 72°F. *unless* my room was at this temperature. This isn't true of your room.

This fact helps explain an (otherwise puzzling) feature of information and, ultimately, of the cognitive attitudes that depend on it (belief, knowledge). For it is by virtue of this fact that a structure (some neural state, say) can carry the information that s (a distal object) is F (spherical) without carrying the information that s is G (plastic), even though (let us suppose) all spheres (in the relevant domain) are plastic. If the fact that all spheres are plastic is sheer accident, not underwritten by any lawful constraint, then the neural state might depend on s's being spherical without depending, in the same way, on its being plastic. Another way of expressing this fact (dear to the heart of philosophers) is to say that the informational content of a structure exhibits *intentional* properties. By saying that it exhibits intentional properties, I mean what philosophers typically mean by this technical term: that the informational content of a signal or structure (like the content of a belief, a desire, or knowledge) depends, not only on the reference (extension) of the terms used in its sentential expression, but on their *meaning* (intension). That is, in the sentential expression of a structure's informational content, one cannot substitute coreferring (i.e., referring to the same thing, coextensional) expressions without (possible) alteration in content. Just as a belief that this man is my cousin differs from a belief that he is Susan's husband, despite the fact that Susan's husband *is* my cousin (these expressions have the same reference), the information (as defined above) that he is my cousin differs from the information that he is Susan's husband. A signal can carry the one piece of information without carrying the other.

We have, then, an account of a signal's informational content that exhibits a degree of intentionality. We have, therefore, an account of information that exhibits some of the attributes we hope eventually to be able to explain in our account of our cognitive states. Perhaps, that is, one can know that *s* is *F* without knowing that *s* is *G*, despite the fact that all *F*s are *G*, *because* knowledge requires information, and one *can* get the information that *s* is *F* without getting the information that it is *G*. If intentionality is "the mark of the mental," then we already have, in the physically objective notion of information defined above (even without *k*), the traces of mentality. And we have it in a form that voltmeters, thermometers, and radios have. What distinguishes us from these more pedestrian processors of information is not our occupation of intentional states, but the sophisticated way we process, encode, and utilize the information we receive. It is our *degree* of intentionality (see part III).

Knowledge

Knowledge is defined (chapter 4) as information-caused (or causally sustained) belief. The analysis is restricted to perceptual knowledge of contingent states of affairs (conditions having an informational measure of something greater than 0) of a *de re* form: seeing (hence, knowing) that this (the perceptual object) is blue, moving, a dog, or my grandmother.

This characterization of knowledge is a version of what has come to be called the "regularity analysis" of knowledge (Armstrong 1973 [3]; Dretske 1969 [31]; 1971 [287]). It is an attempt to get away from the philosopher's usual bag of tricks (justification, reasons, evidence, etc.) in order to give a more realistic picture of what perceptual knowledge is. One doesn't need reasons, evidence, or rational justification for one's belief that there is wine left in the bottle, if the bottle is sitting in good light directly in front of one. One can *see* that it is still half-full. And, rightly or wrongly, I wanted a characterization that would at least allow for the possibility that animals (a frog, rat, ape, or my dog) could know things without my having to suppose them capable of the more sophisticated intellectual operations involved in traditional analyses of knowledge.

What can it mean to speak of information as causing anything—let alone causing a belief? (The analysis of belief, the propositional attitude most often taken as the subjective component of knowledge, is postponed until part III.) Assuming that belief is some kind of internal state with a content expressible as s is F, this is said to be caused by the information that s is F, if and only if those physical properties of the signal by virtue of which it carries this information are the ones that are causally efficacious in the production of the belief. So, for instance, not just any knock on the door tells you it is your friend. The (prearranged) signal is three quick knocks, followed by a pause, and then another three quick knocks. It is that particular signal, that particular temporal pattern, that constitutes the information-carrying property of the signal. The amplitude and pitch are irrelevant. When it is this pattern of knocks that causes you to believe that your friend has arrived, then (it is permissible to say that) the *information* that your friend has arrived causes you to believe he has arrived. The knocks might also frighten away a fly, cause the windows to rattle, and disturb the people upstairs. But what has these effects is not the information, because, presumably, the fly would have been frightened, the windows rattled, and the neighbors disturbed by *any* sequence of knocks of roughly the same amplitude. Hence, the information is not the cause.

In most ordinary situations, there is no explanatory value in talking about the information (in an event) as the cause of something, because there is some easily identifiable physical (nonrelational) property of the event that can be designated as the cause. Why talk of the information (that your friend has arrived) as the cause, when it is clear enough that it is the particular temporal patterns of knocks (or acoustic vibrations) that was the effective agent?

The point of this definition is not to *deny* that there are physical properties of the signal (e.g., the temporal pattern of knocks in the above example) that cause the belief, but to say *which* of these properties must be responsible for the effect if the resultant belief is to qualify as knowledge.[2] If the belief that your friend has arrived is caused by the knock, but the pattern of knocks is irrelevant, then (assuming that someone else could be knocking at your door), though you are caused to believe it by the knock on the door, you do not *know* your friend has arrived. Those properties of the signal that carry the information (that your friend has arrived) are not the ones that are causally responsible for your belief.

The need to speak in this more abstract way—of information (rather than the physical event carrying this information) as the cause of something—becomes much more compelling as we turn to more complex information processing systems. For we then discover that there are an indefinitely large number of different sensory inputs, having no identifiable physical (nonrelational) property in common, that all have the same cognitive outcome. The only way we can capture the relevant causal regularities is by retreating to a more abstract characterization of the cause, a characterization in terms of its relational (informational) properties. We often do this sort of thing in our ordinary descriptions of what we see. Why did he stop? He could see that he was almost out of gas. We speak here of the information (that he was almost out of gas) that is contained in (carried by) the fuel gauge pointer and *not* the fuel gauge pointer itself (which, of course, is what we actually see), because it is a property of this pointer (its position, not its size or color) carrying this vital piece of information that is relevantly involved in the production of the belief. We, as it were, ignore the messenger bringing the information (the fuel gauge indicator) in order to focus on what information the messenger brings. We also ignore the infinite variety of optical inputs (all of varying size, shape, orientation, intensity) in order to focus on the information they carry. Often we have no choice. The only thing they have in common is the information they bear.[3]

A belief that *s* is *F* may not itself carry the information that *s* is *F* just because it is caused by this information (thereby qualifying as knowledge). A gullible person may believe almost anything you tell him—for example, that there are three elephants in your backyard.

His beliefs may not, as a result, have any reliable relation to the facts (this is why we don't believe him when he tells us something). Yet this does not prevent him from knowing something he observes firsthand. When he *sees* the elephants in your backyard, he *knows* they are there, whatever other signal (lacking the relevant information) might have caused him to believe this. If the belief is caused by the appropriate information, it qualifies as knowledge whatever *else* may be capable of causing it.

This definition of knowledge accords, I think, with our ordinary, intuitive judgments about when someone knows something. You can't know that Jimmy is home by seeing him come through the door, if it could be his twin brother Johnny. Even if it is extremely unlikely to be Johnny (for Johnny rarely comes home this early in the afternoon), as long as this remains a relevant possibility, it prevents one from seeing (hence, knowing) *that* it is Jimmy (though one may be caused to *believe* it is Jimmy). The information that it is Jimmy is missing. The optical input is equivocal.

Furthermore, this account of knowledge neatly avoids some of the puzzles that intrigue philosophers (and bore everyone else to death). For example, Gettier-like difficulties (Gettier 1963 [735]) arise for any account of knowledge that makes knowledge a product of some justificatory relationship (having good evidence, excellent reasons, etc.) that *could* relate one to something false. For on all these accounts (unless special ad hoc devices are introduced to prevent it), one can be justified (in a way appropriate to knowledge) in believing something that is, in fact, false (hence, not know it); also know that Q (which happens to be true) is a logical consequence of what one believes, and come to believe Q as a result. On some perfectly natural assumptions, then, one is justified (in a way appropriate to knowledge) in believing the truth (Q). But one obviously doesn't *know* Q is true. This is a problem for justificational accounts. The problem is evaded in the information—theoretic model, because one can get into an appropriate justificational relationship to something false, but one cannot get into an appropriate informational relationship to something false.

Similarly, the so-called lottery paradox (Kyburg 1961 [604]; 1965 [769]) is disarmed. If one could know something without the information (as here defined), one should be able to know *before the drawing* that the 999,999 eventual losers in a (fair) lottery, for which a million tickets have been sold, are going to lose. For they all *are* going to lose, and one knows that the probability of each one's (not, of course, *all*) losing is negligibly less than 1. Hence, one is perfectly justified in believing (truly) that each one is going to lose. But, clearly, one cannot know this. The paradox is avoided by acknowledging what is already inherent in the information—theoretical analysis—that one cannot know one is going to lose in such a lottery no matter how many outstanding tickets there may be. And the reason one cannot is (barring a fixed drawing) the information that one is going to lose is absent. There remains a small, but nonetheless greater than 0, amount of equivocation for each outcome.

There are further, technical advantages to this analysis (discussed in chapter 4), but many will consider these advantages purchased at too great a price. For the feeling will surely be that one never gets the required information. *Not* if information requires a conditional probability of 1. The stimuli are *always* equivocal to some degree. Most of us know about Ames's demonstrations, Brunswik's ecological and functional validities, and the fallibility of our own sensory systems. If knowledge requires information, and information requires 0 equivocation, then precious little, if anything, is ever known.

These concerns are addressed in chapter 5, a chapter that will prove tedious to almost everyone but devoted epistemologists (i.e., those who take skepticism seriously). An example will have to suffice to summarize this discussion.

A perfectly reliable instrument (or one *as* reliable as modern technology can make it) has its output reliably correlated with its input. The position of a mobile pointer on a calibrated scale carries information about the magnitude of the quantity being measured. Communication theorists would (given certain tolerances) have no trouble in describing this as a noiseless channel. If we ask about the conditional probabilities, we note that these are determined by regarding certain parameters as fixed (or simply ignoring them). The spring *could* weaken, it *could* break, its coefficient of elasticity *could* fluctuate unpredictably. The electrical resistance of the leads (connecting the instrument to the apparatus on which measurements are being taken) *could* change. Error would be introduced if any of these possibilities was realized. And who is to say they are not *possibilities?* There *might* even be a prankster, a malevolent force, or a god who chooses to interfere. Should all these possibilities go into the reckoning in computing the noise, equivocation, and information conveyed? To do so, of course, would be to abandon communication theory altogether. For this theory requires for its application a system of fixed, stable, enduring conditions *within* which the degree of covariation in other conditions can be evaluated. If every logical possibility is deemed a possibility, then everything is noise. Nothing is communicated. In the same manner, if everything is deemed a *thing* for purposes of assessing the emptiness of containers (dust? molecules? radiation?), then no room, pocket, or refrigerator is ever empty. The framework of fixed, stable, enduring conditions within which one reckons the flow of information is what I call "channel conditions." Possible variations in these conditions are excluded. They are what epistemologists call "irrelevant alternatives" (Dretske 1970 [286]; Goldman 1976 [339]).

And so it is with our sensory systems. Certainly, in some sense of the word *could*, Herman, a perfectly normal adult, could be hallucinating the entire football game. There is no logical contradiction in this supposition; it is the same sense in which a voltmeter's spring *could* behave like silly putty. But this is not a sense of *could* that is relevant to cognitive studies or the determination of what information these systems are capable of transmitting. The probability of these things happening is set at 0. If they remain possibilities in some sense, they are not possibilities that affect the flow of information.

This discussion merely accentuates the way our talk of information *presupposes* a stable, regular world in which some things can be taken as fixed for the purpose of assessing the covariation in other things. There is here a certain arbitrary or pragmatic element (in what may be taken as permanent and stable enough to qualify as a channel condition), but this element (it is argued) is precisely what we find when we put our cognitive concepts under the same analytical microscope. It is not an objection to regarding the latter as fundamentally information-dependent notions.

Perception

Perception itself is often regarded as a cognitive activity: a form of recognizing, identifying, categorizing, distinguishing, and classifying the things around us (R. N. Haber 1969 [587]). But there is what philosophers (at least *this* philosopher) think of as an *extensional* and an *intensional* way of describing our perceptions (Dretske 1969 [31]). We see the duck (extensional: a concrete noun phrase occurs as object of the verb) and we recognize it (see it) as a duck—see *that* it is a duck (intensional: typically taking a factive nominal as complement of the verb). Too many people (both philosophers and psychologists) tend to think about perception *only* in the latter form, and in so doing they systematically ignore one of the most salient aspects of our mental life: the *experiences* we have when we see, hear, and taste things. The experience in question, the sort of thing that occurs in you when you see a duck (without necessarily recognizing it *as* a duck), the internal state without which (though you may be looking at the duck) you don't *see* the duck, is a stage in the processing of sensory information in which information about the duck is coded in what I call analog form, in preparation for its selective utilization by the cognitive centers (where the *belief* that it is a duck may be generated).

To describe what object you see is to describe what object you are getting information about; to describe what you recognize it as (see it to be) is to describe what information (about that object) you have succeeded in cognitively processing (e.g., that it is a duck). You can see a duck, get information *about* a duck, without getting, let alone cognitively processing, the information that it is a duck. Try looking at one in dim light at such a distance that you can barely see it. To confuse seeing a duck with recognizing it (either as a duck or as something else) is simply to confuse sentience with sapience.

Our experience of the world is rich in information in a way that our consequent beliefs (if any) are not. A normal child of two can *see* as well as I can (probably better). The child's experience of the world is (I rashly conjecture) as rich and as variegated as that of the most knowledgeable adult. What is lacking is a capacity to exploit these experiences in the generation of reliable beliefs (knowledge) about what the child sees. I, my daughter, and my dog can all see the daisy. I see it as a daisy. My daughter sees it simply as a flower. And who knows about my dog?

There are severe limits to our information-processing capabilities (Miller 1956 [790]), but most of these limitations affect our ability to cognitively process the information supplied in such profusion by our sensory systems (Rock 1975 [639]). More information *gets in* than we can manage to digest and get out (in some appropriate response). Glance around a crowded room, a library filled with books, or a garden ablaze with flowers. How much do you see? Is all the information embodied in the sensory representation (experience) given a cognitive form? No. You saw 28 people in a single brief glance (the room was well lit, all were in easy view, and none was occluded by other objects or people). Do you believe you saw 28 people? No. You didn't count and you saw them so briefly that you can only guess. That there were 28 people in the room is a piece of information that was contained *in* the sensory representation without receiving the kind of cognitive transformation (what I call digitalization) associated with conceptualization (belief). This homely example illustrates what is more convincingly demonstrated by masking experiments with brief visual displays (Averbach and Coriell 1961 [675]; Neisser 1967 [622]; Sperling 1960 [834]).

Although it is misleading to put it this way, our sensory experience encodes information in the way a photograph encodes information about the scene at which the camera is pointed. This is *not* to say that our sensory experience is pictorial (consists of sounds, sights, smells, etc.). I don't think there are daisy replicas inside the head, although I *do* think there is information about—and in *this* sense a representation of—daisies in the head. Nor do I mean to suggest (by the picture metaphor) that we are *aware of* (somehow perceive) these internal sensory representations. On the contrary, what we perceive (what we are aware *of*) are the things represented by these internal representations (not the representations themselves), the things *about which* they carry information (see section on "The Objects of Perception" in chapter 6).

I see a red apple in a white bowl surrounded by a variety of other objects. I recognize it as an apple. I come to believe that it is an apple. The belief has a content that we express with the words, "That is an apple." The content of this belief does not represent the apple as red, as large, or as lying next to an orange. I may have (other) beliefs about these matters, but the belief in question abstracts from the concreteness of the sensory representation (icon, sensory information store, experience) in order to represent it simply as an apple. However, these additional pieces of information *are* contained in the sensory experience of the apple. As Haber and Hershenson (1973 [587a]) put it (in commenting on a specific experimental setup), "It appears as if all of the information in the retinal projection is available in the iconic storage, since the perceiver can extract whichever part is asked for."

In passing from the sensory to the cognitive representation (from seeing the apple to realizing that it is an apple), there is a systematic stripping away of components of information (relating to size, color, orientation, surroundings), which makes the experience of the apple the phenomenally rich thing we know it to be, in order to feature *one* component of this information—the information that it is an apple. Digitalization (of, for example, the information that s is an apple) is a process whereby a piece of information is taken from a richer matrix of information in the sensory representation (where it is held in what I call "analog" form) and featured to the exclusion of all else. The difference between the analog and digital coding of information is illustrated by the way a picture of an apple (that carries the information that it is an apple) differs from a statement that it is an apple. Both represent it *as* an apple, but the one embeds this information in an informationally richer representation. Essential to this process of digitalization (the essence of conceptualization) is the *loss* of this excess information.

Digitalization is, of course, merely the information—theoretic version of stimulus generalization. Until information is deleted, nothing corresponding to recognition, classification, or identification has occurred. Nothing distinctively cognitive or conceptual has occurred. To design a pattern-recognition routine for a digital computer, for example, is to design a routine in which information *inessential* to s's being an instance of the letter A (information about its specific size, orientation, color) is systematically discarded (treated as noise) in the production of some single type of internal structure, which, in turn, will produce some identificatory output label (Uhr 1973 [660]). If all the computer could do was pass along the information it received, it could not be credited with recognizing anything at all. It would not be responding to the essential sameness of different inputs. It would be merely a sophisticated transducer. Learning, the acquisition of concepts, is a process whereby we acquire the ability to extract, in this way, information from the sensory representation. Until that happens, we can see but we do not believe.

Belief

The content of a belief, what we believe when we believe (think) that something is so, can be either true or false. If we think of beliefs as internal representations (as I do), then these representations must be capable of *mis* representing how things stand. This is one aspect of intentionality.

Furthermore, if two sentences, S_1 and S_2, mean something different, then the belief we express with S_1 is different from the belief we express with S_2. Believing that a man is your brother is different from believing that he is my uncle (even if your brother is my uncle), because the sentences "He is your brother" and "He is my uncle" mean something different. A difference in meaning is sufficient, not necessary, for a difference in corresponding beliefs. The belief you express with the words "I am sick" is different from the belief I express with these words, despite the fact that the words mean the same thing. They have a different reference. This is a second aspect of intentionality.

But beliefs not only have a content exhibiting these peculiar intentional characteristics; they also, in association with desires, purposes, and fears, help to determine behavior. They are, if we can trust our ordinary ways of thinking, intentional entities with a hand on the steering wheel (Armstrong 1973 [3]).

It is the purpose of part III to give a unified, information—theoretic account of these entities. The account is incomplete in a number of important ways, but the underlying purpose is to exhibit the way meanings (insofar as these are understood to be the conceptual contents of our internal states) are developed out of informational contents.

We have already seen (chapter 3) the way information-bearing structures have a content (the information they carry—e.g., that s is F) exhibiting traces of intentionality. But this is only what I call the first order of intentionality. If two properties are lawfully related in the right way, then no signal can carry information about the one without carrying information about the other. No structure can have the (informational) content that s is F without having the (informational) content that s is G, if it turns out that nothing *can* be F without being G. This is the first respect in which the informational content of a structure fails to display the degree of intentionality of a belief (we can certainly believe that s is F without believing that s is G, despite the nomic connection between F and G).

The second respect in which information-carrying structures are ill prepared to serve as beliefs, despite their possession of content, is that, as we have seen, nothing can carry the information that s is F, nothing can have this informational content, unless, in fact, s is F. But we can certainly believe that something is so without its being so.

Without the details, the basic strategy in part III is quite simple. Consider a map. What makes the symbols on a map *say* or *mean* one thing, not another? What makes a little patch of blue ink on a map mean that there is a body of water in a specific location (whether or not there actually *is* a body of water there)? It seems that it acquires this meaning, this content, by virtue of the information-carrying *role* that that symbol (in this case, a *conventionally* selected and used sign) plays in the production and use of maps. The symbol *means* this because that is the information it was designed to carry. In the case of maps, of course, the flow of information from map-maker to map-user is underwritten by the executive fidelity of the map-makers. A type of structure, in this case blue ink, means there is water there, even though particular instances of that (type of) structure may, through ignorance or inadvertence, fail to carry this information. Misrepresentation becomes possible, because instances (tokens) of a structure (type) that has been assigned (and in this sense has acquired) an information-carrying role may fail to perform in accordance with that role. The instances mean what they do by virtue of their being instances of a certain *type*, and the structure type gets its meaning from its (assigned) communicative function.

Neural structures, of course, are not conventionally assigned an information-carrying role. They are not, in this sense, symbols. Nevertheless, they acquire such a role, I submit, during their development in learning (concept acquisition). In teaching a child what a bird is, for example, in giving the child this concept (so that the youngster can subsequently have beliefs to the effect that this is a bird, that is not), we expose the child to positive and negative instances of the concept in question (with some kind of appropriate feedback) in order to develop a sensitivity to the kind of information (that *s* is a bird) that defines the concept. When the child can successfully identify birds, distinguish them from other animals (how this actually happens is, as far as I am concerned, a miracle), we have created something in the child's head that responds, in some consistent way, to the information that something is a bird. When the learning is successful, we have given the pupil a new concept, a new capacity, to exploit in subsequent classificatory and identificatory activities. If the child then sees an airplane and says "bird," this stimulus has triggered another token of a structure type that was developed to encode the information that the perceptual object was a bird (thereby representing it *as* a bird). We have a case of misrepresentation, a false belief.[4]

But we still have not captured the full intentionality of beliefs. In teaching our child the concept *water*, for instance, why say that the structure that develops to encode information about water is not, instead, a structure that was developed to encode information about the presence of oxygen atoms? After all, any incoming signal that carries the information that *s* is water carries (nested in it) the information that *s* has oxygen atoms in it (since there is a lawful regularity between something's being water and its having oxygen atoms in it).

The answer to this question is, of course, that the child has *not* developed a sensitivity to the information that *s* has oxygen atoms in it just because the pupil has been taught to respond positively to signals *all* of which carry that information. This can easily be demonstrated by testing the child with samples that are not water but do have oxygen atoms in them (rust, air, etc.). The crucial fact is that, although every signal to which the child is taught to respond positively carries information about the presence of oxygen atoms, it is not the properties of the signal carrying *this* information to which the child has acquired a sensitivity. Recall, it is those properties of the signal that are causally responsible for the child's positive response that define what information he is responding to and, hence, what concept he has acquired when he has completed his training. These properties (if the training was reasonably successful) are those carrying the information that the substance is water (or some approximation thereto–as time goes by, the concept may be refined, its information-response characteristics modified, into something more nearly resembling our mature concept of water).

Concept acquisition (of this elementary, ostensive sort) is essentially a process in which a system acquires the capacity to extract a piece of information from a variety of sensory representations *in* which it occurs. The child sees birds in a variety of colors, orientations, activities, and shapes. The sensory representations are infinitely variegated. To learn what a bird is is to learn to recode this analogically held information (that *s* is a bird) into a single form that can serve to determine a consistent, univocal response to these diverse stimuli. Until such structures have been developed, or unless we come into this world with them preformed (see the discussion of innate concepts in chapter 9), nothing of cognitive significance has taken place.

Notes

1. Though I am sympathetic to some of the (earlier) views of the late James Gibson (1950 [579]; 1966 [580]), and though some of my discourse on information (e.g., its availability in the proximal stimulus) is reminiscent of Gibson's language, this work was not intended as support for Gibson's views—certainly not the more extravagant claims (1979) [581]. If criticized for getting

Gibson wrong, I will plead "no contest." I wasn't trying to get him right. If we disagree, so much the worse for one of us at least.

2. This is not so much a denial of Fodor's (1980) [725] formality condition as it is an attempt to say *which* syntactical (formal) properties of the representations must figure in the computational processes if the resulting transformations are to mirror faithfully our ordinary ways of describing them to terms of their semantical relations.

3. I skip here a discussion of information's *causally sustaining* a belief. The idea is simply that one may already believe something when one receives the relevant supporting information. In this case, the belief is not caused or produced by the information. It nonetheless—after acquisition of the relevant information—qualifies as knowledge if it is, later, causally sustained by this information.

4. In my eagerness to emphasize the way conceptual content is determined by etiological factors (the information-response characteristics of the internal structures) and to contrast it with the (behavioristically inspired) functionalist account (where *what* you believe is largely determined by the kind of output it produces), I seriously misrepresented (in chapter 8) Dennett's 1969 [561] position. Dennett stresses, as I do, the importance of the way these internal structures *mediate* input and output. He does, however, trace their ultimate significance, meaning, or content to the kind of (appropriate) behavior they produce.

11

Computational Complexity and the Universal Acceptance of Logic

Christopher Cherniak

When W. V. Quine says, "better translation imposes our logic" upon the beliefs of any agent we try to interpret, and, furthermore, "the logical truths, or the simple ones, will go without saying; everyone will unhesitatingly assent to them if asked,"[1] it is natural to wonder about the universal acceptance of logic. Let us consider the following version of the thesis: Any rational agent must accept a logic, that is, at least a sound and complete first-order deductive system. I shall argue that the thesis is false under some natural and philosophically important interpretations. The discussion identifies relationships between computational-complexity theory, recent psychological studies of the formal incorrectness of everyday reasoning, and more realistic theories of rationality.

Prima facie, the pattern of complexity-theoretic results in recent years constitutes a kind of practical analogue of the classical absolute unsolvability theorems of the 1930s. The project that emerges is to find the philosophical implications of these results, just as we have been trying to interpret the classical unsolvability results. In particular, if complexity theory in some sense "cuts the computational universe at its joints"—providing a principled basis for a hierarchy of qualitative distinctions between practically feasible and unfeasible tasks—then we need to examine the idea that, in at least some interesting cases, rationality models ought not to entail procedures that are computationally intractable. Complexity theory raises the possibility that formally correct deductive procedures may sometimes be so slow as to yield computational paralysis; hence the "quick but dirty" heuristics uncovered by the psychological research may be not

Reprinted from *The Journal of Philosophy*, vol. LXXXI (1984): 739–758, by permission of the author and the publisher. Copyright © 1984, *The Journal of Philosophy*.

irrational sloppiness, but instead the ultimate speed-reliability trade-off to evade intractability. With a theory on nonidealized rationality, complexity theory thereby "justifies the ways of Man" to this extent.

To begin, what is, or would be, a universally accepted logic? At a minimum, the thesis would be that all rational agents accept *some* sound and complete set of laws or axioms and inference rules for first-order logic, as opposed to a claim of the universal acceptance of a particular set of "fundamental" logical laws and rules, or even more strongly, a claim of universal acceptance of all logical truths. The weakest thesis, therefore, could be false either in that: (a) an agent might not accept a complete deductive system; he might have a "cognitive blind spot"; or (b) the agent might accept only an unsound or even inconsistent system; e.g., he might use some rule that did not guarantee preservation of truth in inference, perhaps a "quick but dirty" heuristic; or, more strongly, (c) every law or rule the agent used might be unsound or also inconsistent. I shall deal almost entirely with classical logic. This is not to prejudge the issue of the adequacy of nonstandard logics; the case of classical logic is basic, and the argument should be generalizable to other logics. Whatever one's choice of logic, the prior, and usually unacknowledged, question is whether a sound and complete logic by any standard is in fact the best choice.

I Ideal Rationality

Let us examine the concept of a rational agent which is involved in the thesis of the universal acceptance of logic. Some rationality constraint on an agent's cognitive system of beliefs and desires is the most fundamental law of psychology, more basic than any low-level empirical generalization. It is generally recognized in this philosophy of psychology that, for instance, although consistency may be the hobgoblin of small minds, consistency is a condition for having any mind at all: no rationality, no agent. The conventional strategy in the cognitive sciences has been first to adopt a rather extreme idealization of the rationality required of an agent and, then, perhaps, if they are noticed, to explain away departures of real human behavior from the ideal model.

The models of the agent prevalent in decision, game, and economic theory and in philosophy require that the agent be a maximizer of expected utility, that is, that the agent A satisfy an ideal general rationality condition, a version of which is: If A has a particular belief-desire set, A would undertake all and only actions that are apparently appropriate.[2] Here an action is "apparently appropriate" if, according to A's beliefs, it would tend to satisfy A's desires. An agent who is able to choose his actions so well has to have a great deal of logical insight. In particular, he must satisfy an *ideal inference condition:*

A would make all deductively sound inferences from his belief set which are apparently appropriate and would not mistakenly make any unsound ones.

Otherwise, A might miss some apparently appropriate actions, for instance.

Now, must an ideally rational agent in this sense accept a logic? For the agent to be able to perform all sound inferences that might turn out to be apparently appropriate and not to make unsound ones, he must meet Cartesian standards of perfection: he must in effect be both infallible and able to have an opinion on anything with respect to logic. Such an agent cannot accept an unsound or incomplete deductive system. If he accepts an unsound system for making some of his inferences, he will not be guaranteed to make only sound inferences, appropriate or otherwise; and if he accepts an incomplete system, he will not be able to make some sound inferences that might turn out to be appropriate. In either case, he will not satisfy the ideal inference condition. Therefore, an ideal agent must accept a sound and complete logic if he is to perform required reasoning by means of a formal deductive system.

II Undecidability

If a rationality requirement is the most basic psychological law, the next most basic fact of our psychology is that we are finite objects. The ideal rationality conditions abstract from this fundamental fact of human existence: we are in the finitary predicament of having fixed limits on our cognitive resources, in particular, on our memory capacity and computing time. The standard model in effect assumes, for such purposes as simplification of theory, that a human being has God's brain; for such an ideal agent much of the deductive sciences would be trivial.

If we suppose the agent is finite, there is still another cost for the idea of an ideal agent using only formal deductive procedures. For ideal rationality requires more than just use of a sound and complete logic. The agent has to be able to use that logic very well, so well that any given first-order sentence can be formally proved or disproved in a finite number of steps; otherwise, the ideal agent would not be *guaranteed* always to succeed in making all needed sound inferences (e.g., any arbitrary inference he thought his survival depended upon), and also never to make unsound ones. No heuristic procedure for using the deductive system, however good, would suffice unless it was perfect, with no possibility of failure, and hence in fact algorithmic. (Nor could any recursive enumeration procedure suffice by itself, since the agent would wait forever without finding out that some inferences were unsound.) This finitely represented perfect formal ability, of course, would constitute a decision procedure for first-order logic, which Church's theorem demonstrates to be impossible.

Hence, the ideal rationality conditions are very ideal indeed, in that they entail either the most basic practical impossibility—the use of infinite resources—or else a logical contradiction, like a square circle. Of course, the ideal rationality model remains an indispensable simplification of computational reality for many situations—for example, as one norm or "regulative ideal" for evaluating quick and dirty procedures. But some care is required; using the idealization could be a bit as if Hilbert had retained the presupposition of formalism that all number-theoretic truths are formally provable "as a convenient approximation" in the face of Gödel's incompleteness theorem.

But perhaps the agent might accomplish deductive tasks by some entirely nonformal means, for instance, by immediate synthetic a priori intuition of the deductive relations among the propositions he believed. The agent might do this by direct, quasi-perceptual, Gödelian insight into an independent realm of Platonic entities, or by means of his transcendental ego, situated outside of space, time, causality, and so on, as Kant and intuitionists such as Brouwer have identified it. Conformance to the ideal-inference condition through such faculties of intuition may seem little better than doing so by means of an oracle or miraculously perfect luck in guessing; for example, physicalists and those committed to information-processing models of cognition will not be satisfied with even the form of explanations like these. These procedures remain in need of at least the outlines of a scheme of explanation: The alternative procedure has to be such as to guarantee inferential success nonalgorithmically. With intuitive access to a Platonic realm, it is no longer clear that an agent *is* restricted to finite cognitive resources, e.g., of time and space.

III Computational Complexity

In fact, the deductive ability of the ideal agent is even further removed from computational reality. Even where there is no absolute undecidability, a kind of practical undecidability seems to extend further down, to the most basic parts of logic, to the very core of the notion of computation. In some respects, it is as if Church's theorem applied even to the propositional calculus. Of course, a decision procedure exists for tautological soundness—for example, by use of truth tables. But although a tautology decision procedure is in principle possible, it now appears to be inherently "computationally intractable" and, in some sense, to be extremely unfeasible as a practical matter, e.g., to require computations for relatively simple cases that would exceed the capacities of an ideal computer having the resources of the entire known universe. What is the philosophical significance of such intractability?

The above tautology result is in the field of computational complexity, an area that has grown rapidly during the last decade and is yielding practical unsolvability results which may be as interesting in some ways for philosophy as the classical absolute unsolvability results of the 1930s.[3] (Perhaps philosophy has overlooked the field so far because of a tendency to conclude that if a problem is decidable in principle, then it must be trivial, at least for philosophy conceived of as a "pure" nonempirical discipline.[4]) In complexity theory, feasibility of an algorithm is evaluated in terms of whether its execution time grows as a polynomial function of the size of input instances of the problem. If it does (as does any familiar procedure for arithmetical addition, for example), the algorithm is generally treated as computationally feasible. If it does not and instead increases faster, usually as an exponential function (as does exhaustive search of the game tree in chess, for example), the algorithm is generally regarded as intractable.

Such intractability turns out to a large extent to be independent of how the problem is represented and of the computer model (e.g., random-access or deterministic Turing machine) involved. Just as Turing computability is a formal explication of our intuitive notion of computability, polynomial-time computability can be viewed as one formal specification of a pre-theoretic notion of practical computability. As a first approximation, we can say that complexity theory thereby identifies some of the "natural kinds" of computational difficulty. We shall turn to the question of the "real-world relevance" of complexity theory later; at least important exceptions must be acknowledged to any rule of thumb that equates real-world feasibility with polynomial-time computability.

The ideal agent's procedure for determining whether or not a sentence is a tautological consequence of a set of premises yields a test of whether or not a sentence is truth-functionally consistent. In complexity theory, the latter question is known as the "satisfiability problem." Briefly, the relevant finding here is that the satisfiability problem is a member of the very large and important class of "nondeterministic polynomial time" (NP) problems, which are known to be solvable in polynomial time on a nondeterministic Turing machine, which is allowed to make "guesses" and in effect has an unbounded capacity for some parallel computations. A problem solvable by a nondeterministic Turing machine in polynomial time is solvable by a deterministic machine in exponential time. NP includes P, the class of problems solvable on a standard deterministic Turing machine in just polynomial time.

Most importantly, the satisfiability problem is "NP-complete": *any* NP problem can be efficiently reduced to the satisfiability problem. Each one of the wide variety of known NP-complete problems, numbering in the hundreds, is similarly convertible into any other. In this way, the satisfiability problem is a "universal" NP problem. NP-complete problems have not been proved inherently to require deterministic exponential time; this is the major unanswered question, a "Goldbach's conjecture", of the field, equivalent to the question whether $NP \neq P$ in that some NP problems are not in P. However, NP-complete problems are generally regarded as computationally intractable in this way, since only exponential-time deterministic algorithms for any of them are known, and because if they were not, so many important problems that have long resisted practical solution (such as the "traveling-salesman problem"[5]) would then all turn out to be tractable.

Thus, the ideal agent's perfect capacity even just to make all tautological inferences is the case *par excellence* of a problem-solving capacity that is strongly conjectured to require computationally intractable algorithms. Of course, a "quick but dirty" heuristic procedure for tautological inference will not necessarily yield such apparent exponential explosion of computation—presumably, that is how actual fallible human beings manage, as we shall see. But again, nonalgorithmic procedures would not suffice for the Cartesian perfection of the ideal agent, since *ex hypothesi* they cannot be guaranteed to work in all cases. A surprisingly small and basic fragment of the ideal agent's deducing ability seems by itself to require, for just a finite set of simple cases, resources greater than those available to an ideal computer constructed from the entire universe. There is another layer of impossibility between the idealization and reality, not merely minor exceptions.

IV Minimal Rationality

We can therefore say that, although use of an ideal rationality model is an understandable motivation for arriving at the thesis of universal acceptance of logic, some other argument still is needed for that thesis. Although ideal and more realistic models ought to coexist, for some purposes the idealization strategy seems an overreaction to the "no rationality, no agent" point. The alternative approach is to begin with a somewhat less idealized, more realistic model, of *minimal* rationality, where the agent's ability to choose actions falls between randomness and perfection. A minimal general rationality condition would be: If A has a particular belief-desire set, A would undertake some, but not necessarily all, actions that are apparently appropriate. For an agent to satisfy this condition, he must have some, but not ideal, logical ability—that is, he must satisfy a *minimal inference condition:*

A would make some, but not necessarily all, sound inferences from his belief set which are apparently appropriate.

(A must also *not* attempt enough of the actions that are apparently inappropriate, and inferences that are unsound or apparently inappropriate.)

A useful feature of this less idealized model of rationality is that, as we shall see, it provides a philosophical framework for relating two areas of significant research during the last decade. One is the field of computational complexity just sketched. The other encompasses the many recent psychological experiments that suggest surprisingly ubiquitous use of prima facie sub-optimal "heuristic strategies," rather than formally correct procedures, in everyday intuitive reasoning.[6] Although each of these areas has arisen independently of the others, there seems to be a fundamental connection: (a) Complexity theory provides a principled basis for considering that human beings (indeed, any computational entities) may not be able to perform some very simple reasoning tasks in ways that are guaranteed to be correct. (b) The psychology of "irrationality" suggests how we can do these tasks, by showing something of how we in fact do them—by means of the "quick but dirty" heuristics. (c) The ideal rationality models are at best silent on the normative status of use of these heuristics; the minimal rationality model, to begin with, permits us to acknowledge the basic platitude that human beings are in the finitary predicament, and so *ought* to use some such heuristics—according to this conception, formally incorrect heuristics need not in fact be irrational at all. They are not just inadvisable or unintelligible sloppiness, because they are a means of avoiding computational paralysis while still doing better than guessing.

The increasing interest in computational complexity and also in psychological heuristics makes it important to establish the status of claims of human (or even inherent computer) alogicality or illogicality. In particular, are the claims somehow a priori incoherent and so not a matter open for empirical study, as the rationality idealizations—and even the usual "charity principles"—imply? We thereby return to the issue of the universal acceptance of logic. Given the limitations of the concept of the ideal agent, the main question has now become: If a supposed cognitive system qualifies as minimally rational, is there any sense in which it must include a logic?

To determine in what sense, if any, satisfaction of the minimal rationality conditions implies acceptance of a deductive system, we must ask: What is accepting (or believing) a logical law or rule? Briefly, let us distinguish between strong and weak acceptance of logic. Assent to a logical law, mere lip service, is not enough to constitute strong belief in the law. Assent is neither sufficient nor necessary, although it is one type of evidence for such acceptance. In addition, acting appropriately for, or reasoning in accordance with, a logical law is not enough to constitute such belief. For instance, a sound argument is "in accordance with" *every* valid sentence, in the sense that the argument's conclusion also follows from the premises conjoined with any of these validities; there is then no distinction with regard to accepting logic between idiot and super-savant.

As Donald Davidson has emphasized, a belief must be part of an agent's reason for a decision.[7] Causal efficacy, the "right" role in the decision-making process, also is required here; the minimal agent must actually use the law as a premise in some (not necessarily all) of the practical reasoning, conscious or unconscious, by which he would select apparently appropriate actions (There can be important "generate and test" interplay between heuristic reasoning in the context of discovery, and logic as *post hoc* tribunal in the context of proof.) The key notion in turn, therefore, is that of "using a logical law or rule" (the related notion of "following a rule" has received much attention[8]).

In contrast, to accept or believe a logical law weakly is merely to be usefully (or instrumentalistically) described as using the law; it may be clear that the agent is not in fact using the law at all. This appears to be the sense in which Daniel Dennett says of adaptively behaving creatures from another planet, "in virtue of their rationality they can be supposed to share our belief in logical truths," and further, of "mice and other animals, in virtue of their being intentional systems," "whether or not the animal is said to *believe* the *truths* of logic, it must be supposed to *follow* the *rules* of logic."[9]

Thus, a person might strongly accept a logic—a small set of simple axioms and inference rules from which all logical truths could "in principle" be derived. But such strong acceptance of a complete deductive system for first-order logic is not the same as strong acceptance of "the theory of first-order logic": actual appropriate use of each of the infinitely many assertions derivable by means of those axioms and rules. However, although the latter is not possible for a realistic or minimal agent, the agent can resolve to accept, or be committed to accepting, these truths. Also, a person can endorse a deductive system—for instance, as an object language for the relatively restricted technical purposes of metamathematics. The more limited the use of the system—the more it is preached as a norm on Sunday, but not practiced the rest of the week—the more such endorsement tends to fall below strong acceptance.

V   Practical Adequacy of a Logic

The question of universal acceptance of logic now becomes, Must a minimally rational agent accept a logic either strongly or weakly? The interesting issue is whether an agent's satisfaction of the minimal rationality conditions implies his strong acceptance of a sound and complete deductive system. (The argument below can also be adapted for the weak sense of 'accept.') The question needs further sharpening: One might argue[10] that, though an agent must be able to make some sound inferences—that is, must have some deductive ability—he does not have to be able to make any *particular* inferences, even those which normal human beings find the most obvious. But even if this is true, it does not exclude universal acceptance of logic. It might still turn out that any agent must strongly accept some complete set of valid laws and sound rules; it would just be that agents do not have to accept the laws and rules normal humans do—for instance, those normal humans find obvious. Our question is therefore, Must an agent strongly accept *any* set of valid laws or sound rules that constitute a complete deductive system, much less particular obvious laws or rules? It seems that an agent can have the deductive ability required by the rationality conditions without strongly accepting, i.e., actually using sometimes, even one such law or rule. (We restrict consideration to verbally formulated beliefs.)

We need one more distinction. I shall say that a deductive system is *metatheoretically* adequate if it is sound (and therefore consistent) and complete. In the first paragraph of "The Justification of Deduction," Michael Dummett asserts, "Failure of soundness yields a situation which must be remedied. Failure of completeness cannot always be remedied; a remedy is, however, mandatory whenever it is possible."[11] Dummett accurately describes adherence to such an absolute requirement as "the standard practice of logicians" in constructing and justifying a formal logical theory. However, the metatheoretic adequacy of a deductive system must be explicitly distinguished from its *practical* adequacy: here, its adequacy for accomplishing the deductive tasks required of a minimally rational agent. If one assumes that any possible agent must be ideally rational, it is easy to overlook the difference between the two types of adequacy. But with a minimal rationality model, the overlap of the two types of adequacy becomes much less salient.

What is the relation between metatheoretic and practical adequacy? I shall point out that practical adequacy does not require metatheoretic adequacy, that the former is sometimes preferable to the latter, and that the former may sometimes not even be compatible with the latter. The very quickest possible, but least reliable, way of performing a deductive task is just to guess the answer. We know that a minimal agent does not have to be a perfect logician, but the agent could not accomplish his required sound inferences (while avoiding enough unsound ones) just by a series of lucky guesses. There are, however, other ways to improve above chance the odds of selecting conclusions that follow from premises besides using a sound and complete deductive system. The agent might use what is in effect a better than random, but not perfect, gambling strategy for identifying sound inferences. Though such a rule of thumb would not always succeed, it might work sufficiently often to reach the break-even point of satisfying minimal rationality requirements. I shall argue later that this type of strategy may be indispensable if computational intractability is to be avoided.

VI Against Metatheoretic Adequacy

The concept of such a strategy suggests, to begin with, that it is at least possible for a logically competent agent to have one or more "logical blind spots" which are the result of his exclusively using an incomplete deductive system (whenever he does use a deductive system). Given the difficulties for observer—and agent—in determining the agent's nonconscious cognitive processes, let us consider the overt and explicit steps written out by a person performing a formal derivation (or alternatively, the core dump of a computer running a theorem-proving program). As an uninteresting example, the agent might use a conventional textbook natural-deduction system of independent rules, with a *modus tollens* rule that has a clause that excludes its application to formal sentences with more than 1,000 logical constants. Similarly, it is possible for an agent to perform all required sound inferences by means of an unsound, or even inconsistent, system. Frege's axiomatization of logical theory in *The Fundamental Laws of Arithmetic* and Quine's in *Mathematical Logic* were both inconsistent in ways that did not reveal themselves to many who had used each axiomatization extensively. These two examples suggest that first-order deductive systems can correspondingly be inconsistent in ways that do not yield too many—indeed, any—unsound inferences for the range of deductive tasks required of an agent. And in fact all the early formulations of the substitution rule for the predicate calculus are reported to have been unsound.[12] (Of course, if a deductive system is inconsistent it is complete, but this is no longer metatheoretic virtue.)

Furthermore, an agent who satisfied the minimal rationality condition could use exclusively a deductive system in which *all* axioms were invalid and *all* inference rules were unsound. A natural-deduction system corresponding to a standard textbook one, but composed entirely of unsound rules can easily, if uninterestingly, be constructed. For example, to the original *modus tollens* rule a clause is added: "When one of the premises contains more than 1,000 logical constants, the set of premise-numbers of the line on which the conclusion occurs should be empty; otherwise the premise-numbers are as usually specified." A similar premise-number clause can be added to each of the other rules. Or the original other rules and the new *modus tollens* rule can just be conjoined as a single rule; such a matter of individuating rules seems arbitrary.

The agent would not use the usual shortcut "theorem" rule which permits entering in a derivation a previously proved theorem with an empty set of premise-numbers. The claim here is just that this agent *can* use exclusively this set of unsound basic rules. The agent might happen to be uninterested in using that set to deduce "vacuous" valid sentences; perhaps, as empirical studies indicate for normal human beings, he has difficulty reasoning so abstractly. As proponents of the naturalness of natural-deduction systems often point out, outside of logic courses people rarely seem to use, or at least to cite, logical validities.

The unsound inferences permitted by this system would be performed relatively rarely because they would arise only under a restricted range of conditions: they involve very complex sentences, or might be otherwise unintuitive or difficult for the agent to perform. We know that an agent cannot perform all inferences—in particular, the more complex ones—anyway; so the unsoundness of this system need not detract *at all* from the agent's rationality. We conclude that metatheoretically adequate deductive systems are not the *only* way to achieve practical adequacy. One cannot argue that any possible rational agent must accept logic.

Furthermore, a stronger point against metatheoretic adequacy seems to hold: that in important cases it is antagonistic to practical adequacy. A metatheoretically inadequate system could be superior to any metatheoretically adequate one for the practical purposes of accomplishing an agent's everyday deductive tasks, just as inconsistent naive set theory is often more convenient than one of the consistent axiomatizations. In such a situation, insisting upon use of a metatheoretically adequate system would itself be unreasonable, like trying to use the more correct but hopelessly unwieldly relativity physics instead of classical mechanics for engineering calculations in designing a bridge. Even outside of practical contexts empirical theories are often recognized to be idealizations that are only approximations of reality and apply satisfactorily only over limited ranges of the parameters involved; the kinetic-molecular theory of gases is a standard example of an idealization that is employed because it is much more manageable than more correct theories, e.g., that do not assume molecules are perfectly dimensionless spheres.[13]

Indeed, as mentioned earlier, much evidence has recently emerged indicating that in a remarkably wide range of conditions human beings do not in fact use formally correct procedures in everyday nondeductive reasoning. And occasionally researchers in this field have pointed out, in effect, that use of such quick but dirty heuristics in "applied" as opposed to "pure" situations may be a reasonable speed-accuracy tradeoff.[14] There is also a separate tradition of empirical research suggesting that people do not use formally correct procedures in simple deductive reasoning. In addition, some of my own recent empirical studies indicate that subjects use a "prototypicality heuristic" in deductive reasoning, a set of shortcut strategies that exploit structuring of concepts in terms of prototypes, or best examples, of the concepts; we seem to extend the "context of discovery" in this way into the "context of proof." Furthermore, some of the evidence suggests that using this formally incorrect procedure is in fact rational, in that it pays off with lower error rates. These last findings are significant because they identify a connection between deductive-reasoning heuristics and the important recent research on prototype models of mental representation.[15] Finally, it is worth recalling in this context the widespread occurrence of the simplest classical semantic and set-theoretic antinomies in our conceptual scheme, from the foundations of mathematics to ordinary discourse; this may be another symptom of our use of formally incorrect deductive procedures.

VII   Practical Paralysis

An even stronger point may hold than just that metatheoretically inadequate systems appear to be preferable sometimes to metatheoretically adequate ones. Some of the recent research on computational complexity raises the possibility that metatheoretic adequacy may in important ranges of cases be entirely incompatible with practical adequacy, both for some of the "pure" purposes of the deductive sciences and for the "applied" purposes of maintaining an agent's minimal rationality. Let us begin with an argument of Michael Rabin's[16] for the introduction of a notion of probabilistic proof in mathematics. Of course no decision procedure is possible even in principle for all of elementary number theory, but even in-principle decidability can sometimes be of very limited value. Consider a result of Albert Meyer and Larry Stockmeyer's[17]: Although the set of theorems of a formal system for the weak monadic second-order theory of successor (WSIS), a fragment of elementary number theory, is decidable in principle, its decidability seems extremely unfeasible in practice. The problem requires not just exponential time, but "super-exponential" time. To prove theorems of only 617 symbols or less would require a network with so many boolean elements that, even if each were the size of a proton, the machine would exceed the size of the entire known universe. In effect, the moral Rabin drew from the pattern of such complexity-theoretic results is that, to avoid the problem of unfeasibly long proofs, mathematicians sometimes should make the ultimate speed-accuracy tradeoff: relax the metatheoretic requirement of consistency, even where it is in principle satisfiable, to evade practical paralysis. Rabin recommended, and devised, methods of probabilistic proof which do not guarantee truth, but for which the probability of error can be determined to be, e.g., one in a billion.[18]

Rabin's strategy might be compared with undoing Descartes's bargain; Descartes sought apodeictic certainty, but the cost is recognized to have been epistemic paralysis. We can extend the point from methodology of the deductive sciences to our concern about fundamental constraints on human cognition. There are now two possible extremes for dealing with, e.g., the problem of determining tautological consequence. Just guessing, the quickest but dirtiest procedure, is too dirty for even minimal rationality, since odds of success are chance. The other extreme, a decision procedure, is the most reliable but also seems too slow; it is perfectly infallible, but, as noted earlier, it is probably computationally intractable, which might be too slow for even minimal rationality. Therefore, a compromise between the two extremes seems needed to yield sufficient deductive capacity for minimal rationality.

Various tradeoff strategies are in fact prevalent in computer science in dealing with problems that are found to be computationally intractable. Standards are lowered and "heuristic algorithms" and "approximation algorithms" are sought for the problems instead of perfect optimization algorithms.[19] There is more than one type of compromise with perfect algorithmhood which might evade the apparent intractability of decision procedures for even just tautologous consequence. One might, for instance, use a metatheoretically adequate deductive system, but avoid worst cases by restricting its application to simpler special cases—sets of premises and a possible conclusion that are small enough so that the exponential explosion of operations is not severe. Therefore, the agent could never attempt to make an inference from, or to test for consistency, his entire belief set, or even a large portion of it. The cost, and the eventual limitation, is that the agent would then exhibit the most rationality "locally," within certain neighborhoods of his beliefs, and would be particularly weak on inferences and consistency involving beliefs distributed between such subsets. (In fact, a fundamental feature of human belief systems is that they are "compartmentalized" in this way; thus, an important rationale for this structuring is as a strategy for evading intractability.[20]) Another, simpler strategy would be: Given any case, employ the metatheoretically adequate system; if no answer results within some fixed time limit, just abandon the attempt and flip a coin to pick an answer.

VIII Real-world Relevance

These strategies, however, require that computationally manageable cases involving sufficiently large belief sets be sufficiently frequent to avoid *de facto* computational paralysis. We must therefore turn to the issue of the "real-world relevance" of complexity theory. It should be emphasized that usual complexity measures are not average-case estimates. The typical theorem stating that a problem is computationally complex is of a worst-case form: Given any algorithm for deciding each instance of the problem, each of an infinite number of cases requires exponential time.

This still leaves in limbo an infinite number of *other* cases of the problem. Which of them, if any, requires exponential time? Perhaps every instance of the problem takes exponential time; even then, the exponential blowup might be so slow that the computational cost is not severe for small cases of the problem. Or instead, perhaps no real-world relevant case—of less than colossal size—might require "serious" exponential time; the exponential cases might be of an input size that nothing of human-scale computational resources could ever even encounter. Or again, the problem's complexity profile might fall messily between these two extremes. Therefore information is needed on the "density," or population distribution, of the hard cases. This includes, for example: (a) Do they arise "early" (for cases of about the same order of size as the shortest decision algorithm for the problem)? (b) Do they arise "often," that is, within the population of *interesting* cases; this requires an understanding of which instances are interesting, which of course will be relative to particular goals. (c) How severe is the exponential explosion, when it does occur?

The probability distribution of relevant worst cases is presently not well understood.[21] Indeed, algorithms for linear programming are a well-known counterexample to the assertion: "An algorithm is in fact practically unfeasible if and only if it requires exponential time." On the one hand, the Simplex linear programming algorithm has been proved to require exponential time. Yet for decades the Simplex algorithm has been found very usable in practice—for the population of problems of interest to its users. A recent "empirical" study of running times of the algorithm for actual problems in the banking, steel, and oil industries confirms this; and Steven Smale has just proved that the exponential cases are in a sense rare. On the other hand, the "Khachian" algorithm requires only polynomial time, but its typical running time seems much worse than that of the Simplex algorithm, because its polynomial bounds are so high.[22] The connection of exponential time with in-practice unfeasibility thus needs to be interpreted with some care.

Nonetheless, workers in many areas of computer science certainly continue to accept this connection as a very useful rule of thumb.[23] And some rough estimates do not suggest optimism that methods like the above compartmentalizing and "give up and guess" strategies are by themselves sufficient to avoid intractability in the management of a human belief system. Even decidability of just the monadic predicate calculus (and of some other decidable subclasses of the full predicate calculus) is known to require non-deterministic exponential time.[24]

And, at least as food for thought, it is worth again considering testing for tautological consequence, only a very small part of the general problem here, by means now of the truth-table method (even the more efficient known test procedures such as Wang's algorithm or the resolution method still require as much time in the worst cases). Given the difficulties in individuating beliefs, it is not easy to estimate the number of logically independent atomic propositions in a typical human belief system, but 138 seems much too low—too "small-minded." Yet suppose that each line of the truth table for the conjunction of all these beliefs can be checked in the time a light ray takes to traverse the diameter of a proton, an appropriate cycle time for an ideal computer. At this maximum speed, a consistency test of this very modest belief system would require more time than the estimated twenty billion years from the dawn of the universe to the present. Quinean or Davidsonian charity requirements that a translation be readjusted if it yields an inconsistent belief set seem particularly unrealistic in this light.

Furthermore, it is important to note that some exponential-time problems have been proved to have hard cases of small size (indeed, similar proofs have been emerging for classical absolutely unsolvable problems[25]). As noted above, deciding WSIS sentences of just several hundred symbols is known to require more space (and time) than there is in the known universe. Also, Fischer and Rabin have showed that Presburger arithmetic requires exponential time and, furthermore, that the exponential explosion of proof length sets in early, for sentences of the same order of size as the decision algorithm.[26]

Nonetheless, it is quite easy to show that an early onset of computational complexity—that is, for cases small enough to be humanly relevant—is not an inherent feature of intractability: Given any intractable problem with early-onset complexity, one can always construct another problem with complexity onset only for cases larger than a particular given size.[27] The significant implication here of this point is that "counting the horse's teeth"—empirically observing which are the difficult and interesting cases of a problem—will often be un-avoidable; much of the "real-world" complexity structure of many intractable problems is at least presently a hybrid question, to be approached in the manner of McCall's study of the Simplex algorithm cited earlier. In particular, artificial intelligence workers on automatic theorem proving have uniquely valuable data about what are the "interesting," frequently occurring, cases of a given intractable problem, and which of them in fact require large expenditure of resources. And similar information can correspondingly be obtained for human deductive reasoning. That is, in the hypothetico-deductive manner, we can treat the issue of whether there is real-world relevant complexity at least as an empirical working hypothesis, suppose it is true, and see how well its implications are supported by observations.

In fact, the rather wide range of recent evidence mentioned earlier confirms that people actually do not use formally correct methods in their intuitive reasoning. Instead, they seem to use procedures in nondeductive everyday reasoning such as Kahneman and Tversky's "representativeness" and "availability" heuristics, and related "prototypicality heuristics" in deductive reasoning. Thus, the most fundamental "empirical" suggestion of complexity theory, that algorithmic methods of accomplishing even some very simple deductive tasks are likely to be intractable, would provide a unifying framework for explaining why we use such heuristics instead. It constitutes the ultimate "justification of the ways of Man" here. For a plausible conjecture to begin with is that our quick and dirty shortcut strategies are required to avoid intractability. To the constraint that information-processing models of cognition should be finitary, we could then add that, in at least some interesting cases, they also should not entail certain classes of computationally complex processes. The possibility needs to be explored further that, to a considerable extent, the only way human reasoning (or any agent's) can evade practical paralysis is by not using metatheoretically adequate deductive systems.[28] Ideal rationality requirements seem to exclude even entertaining such a possibility as more than unimportant exceptions to a rule, but a theory of minimal rationality provides a principled basis for relating complexity theory and the psychological studies in this way.

The familiar debate about how to choose between competing logics, e.g., which is more "natural," presupposes as an absolute requirement that we ought not even to consider a logic that is metatheoretically inadequate. But we can now see that the commonplace that Dummett, for example, began with, that metatheoretic adequacy is mandatory whenever "in principle" possible, needs at least to be carefully restricted. If one is engaged in a metatheoretical investigation of a deductive system, rather than generally using the system, Dummett's assertion may be correct. An agent can endorse the use of a metatheoretically adequate system, reason *about* it, and even really use it in some limited contexts. But if the system is actually to be used significantly, metatheoretic inadequacy may be reparable only on pain of intractability; it would then be irrational even to try to adopt exclusively a metatheoretically adequate system, since that would preclude successful reasoning. It would be like insisting upon the perfectionism of the Cartesian methodology of universal doubt, with its resulting cognitive paralysis.

Thus, in contrast to Alfred Tarski's remark, "the appearance of an antinomy is for me a symptom of disease,"[29] there is at least some truth to Wittgenstein's earlier image in his account of the (non)significance of the paradoxes, "a contradiction is not a germ which shows a general illness."[30] The contradiction need not *entirely* vitiate the system. Indeed, this paper has gone further, proposing that such inconsistency may be downright healthy. The moral regarding the thesis of the universal acceptance of logic is that once we begin to take into account at least the most fundamental facts of an agent's psychological reality, that thesis, like a number of other rationality idealizations, seems wrong, and interestingly so. Contrary to the usual charity principles, not only is acceptance of a metatheoretically adequate deductive system not transcendentally indispensable for an agent's rationality, but in important cases it is inadvisable and perhaps even incompatible with that rationality.

Notes

This paper was prepared with support from the American Philosophical Society and the National Endowment for the Humanities. Lenore Blum, Charles Chihara, William Craig, Daniel Dennett, Richard Karp, and Barry Stroud generously helped at various stages of the paper. Some of this material appeared in Cherniak 1977; other material was presented at the University of California, Berkeley, Logic and Methodology Colloquium, February 1982. The paper was read to the Berkeley Philosophy Colloquium, June 1982.

1. Quine 1960 [100], p. 58; and Quine 1970 [102], p. 102. (some of Quine's discussion of logic and translation can be construed as entailing only the universal *nonrejectability* of logic. However, the argument below implies that correct translation might attribute rejection of any particular logical truths.)

2. See Cherniak 1981 [188], pp. 161–183. (If the requirement that A attempt *only* apparently appropriate actions is dropped, a random guesser will satisfy the ideal conditions, given enough time; see the minimal conditions below.)

3. Two key papers are S. Cook 1971 [697], pp. 151–158; and R. Karp 1972 [753], pp. 85–103. A recent review of part of the field is M. Garey and D. Johnson 1979 [577]. Two easily accessible articles are H. Lewis and C. Papadimitriou 1978 [777], pp. 96–109; and L. Stockmeyer and A. Chandra 1979 [840], pp. 140–159.

4. See S. Kleene's discussion of the concept of a decision procedure in sec. 40 of his 1967 [602] for examples of the relegation of such issues to the applied sciences.

5. The traveling-salesman problem, an NP-complete network design problem of considerable practical interest in operations research, is: given a set of cities on a map and all intercity distances, construct the optimum tour, i.e., the shortest round-trip route connecting all the cities by intercity links.

6. For a review of some of their own basic work by two major contributors to the field, see A. Tversky and D. Kahneman 1974 [472], pp. 1124–1131. A recent overview is R. Nisbett and L. Ross 1980 [89].

7. See, for example, Davidson 1980 [29].

8. Cf. Wittgenstein's discussion 1958 [667].

9. Dennett 1978 [562], pp. 9, 11.

10. Cherniak 1981 [188], pp. 248–268. See also sec. 5 of that paper for an argument against the claim that being able to make particular "obvious" inferences, by whatever means, is *constitutive* of understanding the logical constants involved in those inferences; the argument would apply in particular against the assertion that strong acceptance—that is, actual use—of the corresponding obvious valid laws or sound rules is required for an agent to qualify as understanding the logical constants involved.

11. Dummett 1978 [566], p. 290.

12. S. Kleene, 1967 [602] fn, p. 107. See Church 1956 [557], pp. 289–290.

13. The question of adopting convenient but in some sense unsound inference rules in fact sometimes is raised in devising natural-deduction systems for introductory logic texts; see, for example, Mates, *op. cit.*, p. vii.

14. See, for example, the last chapter of Nisbett and Ross, 1980 [89].

15. An early (and controversial) study that suggested subjects use a kind of global impression or "atmosphere" of the logical form of the inference was R. Woodworth and S. Sells 1935 [854], pp. 451–460; see also P. Wason and P. Johnson-Laird 1972 [139], ch. 10. For a review of research on prototypicality, see E. Rosch 1977 [816]. On the use of a prototypicality heuristic in deductive inference, see Cherniak 1984 [459].

16. See Rabin 1974 [809]. On Rabin's concept of a probabilistic algorithm see his 1976 [810]. G. Kolata 1976 [765], pp. 989–990 describes Rabin's argument.

17. See Meyer 1975 [789]; and Stockmeyer and Chandra, 1979 [840].

18. Putnam 1975 [633] has also argued, in a Quinean vein, that "quasi-empirical" methods—resembling those employed in evaluating the plausibility, for instance, of highly theoretical statements in physics—have always been important in mathematics outside of the domain of formal proof.

19. See, e.g., Garey and Johnson, 1979 [577], ch. 6.

20. See Cherniak 1983 [361], pp. 163–186.

21. For an investigation of probability-distribution, as opposed to worst-case, analyses, see R. Karp 1972 [753]. Also relevant for the satisfiability problem is S. Mahaney 1980 [783], pp.54–60.

22. For the proof that the Simplex algorithm requires exponential time, see V. Klee and G. Minty 1972 [764]. The "empirical" study of running times is in E. McCall 1982 [781], pp. 207–212. Smale's proof has been reported in his 1982. A short review of the so-called "Khachian" algorithm: L. Lovacs 1980 [778].

23. See, for example, pp. 8–9, Garey and Johnson, 1979 [577].

24. For a review of these results, see H. Lewis 1978 [776], pp. 35–47.

25. Undecidability for elementary arithmetic is now known not to arise only for extremely complex and mathematically uninteresting sentences: See J. Jones 1978 [750], for an undecidable, unabbreviated sentence (based on the solution of Hilbert's Tenth Problem) of about 100 symbols in length; and his 1982 [751], pp. 549–571, for the basis for constructing still shorter sentences. See also G. Chaitin 1974 [691], pp. 403–424. In addition, a "mathematically simple and interesting" theorem (an extension of the finite Ramsey theorem) is not provable in Peano arithmetic; see J. Paris and L. Harrington 1977 [797]. The present paper further motivates study of the "density," or distribution, of undecidable sentences.

26. See M. Fischer and M. Rabin 1974 [721], pp. 27–41.

27. For example, as noted, the set of theorems of Presburger arithmetic has early-onset complexity. However, the set of Presburger arithmetic theorems, each of length more than 10,000 symbols, can be quickly decided for any case of length less than 10,000 symbols; the algorithm will just count the number of symbols in any sentence to be decided and immediately reject it if that length is less than 10,000. Another question concerns the "naturalness" of such truncated problems.

28. Correspondingly in artificial intelligence, the algorithmic approach of seeking classical decision procedures, or even just complete proof procedures, for theoremhood needs to be reevaluated in light of the problem of

combinatorial explosions of branchings in proofs. For a brief discussion of the issue, see A. Newell and H. Simon 1976 [795], pp. 113–126. See also Rabin, 1976 [810]. An extensive review of practical limitations on theorem-proving programs (and program verifiers) still is needed.

29. A. Tarski 1969 [844], pp. 63–77.

30. Wittgenstein 1976 [668], p. 211.

12

Judgmental Heuristics and Knowledge Structures

Richard Nisbett and Lee Ross

The most characteristic thing about mental life, over and beyond the fact that one apprehends the events of the world around one, is that one constantly goes beyond the information given.

Jerome Bruner

The perceiver, as Bruner (1957) [445] recognized, is not simply a dutiful clerk who passively registers items of information. Rather, the perceiver is an active interpreter, one who resolves ambiguities, makes educated guesses about events that cannot be observed directly, and forms inferences about associations and causal relations. In this chapter we explore the strategies that permit and encourage the perceiver to "go beyond the information given," that is, to venture beyond the most immediate implications of the data. We sketch some of the "knowledge structures" applied to understanding the world. These range from broad propositional theories about people in general to more schematic representations of objects, events, and actors. These structures house the person's generic knowledge and preconceptions about the world and provide the basis for quick, coherent, but occasionally erroneous interpretations of new experience.

Before discussing these structures, we will introduce the reader to the "availability heuristic" and the "representativeness heuristic"—two simple judgmental strategies on which people seem to rely, and by which they sometimes are misled, in a variety of inferential tasks. In so doing, the chapter introduces the reader to a set of extraordinarily important contributions by Daniel Kahneman and Amos Tver-

Reprinted form *Human Inference: Strategies and Shortcomings of Social Judgment,* by Richard Nisbett and Lee Ross (Englewood Cliffs, N.J.: Prentice-Hall, Inc., 1980), pp. 17–42, by permission of the publisher. Copyright © 1980, Prentice-Hall, Inc.

sky (1972 [473], 1973 [474], in press; Tversky and Kahneman, 1971 [475], 1973 [474], 1974 [472]). . . .

The heuristics to be explored are relatively primitive and simple judgmental strategies. They are not irrational or even nonrational. They probably produce vastly more correct or partially correct inferences than erroneous ones, and they do so with great speed and little effort. Indeed, we suspect that the use of such simple tools may be an inevitable feature of the cognitive apparatus of any organism that must make as many judgments, inferences, and decisions as humans have to do. Each heuristic or, more properly, the misapplication of each heuristic, does lead people astray in some important inferential tasks. . . . It is the misuse of the heuristics—their application in preference to more normatively appropriate strategies—that we will emphasize.

Although we characterize the heuristics as "judgmental strategies," the term is misleading in that it implies a conscious and deliberate application of well-defined decision rules. The heuristics to be explored should be distinguished from straightforward computational or judgmental "algorithms" (such as the method for finding square roots or deciding whether one's bridge hand merits an opening bid), which generally are explicit and invariant both in the criteria for their use and the manner of their application. The intuitive psychologist probably would not assent to, much less spontaneously express, any general formulation of either heuristic. Instead, the utilization of the heuristics is generally automatic and nonreflective and notably free of any conscious consideration of appropriateness. As we shall see, the heuristics are not applied in a totally indiscriminate fashion. In many contexts in which a given heuristic would promote error, people refrain from using it and probably could articulate why its use would be foolish. On other logically equivalent and equally unpropitious occasions, people readily apply the same heuristic and may even attempt to justify its use.

The Availability Heuristic

When people are required to judge the relative frequency of particular objects or the likelihood of particular events, they often may be influenced by the relative *availability* of the objects or events, that is, their accessibility in the processes of perception, memory, or construction from imagination (cf. Tversky and Kahneman 1973 [474]).

Such availability criteria often will prove accurate and useful. To the extent that availability is actually associated with objective frequency, the availability heuristic can be a useful tool of judgment. There are many factors uncorrelated with frequency, however, which can influence an event's immediate perceptual salience, the vividness or completeness with which it is recalled, or the ease with which it is imagined. As a result, the availability heuristic can be misleading.

Availability Biases in Frequency Estimation

Let us proceed first by introducing and then exploring in some detail three judgmental tasks for which application of the availability heuristic might lead one to biased estimates of the relative frequency of various objects or events. The first two examples are hypothetical. . . .

1. A pollster who asks a sample of American adults to estimate the "percentage of the work force who are currently unemployed" finds an "egocentric bias." That is, currently unemployed workers tend to overestimate the rate of unemployment, but currently employed workers tend to underestimate it.

2. An Indiana businessman confides to a friend, "Did you ever notice how many Hoosiers become famous or important? Look anywhere—politics, sports, Hollywood, big business, even notorious bank robbers—I couldn't guess the exact figures, but I bet we Hoosiers have far more than our fair share on just about any list in *Who's Who.*"

3. A group of subjects consistently errs in judging the relative frequency of two kinds of English words. Specifically, they estimate the number of words beginning with particular letters (for example, *R* or *K*) to be greater than the number of words with those letters appearing third, although words of the latter type actually are far more numerous.

Examples 1 and 2 seem to present common and familiar errors, although one might not immediately recognize the role of availability factors in producing them. In fact, some readers might hasten to cite motivational or even "psycho-dynamic" factors that could induce unemployed workers to overestimate the commonness of their plight or that could prompt proud Indiana residents to exaggerate their share of the limelight. Example 3 seems less intuitively obvious and at first seems quite unconnected to the other two examples. Nevertheless, the chief source of error in all three cases seems to us to be the availability heuristic.

Consider Example 1, about estimates of unemployment. Here the bias in subjective availability can be traced to a bias in initial sampling. Unemployed people are more likely to know and meet other unemployed people than are job-holders, and vice versa. The reasons for such a sampling bias are hardly mysterious: The unemployed individual is likely to share the neighborhood, socioeconomic background, and occupation of other jobless individuals. He also is likely to encounter other unemployed people in such everyday endeavors as job-hunting, visiting employment agencies, collecting unemployment benefits, and shopping at stores offering cut-rate prices or easy credit. Indeed, he even may seek out such individuals for social comparison, information exchange, or general commiseration. Thus, to the extent that the unemployed person relies upon the sample generated by his personal experience, he will be misled about the commonness of unemployment. In the same manner, employed people, who are apt to live, work, and shop near one another, are apt to err in the opposite direction.

It is important to emphasize that the people in this hypothetical example would not be compelled to rely upon biased availability criteria in estimating the frequency of unemployment. They could try to recall media presentations of data, could apply some popular rule of thumb ("When there's an energy shortage, jobs disappear"), or could employ some more appropriate "sampling procedure" ("How many people have I seen lining up outside my neighborhood unemployment office on the first of the month this year as compared with last year?"). They even could attempt to compensate for the biases distorting their samples of available data ("Hardly anyone I know is jobless, but of course, I don't get to meet many unemployed people, do I? I guess I'd better adjust my estimate upward!"). Indeed, it is quite likely that some people *would* avoid availability criteria or at least would attempt the necessary adjustments. Throughout this book, however, we present experimental evidence showing that simple, tempting, availability criteria are used in contexts in which availability and frequency are poorly correlated and are used without appropriate adjustments for the factors that bias subjective experience.

Now let us consider Example 2, about the relative prominence of Indiana natives. The Hoosier's egocentric estimate clearly contains some of the same features as in our initial example. That is, people from Indiana are disproportionately likely to know or hear about famous fellow Hoosiers. Beyond such biases in initial exposure, however, this example introduces the potential influence of additional biases in *storage*. When a national sportscaster says "Myra Swift of Grandville, Indiana and Mary Speed of Bigtown, Florida won gold medals in the Olympics yesterday," it is the accomplishment of his fellow Hoosier that the Indiana businessman is more likely to notice and to remember. Accordingly, the sample of famous people he subsequently can recall from memory will reflect biases at the "storage" stage as well as at the sampling stage.

Biases in exposure, attention, and storage can arise, of course, from many factors besides the kinship between the perceiver and the object. . . . For instance, oddity or newsworthiness could accomplish the same end. Thus, people from all states might overestimate the number of very big, very small, very young, very pretty, or very hirsute Olympic gold medalists because such factors would bias the rater's likelihood of sampling, storing, and recalling the pertinent instances.

Example 3, about estimates of the frequency of the letter R in the first versus the third position, is subtler. In fact, readers who try the experiment themselves may find that they make the same incorrect assessments of relative frequency as did the original subjects. Once again, an inappropriate application of the availability criterion is the source of the difficulty. Like the subjects in Tversky's and Kahneman's (1973) [474] demonstration, the reader probably finds that instances of words beginning with R are easier to generate spontaneously (at least in a casual first attempt) than are instances of words that have R as their third letter. But the differences in ease of generation do not reflect corresponding differences in word frequency. Any truly *random* sample of English words would reveal words beginning with R to be much *less* common than words with R as their third letter. The relative difficulty of generating words like "care," "street," and "derail," may give interesting hints of the storage and retrieval of one's vocabulary, but it says virtually nothing about objective word frequencies.

An analogy may be instructive here: In a quick search of the library, one would find it easier to find books by authors named Woolf than by authors named Virginia, or to find books about Australia than books by authors born in Australia. Such differences obviously would indicate little about the relative frequencies of such books in the library's collection. Instead, they would reflect the library's system for referencing books and granting access to them. By the same token, first letters apparently are more useful cues than third letters are for referencing and permitting access to the items in one's personal word collection. Once again, the use of criteria other than the subjective ease of generation (or, alternatively, recognition of relevant biases and adequate compensation) could lead people to a more accurate estimate.

Availability of Event Relationships and of Causal Explanations

Kahneman's and Tversky's work has been largely on the use of the availability heuristic in judgments involving the frequency or probability of individual events. Other research indicates that subjective availability may influence judgments of *relationships* between events, particularly *causal* relationships.

Jones's and Nisbett's (1972) [752] account of the divergent causal interpretations of actors and observers—from which observers cite "dispositional" factors (traits, abilities, attitudes, etc.) to explain behaviors and outcomes that the actors themselves attribute to "situational" factors—is one case in point. For example, the actor who gives a dollar to a beggar is apt to attribute his behavior to the sad plight of the beggar, but the observer of the behavior is apt to attribute it to the actor's generosity. From the actor's perspective, it is the constantly changing features of the environment that are particularly salient or "available" as potential causes to which his behavior can be attributed. From the observer's perspective, the actor is the perceptual "figure" and the situation merely "ground," so that the actor himself provides the most available causal candidate. Indeed, by altering actors' and observers' perspectives through videotape replays, mirrors, or other methods, one can correspondingly alter the actors' and observers' causal assessments (cf. Arkin and Duval 1975 [674]; Duval and Wicklund 1972 [567]; Regan and Totten 1975 [811]; Storms 1973 [841]).

Subsequent research by a number of investigators, most notably Taylor and her associates (for example, Taylor and Fiske 1975 [846], 1978 [847]), has demonstrated a more general point regarding availability and causal assessment. It appears that almost *any* manipulation that focuses the perceiver's attention on a potential cause, for example, on a particular participant in a social interaction, affects causal assessment. Whether the attentional manipulation is achieved

by a blunt instruction about which participant to watch, subtle variations in seating arrangement, or by "solo" versus "nonsolo" status
of, for example, female or black participants, the person made disproportionately "available" to onlookers is seen to be a disproportionately potent causal agent. (See also McArthur and Post 1977 [779];
McArthur and Solomon 1978 [780].)

Availability effects also may account for other biases involving perceived causality. Consider Fischhoff's (1975 [722]; Fischhoff and
Beyth 1975 [723]) reports on the subjective certainty of hindsight
knowledge. These reports show that outcomes often seem in retro-
spect to have been inevitable. This may be because the antecedents
and causal scenarios that "predicted" such outcomes have far greater
"after-the-fact" availability than do antecedents or scenarios that predicted alternative outcomes that did not in fact occur. In a similar
vein, Ross, Lepper, Strack, and Steinmetz (1977) [821] demonstrated
that *explaining* why some event is consistent with known preceding
events (for example, explaining the suicide of a clinical patient whose
case history one has examined) tends to increase the subjective likelihood that the event actually did occur. Again the relevant mechanism
appears to be the availability heuristic. The explanation creates a particular causal scenario, and its causal factors are disproportionately
available to the perceiver when predictions are made later.

In both hindsight and explanation, the subjective ease of generation appears to be important. The subjects seem to respond not only
to the mere presence of potential causal scenarios but also to the relative ease with which they were detected or invented. People probably
implicitly assume this subjective ease of generation to be somehow
symptomatic of the scenario's likelihood or of the explanation's
aptness.

Appropriate and Inappropriate Applications of the Availability Heuristic

An indiscriminate use of the availability heuristic clearly can lead people into serious judgmental errors. It is important to reemphasize that
in many contexts perceptual salience, memorability, and imaginability may be relatively unbiased and therefore well correlated with true
frequency, probability, or even causal significance. In such cases, of
course, the availability heuristic often can be a helpful and efficient
tool of inference.

The same jobless individuals whose estimates of unemployment rates were distorted by the availability heuristic could make a reasonably accurate estimate of the preponderance of oak trees to maple trees in their neighborhood by using the same strategy. In estimating the frequencies of various types of trees, the individual's personal experiences and subsequent recollections would constitute generally unbiased samples. Similarly, the Indiana resident who was misled by the disproportionate availability of instances of famous fellow Hoosiers might have fared quite well if the same heuristic had been applied in estimating the success of German Olympians relative to Italian Olympians. Furthermore, the "ease of generation" criterion would have helped rather than hindered Tversky's and Kahneman's subjects if the experimental task had been to estimate the relative frequencies either of a) words beginning with R versus words beginning with L, or b) words with R versus L in the third position. In either of these cases, differences in the relative ease of generation would have reflected differences in frequency quite accurately.

The normative status of using the availability heuristic, and the pragmatic utility of using it, thus depend on the judgmental domain and context. People are not, of course, totally unaware that simple availability criteria must sometimes be discounted. For example, few people who were asked to estimate the relative number of moles versus cats in their neighborhood would conclude "there must be more cats because I've seen several of them but I've never seen a mole." Nevertheless, as this book documents, people often fail to distinguish between legitimate and superficially similar, but illegitimate, uses of the availability heuristic.

The Representativeness Heuristic

The second judgmental heuristic to be introduced is one which Kahneman and Tversky (1972 [473], 1973 [474]; Tversky and Kahneman 1974 [472]) termed the *representativeness* heuristic. This heuristic involves the application of relatively simple resemblance or "goodness of fit" criteria to problems of categorization. In making a judgment, people assess the degree to which the salient features of the object are representative of, or similar to, the features presumed to be characteristic of the category.

In the following sections we try to provide a coherent grouping of examples. It should be emphasized, however, that our classification system is neither exhaustive nor theoretically derived. We also should note that we make no attempt to specify the precise criteria by which individuals calculate the representativeness of one object or event to another. (For the interested reader, a recent but already classic paper by Tversky 1977 [849], takes a first step in this direction by introducing a formal theory of similarity judgments.)

Judgments of the Degree to Which Outcomes Are Representative of Their Origins

People often are required to predict some outcome or judge the likelihood of some event on the basis of information about the "generating process" that produced it. On such occasions, the judgment is likely to reflect the degree to which the specified outcome represents its origin. Let us consider an example adapted from one used by Kahneman and Tversky (1972) [473]:

Subjects are asked to assess the relative likelihood of three particular sequences of births of boys (B) and girls (G) for the next six babies born in the United States. These sequences are i) BBBBBB, ii) GGGBBB, iii) GBBGGB.

According to the conventional probability calculation, the likelihood of each of these sequences is almost identical. (Actually, the first sequence is slightly more likely than either the second or third sequence, since male births are slightly more common than female births. The latter two sequences are simply different orderings of identical, independent events.) Subjects who rely upon their intuitions and upon the representativeness criteria which guide such intuitions, are apt to regard the GBBGGB sequence as far more likely than either of the other two. In doing so, they are responding to what they know about the population of babies and about the processes of "generation," that is, that each birth is a "random" event in which the probability of "boy" and "girl" are nearly equal. Only the GBBGGB sequence is "representative" of the generating process. The GGGBBB sequence seems too "orderly" to represent a random process. The BBBBBB sequence satisfies the criteria even less: It captures neither the randomness of the birth process nor the equal sex distribution of the population from which the six births were "sampled."

The representativeness heuristic also accounts for the familiar "gamblers' fallacy." After observing a long run of "red" on a roulette wheel, people believe that "black" is now due, because the occurrence of black would make the overall sequence of events more representative of the generating process than would the occurrence of another red. In a similar vein, any researcher who has ever consulted a random number table for an unbiased ordering of events has probably felt that the result was somehow insufficiently "representative" of a chance process, that it contained suspiciously orderly sequences, suspiciously long runs, suspicious overrepresentations or underrepresentations of particular numbers early or late in the sequence, and so forth (cf. Tversky and Kahneman 1971 [475]).

Judgments of the Degree to Which Instances Are Representative of Categories

Many everyday judgments require people to estimate the likelihood that some object or event with a given set of characteristics is an instance of some designated category or class. Typically, the judgments are made in relative terms, that is, is Event X more likely to be an instance of Class A or of Class B? Consider the following problem, which is similar in form to those in the empirical work by Kahneman and Tversky. . . .

The present authors have a friend who is a professor. He likes to write poetry, is rather shy, and is small in stature. Which of the following is his field: (a) Chinese studies or (b) psychology?

Those readers who quickly and confidently predicted "psychology" probably applied some version, whether sophisticated or crude, of conventional statistical canons. We congratulate these readers. We suspect, however, that many readers guessed "Chinese studies," or at least seriously considered that such a guess might be reasonable. If so, they probably were seduced by the representativeness heuristic. Specifically, they assessed the relative "goodness of fit" between the professor's personality profile and the predominant features of their stereotypes of Sinologists and psychologists. Finding the fit better for the former than for the latter, they guessed the professor's field to be Chinese studies.

In succumbing to the lure of the representativeness heuristic, what the reader likely has overlooked or not appreciated is some relevant category *baserate* information. Let the reader who guessed "Chinese studies" now reconsider that guess in light of the relative numbers of psychologists and Sinologists in the population. Then consider the more restricted population of people likely to be friends of the authors, who themselves are psychologists. Surely *no* reader's implicit personality theory of the strength of association between academic discipline and the professor's various characteristics, that is, poetry-writing, shyness, and slightness of stature, warrants overriding such base-rate considerations.

Errors in problems of the Sinologist/psychologist variety may reflect that the judge has been led to answer the wrong question or, more specifically, to ponder the wrong conditional probability. The judge seems to be responding to the question "How likely is it that a psychologist (versus a Sinologist) would resemble the personal profile provided?" when the actual question posed is "How likely is someone resembling the personality profile to be a psychologist (versus a Sinologist)?" The representativeness heuristic leads people to give a similar answer to the two questions, since it entails consideration only of the resemblance of the two occupational stereotypes to the given personality description. The error is the failure to consider the relevant base rates or marginal probabilities, a consideration which is irrelevant to the first question but critical to the second. Although a much higher proportion of Sinologists than of psychologists may fit the profile, there would still be a much greater *absolute* number of psychologists than of Sinologists who fit it, because of the vastly greater number of psychologists than of Sinologists in the population. . . .

Judgments of the Degree to Which Antecedents Are Representative of Consequences

Earlier we contended that the availability of causal candidates, or of causal scenarios linking outcomes to potential antecedents, influences assessments of causality. We contend that representativeness criteria also may be important to such inferences. That is, a person who is required to account for some observed action or outcome may search the list of *available* antecedents for those that seem to be the most *representative* "causes" of the known "consequences."

Simple resemblance criteria appear to influence causal assessment just as they influence judgments of the representativeness of outcomes to origins or instances to classes. . . . Sometimes the resemblance criterion is used in a crude and unsophisticated way, as it is in primitive medical beliefs attributing a particular illness to an environmental agent with features resembling the illness. Sometimes its influence is less patent, as in the preference for motivational causes in explaining events with strong motivational or affective consequences or the preference for complicated, multifaceted causes for complicated, multifaceted outcomes.

Generally, the use of the representativeness heuristic in causal assessment is more than a simple comparison of the features of effects with those of their potential causes. Normally, people also use *theories* or general *knowledge* of the particular antecedents likely to cause or explain given outcomes and of the specific outcomes likely to follow given antecedents. A person's belief that the cause of Egypt's diplomatic initiative toward Israel was an heroic vision of Egypt's leader rather than economic exigency does not reflect merely a crude assessment of the similarity between historic gestures and heroic visions. Instead, such assessments reflect judgments of the similarity of known effects and potential causes to tacit or explicit models of cause-and-effect relations in international conduct. Application of the representativeness heuristic to the assessment of causality thus ranges from the crude and questionable requirement that potential causes resemble effects, to normatively proper strategies based on a comparison of the similarity of observed effects and potential causes to generalized cause-and-effect models in the given domain.

Appropriate and Inappropriate Applications of the Representativeness Heuristic

Even more than the availability heuristic, the representativeness heuristic is a legitimate, indeed absolutely essential, cognitive tool. Countless inferential tasks, especially those requiring induction or generalization, depend on deciding what class or category of event one is observing; such judgments inevitably hinge upon assessments of resemblance or representativeness (cf. Tversky 1977). Even in our examples, the use of the representativeness heuristic produced errors only because it was overapplied or misapplied while normatively important criteria were overlooked. Let us briefly reconsider each of those examples.

In the case of the representativeness of the outcome to the origin, the problem is clearly one of overapplication. The insight that the features of the sample ought to resemble those of the population or the generating process is generally valid. It leads people to recognize that an all-male or an all-white jury is more likely to reflect a biased selection procedure than will a jury with a more proportionate representation of the overall population. It also leads people to cry foul when a politician's cronies seem to enjoy a disproportionate share of good luck in their transactions with local or state agencies. Unfortunately, when people's understanding of the generating process and its implications is deficient—as when there are misconceptions about randomness—the representativeness heuristic will mislead.

In the second example, the sinologist/psychologist problem, people are foiled mainly because important information is neglected, that is, the relevant base rates are ignored. In many circumstances, of course, such information is absent, and the representativeness heuristic has no serious contender. In other circumstances, base-rate information may have little practical significance. Sometimes the feature-matching process results in a category determination with a probability near 1.0, and when features are as powerfully diagnostic as that, there is little practical need to consider base rates. For example, in the sinologist/psychologist problem, if the profile were extended to include the information that the person speaks Chinese, knows no statistics, and has never heard of B. F. Skinner, the relevance of base-rate frequencies would dwindle to triviality. There are also occasions when representativeness criteria can be used directly without violating normative standards because the base rates or marginal probabilities are approximately equal. If the sinologist/psychologist problem were altered to a decision between a sociologist and an historian, the representativeness heuristic would serve the judge quite well, providing that the relevant occupational stereotypes had at least some validity.

Knowledge Structures: Theories And Schemas

We have discussed some of the judgmental strategies that people use in a variety of social inference tasks. Often, however, people's understanding of the rapid flow of continuing social events may depend less on such judgmental procedures than on a rich store of general knowledge of objects, people, events, and their characteristic relationships. Some of this knowledge may be represented as beliefs or *theories*, that is, reasonably explicit "propositions" about the characteristics of objects or object classes. (For example: Joe is kind to small animals. Rotarians are public spirited. Adult neuroses have their "origin" in childhood trauma. Decision makers prefer minimax strategies.) People's generic knowledge also seems to organized by a variety of less "propositional," more *schematic*, cognitive structures (for example, the knowledge underlying one's awareness of what happens in a restaurant, one's understanding of the Good Samaritan parable, or one's conception of what an introvert is like). To describe such knowledge structures, psychologists refer to a growing list of terms, including "frames" (Minsky 1975 [791]), "scripts" (Abelson 1976 [671]; Schank and Abelson 1977 [649]), "nuclear scenes" (Thomkins 1979 [848]), and "prototypes" (Cantor and Mischel 1977, in press), in addition to the earlier and more general term "schemas" (Bartlett 1932 [542]; Piaget 1936 [629]; also Rumelhart 1976 [823]).

In the following discussion we largely forsake any attempt at classifying or defining the possible structures. (See Schank and Abelson 1977 [649], Abelson 1978 [672], and Taylor and Crocker 1980 [845].) We do, however, observe the distinction between beliefs or theories that can be summarized in one or more simple propositions, and other more schematic structures. Both types of knowledge structures are important because they provide an interpretative framework for the lay scientist—one that resolves ambiguity and supplements the information "given" with much "assumed" information.

Theories and Their Impact

. . . [Here] we restrict ourselves to emphasizing the role of lay psychological theory first in the application of the representativeness heuristic and then in a variety of attributional judgments. The types of theories to be considered vary from the relatively narrow generalizations that people make about particular individuals or groups, to the broadest conceptions of human nature and the determinants of human behavior.

Theory-based Judgments of Representativeness

As we noted earlier, assessments of representativeness often depend less on simple similarity criteria than on more sophisticated "theories" of the types of attributes and events that occur together, or that cause each other. For example, scandal in a parliamentary government is a "representative" cause of an impending election. When a

scandal occurs we expect an election and when an election is called
we are apt to cite any previous scandal as a contributing cause. The
reason for such judgments clearly is not in the relative similarity of
the outstanding features of political scandals and parliamentary elec-
tions. Rather, the judgment reflects one's adherence to a pair of "theoretical" propositions, first, that scandals weaken governments and
second, that weakened governments in parliamentary democracies
often must go to the electorate for a vote of confidence. Sometimes,
as we shall see, the preconceptions governing causal inferences
and likelihood assessments may best be regarded not as a set of
propositions but as a schema or "script" (cf. Abelson 1976 [671]) in
which a succession of "scenes" is linked in a single coherent structure—for example, accusations, denials, fresh accusations, limited ac-
knowledgments of bad judgment and mendacity, resignations, and
a final emotional appeal by the political leader for support at the
polls.

People rely upon an enormous number of such theories, which are
derived from personal experience and from the accumulated wisdom
of one's culture, to decide on the representativeness of causes and
effects, outcomes and outcome-generating processes, and objects and
classes. The costs and benefits of relying upon such specific prior theories, rather than collecting and analyzing further data, for instance,
depend both on the accuracy of the theories and on the feasibility of
employing other, more empirical procedures.

Global Theories and Situational versus Dispositional Attribution

Perhaps the most significant and far-reaching of the intuitive scientist's theories are those addressing the general causes of human behavior. These theories determine the meaning we extract from social
interaction, and, in large measure, they determine the way we behave in response to the actions of our fellows. For example, the lay
scientist, like the professional psychologist, believes that rewards for
particular behaviors increase the subsequent likelihood of such behaviors and that punishment decreases their likelihood. The lay scientist, like the professional, believes that people's behavior is guided
by plans and goals and believes that people seek to maximize pleasure and minimize pain. Such tacit, "global" theories, as well as
many more specific theories, including theories about specific
individuals or classes of individuals, govern our understanding of

behavior—our causal explanations of past behavior and our predictions of future behavior.

There has been surprisingly little research on those beliefs and theories shared by the mass of people in our culture. Heider (1958) [592] was perhaps the first to emphasize their importance, and Abelson (1968) [670] was the first (and very nearly the only) investigator to attempt to study them empirically. What little research has been done on people's theories has focused on individual differences in the beliefs and theories. Christie and Geis (1970) [556], for example, identified a set of cynical views about human nature that characterizes the highly "Machiavellian" individual and explains his success in manipulating his more trusting peers. Even more relevant to present concerns, Rotter and others (Rotter 1966 [822]; Collins 1974 [696]; Crandall, Katkovsky, and Crandall 1965 [669]; Lefcourt 1972 [770]) investigated general inclinations toward internal versus external explanations (that is, personal effort and ability versus the vicissitudes of chance) in accounting for personal and social outcomes. More recently, Seligman (1975 [652]), discussed the part that people's theories of the controllability of outcomes and of the causes of success and failure may have in the clinical syndrome of depression.

The most general and encompassing lay theory of human behavior—so broadly applied that it might more aptly be termed a "meta-theory"—is the assumption that behavior is caused primarily by the enduring and consistent dispositions of the actor, as opposed to the particular characteristics of the situation to which the actor responds. Throughout this book we refer to what Ross (1977 [481], 1978 [819]; Ross and Anderson 1980 [820]) called the "fundamental attribution error"—the tendency to attribute behavior exclusively to the actor's dispositions and to ignore powerful situational determinants of the behavior. [Later] we argue that such errors are determined partially by perceptual factors. Such errors probably are also prompted partially by domain-specific theories, for example: "Successful people are ambitious and motivated"; "People who hurt others' feelings are rude and not well 'brought up.' " But in large measure the error, we suspect, lies in a very broad proposition about human conduct, to wit, that people behave as they do because of a general disposition to behave in the way that they do.

It is difficult to prove that people adhere to anything like an overarching "general theory" of the relative impact of dispositional versus situational factors. There is reason to suspect, nevertheless, that a rather general, "dispositionalist theory" is shared by almost everyone socialized in our culture. Certainly, it is a part of the world view of the so-called Protestant ethic that one's virtues and successes ultimately reflect one's worthiness and, conversely, that one's vices and failings reflect one's unworthiness. According to this view, good or bad luck, accidents of birth, and situational adversities may forestall matters but one's fate will eventually mirror one's character, and one's personal traits and abilities will ultimately prevail over circumstances. This message is as present in Henry Fielding's novels as it is in Horatio Alger's sentimental doggerel. It is the set of beliefs which Max Weber (1904) [663] long ago identified as a precondition for the rise of capitalism, and it is consistent with the many philosophical positions that have assigned central roles to the concepts of personal responsibility and free will. The "dispositionalist theory," in short, is thoroughly woven into the fabric of our culture. Not surprisingly, therefore, children growing up in our culture come to hold an increasingly dispositional view of the causes of behavior (Ross, Turiel, Josephson, and Lepper 1979 [643]).

The opposite view, the "situationalist" position, does not lack advocates. It is espoused by most contemporary experimental social psychologists, behaviorists, and role-theory sociologists. (In a sense, the view is also part of the economic determinism of classical Marxism.) This alternative view, which was perhaps first explicitly articulated by Lewin (1935) [608] maintains that behavior is understood best in terms of states and intentions that are themselves the product of those situational stimuli pertinent to the individual at the moment of action. Such a view garners support, . . . from two sources: One is the failure of researchers to demonstrate anything like the cross-situational consistency in behavior demanded by the dispositionalist view (cf. Hartshorne and May 1928 [590]; Newcomb 1929 [624]; and more generally Mischel 1968 [618]). The second source of support for the situationalist position is the many studies that demonstrate that seemingly insubstantial manipulations of situational factors can control behavior dramatically and can greatly restrict individual differences. The mass of people may be seen to act in ways that seem either cowardly or brave, honest or dishonest, prejudiced or unprejudiced, or apathetic or concerned, depending on the situational constraints and opportunities present at the time of action.

We do not wish to imply that the evidence massively or unambiguously supports a situationalist view. The recent "metatheory shift" in the social sciences, like all such metatheory shifts or new "paradigms" (Kuhn 1962) [1975]) is currently quite underdetermined by the available data. Perhaps the chief evidence supporting the situationalist view is the continuing ability of social scientists, even those who subscribe to the situationalist view, to be surprised by evidence both of the lack of individual consistency in dispositional tendencies and of the power of manifestly "weak" situational factors to control behavior.

Whether it is the layperson's metatheory or the social scientist's that is correct (cf. Bem and Allen 1974 [676], Bem and Funder 1978 [677]), the metatheory exerts a pronounced influence on people's judgments of the causes and meanings of behavior. Often, as we will demonstrate, this marked dispositional bias can be shown to be incorrect.

Schemas, Scripts, and Personae

To understand the social world, the layperson makes heavy use of a variety of knowledge structures normally not expressed in propositional terms and possibly not stored in a form even analogous to propositional statements. In describing these cognitive structures we shall use the generic designation "schema" and will comment in detail about only two types of schemas—event-schemas, or "scripts," and person-schemas, or "personae."

The most basic type of schema is probably that which underlies the use of common concepts or categories such as *dog, tree* or *chair*, or concepts of far greater or lesser generality *(animals, flora*, and *furniture*, or *Airedales, Ponderosa pines*, and *Chippendales)*. In recent years there has been an explosion of interest in and research on people's use of categories, and we cannot digress to summarize this important and ever-expanding literature. Let us note merely that the "classic" view of a category, one that entails clearly specified boundaries and a set of defining characteristics necessary to and sufficient for category membership, has come under increasingly devastating attack (cf. Wittgenstein 1953 [666]; Rosch 1978 [817]; Tversky 1977 [849]). Gradually it has been supplanted by a more lenient and catholic view—one that allows ambiguous boundaries, recognizes a variety of differing bases for assessing category membership, and permits individual members to differ in their prototypicality. What both the traditional and newer views have in common is the notion that the category and the concept underlying it form an important basis for inference. That is, once the criteria for applying the concept have been met, the concept user readily assigns a number of additional characteristics to the entity. For example, upon deciding on the basis of a particular animal's appearance that it is a "dog," one makes the inferential leaps that it is trainable, capable of loyalty, able to bark, and likely to chase cats but is unlikely to climb trees, purr, or wash its coat.

In principle one could speak of a dog "schema," or even an Airedale schema or an animal schema. In practice, however, the term "schema" has come to be differentiated from the term "concept." Since its introduction in the 1930s by Bartlett (1932) [542] and by Piaget (1936) [629], the term "schema" has been used more and more to refer to those mental structures having a *dynamic* or *relational* aspect. For example, Piaget refers to a "thumb-sucking" schema and a "conservation" schema, both of which, despite the enormous difference in their level of abstractness, have dynamic relationships among the schema's components. In the former, the schema is a kind of mental summary of the sensory, cognitive, and motor experiences in a sequence of actions involving body parts. In the latter, the schema represents experiential knowledge of the relationship between mass and volume (or number and position) and the outcomes likely to result from various action sequences involving a fixed mass of material (or a fixed number of objects).

Kelly (1972) [756] introduced to the attribution literature the notion of a causal schema. Kelley used the term to refer primarily to a highly abstract, content-free notion of the formal relations among causes and effects. He proposed that people possess in very abstract and general form the notions of sufficiency and necessity in causal relations. This distinction underlies a number of specific causal schemas, such as the single necessary cause schema (in which the existence of the effect carries with it the certainty that a particular cause was present) and the multiple sufficient cause schema (in which the existence of the effect implies the possibility of each of several causes). There also are more complicated general schemas. For example, people may have a "discounting" schema: Given an effect capable of being produced by several causes and certain knowledge of the operation of a particular cause, people reduce their subjective probability that each of the other sufficient causes was operative. People also may possess an inhibitory cause schema: Given knowledge of the existence of a factor operating to block the occurrence of the effect, people infer that one or more facilitative causes were unusually powerful.

Though we are not confident that people actually possess such content-free causal schemas, we will use the term occasionally, to refer primarily to causal-analytic strategies that people do *not* seem to understand or to use in situations in which they would be helpful.

Scripts

The lexicons of cognitive social psychology and artificial intelligence recently were enriched by the introduction of the "script" concept (Abelson 1976 [671], 1978 [672]; Schank and Abelson 1977 [649]). A script is a type of schema in which the related elements are social objects and events involving the individual as actor or observer. Unlike most schemas, scripts generally are event sequences extended over time, and the relationships have a distinctly causal flavor, that is, early events in the sequence produce or at least "enable" the occurrence of later events. A script can be compared to a cartoon strip with two or more captioned "scenes," each of which summarizes some basic actions that can be executed in a range of possible manners and contexts (for instance, the "restaurant script" with its "entering," "ordering," "eating," and "exiting" scenes). Alternatively, a script can be represented as a computer program with a set of tracks, variables, relationships, operations, subroutines, loops, and the like, which are "instantiated" with particular values for any particular application of the script. Thus, the restaurant script has a coffee shop track, a Chinese restaurant track, a cafeteria track, perhaps even a McDonald's track. The variable representing the decor may take on the value "fancy" or "crummy." The waiter values include "polite," "surly," and "bad enough to prompt a complaint." Exiting entails the operational options "pay waiter" or "pay cashier," and so forth.

Scripts can vary in many ways. They can be highly abstract, culturally pervasive, and may owe their existence only slightly to direct personal experience (for example, the script that links "temptation," "transgression," and "retribution"). Or they may be highly concrete, idiosyncratic, and directly tied to experience (for example, the scripted episode in which Daddy comes home from work, asks Mommy what's for dinner, she gets annoyed and sulks **and, de-**

pending on what his day has been like, he either apologizes or gets angry too). The importance of scripts to the intuitive scientist lies in the speed and ease with which they make events (or secondhand accounts of events) readily comprehensible and predictable. Their potential cost, as always, is the possibility of erroneous interpretations, inaccurate expectations, and inflexible modes of response.

Personae

Central to any dramatic script is the *dramatis personae,* or cast of characters. Indeed, to specify the characters is often sufficient to convey much of the action of the script (for example, "the prostitute with the heart of gold and the scholarly but naive young man" or "the crusty but benign older physician and the hot-headed, idealistic young surgeon").

Social judgments and expectations often are mediated by a class of schemas which we shall term "personae," that is, cognitive structures representing the personal characteristics and typical behaviors of particular "stock characters." Some personae are the unique products of one's own personal experience (good old Aunt Mary, Coach Whiplasch). Others are shared within the culture or subculture (the sexpot, the earth-mother, the girl-next-door, the redneck, the schlemiel, the rebel-without-a-cause). Many of the shared personae are borrowed from fiction (Shakespeare's tortured Hamlet or television's bigoted Archie Bunker) or even from the popularized professional jargon of psychology and psychiatry (the authoritarian, the "Type A" personality, the anal-compulsive).

Our store of personae is augmented further by metaphors drawn from the animal kingdom and from the many occupational roles in our society. Animal or occupational personae are apt to be very simple and "concept-like," primarily highlighting a limited set of physical or behavioral characteristics. Hence, we readily understand, and are apt to be strongly influenced by, remarks like, "What do you see in that big *ox,*" or "I wouldn't trust that *viper* if I were you," or "He wants you to be his Haldeman," or "Surgeon Blochit is a real butcher" (or, alternatively, "Butcher Phelps is a real surgeon").

In each instance the persona constitutes a knowledge structure which, when evoked, influences social judgments and behaviors. Once the principal features or behaviors of a given individual suggest a particular persona, subsequent expectations of and responses to that individual are apt to be dictated in part by the characteristics of the persona.

The concept of a persona is not essentially different from that of a stereotype. We prefer the term "persona," however, because it lacks the pejorative implications of the term "stereotype," which has been used to describe culturally shared, indeed hackneyed, notions of particular groups of people. The persona is also similar to the notion of a "person-prototype," proposed and investigated by Cantor and Mischel (1977 [685], in press [686]).

Availability, Representativeness, and the Arousal of Knowledge Structures

The notion that the layperson's experience, understanding, and inferences are structured by a great and varied store of schemas is intuitively satisfying. Indeed, it has become increasingly clear to theorists working in almost all areas of psychology that the schema construct is a cornerstone of psychological theory (Neisser 1976 [623]). Workers in social interaction (Berne 1964 [547]; Goffman 1959 [583]), personality and psychopathology (G. Kelly 1955 [601], 1958 [758]), visual perception (Minsky 1975 [791]), and especially in language comprehension and artificial intelligence (Abelson 1978 [672]; Bobrow and Collins 1976 [549]; Bower, Black, and Turner in press [682]; Rumelhart, 1976 [823]; Rumelhart and Ortony 1976 [824]; Schank 1975 [648]) all have made essentially the same point—that objects and events in the phenomenal world are almost never approached as if they were *sui generis* configurations but rather are assimilated into preexisting structures in the mind of the perceiver.

Unfortunately, the increasing conviction that schemas exist and are important has not been accompanied by a commensurate increase in our knowledge of them. There still is little evidence that might clarify their properties or define the type of work they perform. Most critical of all, perhaps, is our ignorance of the conditions of their instigation and use. In 1961, De Soto wrote of our "crippling ignorance of the dynamics of schema arousal" (p. 22), and a decade later Kelley (1972 [756]) was obliged to echo De Soto's complaint. Recently, however, matters have begun to improve. For instance, Markus (1977) [787] showed that the speed with which information about the self is processed may be predicted by the presence or absence of schematic self-concepts or "self-schemas." Similarly, Cantor's and Mischel's work (1977 [685] in press [686]) documented the biasing effects of person schemas or "prototypes" on the interpretation of ambiguous information and the recall of specific details about people.

Perhaps the most encouraging development for the question of schema arousal is the theoretical one in Kahneman's and Tversky's work on heuristics. It is obvious that a schema can be aroused only if it exists in the person's long-term repertoire of schemas. What is not so obvious is that the *acute or transient availability* of a schema also may be an important determinant of its application to a particular instance. Two recent experiments support this possibility.

Higgins, Rholes, and Jones (1977) [746] asked subjects to read a brief paragraph describing a young man and then to evaluate him on a number of dimensions. The young man was described as having many risky hobbies, having a high opinion of his abilities, having limited relationships with other people, and being unlikely to change his mind or turn back from a chosen course of action. Before reading about the young man, subjects had participated in a "learning experiment" in which some were exposed to the words "adventurous," "self-confident," "independent," and "persistent," and some were exposed to the words "reckless," "conceited," "aloof," and "stubborn." Subjects exposed to the positive words later evaluated the young man more highly than did those exposed to the negative words. (Subjects exposed to equally positive or negative but conceptually irrelevant words were uninfluenced.) As Higgins and colleagues suggest, this effect is most likely mediated by the transient availability of different concepts or "personae."

Hornstein, LaKind, Frankel, and Manne (1975) [748] performed an experiment with similar implications. Before playing a prisoner's dilemma game, subjects were left seated in a waiting room listening to what they believed was a piped-in radio program. The music was interrupted for a "human interest" story. In one instance this was a heart-warming account of someone who offered a kidney to someone whom he did not know who was in need of a transplant. In another instance, subjects heard a ghastly account of an urban atrocity. The vignette had pronounced effects on subsequent strategy in the prisoner's dilemma game. Subjects who had heard the heart-warming vignette played the game in a much more cooperative way than did those who had heard the horror. The authors argued persuasively

(and with data) against a mood interpretation of the subsequent behavior. Instead, it seems likely that it was an acute manipulation of
the availability of different personae or "schemas for the human race"
that accounted for the results ("most people are basically decent and
kind" versus "it's dog eat dog out there").

It seems equally clear that the representativeness heuristic takes
part in the selection of schemas. Indeed, the similarity of the data at
hand to some stored representation of objects and events always has
been presumed to be the chief determinant of schema arousal and
application. But it also seems likely that purely incidental and irrelevant features of the stimulus may prompt the arousal of schemas
tagged with similar incidental features. Thus, we have it on the testimony of Colonel House (May 1973 [614]) that, on the eve of World
War I, President Woodrow Wilson was anguishing over the possibility of war with *Great Britain*. Why? Because, as on the eve of the War
of 1812, the British were illegally searching American ships and, as
Wilson agonized to House, "Madison and I are the only Princeton
men to become President" (!) Apparently, the "search-ships/war with
England" schema was a representative one for Wilson in part because
of the irrelevant surface detail of the alma mater of the incumbent
president.

Availability and representativeness determinants of schema
arousal appear to be the probable focal guides of future research in
this area. It will be fascinating to see whether these determinants operate in a normatively appropriate way, or whether, as in the Wilson
anecdote, they operate so as to leave us at the mercy of arbitrary and
incidental features of stimuli and structures.

Appropriate and Inappropriate Utilization of Knowledge Structures

It would be even more foolish to criticize people's general tendency
to employ schemas and other knowledge structures than it would
be to criticize their general tendency to rely on the availability and
representativeness heuristics. Indeed, the primary reason for the
widespread acceptance of the notion of schematic knowledge structures is that it is almost impossible to imagine how mental life could
be managed without them. In a world characterized by recurrent
stimuli presenting important functional equivalencies, any cognitive
system that places a premium on minimizing computing time and

effort must take advantage of such redundancy by storing generic concepts, events, event-sequences, and the like.

Despite the important efficiencies that accrue to the schema user, there seems little doubt there often are serious costs as well. Schemas are apt to be overused and misapplied, particularly to the social sphere, and they are apt to be used when other, less rapid and intuitive methods of judgment would fully merit the additional time and effort required.

In the physical world, stimuli categorized in a particular way, or events interpreted in terms of a given schema, may be similar to an extent rarely true in the social domain. In many important respects, it is only a slight overstatement to say that "if you've seen one oak tree, you've seen them all." The number of properties necessary to define uniquely many types of physical objects is highly limited. As a consequence, the number of properties of a particular object that must be perceived in order to place the object in its correct category also is limited. Moreover, once a physical object has been placed in some conceptual category, one can usually disregard much of the information that dicated the categorization (that is, information specifying exactly how, when, and under what observation conditions a particular tree satisfied the requirements for assignment to the "oak" category). Most important of all, classification of a physical object usually permits one to adduce or predict confidently additional properties of the object. Thus, once an object is correctly characterized as an oak tree, it is nearly certain that the tree will provide shade and acorns, that its wood will be hard and burn slowly, that all its leaves will drop in the fall, and so on.

It is quite different in the social domain, in which the observed properties are less diagnostic, in which the number of properties suggestive of a given category are not so sharply delineated, and in which the number of properties that can be inferred confidently, given correct categorization of the object, is very small. To appreciate these differences, let us note how the categorization of a person as a "bigot" differs from the categorization of an object as an oak tree. First, the number of properties that might indicate bigotry is, for all practical purposes, infinite, and information about the circumstances in which a particular person satisfied the "bigot" criterion can be ignored or forgotten only at one's peril. Similarly, the number of properties dicated by the categorization of someone as a bigot is large only in proportion to the naiveté of the perceiver. Few characteristics or behaviors can be confidently assumed about any particular "bigot." Schemas in the social domain rarely are more than rough outlines and tentative guides for perception and behavior. When they are relied on heavily, there are bound to be inferential errors and misguided actions.

E. R. May, in his fascinating book entitled *"Lessons" of the Past* (1973) [614], presented some thought-provoking examples of erroneous political judgments and policies that seem to have originated in the overutilization or misapplication of particular schemas. For example, May describes how a schema, which might be termed the "Munich Conference" script, exerted an undue influence on the thinking of politicians (most notably President Lyndon Johnson), who invoked the specter of the infamous "Munich Conference" to defend the aggressiveness of their military policy or the intransigence of their diplomacy. These politicians seem to have been influenced greatly by—or perhaps hoped to influence the public and their potential detractors through—a particularly vivid, historic script. The script has two scences or vignettes, *"The Political Compromise,"* in which one yields to a power-hungry and unprincipled foe, and *"The Military Consequence,"* in which one's country or that of one's ally is subsequently overrun by the foe. To the extent that politicians rely on such historical scripts, they may be unduly dogmatic and constrained and may be unresponsive to features that ought to distinguish a current political decision from an historical one. They may even be unduly responsive to prominent but superficial considerations of script representativeness, that is, the Munich script may be particularly likely to be evoked if the foreign leader requests the conference in his own country rather than on neutral grounds or if he has a small moustache!

A "persona" can mislead as badly as a script can, as other examples from May's book show. President Harry Truman, a man not given to speaking kindly of all whom he met, demonstrated a peculiar willingness to trust his wartime ally, Joseph Stalin. His personal correspondences reveal a surprising source of this trust. To Truman, Stalin evoked the persona of Tom Pendergast, his former Missouri benefactor. Pendergast was a ruthless and corrupt political kingmaker, but he had always been completely trustworthy in his relations with Truman. Apparently because some of Stalin's characteristics were representative of the Pendergast persona, Truman seemed to feel that other Pendergast characteristics also could be assumed—specifically, trustworthiness in matters relating to Truman.

To May's examples of schema-induced errors in the judgment of politicians, we add one related to us by Dorwin Cartwright. Cartwright told us that spokesmen for the pure sciences, lobbying for financial aid in the postwar period of the late forties and early fifties, effectively argued that the technological innovations of World War II had "depleted the stockpile of basic knowledge." Congressmen, accustomed to arguments about the depletion of stockpiles and the need for replenishing them, apparently accepted the idea that the "basic knowledge stockpile" was one of those depleted. The "stockpile" concept, as applied to basic scientific knowledge, is not entirely invalid, that is, the more knowledge the better, the more money and effort spent, the faster it will grow, and so on. But the "depletion" schema is invalid and highly misleading. For heavy use of basic scientific knowledge, far from exhausting the "stockpile," makes it grow.

Our examples so far have been of the misapplication of particular schemas when more cautious and critical application of the same schemas would have served the intuitive scientist quite well. It is possible, however, to describe particular conceptual categories, scripts, or personae that are so lacking in foundation and predictive value that they almost invariably serve the user badly. Many racial or ethnic stereotypes fit this designation. The Volvo-Saab "thought experiment" described in chapter 1 is another example. [Editor's note: The thought experiment is as follows. You have decided to buy either a Volvo or a Saab. On looking in *Consumer Reports*, you find that Volvo is the more reliable car, and so you decide to buy the Volvo. Your brother-in-law then details his many problems with a single Volvo. What is the likely effect of this new information on your decision?] The brother-in-law's litany of mechanical woes derives its impact, in part, from its ability to evoke the familiar "lemon" schema that haunts most prospective car buyers. Such a schema invites the assumption that mechanical difficulties are not distributed in a normal curve but that there is instead a distinct "bump" at the high-difficulty end of the continuum. It is doubtful that there is such a bump, and if there is not then it is clearly counterproductive to direct one's efforts toward avoiding a mythical lemon when one's efforts could be better directed toward obtaining a car with the best overall record for trouble-free performance. But even if the lemon schema is true, the anecdote about the brother-in-law's Volvo provides far less evidence about the distribution of lemons across car makes than do drab statistical surveys of repair records.

An example of inappropriate schema usage that may hit even closer to home is the behavior of the typical faculty committee charged to select students for a graduate program. A letter of recommendation for Elsa Doud may note that Ms. Doud was shy in Professor Smith's class at Ohio State. Doud's shyness and "midwesternness" may call to mind Priscilla Frimp, another shy midwestern woman who never made it through the program. The Frimp persona may then be used as a basis to reject Doud. Any reliance on personae in such a situation is utterly without foundation. The only currently valid grounds for predicting graduate performance seem to be the candidate's GRE (Graduate Record Examination) scores, grades, research experience, quality of undergraduate institution, and evaluations in letters of recommendation. Of course, if the anti-Doud professor wishes to construct a shyness measure and can show that it is related to quality of graduate performance, then the professor may administer this measure to the entire pool of applicants and reject those scoring high on it. If an interaction among shyness, sex, and region of the country is found, such that shyness is particularly crippling to the performance of midwestern females, then a lower cutoff point on the shyness scale may be set for midwestern females than for male or female students from other parts of the country. Unless the professor is willing to perform the requisite validation research, however, any persona ruminations should be kept out of the student selection procedure.

Inferential Adjustment And Its Limitations

In this chapter we described some inferential strategies on which the lay scientist seems to rely in forming judgments of the social world. There were two common themes in our observations. The first and more obvious—that people's errors and insights are intimately linked together and are typically a matter of appropriate versus inappropriate application of a given heuristic, theory, or schema—was reiterated often enough that we trust it needs no reemphasis. There was a second and less obvious theme that merits some elaboration. At several points we emphasized that it is not only people's eagerness to apply simple heuristics and immediately available knowledge structures that leads to grief; it is also the failure to make necessary *adjustments* of initial judgments. That is, once a simple heuristic or schema has been used, subsequent considerations fail to exert as much impact as common sense or normative considerations might dictate that it should.

Some simple, direct demonstrations of inadequate adjustment or "anchoring" effects were provided in work by Tversky and Kahneman (1974) [472]. In one study, for example, subjects were asked to adjust an arbitrary initial estimate of the percentage of African countries in the United Nations. Those starting with "anchors" of 10 percent and 65 percent produced "adjusted" estimates of 25 percent and 45 percent, respectively. The same anchoring effects were demonstrated with initial "estimates" dictated by the subject's own previous spin of a roulette wheel! Even though it would have been obvious to the subjects that these "starting points" were wholly arbitrary and unrelated to the judgment task, they nevertheless had an influence on final estimates.

Our present contention is essentially an extension of Tversky's and Kahneman's point about the effects of a cognitive "anchor." That is, once subjects have made a first pass at a problem, the initial judgment may prove remarkably resistant to further information, alternative modes of reasoning, and even logical or evidential challenges. Attempts to integrate new information may find the individual surprisingly "conservative," that is, willing to yield ground only grudgingly and primed to challenge the relevance, reliability, or authority of subsequent information or logical consideration. As a result, the method of first choice—and we believe heuristics and schemas to be such methods of first choice—may have disproportionate impact, while other methods (notably, methods considering pallid base lines, mitigating situational factors, possible sources of unreliability in the data, and the like) have relatively little impact.

Summary

The chapter describes two of the general tools that people use to "go beyond the information given," judgmental heuristics and knowledge structures.

The availability heuristic is used to judge the frequency and likelihood of events and event-relations. Since the availability of remembered events is sometimes biased at the stage of sampling, sometimes at the stage of encoding and storage, and sometimes at the stage of retrieval, frequency and likelihood estimates often will be biased correspondingly.

The representativeness heuristic is used to estimate the likelihood of some state of affairs given knowledge of some other state of affairs, for example, the likelihood that an object is a member of some category because it has certain characteristics. Such judgments are based on the perceived similarity of the known characteristics of the object to the presumed essential characteristics of the category. The heuristic sometimes misleads because, in some circumstances, notably when diagnosticity is low or category base rates differ widely, mere similarity is an unreliable guide to likelihood.

In addition to heuristics, people use certain knowledge structures in approaching judgment tasks. These include relatively propositional structures such as theories and beliefs, and more schematic structures like scripts and personae. These knowledge structures are invaluable aids to understanding social events, but they may mislead to the extent that they are poor representations of external reality and to the extent that they preclude attention to the details of the actual object at hand.

The judgmental heuristics may prove to be the primary determinants of the arousal and application of the various knowledge structures. Availability of a given structure, including transient, arbitrary increments in its availability, may increase the likelihood of its application. The representativeness of a given structure, including the similarity of quite superficial and incidental features of the stimulus to features of the structure, may be a chief determinant of the arousal and application of a given structure.

It is emphasized that it is not the existence of heuristics and knowledge structures that can be criticized but rather, their overuse, misuse, and use in preference to more appropriate strategies. Even when more appropriate strategies are subsequently employed for a given judgmental task, the undue influence of the simpler, more intuitive strategies may persist.

13 Epistemic Folkways and Scientific Epistemology

Alvin I. Goldman

I

What is the mission of epistemology, and what is its proper methodology? Such meta-epistemological questions have been prominent in recent years, especially with the emergence of various brands of "naturalistic" epistemology. In this paper, I shall reformulate and expand upon my own meta-epistemological conception (most fully articulated in Goldman 1986 [49]), retaining many of its former ingredients while reconfiguring others. The discussion is by no means confined, though, to the meta-epistemological level. New substantive proposals will also be advanced and defended.

Let us begin, however, at the meta-epistemological level, by asking what role should be played in epistemology by our ordinary epistemic concepts and principles. By some philosophers' lights, the sole mission of epistemology is to elucidate commonsense epistemic concepts and principles: concepts like knowledge, justification, and rationality, and principles associated with these concepts. By other philosophers' lights, this is not even part of epistemology's aim. Ordinary concepts and principles, the latter would argue, are fundamentally naive, unsystematic, and uninformed by important bodies of logic and/or mathematics. Ordinary principles and practices, for example, ignore or violate the probability calculus, which ought to be the cornerstone of epistemic rationality. Thus, on the second view, proper epistemology must neither *end* with naive principles of justification or rationality, nor even *begin* there.

My own stance on this issue lies somewhere between these extremes. To facilitate discussion, let us give a label to our common-

Reprinted from *Liaisons: Philosophy Meets the Cognitive and Social Sciences*, by Alvin I. Goldman (Cambridge, Mass.: MIT Press, 1992), pp. 155–175, by permission of the publisher. Copyright © 1992, MIT Press.

sense epistemic concepts and norms; let us call them our *epistemic folkways*. In partial agreement with the first view sketched above, I would hold that *one* proper task of epistemology is to elucidate our epistemic folkways. Whatever else epistemology might proceed to do, it should at least have its roots in the concepts and practices of the folk. If these roots are utterly rejected and abandoned, by what rights would the new discipline call itself 'epistemology' at all? It may well be desirable to reform or transcend our epistemic folkways, as the second of the views sketched above recommends. But it is essential to preserve continuity; and continuity can only be recognized if we have a satisfactory characterization of our epistemic folkways. Actually, even if one rejects the plea for continuity, a description of our epistemic folkways is in order. How would one know what to criticize, or what needs to be transcended, in the absence of such a description? So a first mission of epistemology is to describe or characterize our folkways.

Now a suitable description of these folk concepts, I believe, is likely to depend on insights from cognitive science. Indeed, identification of the semantic contours of many (if not all) concepts can profit from theoretical and empirical work in psychology and linguistics. For this reason, the task of describing or elucidating folk epistemology is a *scientific* task, at least a task that should be informed by relevant scientific research.

The second mission of epistemology, as suggested by the second view above, is the formulation of a more adequate, sound, or systematic set of epistemic norms, in some way(s) transcending our naive epistemic repertoire. How and why these folkways might be transcended, or improved upon, remains to be specified. This will partly depend on the contours of the commonsense standards that emerge from the first mission. On my view, epistemic concepts like knowledge and justification crucially invoke psychological faculties or processes. Our folk understanding, however, has a limited and tenuous grasp of the processes available to the cognitive agent. Thus, one important respect in which epistemic folkways should be transcended is by incorporating a more detailed and empirically based depiction of psychological mechanisms. Here too epistemology would seek assistance from cognitive science.

Since both missions of epistemology just delineated lean in important respects on the deliverances of science, specifically cognitive science, let us call our conception of epistemology *scientific epis-*

temology. Scientific epistemology, we have seen, has two branches: *descriptive* and *normative*. While descriptive scientific epistemology aims to describe our ordinary epistemic assessments, normative scientific epistemology continues the practice of making epistemic judgments, or formulating systematic principles for such judgments.[1] It is prepared to depart from our ordinary epistemic judgments, however, if and when that proves advisable. (This overall conception of epistemology closely parallels the conception of metaphysics articulated in Goldman 1992 [50], chapters 2 and 3. The descriptive and normative branches of scientific epistemology are precise analogues of the descriptive and prescriptive branches of metaphysics, as conceptualized there.) In the remainder of this paper, I shall sketch and defend the particular forms of descriptive and normative scientific epistemology that I favor.

II

Mainstream epistemology has concentrated much of its attention on two concepts (or terms): knowledge and justified belief. The preceding essay primarily illustrates the contributions that cognitive science can make to an understanding of the former; this essay focuses on the latter. We need not mark this concept exclusively by the phrase 'justified belief'. A family of phrases pick out roughly the same concept: 'well-founded belief', 'reasonable belief', 'belief based on good grounds', and so forth. I shall propose an account of this concept that is in the reliabilist tradition, but departs at a crucial juncture from other versions of reliabilism. My account has the same core idea as Ernest Sosa's *intellectual virtues* approach, but incorporates some distinctive features that improve its prospects.[2]

The basic approach is, roughly, to identify the concept of justified belief with the concept of belief obtained through the exercise of intellectual virtues (excellences). Beliefs acquired (or retained) through a chain of "virtuous" psychological processes qualify as justified; those acquired partly by cognitive "vices" are derogated as unjustified. This, as I say, is a *rough* account. To explain it more fully, I need to say things about the psychology of the epistemic evaluator, the possessor and deployer of the concept in question. At this stage in the development of semantical theory (which, in the future, may well be viewed as part of the "dark ages" of the subject), it is difficult to say just what the relationship is between the meaning or "content" of concepts and the form or structure of their mental representation. In the present case, however, I believe that an account of the form of representation can contribute to our understanding of the content, although I am unable to formulate these matters in a theoretically satisfying fashion.

The hypothesis I wish to advance is that the epistemic evaluator has a mentally stored set, or list, of cognitive virtues and vices. When asked to evaluate an actual or hypothetical case of belief, the evaluator considers the processes by which the belief was produced, and matches these against his list of virtues and vices. If the processes match virtues only, the belief is classified as justified. If the processes are matched partly with vices, the belief is categorized as unjustified. If a belief-forming scenario is described that features a process not on the evaluator's list of either virtues or vices, the belief may be categorized as neither justified nor unjustified, but simply *non*justified. Alternatively (and this alternative plays an important role in my story), the evaluator's judgment may depend on the (judged) *similarity* of the novel process to the stored virtues and vices. In other words, the "matches" in question need not be perfect.

This proposal makes two important points of contact with going theories in the psychology of concepts. First, it has some affinity to the *exemplar* approach to concept representation (cf. Medin and Schaffer 1978 [788]; Smith and Medin 1981 [657]; Hintzman 1986 [747]). According to that approach, a concept is mentally represented by means of representations of its positive instances, or perhaps types of instances. For example, the representation of the concept *pants* might include a representation of a particular pair of faded blue jeans and/ or a representation of the type *blue jeans*. Our approach to the concept of justification shares the spirit of this approach insofar as it posits a set of examples of virtues and vices, as opposed to a mere abstract characterization—e.g., a definition—of (intellectual) virtue or vice. A second affinity to the exemplar approach is in the appeal to a similarity, or matching, operation in the classification of new target cases. According to the exemplar approach, targets are categorized as a function of their similarity to the positive exemplars (and dissimilarity to the foils). Of course, similarity is invoked in many other approaches to concept deployment as well (see E. E. Smith 1990 [830]). This makes our account of justification consonant with the psychological literature generally, whether or not it meshes specifically with the exemplar approach.

Let us now see what this hypothesis predicts for a variety of cases. To apply it, we need to make some assumptions about the lists of virtues and vices that typical evaluators mentally store. I shall assume that the virtues include belief formation based on sight, hearing, memory, reasoning in certain "approved" ways, and so forth. The vices include intellectual processes like forming beliefs by guesswork, wishful thinking, and ignoring contrary evidence. *Why* these items are placed in their respective categories remains to be explained. As indicated, I plan to explain them by reference to reliability. Since the account will therefore be, at bottom, a reliabilist type of account, it is instructive to see how it fares when applied to well-known problem cases for standard versions of reliabilism.

Consider first the demon-world case. In a certain possible world, a Cartesian demon gives people deceptive visual experiences, which systematically lead to false beliefs. Are these vision-based beliefs justified? Intuitively, they are. The demon's victims are presented with the same sorts of visual experiences that we are, and they use the same processes to produce corresponding beliefs. For most epistemic evaluators, this seems sufficient to induce the judgment that the victims' beliefs are justified. Does our account predict this result? Certainly it does. The account predicts that an epistemic evaluator will match the victims' vision-based processes to one (or more) of the items on his list of intellectual virtues, and therefore judge the victims' beliefs to be justified.

Turn next to Laurence BonJour's (1985) [14] cases in which hypothetical agents are assumed to possess a perfectly reliable clairvoyant faculty. Although these agents form their beliefs by this reliable faculty, BonJour contends that the beliefs are not justified; and apparently most (philosophical) evaluators agree with that judgment. This result is not predicted by simple forms of reliabilism.[3] What does our present theory predict? Let us consider the four cases in two groups. In the first three cases (Samantha, Casper, and Maud), the agent has contrary evidence that he or she ignores. Samantha has a massive amount of apparently cogent evidence that the president is in Washington, but she nonetheless believes (through clairvoyance) that the president is in New York City. Casper and Maud each has large amounts of ostensibly cogent evidence that he/she has no reliable clairvoyant power, but they rely on such a power nonetheless. Here our theory predicts that the evaluator will match these agent's belief-forming processes to the vice of ignoring contrary evidence.

Since the processes include a vice, the beliefs will be judged to be unjustified.

BonJour's fourth case involves Norman, who has a reliable clairvoyant power but no reasons for or against the thesis that he possesses it. When he believes, through clairvoyance, that the president is in New York City, while possessing no (other) relevant evidence, how should this belief be judged? My own assessment is less clear in this case than the other three cases. I am tempted to say that Norman's belief is *non*justified, not that it is thoroughly *un*justified. (I construe unjustified as "having negative justificational status," and nonjustified as "lacking positive justificational status.") This result is also readily predicted by our theory. On the assumption that I (and other evaluators) do not have clairvoyance on my list of virtues, the theory allows the prediction that the belief would be judged neither justified nor unjustified, merely nonjustified. For those evaluators who would judge Norman's belief to be *un*justified, there is another possible explanation in terms of the theory. There is a class of putative faculties, including mental telepathy, ESP, telekinesis, and so forth that are scientifically disreputable. It is plausible that evaluators view any process of basing beliefs on the supposed deliverances of such faculties as vices. It is also plausible that these evaluators judge the process of basing one's belief on clairvoyance to be *similar* to such vices. Thus, the theory would predict that they would view a belief acquired in this way as unjustified.[4]

Finally, consider Alvin Plantinga's (1988) [317] examples that feature disease-triggered or mind-malfunctioning processes. These include processes engendered by a brain tumor, radiation-caused processes, and the like. In each case Plantinga imagines that the process is reliable, but reports that we would not judge it to be justification conferring. My diagnosis follows the track outlined in the Norman case. At a minimum, the processes imagined by Plantinga fail to match any virtue on a typical evaluator's list. So the beliefs are at least nonjustified. Furthermore, evaluators may have a prior representation of pathological processes as examples of cognitive vices. Plantinga's cases might be judged (relevantly) similar to these vices, so that the beliefs they produce would be declared unjustified.

In some of Plantinga's cases, it is further supposed that the hypothetical agent possesses countervailing evidence against his belief, which he steadfastly ignores. As noted earlier, this added element would strengthen a judgment of unjustifiedness according to our theory, because ignoring contrary evidence is an intellectual vice. Once again, then, our theory's predictions conform with reported judgments.

Let us now turn to the question of how epistemic evaluators acquire their lists of virtues and vices. What is the basis for their classification? As already indicated, my answer invokes the notion of reliability. Belief-forming processes based on vision, hearing, memory, and ("good") reasoning are deemed virtuous because they (are deemed to) produce a high ratio of true beliefs. Processes like guessing, wishful thinking, and ignoring contrary evidence are deemed vicious because they (are deemed to) produce a low ratio of true beliefs.

We need not assume that each epistemic evaluator chooses his/her catalogue of virtues and vices by direct application of the reliability test. Epistemic evaluators may partly inherit their lists of virtues and vices from other speakers in the linguistic community. Nonetheless, the hypothesis is that the selection of virtues and vices rests, ultimately, on assessments of reliability.

It is not assumed, of course, that all speakers have the same lists of intellectual virtues and vices. They may have different opinions about the reliability of processes, and therefore differ in their respective lists.[5] Or they may belong to different subcultures in the linguistic community, which may differentially influence their lists. Philosophers sometimes seem to assume great uniformity in epistemic judgments. This assumption may stem from the fact that it is mostly the judgments of philosophers themselves that have been reported, and they are members of a fairly homogeneous subculture. A wider pool of "subjects" might reveal a much lower degree of uniformity. That would conform to the present theory, however, which permits individual differences in catalogues of virtues and vices, and hence in judgments of justifiedness.

If virtues and vices are selected on the basis of reliability and unreliability, respectively, why doesn't a hypothetical case introducing a novel reliable process induce an evaluator to add that process to his list of virtues, and declare the resulting belief justified? Why, for example, doesn't he add clairvoyance to his list of virtues, and rule Norman's beliefs to be justified?

I venture the following explanation. First, people seem to have a trait of *categorial conservation*. They display a preference for "entrenched" categories, in Nelson Goodman's (1955) [53] phraseology, and do not lightly supplement or revise their categorial schemes. An isolated single case is not enough. More specifically, merely imaginary cases do not exert much influence on categorial structures. People's cognitive systems are responsive to live cases, not purely fictional ones. Philosophers encounter this when their students or nonphilosophers are unimpressed with science fiction-style counterexamples. Philosophers become impatient with this response because they presume that possible cases are on a par (for counterexample purposes) with actual ones. This phenomenon testifies, however, to a psychological propensity to take an invidious attitude toward purely imaginary cases.

To the philosopher, it seems both natural and inevitable to take hypothetical cases seriously, and if necessary to restrict one's conclusions about them to specified "possible worlds." Thus, the philosopher might be inclined to hold, "If reliability is the standard of intellectual virtue, shouldn't we say that clairvoyance is a virtue *in the possible worlds* of BonJour's examples, if not a virtue in general?" This is a natural thing for philosophers to say, given their schooling, but there is no evidence that this is how people naturally think about the matter. There is no evidence that "the folk" are inclined to relativize virtues and vices to this or that possible world.

I suspect that concerted investigation (not undertaken here) would uncover ample evidence of conservatism, specifically in the normative realm. In many traditional cultures, for example, loyalty to family and friends is treated as a cardinal virtue.[6] This view of loyalty tends to persist even through changes in social and organizational climate, which undermine the value of unqualified loyalty. Members of such cultures, I suspect, would continue to view personal loyalty as a virtue even in *hypothetical* cases where the trait has stipulated unfortunate consequences.

In a slightly different vein, it is common for both critics and advocates of reliabilism to call attention to the relativity of reliability to the domain or circumstances in which the process is used. The question is therefore raised, what is the relevant domain for judging the reliability of a process? A critic like John Pollock (1986 [98], pp. 118–119), for example, observes that color vision is reliable on earth but unreliable in the universe at large. In determining the reliability of color vision, he asks, which domain should be invoked? Finding no satisfactory reply to this question, Pollock takes this as a serious difficulty for reliabilism. Similarly, Sosa (1988 [329] and 1991 [125]) notes that an intellectual structure or disposition can be reliable with respect to one field of propositions but unreliable with respect to another, and reliable in one environment but unreliable in another. He does not view this as a difficulty for reliabilism, but concludes that any talk of intellectual virtue must be relativized to field and environment.

Neither of these conclusions seems apt, however, for purposes of *description* of our epistemic folkways. It would be a mistake to suppose that ordinary epistemic evaluators are sensitive to these issues. It is likely—or at least plausible—that our ordinary apprehension of the intellectual virtues is rough, unsystematic, and insensitive to any theoretical desirability of relativization to domain or environment. Thus, as long as we are engaged in the description of our epistemic folkways, it is no criticism of the account that it fails to explain what domain or environment is to be used. Nor is it appropriate for the account to introduce relativization where there is no evidence of relativization on the part of the folk.

Of course, we do need an explanatory story of how the folk arrive at their selected virtues and vices. And this presumably requires some reference to the domain in which reliability is judged. However, there may not be much more to the story than the fact that people determine reliability scores from the cases they personally "observe." Alternatively, they *may* regard the observed cases as a sample from which they infer a truth ratio in some wider class of cases. It is doubtful, however, that they have any precise conception of the wider class. They probably don't address this theoretical issue, and don't do (or think) anything that commits them to any particular resolution of it. It would therefore be wrong to expect descriptive epistemology to be fully specific on this dimension.

A similar point holds for the question of process individuation. It is quite possible that the folk do not have highly principled methods for individuating cognitive processes, for "slicing up" virtues and vices. If that is right, it is a mistake to insist that descriptive epistemology uncover such methods. It is no flaw in reliabilism, considered as descriptive epistemology, that it fails to unearth them. It may well be desirable to develop sharper individuation principles for purposes of normative epistemology (a matter we shall address in section III). But the missions and requirements of descriptive and normative epistemology must be kept distinct.

This discussion has assumed throughout that the folk have lists of intellectual virtues and vices. What is the evidence for this? In the moral sphere ordinary language is rich in virtues terminology. By contrast, there are few common labels for intellectual virtues, and those that do exist—'perceptiveness', 'thoroughness', 'insightfulness', and so forth—are of limited value in the present context. I propose to identify the relevant intellectual virtues (at least those relevant to *justification*) with the belief-forming capacities, faculties, or processes that would be accepted as answers to the question "How does X know?" In answer to this form of question, it is common to reply, "He saw it," "He heard it," "He remembers it," "He infers it from such-and-such evidence," and so forth. Thus, basing belief on seeing, hearing, memory, and (good) inference are in the collection of what the folk regard as intellectual virtues. Consider, for contrast, how anomalous it is to answer the question "How does X know?" with "By guessing," "By wishful thinking," or "By ignoring contrary evidence." This indicates that *these* modes of belief formation—guessing, wishful thinking, ignoring contrary evidence—are standardly regarded as intellectual *vices*. They are not ways of obtaining knowledge, nor ways of obtaining justified belief.

Why appeal to "knowledge"-talk rather than "justification"-talk to identify the virtues? Because 'know' has a greater frequency of occurrence than 'justified', yet the two are closely related. Roughly, justified belief is belief acquired by means of the same sorts of capacities, faculties, or processes that yield knowledge in favorable circumstances (i.e., when the resulting belief is true and there are no Gettier complications, or no relevant alternatives).

To sum up the present theory, let me emphasize that it depicts justificational evaluation as involving two stages. The first stage features the acquisition by an evaluator of some set of intellectual virtues and vices. This is where reliability enters the picture. In the second stage, the evaluator applies his list of virtues and vices to decide the epistemic status of targeted beliefs. At this stage, there is no direct consideration of reliability.

There is an obvious analogy here to rule utilitarianism in the moral sphere. Another analogy worth mentioning is Saul Kripke's (1980) [603] theory of *reference-fixing*. According to Kripke, we can use one property to fix a reference to a certain entity, or type of entity; but once this reference has been fixed, that property may cease to play a role in identifying the entity across various possible worlds. For example, we can fix a reference to heat as the phenomenon that causes certain sensations in people. Once heat has been so picked out, this property is no longer needed, or relied upon, in identifying heat. A phenomenon can count as heat in another possible world where it doesn't cause those sensations in people. Similarly, I am proposing, we initially use reliability as a test for intellectual quality (virtue or vice status). Once the quality of a faculty or process has been determined, however, it tends to retain that status in our thinking. At any rate, it isn't reassessed each time we consider a fresh case, especially a purely imaginary and bizarre case like the demon world. Nor is quality relativized to each possible world or environment.

The present version of the virtues theory appears to be a successful variant of reliabilism, capable of accounting for most, if not all, of the most prominent counterexamples to earlier variants of reliabilism.[7] The present approach also makes an innovation in naturalistic epistemology. Whereas earlier naturalistic epistemologists have focused exclusively on the psychology of the epistemic agent, the present paper also highlights the psychology of the epistemic evaluator.

III

Let us turn now to *normative* scientific epistemology. It was argued briefly in section I that normative scientific epistemology should preserve continuity with our epistemic folkways. At a minimum, it should rest on the same types of evaluative criteria as those on which our commonsense epistemic evaluations rest. Recently, however, Stephen Stich (1990) [128] has disputed this sort of claim. Stich contends that our epistemic folkways are quite idiosyncratic and should not be much heeded in a reformed epistemology. An example he uses to underline his claim of idiosyncracy is the notion of justification as rendered by my "normal worlds" analysis in Goldman 1986 [49]. With hindsight, I would agree that that particular analysis makes our ordinary notion of justification look pretty idiosyncratic. But that was the fault of the analysis, not the analysandum. On the present rendering, it looks as if the folk notion of justification is keyed to dispositions to produce a high ratio of true beliefs in the actual world, not in "normal worlds"; and there is nothing idiosyncratic about that. Furthermore, there seem to be straightforward reasons for thinking that true belief is worthy of positive valuation, if only from a pragmatic point of view, which Stich also challenges. The pragmatic utility of true belief is best seen by focusing on a certain subclass of beliefs, viz., beliefs about one's own *plans of action*. Clearly, true beliefs about which courses of action would accomplish one's ends will help secure these ends better than false beliefs. Let proposition P = "Plan N will accomplish my ends" and proposition P' = "Plan N'' will accomplish my ends." If P is true and P' is false, I am best off believing the former and not believing the latter. My belief will guide my choice of a plan, and belief in the true proposition (but not the false one) will lead me to choose a plan that *will* accomplish my ends. Stich has other intriguing arguments that cannot be considered here, but it certainly appears that true belief is a perfectly sensible and stable value, not an idiosyncratic one.[8] Thus, I shall assume that normative scientific epistemology should follow in the footsteps of folk practice and use reliability (and other truth-linked standards) as a basis for epistemic evaluation.

If scientific epistemology retains the fundamental standard(s) of folk epistemic assessment, how might it diverge from our epistemic folkways? One possible divergence emerges from William Alston's (1988) [1] account of justification. Although generally sympathetic with reliabilism, Alston urges a kind of constraint not standardly imposed by reliabilism (at least not process reliabilism.). This is the requirement that the processes from which justified beliefs issue must have as their input, or basis, a state *of which the cognizer is aware* (or can easily become aware). Suppose that Alston is right about this as an account of our folk conception of justification. It may well be urged that this ingredient needn't be retained in a scientifically sensitive epistemology. In particular, it may well be claimed that one thing to be learned from cognitive science is that only a small proportion of our cognitive processes operate on consciously accessible inputs. It could therefore be argued that a reformed conception of intellectually virtuous processes should dispense with the "accessibility" requirement.

Alston aside, the point of divergence I wish to examine concerns the psychological units that are chosen as virtues or vices. The lay epistemic evaluator uses casual, unsystematic, and largely introspective methods to carve out the mental faculties and processes responsible for belief formation and revision. Scientific epistemology, by contrast, would utilize the resources of cognitive science to devise a more subtle and sophisticated picture of the mechanisms of belief acquisition. I proceed now to illustrate how this project should be carried out.

An initial phase of the undertaking is to sharpen our conceptualization of the types of cognitive units that should be targets of epistemic evaluation. Lay people are pretty vague about the sorts of entities that qualify as intellectual virtues or vices. In my description of epistemic folkways, I have been deliberately indefinite about these entities, calling them variously "faculties," "processes," "mechanisms," and the like. How should systematic epistemology improve on this score?

A first possibility, enshrined in the practice of historical philosophers, is to take the relevant units to be cognitive *faculties*. This might be translated into modern parlance as *modules*, except that this term has assumed a rather narrow, specialized meaning under Jerry Fodor's (1983) [38] influential treatment of modularity. A better translation might be (cognitive) *systems*, e.g., the visual system, long-term memory, and so forth. Such systems, however, are also suboptimal candidates for units of epistemic analysis. Many beliefs are the outputs of two or more systems working in tandem. For example, a belief consisting in the visual classification of an object ("That is a chair") may involve matching some information in the visual system with a category stored in long-term memory. A preferable unit of analysis, then, might be a *process*, construed as the sort of entity depicted by familiar flow charts of cognitive activity. This sort of diagram depicts a sequence of operations (or sets of parallel operations), ultimately culminating in a belief-like output. Such a sequence may span several cognitive systems. This is the sort of entity I had in mind in previous publications (especially Goldman 1986 [49]) when I spoke of "cognitive processes."

Even this sort of entity, however, is not a fully satisfactory unit of analysis. Visual classification, for example, may occur under a variety of degraded conditions. The stimulus may be viewed from an unusual orientation; it may be partly occluded, so that only certain of its parts are visible; and so forth. Obviously, these factors can make a big difference to the reliability of the classification process. Yet it is one and the same process that analyzes the stimulus data and comes to a perceptual "conclusion." So the same process can have different degrees of reliability depending on a variety of parameter values. For purposes of epistemic assessment, it would be instructive to identify the parameters and parameter values that are critically relevant to degrees of reliability. The virtues and vices might then be associated not with processes per se, but with processes operating *with specified parameter values*. Let me illustrate this idea in connection with visual perception.

Consider Irving Biederman's (1987 [679], 1990 [680]) theory of object recognition, recognition-by-components (RBC). The core idea of Biederman's theory is that a common concrete object like a chair, a giraffe, or a mushroom is mentally represented as an arrangement of simple primitive volumes called *geons (geometrical ions)*. These geons, or primitive "components" of objects, are typically symmetrical volumes lacking sharp concavities, such as blocks, cylinders, spheres, and wedges. A set of twenty-four types of geons can be differentiated on the basis of dichotomous or trichotomous contrasts of such attributes as curvature (straight versus curved), size variation (constant versus expanding), and symmetry (symmetrical versus asymmetrical). These twenty-four types of geons can then be combined by means of six relations (e.g., top-of, side-connected, larger-than, etc.) into various possible multiple-geon objects. For example, a cup can be represented as a cylindrical geon that is side-connected to a curved, handle-like geon, whereas a pail can be represented as the same two geons bearing a different relation; the curved, handle-like geon is at the top of the cylindrical geon.

Simplifying a bit, the RBC theory of object recognition posits five stages of processing. (1) In the first stage, low-level vision extracts edge characteristics, such as L's, Y-vertices, and arrows. (2) On the basis of these edge characteristics, viewpoint-independent attributes are detected, such as curved, straight, size-constant, size-expanding, etc. (3) In the next stage, selected geons and their relations are activated. (4) Geon activation leads to the activation of object models, that is, familiar models of simple types of objects, stored in long-term memory. (5) The perceived entity is then "matched" to one of these models, and thereby identified as an instance of that category or classification. (In this description of the five stages, all processing is assumed to proceed bottom-up, but in fact Biederman also allows for elements of top-down processing.)

Under what circumstances, or what parameter values, will such a sequence of processing stages lead to *correct*, or *accurate*, object identification? Biederman estimates that there are approximately 3,000 common basic-level, or entry-level, names in English for familiar concrete objects. However, people are probably familiar with approximately ten times that number of object models because, among other things, some entry-level terms (such as *lamp* and *chair*) have several readily distinguishable object models. Thus, an estimate of the number of familiar object models would be on the order of 30,000.

Some of these object models are simple, requiring fewer than six components to appear complete; others are complex, requiring six to nine components to appear complete. Nonetheless, Biederman gives theoretical considerations and empirical results suggesting that an arrangement of only *two* or *three* geons almost always suffices to specify a simple object and even most complex ones. Consider the number of possible two-geon and three-geon objects. With twenty-four possible geons, Biederman says, the variations in relations can produce 186,624 possible two-geon objects. A third geon with its possible relations to another geon yields over 1.4 billion possible three-geon objects. Thus, if the 30,000 familiar object models were distributed homogeneously throughout the space of possible object models, Biederman reasons, an arrangements of two or three geons would almost always be sufficient to specify any object. Indeed, Biederman puts forward a *principle of geon recovery:* If an arrangement of two or three geons can be recovered from the image, objects can be quickly recognized even when they are occluded, rotated in depth, novel, extensively degraded, or lacking in customary detail, color, and texture.

The principle of three-geon sufficiency is supported by the following empirical results. An object such as an elephant or an airplane is complex, requiring six or more geons to appear complete. Nonetheless, when only three components were displayed (the others being occluded), subjects still made correct identifications in almost 80 percent of the nine-component objects and more than 90 percent of the six-component objects. Thus, the reliability conferred by just three geons and their relations is quite high. Although Biederman doesn't give data for recovery of just one or two geons of complex objects, presumably the reliability is much lower. Here we presumably have examples of parameter values—(1) number of components in the complete object, and (2) number of recovered components—that make a significant difference to reliability. The same process, understood as an instantiation of one and the same flow diagram, can have different levels of reliability depending on the values of the critical parameters in question. Biederman's work illustrates how research in cognitive science can identify both the relevant flow of activity and the crucial parameters. The quality (or "virtue") of a particular (token) process of belief-acquisition depends not only on the flow diagram that is instantiated, but on the parameter values instantiated in the specific tokening of the diagram.

Until now reliability has been my sole example of epistemic quality. But two other dimensions of epistemic quality—which also invoke truth or accuracy—should be added to our evaluative repertoire. These are *question-answering power* and *question-answering speed*. (These are certainly reflected in our epistemic folkways, though not well reflected in the concepts of knowledge or justification.) If a person asks himself a question, such as "What kind of object is that?" or "What is the solution to this algebra problem?" there are three possible outcomes: (A) he comes up with *no answer* (at least none that he believes), (B) he forms a belief in an answer which is *correct*, and (C) he forms a belief in an answer which is *incorrect*. Now reliability is the ratio of cases in category (B) to cases in categories (B) and (C), that is, the proportion of true beliefs to beliefs. Question-answering *power*, on the other hand, is the ratio of (B) cases to cases in categories (A), (B), and (C). Notice that it is possible for a system to be highly reliable but not very powerful. An object-recognition system that never yields outputs in category (C) is perfectly reliable, but it may not be very powerful, since most of its outputs could fall in (A) and only a few in (B). The human (visual) object-recognition system, by-contrast, is very powerful as well as quite reliable. In general, it is power and not just reliability that is an important epistemic desideratum in a cognitive system or process.

Speed introduces another epistemic desideratum beyond reliability and power. This is another dimension on which cognitive science can shed light. It might have been thought, for example, that correct identification of complex objects like an airplane or an elephant requires more time than simple objects such as a flashlight or a cup. In fact, there is no advantage for simple objects, as Biederman's empirical studies indicate. This lack of advantage for simple objects could be explained by the geon theory in terms of parallel activation: geons are activated in parallel rather than through a serial trace of the contours of the object. Whereas more geons would require more processing time under a serial trace, this is not required under parallel activation.

Let us turn now from perception to learning, especially language learning. Learnability theory (Gold 1967 [738]; Osherson, Stob, and

Weinstein 1985 [628]) uses a criterion of learning something like our notion of power, viz., the ability or inability of the learning process to arrive at a correct hypothesis after some fixed period of time. This is called *identification in the limit*. In language learning, it is assumed that the child is exposed to some information in the world, e.g., a set of sentences parents utter, and the learning task is to construct a hypothesis that correctly singles out the language being spoken. The child is presumed to have a learning strategy: an algorithm that generates a succession of hypotheses in response to accumulating evidence. What learning strategy might lead to success? *That* children learn their native language is evident to common sense. But *how* they learn it—what algorithm they possess that constitutes the requisite intellectual virtue—is only being revealed through research in cognitive science.

We may distinguish two types of evidence that a child might receive about its language (restricting attention to the language's grammar): positive evidence and negative evidence. Positive evidence refers to information about which strings of words *are* grammatical sentences in the language, and negative evidence refers to information about which strings of words are *not* grammatical sentences. Interestingly, it appears that children do not receive (much) negative evidence. The absence of negative evidence makes the learning task much harder. What algorithm might be in use that produces success in this situation?

An intriguing proposal is advanced by Robert Berwick (1986 [678]; cf. Pinker 1990 [802]). In the absence of negative evidence, the danger for a learning strategy is that it might hypothesize a language that is a superset of the correct language, i.e., one that includes all grammatical sentences of the target language plus some additional sentences as well. Without negative evidence, the child will be unable to learn that the "extra" sentences are incorrect, i.e., don't belong to the target language. A solution is to avoid ever hypothesizing an overly general hypothesis. Hypotheses should be *ordered* in such a way that the child always guesses the narrowest possible hypothesis or language at each step. This is called the *subset principle*. Berwick finds evidence of this principle at work in a number of domains, including concepts, sound systems, and syntax. Here, surely, is a kind of intellectual disposition that is not dreamed of by the "folk."

IV

We have been treating scientific epistemology from a purely reliabil-ist, or veritistic (truth-linked), vantage point. It should be stressed, however, that scientific epistemology can equally be pursued from other evaluative perspectives. You need not be a reliabilist to accept the proposed role of cognitive science in scientific epistemology. Let me illustrate this idea with the so-called *responsibilist* approach, which characterizes a justified or rational belief as one that is the product of epistemically responsible action (Kornblith 1983 [429]; Code 1987 [26]), or perhaps epistemically responsible processes (Talbott 1990 [133]). Actually, this conception of justification is approximated by my own *weak* conception of justification, as presented in chapter 7. Both depict a belief as justified as long as its acquisition is *blameless* or *nonculpable*. Given limited resources and limited information, a belief might be acquired nonculpably even though its generating processes are not virtuous according to the reliabilist criterion.

Let us start with a case of Hilary Kornblith. Kornblith argues that the justificational status of a belief does not depend exclusively on the *reasoning* process that produces that belief. Someone might reason perfectly well from the evidence he possesses, but fail to be epistemi-cally responsible because he neglects to acquire certain further evi-dence. Kornblith gives the case of Jones, a headstrong young physicist eager to hear the praise of his colleagues. After Jones pres-ents a paper, a senior colleague makes an objection. Unable to toler-ate criticism, Jones pays no attention to the objection. The criticism is devastating, but it makes no impact on Jones's beliefs because he does not even hear it. Jones's conduct is epistemically irresponsible. But his reasoning process from the evidence he actually possesses— which does not include the colleague's evidence—may be quite impeccable.

The general principle suggested by Kornblith's example seems to be something like this. Suppose that an agent (1) believes P, (2) does not believe Q, and (3) would be unjustified in believing P if he did believe Q. If, finally, he is *culpable* for failing to believe Q (for being ignorant of Q), then he is unjustified in believing P. In Kornblith's case, P is the physics thesis that Jones believes. Q consists in the criti-cisms of this thesis presented by Jones's senior colleague. Jones does not believe Q, but if he did believe Q, he would be unjustified in believing P. However, although Jones does not believe Q, he is culpable for failing to believe it (for being ignorant of these criticisms), because he *ought* to have paid attention to his colleague and acquired belief in Q. Therefore, Jones's belief in P is unjustified.

The provision that the agent be *culpable* for failing to believe Q is obviously critical to the principle in question. If the criticisms of Jones's thesis had never been presented within his hearing, nor published in any scientific journal, then Jones's ignorance of Q would not be culpable. And he might well be justified in believing P. But in Kornblith's version of the case, it seems clear that Jones *is* culpable for failing to believe Q, and that is why he is unjustified in believing P.

Under what circumstances is an agent culpable for failing to believe something? That is a difficult question. In a general discussion of culpable ignorance, Holly Smith (1983) [831] gives an example of a doctor who exposes an infant to unnecessarily high concentrations of oxygen and thereby causes severe eye damage. Suppose that the latest issue of the doctor's medical journal describes a study establishing this relationship, but the doctor hasn't read this journal. Presumably his ignorance of the relationship would be culpable; he *should* have read his journal. But suppose that the study had appeared in an obscure journal to which he does not subscribe, or had only appeared one day prior to this particular treatment. Is he still culpable for failing to have read the study by the time of the treatment?

Smith categorizes her example of the doctor as a case of *deficient investigation*. The question is (both for morals and for epistemology), What amounts and kinds of investigation are, in general, sufficient or deficient? We may distinguish two types of investigation: (1) investigation into the physical world (including statements that have been made by other agents), and (2) investigation into the agent's own storehouse of information, lodged in long-term memory. Investigation of the second sort is particularly relevant to questions about the role of cognitive science, so I shall concentrate here on this topic. Actually, the term 'investigation' is not wholly apt when it comes to long-term memory. But it is adequate as a provisional delineation of the territory.

To illustrate the primary problem that concerns me here, I shall consider two examples drawn from the work of Amos Tversky and Daniel Kahneman. The first example pertains to their study of the "conjunction fallacy" (Tversky and Kahneman 1983 [483]). Suppose that a subject assigns a higher probability to a conjunction like "Linda is a bank teller and is active in the feminist movement" than to one of its own conjuncts, "Linda is a bank teller." According to the standard probability calculus, no conjunction can have a higher probability than one of its conjuncts. Let us assume that the standard probability calculus is, in some sense, "right." Does it follow that a person is irrational, or unjustified, to make probability assignments that violate this calculus? This is subject to dispute. One might argue that it does not follow, in general, from the fact that M is an arbitrary mathematical truth, that anyone who believes something contrary to M is ipso facto irrational or unjustified. After all, mathematical facts are not all so transparent that it would be a mark of irrationality (or the like) to fail to believe any of them. However, let us set this issue aside. Let us imagine the case of a subject who has studied probability theory and learned the conjunction rule in particular. Let us further suppose that this subject would retract at least one of his two probability assignments if he recognized that they violate the conjunction rule. (This is by no means true of all subjects that Tversky and Kahneman studied.) Nonetheless, our imagined subject fails to think of the conjunction rule in connection with the Linda example. Shall we say that the failure to recover the conjunction rule from long-term memory is a *culpable omission*, one that makes his maintenance of his probability judgments unjustified? Is this like the example of Jones who culpably fails to learn of his senior colleague's criticism? Or is it a case of non-culpable nonrecovery of a relevant fact, a fact that is, in some sense "within reach," but legitimately goes unnoticed?

This raises questions about when a failure to recover or activate something from long-term memory is culpable, and that is precisely a problem that invites detailed reflection on mechanisms of memory retrieval. This is not a matter to which epistemologists have devoted much attention, partly because little has been known about memory retrieval until fairly recently. But now that cognitive science has at least the beginnings of an understanding of this phenomenon, normative epistemology should give careful attention to that research. Of course, we cannot expect the issue of culpability to be resolved directly by empirical facts about cognitive mechanisms. Such facts are certainly relevant, however.

The main way that retrieval from memory works is by *content addressing* (cf. Potter 1990). Content addressing means starting retrieval with part of the content of the to-be-remembered material, which provides an "address" to the place in memory where identical or similar material is located. Once a match has been made, related information laid down by previously encoded associations will be retrieved, such as the name or appearance of the object. For example, if you are asked to think of a kind of bird that is yellow, a location in memory is addressed where "yellow bird" is located. "Yellow bird" has previously been associated with "canary," so the latter information is retrieved. Note, however, that there are some kinds of information that cannot be used as a retrieval address, although the information is in memory. For example, what word for a family relationship (e.g., *grandmother*) ends in *w*? Because you have probably never encoded that piece of information explicitly, you may have trouble thinking of the word (hint: not *niece*). Although it is easy to move from the word in question *(nephew)* to "word for a family relationship ending in *w*," it is not easy to move in the opposite direction.

Many subjects who are given the Linda example presumably have not established any prior association between such pairs of propositions ("Linda is a bank teller and is active in the feminist movement" and "Linda is a bank teller") and the conjunction rule. Furthermore, in some versions of the experiment, subjects are not given these propositions adjacent to one another. So it may not occur to the subject even to *compare* the two probability judgments, although an explicit comparison would be more likely to address a location in memory that contains an association with the conjunction rule. In short, it is not surprising, given the nature of memory retrieval, that the material provided in the specified task does not automatically yield retrieval of the conjunction rule for the typical subject.

Should the subject deliberately search memory for facts that might retrieve the conjunction rule? Is omission of such deliberate search a culpable omission? Perhaps, but how much deliberate attention or effort ought to be devoted to this task? (Bear in mind that agents typically have numerous intellectual tasks on their agendas, which vie for attentional resources.) Furthermore, what form of search is obligatory? Should memory be probed with the question, "Is there any rule of probability theory that my (tentative) probability judgments violate?" This is a plausible search probe for someone who has already been struck by a thought of the conjunction rule and its possible violation, or whose prior experiences with probability experiments make him suspicious. But for someone who has not already retrieved the conjunction rule, or who has not had experiences with probability experiments that alert him to such "traps," what reason is there to be on the lookout for violations of the probability calculus?

It is highly questionable, then, that the subject engaged in "deficient investigation" in failing to probe memory with the indicated question.

Obviously, principles of culpable retrieval failure are not easy to come by. Any principles meriting our endorsement would have to be sensitive to facts about memory mechanisms.

A similar point can be illustrated in connection with the so-called *availability heuristic*, which was formulated by Tversky and Kahneman (1973) [474] and explored by Richard Nisbett and Lee Ross (1980) [89]. A cognizer uses the availability heuristic when he estimates the frequency of items in a category by the instances he can *bring to mind* through memory retrieval, imagination, or perception. The trouble with this heuristic, as the above mentioned researchers indicate, is that the instances one brings to mind are not necessarily well correlated with objective frequency. Various *biases* may produce discrepancies: biases in initial sampling, biases in attention, or biases in manner of encoding or storing the category instances.

Consider some examples provided by Nisbett and Ross: one hypothetical example and one actual experimental result. (1) (Hypothetical example) An Indiana businessman believes that a disproportionate number of Hoosiers are famous. This is partly because of a bias in initial exposure, but also because he is more likely to notice and remember when the national media identify a famous person as a Hoosier. (2) (Actual experiment) A group of subjects consistently errs in judging the relative frequency of words with R in first position versus words with R in third position. This is an artifact of how words are encoded in memory (as already illustrated in connection with *nephew*). We don't normally code words by their third letters, and hence words having R in the third position are less "available" (from memory) than words beginning with R. But comparative availability is not a reliable indicator of actual frequency.

Nisbett and Ross (p. 23) view these uses of the availability heuristic as normative errors. "An indiscriminate use of the availability heuristic," they write, "clearly can lead people into serious judgmental errors." They grant, though, that in many contexts perceptual salience, memorability, and imaginability may be relatively unbiased and well correlated with true frequency or causal significance. They conclude: "The normative status of using the availability heuristic . . . thus depend[s] on the judgmental domain and context. People are not, of course, totally unaware that simple availability criteria must sometimes be discounted. For example, few people who were asked to estimate the relative number of moles versus cats in their neighborhood would conclude 'there must be more cats because I've seen several of them but I've never seen a mole.' Nevertheless, as this book documents, people often fail to distinguish between legitimate and superficially similar, but illegitimate, uses of the availability heuristic."

We can certainly agree with Nisbett and Ross that the availability heuristic can often lead to incorrect estimates of frequency. But does it follow that uses of the heuristic are often *illegitimate* in a sense that implies the epistemic *culpability* of the users? One might retort, "These cognizers are using all the evidence that they possess, at least *consciously* possess. Why are they irresponsible if they extrapolate from this evidence?" The objection apparently lurking in Nisbett and Ross's minds is that these cognizers *should* be aware that they are using a systematically biased heuristic. This is a piece of evidence that they *ought* to recognize. And their failure to recognize it, and/or their failure to take it into account, makes their judgmental performance culpable. Nisbett and Ross's invocation of the cat/mole example makes the point particularly clear. If someone can appreciate that the relative number of cats and moles *he has seen* is not a reliable indicator of the relative number of cats and moles in the neighborhood, surely he can be expected to appreciate that the relative number of famous Hoosiers *he can think of* is not a reliable indicator of the proportion of famous people who are Hoosiers!

Is it so clear that people *ought* to be able to appreciate the biased nature of their inference pattern in the cases in question? Perhaps it seems transparent in the mole and Hoosier cases; but consider the letter *R* example. What is (implicitly) being demanded here of the cognizer? First, he must perform a feat of meta-cognitive analysis: he must recognize that he is inferring the relative proportion of the two types of English words from his own constructed samples of these types. Second, he must notice that his construction of these samples depends on the way words are encoded in memory. Finally, he must realize that this implies a bias in ease of retrieval. All these points may seem obvious in hindsight, once pointed out by researchers in the field. But how straightforward or obvious are these matters if they haven't already been pointed out to the subject? Of course, we currently have no "metric" of straightforwardness or obviousness. That is precisely the sort of thing we need, however, to render judgments of culpability in this domain. We need a systematic account of how difficult it is, starting from certain information and preoccupations, to generate and apprehend the truth of certain relevant hypotheses. Such an account clearly hinges on an account of the inferential and hypothesis-generating strategies that are natural to human beings. This is just the kind of thing that cognitive science is, in principle, capable of delivering. So epistemology must work hand in hand with the science of the mind. The issues here are not purely scientific, however. Judgments of justifiedness and unjustifiedness, on the responsibilist conception, require assessments of culpability and nonculpability. Weighing principles for judgments of culpability is a matter for philosophical attention. (One question, for example, is how much epistemic culpability depends on voluntariness.) Thus, a mix of philosophy and psychology is needed to produce acceptable principles of justifiedness.

Notes

I wish to thank Tom Senor, Holly Smith, and participants in a conference at Rice University for helpful comments on earlier versions of this paper.

1. Normative scientific epistemology corresponds to what I elsewhere call *epistemics* (see Goldman 1986 [49]). Although epistemics is not restricted to the assessment of *psychological* processes, that is the topic of the present paper. So we are here dealing with what I call *primary epistemics*.

2. Sosa's approach is spelled out most fully in Sosa 1985 [299], 1988 [329], and 1991 [125].

3. My own previous formulations of reliabilism have not been so simple. Both "What Is Justified Belief?" (chapter 6 of this volume) and *Epistemology and Cognition* (Goldman 1986 [49]) had provisions—e.g., the non-undermining provision of *Epistemology and Cognition*—that could help accommodate BonJour's examples. It is not entirely clear, however, how well these qualifications succeeded with the Norman case, described below.

4. Tom Senor presented the following example to his philosophy class at the University of Arkansas. Norman is working at his desk when out of the blue he is hit (via clairvoyance) with a very distinct and vivid impression of the president at the Empire State Building. The image is phenomenally distinct from a regular visual impression but is in some respects similar and of roughly equal force. The experience is so overwhelming that Norman just can't help but form the belief that the president is in New York. About half of Senor's class judged that in this case Norman justifiably believes that the president is in New York. Senor points out, in commenting on this paper, that their judgments are readily explained by the present account, because

the description of the clairvoyance process makes it sufficiently similar to vision to be easily "matched" to that virtue.

5. Since some of these opinions may be true and others false, people's lists of virtues and vices may have varying degrees of accuracy. The "real" status of a trait as a virtue or vice is independent of people's opinions about that trait. However, since the enterprise of descriptive epistemology is to describe and explain evaluators' judgments, we need to advert to the traits they *believe* to be virtues or vices, i.e., the ones on their mental lists.

6. Thanks to Holly Smith for this example. She cites Riding 1989 [638] (chap. 6) for relevant discussion.

7. It should be noted that this theory of justification is intended to capture what I call in chapter 7 the *strong* conception of justification. The complementary conception of *weak* justification will receive attention in section IV of this essay.

8. For further discussion of Stich, see Goldman 1991 [50].

14

Positive versus Negative Undermining in Belief Revision

Gilbert Harman

I am going to compare two competing theories of reasoning or, as I prefer to say, two competing theories of (reasoned) belief revision. I prefer to speak of belief revision rather than reasoning because the theories I am going to talk about are meant to apply as well to the decision to stop believing something one has previously believed as to the decision to start believing something new. The term "reasoning" may suggest inferring something new from premises one previously accepts and I do not want to restrict the comparison to that case. I will be concerned with reasoning as a way of changing one's view both by addition and by subtraction. Indeed I shall try to show that the difference between the theories I will discuss is clearest when the issue is whether to *stop* believing something.

I would really prefer to call these theories theories of "change in view" to allow for changes in plans and intentions as well as changes in beliefs. But I will for the most part restrict discussion to the case of changing one's beliefs.

I will call the theories I am concerned with the "foundations theory of belief revision" and the "coherence theory of belief revision," respectively, since there are similarities between these theories and certain philosophical theories of justification sometimes called "foundations" and "coherence" theories (Sosa 1980 [833]; Pollock 1980 [803]). But the theories I am concerned with are not precisely the same as the corresponding philosophical theories of justification, which are not normally presented as theories of belief revision. Actually, I am not sure what such theories of justification are supposed to be concerned with. So, although I will be using the *term* "justifica-

Reprinted from *Change in View: Principles of Reasoning*, by Gilbert Harman (Cambridge, Mass.: MIT Press, 1986, pp. 29–42, by permission of the publisher. Copyright © 1986, MIT Press.

tion" in what follows, as well as the terms "coherence" and "foundations," I do not claim that my use of any of these terms is the same as its use in these theories of justification. I mean to be raising a new issue, not discussing an old one.

The key point in what I am calling the *foundations* theory is that some of one's beliefs "depend on" others for their "justification"; these other beliefs may depend on still others, until one gets to foundational beliefs that do not depend on any further beliefs for their justification. In this theory, reasoning on belief revision should consist, first, in subtracting any of one's beliefs that do not now have a satisfactory justification and, second, in adding new beliefs that either need no justification or are justified on the basis of other justified beliefs one has.

On the other hand, according to what I am calling the *coherence* theory, it is not true that one's beliefs have, or ought to have, the sort of justificational structure required by the foundations theory. For one thing, in this view beliefs do not usually require any sort of justification at all. Justification is taken to be required only if one has a special reason to doubt a particular belief. Such a reason might consist in a conflicting belief or in the observation that one's beliefs could be made more "coherent," that is, more organized or simpler or less ad hoc, if the given belief were abandoned (and perhaps certain other changes were made). According to the coherence theory, belief revision should involve minimal changes in one's beliefs in a way that sufficiently increases overall coherence.

In this chapter I will elaborate these two theories in order to compare them with actual reasoning and intuitive judgments about such reasoning. As I have already said, it turns out that the theories are most easily distinguished by the conflicting advice they occasionally give concerning whether one should *give up* a belief P from which many other of one's beliefs have been inferred, when P's original justification has to be abandoned. Here a surprising contrast seems to emerge—"is" and "ought" seem to come apart. The foundations theory seems, at least at first, to be more in line with our intuitions about how people *ought* to revise their beliefs; the coherence theory is more in line with what people *actually do* in such situations. Intuition seems strongly to support the foundations theory over the coherence theory as an account of what one is *justified* in doing in such cases; but *in fact* one will tend to act as the coherence theory advises.

After I explain this, I will go on to consider how this apparent discrepancy might be resolved. I will conclude by suggesting that the coherence theory is normatively correct after all, despite initial appearances.

Taking each of these theories in turn, I begin with the foundations theory.

The Foundations Theory of Belief Revision

The basic principle of the foundations theory, as I will interpret it, is that one's beliefs have a justificational structure, some serving as reasons or justifications for others, these justifying beliefs being more basic or fundamental for justification than the beliefs they justify.

The justifications are *prima facie* or defeasible. The foundations theory allows, indeed insists, that one can be justified in believing something P and then come to believe something else that undermines one's justification for believing P. In that case one should stop believing P, unless one has some further justification that is not undermined.

I say "unless one has some further justification," because, in this view, a belief may have more than one justification. To be justified, a belief must have *at least* one justification, but it may have more than one. That is, if a belief in P is to be justified, it is required, either that P be a foundational belief whose intrinsic justification is not defeated, or that there be at least one undefeated justification of P from other beliefs one is justified in believing. If one believes P and it happens that all of one's justifications for believing P come to be defeated, one is no longer justified in continuing to believe P and one should subtract P from one's beliefs.

Furthermore, and this is very important, if one comes not to be justified in continuing to believe P in this way, then not only is it true that one must abandon belief in P but justifications one has for other beliefs are also affected if these justifications appeal to one's belief in P. Justifications appealing to P must be abandoned when P is abandoned. If that means further beliefs are left without justification, then these beliefs too must be dropped, along with any justifications appealing to them. So there will be a chain reaction when one loses justification for a belief on which other beliefs depend for their justification. (This is worked out in more detail for an artificial intelligence system in Doyle 1979 [711], 1980 [565].)

Now, it is an important aspect of the foundations theory of reasoning that justifications cannot legitimately be circular. P cannot be part of one's justification for Q, while Q is part of one's justification for P, (unless one of these beliefs has a different justification that does not appeal to the other belief).

The foundations theory also disallows infinite justifications. It does not allow P to be justified by appeal to Q, which is justified by appeal to R, and so on forever. Since justification cannot be circular, this means justification must eventually come to an end in beliefs that themselves, either need no justification, or are justified but not by appeal to other beliefs. Let us say that such basic or foundational beliefs are "intrinsically" justified.

For our purposes, it does not matter exactly which beliefs are taken to be intrinsically justified in this sense. Furthermore, I emphasize that the foundations theory allows for situations in which a basic belief has its intrinsic justification defeated by one or more other beliefs, just as it allows for situations in which the justification of one belief in terms of other beliefs is defeated by still other beliefs one has. Foundationalism, as I am interpreting it anyway, is not committed to the *incorrigibility* of basic beliefs.

A belief is a basic belief if it has an intrinsic justification which does not appeal to other beliefs. A basic belief may also have one or more nonintrinsic justifications which do appeal to other beliefs. So a basic belief can have its intrinsic justification defeated and still remain justified as long as it retains at least one justification that is not defeated.

The existence of basic beliefs follows from the restrictions against circular and infinite justifications. Infinite justifications are to be ruled out because a finite creature can only have a finite number of beliefs, or at least only a finite number of *explicit beliefs*, whose content is explicitly represented in the brain. (Explicit beliefs do not have to be conscious as long as there is somewhere in the brain or mind an explicit representation of the content of the belief.)

Now, in believing various things explicitly, one believes various other things *implicitly*; one's belief in these further matters is implicit in one's explicitly believing what one believes. For example in virtue of one's explicit beliefs about arithmetic one will implicitly believe that $1002 + 3 = 1005$. And there might well be infinitely many such implicit beliefs, since infinitely many things may be obviously implied by, and therefore implicit in, what one explicitly believes. But in the first instance what one believes is what one believes explicitly, and so what one is justified in believing depends entirely on what one is justified in believing explicitly. To consider whether one's implicit beliefs are justified is to consider whether one is justified in believing the explicit beliefs on which the implicit beliefs depend. A justification for a belief that appeals to other beliefs must always appeal to things one believes explicitly. Since one has only finitely many explicit beliefs, there are only finitely many beliefs that can be appealed to for purposes of justification, and so infinite justifications are ruled out.

So much then for the foundations theory. Let me turn now to the coherence theory.

The Coherence Theory of Belief Revision

The coherence theory is a *conservative* theory in a way the foundations theory is not. The coherence theory supposes one's present beliefs are justified just as they are in the absence of special reasons to change them, where changes are allowed only to the extent that they yield sufficient increases in coherence. This is a striking difference from the foundations theory. The foundations theory takes one to be justified in continuing to believe something only if one has a special reason to continue to accept that belief. The coherence theory, on the other hand, takes one to be justified in continuing to believe something as long as one has no special reason to stop believing it.

According to the coherence theory, if one's beliefs are incoherent in some way, either because of outright inconsistency or perhaps because of simple *ad hoc*ness, then one should try to make minimal changes in those beliefs in order to eliminate the incoherence. More generally, small changes in one's beliefs are justified to the extent these changes add to the coherence of one's beliefs.

For our purposes, we do not need to be too specific as to exactly what coherence involves, except to say it includes not only consistency but also a network of relations among one's beliefs, especially relations of implication and explanation.

It is important that coherence competes with conservatism. It is as if there are two aims or tendencies of reasoned revision, one being to maximize coherence, the other to minimize change. Both tendencies are important. Without conservatism, one would be led to reduce one's beliefs to the single Parmenidean thought that all is one. Without the tendency towards coherence, we would have what Peirce (1877) [628a] called "the method of tenacity," in which one holds to one's initial convictions no matter what evidence may accumulate against them.

According to the coherence theory, the assessment of a challenged belief is always holistic. Whether such a belief is justified depends on how well it fits together with everything else one believes. If one's beliefs are coherent, they are mutually supporting. All of one's beliefs are, in a sense, equally fundamental. In the coherence theory there are not the asymmetrical justification relations among one's beliefs that there are in the foundations theory. It can happen in the coherence theory that P is justified because of the way it coheres with Q and Q is justified because of the way it coheres with P. In the foundations theory, such a pattern of justification would be ruled out by the restriction against circular justification. But there is nothing wrong with circular justification in the coherence theory, especially if the circle is a large one!

Here then is a brief sketch of the coherence theory. I turn now to testing these theories against our intuitions about cases. This raises an immediate problem for the coherence theory.

An Objection to the Coherence Theory: Karen's Aptitude Test

The problem is that, contrary to what is assumed in the coherence theory, there do seem to be asymmetrical justification relations among one's beliefs.

Consider Karen, who has taken an aptitude test and has just been told her results show she has a considerable aptitude for science and music, but little aptitude for history and philosophy. This news does not correlate perfectly with her previous grades. She had previously done very well, not only in physics, for which her aptitude scores are reported to be high, but also in history, for which her aptitude scores are reported to be low. Furthermore, she had previously done poorly, not only in philosophy, for which her aptitude scores are reported to be low, but also in music, for which her aptitude scores are reported to be high.

After carefully thinking over these discrepancies, Karen concludes (1) her reported aptitude scores accurately reflect and are explained by her actual aptitudes, so (2) she has an aptitude for science and music and no aptitude for history and philosophy, so (3) her history course must have been an easy one, and (4) she did not work hard enough in the music course. She decides (5) to take another music course but not take any more history.

It seems quite clear that, after Karen reaches these conclusions, some of her beliefs are based on others. Her belief that the history course was very easy depends for its justification on her belief that she has no aptitude for history, a belief which depends in turn for its justification on her belief that she got a low score for history aptitude in her aptitude test. There is not a dependence in the other direction. For example, her belief about her aptitude test score in history is not based on her belief that she has no aptitude for history or her belief that the history course was an easy one.

This asymmetry would seem to conflict with the coherence theory which denies there are such relations of asymmetrical dependency among one's beliefs.

It might be suggested on behalf of the coherence theory, that the relevant relations here are merely *temporal* or *causal* relations. We can agree that Karen's belief about the outcome of her aptitude test precedes and is an important cause of her belief that the history course she took was a very easy one, without our having to agree that a relation of dependence or justification holds or ought to hold among these two beliefs once the new belief has been accepted.

In order to test this suggestion, it is sufficient to tell more of Karen's story. Some days later she is informed that the report about her aptitude scores was incorrect! The scores reported were those of someone else whose name was confused with hers. Unfortunately, her own scores have now been lost. How should Karen revise her views, given this new information?

The foundations theory says she should abandon all beliefs whose justifications depend in part on her prior belief about her aptitude test scores. The only exception is for beliefs for which she can now find another and independent justification which does not depend on her belief about her aptitude test scores. She should continue to believe only those things she would have been justified in believing if she had never been given the false information about those scores. The foundations theory says this because it does not accept a principle of conservatism. The foundations theory does not allow that a belief might acquire justification simply by being believed.

Let us assume that, if Karen had not been given the false information about her aptitude test scores, she could not have reasonably reached any of the conclusions she did reach about her aptitudes in physics, history, philosophy, and music; and let us also assume that without those beliefs, Karen could not have reached any of her further conclusions about the courses she has already taken. Then, according to the foundations theory, Karen should abandon her beliefs about her relative aptitudes in these subjects; and she should give up her belief that the history course she took was very easy, as well as her belief that she did not work hard enough in the music course. She should also reconsider her decisions to take another course in music and not take any more history courses.

Now, the coherence theory does not automatically yield the same advice that the foundations theory gives about this case. Karen's new information does produce a loss of overall coherence in her beliefs, since she can no longer coherently suppose that her aptitudes in science, music, philosophy, and history are in any way responsible for the original report she received about the results of her aptitude test. So she must abandon that particular supposition about the explanation of the original report of her scores. Still, there is considerable coherence among the beliefs she inferred from this false report. For example, there is a connection between her belief that she has little aptitude for history, her belief that her high grade on the history course was the result of the course's being an easy one, and her belief that she will not take any more courses in history. There are similar connections between her beliefs about her aptitudes in other subjects, how well she did in courses in those subjects, and her plans for the future in those areas. Let us suppose Karen inferred a great many other things that we haven't mentioned from that original report so there are a great many beliefs involved here. Abandoning all of these beliefs is costly from the point of view of conservatism, which says to minimize change. Let us suppose it turns out that there are so many of these beliefs, and they are so connected with each other and with other things Karen believes, that the coherence theory implies Karen should retain all these new beliefs even though she must give up her beliefs about the explanation of the report of her aptitude scores.

Then the foundations theory says Karen should give up all these beliefs, while the coherence theory says Karen should retain them. Which theory is right about what Karen ought to do? Almost everyone who I have asked about this issue sides with the foundations theory: Karen should not retain any beliefs she inferred from the false report of her aptitude test scores that she would not have been justified in believing in the absence of that false report. That does seem to be the intuitively right answer. The foundations theory is in accordance with our intuitions about what Karen *ought* to do in a case like this. The coherence theory is not.

Belief Perseverance

But now I must remark on an important complication, to which I have already referred. In fact, Karen would almost certainly keep her new beliefs! That is what people actually do in situations like this. Although the foundations theory gives intuitively satisfying advice about what Karen *ought* to do in such a situation, the coherence theory is more in accord with what people actually do!

To document the rather surprising facts here, let me quote at some length from a recent survey article (Ross and Anderson 1982 [820], pp. 147–149), which speaks of

the dilemma of the social psychologist who has made use of deception in the course of an experiment and then seeks to debrief the subjects who had been the target of such deception. The psychologist reveals the totally contrived and inauthentic nature of the information presented presuming that this debriefing will thereby eliminate any effects such information might have exerted upon the subjects' feelings or beliefs. Many professionals, however, have expressed public concern that such experimental deception may do great harm that is not fully undone by conventional debriefing procedures.

The authors go on to describe experiments designed to "explore" what they call "the phenomenon of belief perseverance in the face of evidential discrediting." In one experiment,

Subjects first received continuous false feedback as they performed a novel discrimination task (i.e., distinguishing authentic suicide notes from fictitious ones) . . . [Then] the actor . . . received a standard debriefing session in which he learned that his putative outcome had been predetermined and that his feedback had been totally unrelated to actual performance . . . Every subject was led to explicitly acknowledge his understanding of the nature and purpose of the experimental deception.

Following this total discrediting of the original information, the subjects completed a dependent variable questionnaire dealing with the actors' performance and abilities. The evidence for postdebriefing impression perseverance was unmistakable . . . On virtually every measure . . . the totally discredited initial outcome manipulation produced significant "residual" effects upon actors' . . . assessments . . .

Follow-up experiments have since shown that a variety of unfounded personal impressions, once induced by experimental procedures, can survive a variety of total discrediting procedures. For example, Jennings, Lepper, and Ross . . . have demonstrated that subjects' impressions of their ability at interpersonal persuasion (having them succeed or fail to convince a confederate to donate blood) can persist after they have learned that the initial outcome was totally inauthentic. Similarly, . . . two related experiments have shown that students' erroneous impressions of their "logical problem solving abilities" (and their academic choices in a follow-up measure two months later) persevered even after they had learned that good or poor teaching procedures provided a totally sufficient explanation for the successes or failures that were the basis for such impressions.

Other studies first manipulated and then attempted to undermine subjects' theories about the functional relationship between two measured variables: the adequacy of firefighters' professional performances and their prior scores on a paper and pencil test of risk preference. . . . such theories survived the revelations that the cases in question had been totally fictitious and the different subjects had, in fact, received opposite pairings of riskiness scores and job outcomes . . . Over 50% of the initial effect of the "case history" information remained after debriefing.

In summary [the authors conclude] it is clear that beliefs can survive . . . the total destruction of their original evidential bases.

It is therefore quite likely that Karen will continue to believe many of the things she inferred from the false report about her aptitude test scores. She will continue to believe these things even after learning that the report was false.

The Habit Theory of Belief

I now want to consider why this is likely to be so. Why is it so hard for subjects to be debriefed? Why do people retain conclusions they have drawn from evidence that is now discredited?

One possibility is that belief is a kind of habit. This would be an implication of behaviorism, the view that beliefs and other mental attitudes are habits of behavior. Of course, behaviorism is not currently fashionable. But the suggestion that beliefs are habits might be correct even apart from behaviorism. The relevant habits need not be overt behavioral habits. They might be habits of thought. Perhaps, to believe that P is to be disposed to *think* that P under certain conditions, to be disposed to use this thought as a premise or assumption in reasoning and in deciding what to do. Then, once a belief has become established, considerable effort might be needed to get rid of it, even if one should come to see one ought to get rid of it, just as it is hard to get rid of other bad habits. One can't simply decide to get rid of a bad habit; one must take active steps to ensure that the habit does not reassert itself. Perhaps it is just as difficult to get rid of a bad belief.

Alvin Goldman (1978) [203] mentions a related possibility, observing that Anderson and Bower (1973) [535] treat coming to believe something as the establishing of connections, or "associative links," between relevant conceptual representations in the brain. Now, it may be that such connections or links, once set up, cannot easily be broken unless competing connections are set up that overwhelm the original ones. The easiest case might be that in which one starts by believing P and then comes to believe $not\text{-}P$ by setting up stronger connections involving $not\text{-}P$ than those involved in believing P. It might be much harder simply to give up one's belief in P without substituting a contrary belief. According to this model of belief, then, in order to stop believing P, it would not be enough simply to notice passively that one's evidence for P had been discredited. One would have to take positive steps to counteract the associations that constitute one's belief in P. The difficulties in giving up a discredited belief would then be similar in this view to the difficulties envisioned in the habit theory of belief.

Here then is one possible reason why beliefs might survive after the evidence for them has been discredited: it may be hard to get rid of a belief once one has stored that belief. If so, foundationalism could be normatively correct as an ideal, even though the ideal is one it takes considerable effort to live up to.

But this cannot be the explanation. Of course, there are cases in which one has to struggle in order to abandon a belief one takes to be discredited. One finds oneself coming back to thoughts one realizes one should no longer accept. There are such habits of thought. But this is not what is happening in the debriefing studies. Subjects in these studies are not struggling to abandon beliefs they see are discredited. On the contrary, the problem is that subjects do not see that the beliefs they have acquired have been discredited. They see all sorts of reasons for the beliefs, where the reasons consist in connections with other beliefs of a sort that the coherence theory might approve, but not the foundations theory. So the correct explanation of belief perseverance in these studies is not that beliefs that have lost their evidential grounding are like bad habits.

Positive versus Negative Undermining

So I now want to consider another and I think more plausible hypothesis as to why beliefs might survive after the evidence for them has been discredited, namely the hypothesis that people simply do not keep track of the justification relations among their beliefs. They continue to believe things after the evidence for them has been discredited because they do not realize what they are doing. They do not understand that the discredited evidence was the sole reason why they believe as they do. They do not see they would not have been justified in forming those beliefs in the absence of the now discredited evidence. They do not realize these beliefs have been undermined. My suggestion is that it is this, rather than the difficulty of giving up bad habits, which is responsible for belief perseverance.

This is to suppose people do not in fact proceed in accordance with the advice of the foundations theory. The foundations theory says people should keep track of their reasons for believing as they do and should stop believing anything that is not associated with adequate evidence. So the foundations theory implies that, if Karen has not kept track of her reason for believing her history course to have been an easy one, she should have abandoned her belief even before she was told about the mix up with her aptitude test scores.

This implication of the foundations theory is not obviously right. Indeed, if, as I suggest, people rarely keep track of their reasons, the implication would be that people are unjustified in almost all their beliefs, which seems to me an absurd result. In this case, foundationalism seems wrong even as a normative theory. So let us see whether we cannot defend the coherence theory as a normative theory.

Now, although justification in a coherence theory is always "holistic" in the sense that whether one is justified in coming to adopt a new belief depends on how that belief would fit in with everything else one believes, we have already seen how appeal might be made to a nonholistic *causal* notion of "local justification" by means of a limited number of one's prior beliefs, namely those prior beliefs that are most crucial to one's justification for adding the new belief. To be sure, the coherence theory must not suppose there are *continuing* links of justification dependency among beliefs once these beliefs are accepted, links that can be consulted when revising one's beliefs. But the theory can admit that Karen's coming to believe certain things

depended on certain of her prior beliefs in a way that it did not depend on others, where this dependence represents a kind of local
justification, even though in another respect whether Karen was justified in coming to believe those things depended on everything she
then believed.

Given this point, I suggest that the coherence theory might incor-
porate the principle that it is incoherent to believe both P and also
that one would not be justified in believing P if one had relied only
on true beliefs. Within the coherence theory, this implies, roughly
speaking

Principle of Positive Undermining: One should stop believing P
whenever one positively believes one's reasons for believing P are
no good.

I want to compare this with the analogous principle within a foundations theory:

Principle of Negative Undermining: One should stop believing P
whenever one does not associate one's belief in P with an adequate
justification (either intrinsic or extrinsic).

The principle of positive undermining is much more plausible than
the principle of negative undermining. The principle of negative undermining implies that, as one loses track of the justifications of one's
beliefs, one should give up those beliefs. But one does not seem to
keep track of one's justifications for most of one's beliefs. If so, the
principle of negative undermining would say one should stop believing almost everything one believes, which is absurd. On the other
hand, the principle of positive undermining does not have this absurd implication. The principle of positive undermining does not suppose the absence of a justification is a reason to stop believing
something. It only supposes one's belief in P is undermined by the
positive belief that one's reasons for P are no good.

In this connection it is relevant that subjects *can* be successfully
debriefed after experiments involving deception, if the subjects are
made vividly aware of this very phenomenon, that is, if they are
made vividly aware of this very tendency for people to retain false
beliefs after the evidence for them has been undercut and are also
made vividly aware of how this phenomenon has acted in their own
case (Nisbett and Ross 1980 [89]). Now, someone might suggest this

shows that under ideal conditions people really do act in accordance with the foundations theory after all, so that the foundations theory *is* normatively correct as an account of how one ought ideally to revise one's beliefs. But in fact this further phenomenon seems clearly to support the coherence theory, with its principle of positive undermining, and not the foundations theory, with its principle of negative undermining. The so-called full debriefing cannot merely undermine the evidence for the conclusions subjects have reached but must also directly attack each of these conclusions themselves. It seems clear, then, that the full debriefing works, not just by getting subjects to give up the beliefs that originally served as evidence for the conclusions they have reached, but by getting them to accept certain further positive beliefs about their lack of good reasons for each of these conclusions.

What about Our Intuitions?

This may seem counterintuitive. It may seem to fly in the face of common sense to suppose that the coherence theory is normatively correct in cases like this. After carefully considering Karen's situation, almost everyone agrees she should give up all beliefs of hers she inferred from the original false report, excepting only those beliefs which would have been justified apart from any appeal to evidence tainted by that false information. Almost everyone's judgment about what Karen ought to do coincides with what the foundations theory says she ought to do. Indeed, psychologists who have studied the phenomenon of "belief perseverance" in the face of debriefing consider it to be a paradigm of irrationality. How *could* these very strong normative intuitions possibly be taken to be mistaken here, as they must be if the coherence theory is to be accepted as normatively correct?

The answer is that, when people think about Karen's situation, they ignore the possibility that she may have failed to keep track of the justifications of her beliefs. They imagine Karen is or ought to be aware she no longer has any good reasons for the beliefs she inferred from the false report. And, of course, this is to imagine Karen is violating the principle of positive undermining. It is very hard to allow for the possibility that she may be violating not that principle but only the foundationalist's principle of negative undermining.

Keeping Track of Justification

I have said several times that people do not seem to keep track of the justifications of their beliefs. Indeed, it seems obvious that they do not. If we tried to suppose people did keep track of their justifications, we would have to suppose either that they fail to notice when their justifications are undermined or that they do notice this but have great difficulty in abandoning the unjustified beliefs in the way a person has difficulty in abandoning a bad habit. Neither of these possibilities offers a plausible account of the sort of belief persistance I have been discussing.

It stretches credulity to suppose people always keep track of the sources of their beliefs but fail to notice when these sources are undermined. That is like supposing people always remember everything that has ever happened to them but cannot always retrieve the stored information from where they placed it in memory. To say one remembers something is to say one has stored it in a way that normally allows it to be retrieved on the appropriate occasion. Similarly, to say people keep track of the sources of their beliefs must be to say they can normally use this information when it is appropriate to do so.

I have already remarked that the other possibility seems equally incredible, namely, that people have trouble abandoning the undermined beliefs in the way they have trouble getting rid of bad habits. To repeat, participants in belief perseverance studies show no signs of knowing their beliefs are ungrounded. They do not act like people struggling with their beliefs as with bad habits. Again, I agree it sometimes happens that one keeps returning to thoughts after one has seen there can be no reason to accept those thoughts. There are habits of thought that can be hard to get rid of. But that is not what is going on in the cases psychologists study under the name of "belief perseverance."

This leaves the issue whether one should *try* always to keep track of the local justifications of one's beliefs, even if, in fact, people do not seem to do this. I want to conclude my discussion by considering the possibility that there is a good reason for not keeping track of these justifications.

On Not Reasoning Probabilistically

Consider an analogous case. It can seem that one ought not to accept beliefs in a yes-no fashion, but should believe things to various degrees, having more confidence in some things than others, where one's degree of belief represents the "subjective probability" one assigns to the truth of that belief. It can seem, furthermore, that one should also assign degrees of desirability or "utility" to various outcomes of action and decide what to do by considering how likely the person thinks one or another act will make this or that outcome. In other words, it can seem one should determine the "expected utility" of each act by adding together the utilities of the possible outcomes of the act, each multiplied by the probability that the act will lead to that outcome; and then one should do that act which has the greatest expected utility. It can also seem clear that one should assign degrees of belief, or subjective probabilities, in accordance with the principles of probability theory and, as new evidence comes in, one should "update" one's subjective probabilities by "conditionalization" on the new evidence or by using some generalization of conditionalization (Jeffrey 1983 [597]).

However, there is considerable empirical evidence that people do not do very well by these standards (Kahneman, Slovic, and Tversky 1982 [68]; Nisbett and Ross 1980 [89]). People have great difficulty with probability and make the most elementary mistakes from this point of view. Probabilistic reasoning is not something that comes naturally to people. Indeed, even experts in probability make all sorts of mistakes if they are not consciously thinking of a problem as one that should be analyzed statistically.

Now, I believe that there is a deep reason for this inability to deal with probabilities. It would be impossible to design finite creatures to operate purely probabilistically. The impossibility arises from a combinatorial explosion that occurs in probabilistic thinking (Harmon 1986 [60]). In order to have useful degrees of belief concerning N different matters it is not enough to assign probabilities to N propositions. One has to assign various conditional probabilities as well, or (equivalently) one has to assign probabilities to various conjunctions consisting in some of the original propositions and of negations of some of these propositions, and in the general case, $2^N - 1$ independent assignments must be recorded. This means that to have useful degrees of belief concerning ten matters, one needs to record a thousand probabilities; to have useful degrees of belief concerning twenty matters, one needs a million probability assignments; for thirty matters, one needs a billion probability assignments; and so forth.

The problem cannot be avoided by using general principles to assign probabilities. One idea along these lines would be to specify a general principle determining an initial probability distribution and to otherwise record only new evidence taken to be certain, where one's other degrees of belief are then determined by conditionalization on that evidence. The problem is that, since such evidence would have to be certain, most of it would have to be evidence about one's immediate perceptual experience, about how exactly things look, sound, smell and so forth. This is a problem because this idea would work only if one remembered all such perceptual evidence, or at least all such evidence that affected one's degrees of belief; and that is something one simply does not do. One normally does not recall one's immediate perceptual experiences of an hour ago, to say nothing of the experiences of the past week, year, or decade. One is more apt to remember the position of the furniture and whether something was moved than how things looked from where one was standing, even though one's beliefs about the position of the furniture were based on how things looked. Of course, there are exceptions to this. Sometimes one does remember one's immediate experiences. But only in exceptional cases.

The evidence one remembers tends not to be the absolutely certain evidence of one's immediate experience but rather the somewhat less certain evidence concerning the placement of objects in the environment. But then one's current degree of belief cannot be specified by simple conditionalization on this evidence. One must instead use something like Jeffrey's (1983) [597] generalization of conditionalization. But that requires keeping track of the probabilities of various conjunctions of evidence statements and /or their denials, which brings back the combinatorial explosion.

So the problem cannot be avoided by specifying a general principle determining an initial probability distribution together with the evidence that has accumulated since the beginning. An alternative idea would be *always* to specify a new general principle determining one's current probability distribution. But, this won't be any improvement, either. For one thing, the problem of discovering such a general principle each time is intractable. Furthermore, if one's degrees of belief arise from Jeffrey's generalized conditionalization from one's prior degrees of belief, there will normally be no very much simpler way to specify them than that just mentioned in the previous paragraph. So the complexity of one's current principle for assigning probabilities will be affected by the same combinatorial explosion.

Clearly, this severely limits the amount of probabilistic reasoning a finite creature can do. It is therefore no wonder people are not very good at such reasoning. We cannot operate purely probabilistically. We have to reason in a different and more manageable way.

The problem does not arise with yes-no all-or-nothing belief within the framework of a coherence theory of belief revision. One's beliefs in N topics can be represented by the acceptance of N representations rather than the $2^N - 1$ representations required by a probabilistic approach. The calculations needed for updating one's views in the face of new evidence similarly do not involve the sort of combinatorial explosion that occurs in the probabilistic framework.

Clutter Avoidance

Now, the issue before us is not whether people should reason in a purely probabilistic fashion but rather whether within the sort of non-probabilistic framework in which people must operate they should keep track of the justifications of their beliefs. I want to suggest that there are practical considerations that tell against keeping track of justifications.

In particular, there is a practical reason to avoid too much clutter in one's beliefs. There is a limit to what one can remember, a limit to the number of things one can put into long term storage, and a limit to what one can retrieve. It is important to save room for important things and not clutter one's mind with a lot of unimportant matters. This is one very important reason why one does not try to believe all sorts of logical consequences of one's beliefs. One should not try to infer all one can from one's beliefs. One should try not to retain too much trivial information. Furthermore, one should try to store in long-term memory only the key matters that one will later need to recall. When one reaches a significant conclusion from one's other beliefs, one needs to remember the conclusion but does not normally need to remember all the intermediate steps involved in reaching that conclusion. Indeed, one should not try to remember those intermediate steps; one should try to avoid too much clutter in one's mind.

Similarly, even if much of one's knowledge of the world is inferred ultimately from what one believes oneself to be immediately perceiving at one or another time, one does not normally need to remember these original perceptual beliefs or many of the various intermediate conclusions drawn from them. It is enough to recall the more important of one's conclusions about the location of the furniture, etc.

This means one should not be disposed to try to keep track of the local justifications of one's beliefs. One could keep track of these justifications only by remembering an incredible number of mostly perceptual original premises, along with many, many intermediate steps which one does not want and has little need to remember. One will not want to link one's beliefs to such justifications because one will not in general want to try to retain the prior beliefs from which one reached one's current beliefs.

The practical reason for not keeping track of the justifications of one's beliefs is not as severe as the reason that prevents one from operating purely probabilistically. The problem is not that there would be a combinatorial explosion. Still, there are important practical constraints. It is more efficient not to try to retain these justifications and the accompanying justifying beliefs. This leaves more room in memory for important matters.

Summary and Final Conclusions

To sum up: I have discussed two theories of belief revision, the foundations theory and the coherence theory. The foundations theory says one's beliefs are to be linked by relations of justification that one is to make use of in deciding whether to stop believing something. The coherence theory denies that there should be this sort of justificational structure to one's beliefs. The coherence theory takes conservatism to be an important principle—one's beliefs are justified in the absence of a special reason to doubt them. The foundations theory rejects any such conservatism.

When we consider a case like Karen's, our intuitive judgments may seem to support foundationalism. But it is important to distinguish two different principles, the coherence theory's principle of positive undermining and the foundations theory's much stronger principle of negative undermining. Once we distinguish these principles we see it is really the foundations theory that is counterintuitive, since that theory would have one give up almost everything one believes, if, as I have argued, one does not keep track of one's justifications. Furthermore, there is a very good practical reason not to keep track of justifications, namely that in the interests of clutter avoidance one should not normally even try to retain the beliefs from which one's more important beliefs were inferred.

Note

I am indebted to Jens Kulenkampff and John Pollack for helpful comments on an earlier draft of this paper.

15

Could Man Be an Irrational Animal? Some Notes on the Epistemology of Rationality

Stephen P. Stich

I

Aristotle thought man was a rational animal. From his time to ours, however, there has been a steady stream of writers who have dissented from this sanguine assessment. For Bacon or Hume or Freud or D. H. Lawrence, rationality is at best a sometimes thing. On their view, episodes of rational inference and action are scattered beacons on the irrational coastline of human history. During the last decade or so, these impressionistic chroniclers of man's cognitive foibles have been joined by a growing group of experimental psychologists who are subjecting human reasoning to careful empirical scrutiny. Much of what they have found would appall Aristotle. Human subjects, it would appear, regularly and systematically invoke inferential and judgmental strategies ranging from the merely invalid to the genuinely bizarre.

Recently, however, there have been rumblings of a reaction brewing—a resurgence of Aristotelian optimism. Those defending the sullied name of human reason have been philosophers, and their weapons have been conceptual analysis and epistemological argument. The central thrust of their defense is the claim that empirical evidence could not possibly support the conclusion that people are systematically irrational. And thus the experiments which allegedly show that they are must be either flawed or misinterpreted.

In this paper I propose to take a critical look at these philosophical defenses of rationality. My sympathies, I should note straightaway, are squarely with the psychologists. My central thesis is that the philosophical arguments aimed at showing irrationality cannot be experimentally demonstrated are mistaken. Before considering these

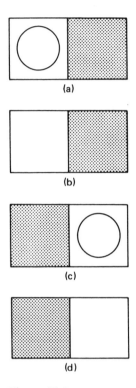

Figure 15.1

arguments, however, we would do well to set out a few illustrations of the sort of empirical studies which allegedly show that people depart from normative standards of rationality in systematic ways. This is the chore that will occupy us in the following section.

II

One of the most extensively investigated examples of inferential failure is the so-called "selection task" studied by P. C. Wason, P. N. Johnson-Laird and their colleagues.[1] A typical selection task experiment presents subjects with four cards like those in figure 15.1. Half of each card is masked. Subjects are then given the following instructions:

Which of the hidden parts of these cards do you need to see in order to answer the following question decisively?

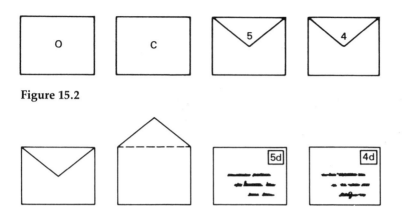

Figure 15.2

Figure 15.3

FOR THESE CARDS IS IT TRUE THAT IF THERE IS A CIRCLE ON THE LEFT THERE IS A CIRCLE ON THE RIGHT?

You have only one opportunity to make this decision; you must not assume that you can inspect cards one at a time. Name those cards which it is absolutely essential to see.

Wason and Johnson-Laird discovered that subjects, including very intelligent subjects, find the problem remarkably difficult. In one group of 128 university students, only *five* got the right answer. Moreover, the mistakes that subjects make are not randomly distributed. The two most common wrong answers are that one must see both (a) and (c), and that one need only see (a). The phenomenon turns out to be a remarkably robust one, producing essentially the same results despite significant variation in the experimental design, the wording of the question and the details of the problem. For example, subjects presented with the four envelopes in figure 15.2 and asked which must be turned over to determine the truth of the rule:

IF IT HAS A VOWEL ON ONE SIDE IT HAS AN EVEN NUMBER ON THE OTHER

do just as badly as subjects given the cards in figure 15.1. However, there are variations in the experimental design which substantially improve inferential performance. One of these is making the relation between the antecedent and the consequent of the conditional rule in the instructions more "realistic." So, for example, subjects presented with the envelopes in figure 15.3, and asked which must be turned over to determine the truth of the rule:

IF IT IS SEALED THEN IT HAS A 5d STAMP ON IT

do vastly better than subjects presented with the envelopes in figure 15.2. In one experiment using the "realistic" material, 22 out of 24 subjects got the right answer.[2]

Wason and Johnson-Laird have also explored the ways in which subjects react when they are shown that their initial inferences are mistaken. In figure 15.1, for example, a subject who said he must see only the hidden side of (a) might be asked to remove the masks on both (a) and (d), discovering a circle under each mask. Many subjects have a startling reaction. They note that the rule is false for these cards—in virtue of card (d)—and they continue to insist that it was only necessary to see card (a)! In further work Wason, Johnson-Laird and their colleagues have looked at the ways in which subjects react when the apparent contradiction in their claims is pointed out. The intriguing details of these studies need not detain us here.

My second example of research revealing prima facie deviation from normative standards of inference focuses on the way people assess the probability of logically compound events or states of affairs. It is a truism of probability theory that the likelihood of a compound event or state of affairs must be less than or equal to the likelihood of the component events or states of affairs. If the components are probabilistically independent, the probability of the compound is equal to the product of the probabilities of the components. If the components are not probabilistically independent, matters are more complicated. But in no case will the probability of the compound be *greater* than the probability of the components. There are, however, a number of experiments which demonstrate that people regularly violate this basic tenet of probabilistic reasoning. In one such experiment Kahneman and Tversky gave subjects personality profiles of various target persons. Subjects were then asked to assess the likelihood that the persons described in the profiles belonged to various groups. One group of subjects was asked to estimate the likelihood that profiled persons were member of noncompound groups like *lawyers* or *Republicans*. Another group of subjects was asked to estimate the probability that the profiled persons were members of compound groups like *Republican lawyers*. What Kahneman and Tversky found is that if a profiled person is judged rather unlikely to be, say, a lawyer, and rather likely to be a Republican, he will be judged moderately likely to be a Republican lawyer. That is, the likelihood of the target being a Republican lawyer is judged significantly higher than the likelihood of his being a lawyer! The explanation that Kahneman and Tversky offer for these peculiar judgments turns on what they call the representativeness heuristic. Subjects, they hypothesize, assess the likelihood that a target person is a Republican lawyer by assessing the similarity between the profile and the stereotypical Republican, assessing the similarity between the profile and the stereotypical lawyer, and then *averaging* these two likelihoods.[3]

In a similar study with alarming implications for public policy judgments, Slovic, Fischoff and Lichtenstein showed that subjects estimate the probability of a compound sequence of events to be greater than the least likely of the events in the sequence.[4] It is disquieting to speculate on how large an impact this inferential failing may have on people's assessments of the chance of such catastrophes as nuclear reactor failures which require a number of distinct events to occur in sequence.[5]

My final example of an experimental program exploring human irrationality is the work on belief perseverance by Ross, Lepper and their colleagues.[6] One of the experimental strategies used in this work is the so-called "debriefing" paradigm. In these experiments subjects are given evidence which is later completely discredited. But despite being "debriefed" and told exactly how they had been duped, subjects tend to retain to a substantial degree the beliefs they formed on the basis of the discredited evidence. In one such experiment subjects were presented with the task of distinguishing between authentic and inauthentic suicide notes. As they worked they were provided with false feedback indicating that overall they were performing at close to the average level or (for other subjects) much above the average level, or (for a third group of subjects) much below the average level. Following this, each subject was debriefed, and the predetermined nature of the feedback was explained to him. They were not only told that their feedback had been false but were also shown the experimenter's instruction sheet assigning them to the success, failure or average group, and specifying the feedback to be presented. Subsequent to this, and allegedly for quite a different reason, subjects were asked to fill out a questionnaire on which they were asked to estimate their actual performance at the suicide note task, to predict their probable success on related future tasks and to rate their ability at suicide note discrimination and other related tasks. The results revealed that even after debriefing subjects who had initially been assigned to the success group continued to rate their performance and abilities far more favorably than did subjects in the average group. Subjects initially assigned to the failure group showed the opposite pattern of results. Once again, these results appear to reflect a robust phenomenon which manifests itself in many variations on the experimental theme, including some conducted outside the laboratory setting.

The three examples I have sketched could easily be supplemented by dozens more, all apparently demonstrating that human reasoning often deviates substantially from the standard provided by normative canons of inference. Let us now turn our attention to the arguments aimed at showing that these experiments are being misinterpreted.

III

Of the three arguments I shall consider, two are due to D. C. Dennett. Both arguments are embedded in Dennett's much more elaborate theory about the nature of intentional attributions, though neither argument is developed in much detail. In a pair of previous papers I have tried to give a systematic critique of Dennett's views with due attention to problems of interpretation and the possibilities of alternative construals.[7] In the present paper I will sidestep most of these niceties. What I wish to show is that a pair of arguments are mistaken. I think it is clear that Dennett has at least flirted with each of these arguments. But for the purposes at hand, pinning the tail on the donkey is of little importance.

The first of the arguments I am attributing to Dennett might be called *the argument from the inevitable rationality of believers.* On Dennett's view, when we attribute beliefs, desires and other states of commonsense psychology to a person—or for that matter to an animal or an artifact—we are assuming or presupposing that the person or object can be treated as what Dennett calls an *intentional system.* An intentional system is one which is rational through and through; its beliefs are "those it ought to have, given its perceptual capacities, its epistemic needs, and its biography. . . . [Its desires] are those it ought to have, given its biological needs and the most practicable means of satisfying them. . . . [And its] behavior will consist of those acts that it *would be rational* for an agent with those beliefs and desires to perform."[8] According to Dennett it is in the context of this set of assumptions about rationality that our ordinary talk about beliefs, desires and other intentional states gains its meaning. If this is right, then we should expect that when a person's behavior is less than fully rational the intentional scheme would no longer apply. We could not rest content with a description of a person as holding an incoherent or irrational set of beliefs, for absent rationality we cannot coherently ascribe beliefs at all. Dennett puts the matter as follows:

Conflict arises . . . when a person falls short of perfect rationality, and avows beliefs that either are strongly disconfirmed by the available empirical evidence or are self-contradictory or contradict other avowals he has made. If we lean on the myth that a man is perfectly rational, we must find his avowals less than authoritive: "You can't mean—understand—what you're saying!"; if we lean on his right as a speaking intentional system to have his word accepted, we grant him an irrational set of beliefs. Neither position provides a stable resting place; for, as we saw earlier, intentional explanation and prediction cannot be accommodated either to breakdown or to less than optimal design, so there is no coherent intentional description of such an impasse.[9]

Given this much of Dennett's view, it follows straightforwardly that no experiment could demonstrate that people systematically invoke invalid or irrational inferential strategies. The point is not that people *must* be rational. No such conclusion follows from Dennett's view. What does follow from Dennett's view is that people must be rational *if they can usefully be viewed as having any beliefs at all.* We have no guarantee that people will behave in a way that makes it profitable for us to assume the intentional stance toward them. But intentional descriptions and rationality come in the same package; there is no getting one without the other. Thus if people infer at all, that is, if they generate new beliefs from old ones, from perceptual experience, or what have you, then they must do so rationally. Dennett is, in effect, offering us a *reductio* on the claim that people infer irrationally. If a system infers irrationally, it cannot be an intentional system; thus we cannot ascribe beliefs and desires to it. But since inference is a belief generating process, the system does not infer at all.

Now as I see it, the problem with Dennett's argument comes right at the beginning. He is simply wrong about the relationship between our ordinary notions of belief and desire and his notion of an idealized fully rational intentional system. *Pace* Dennett, it is simply not the case that our ordinary belief and desire ascriptions presuppose full rationality. There is nothing in the least incoherent or unstable about a description, cast in intentional terms, of a person who has inconsistent beliefs. The subjects in Wason and Johnson-Laird's experiments provide a clear example, one among endlessly many. Some of these subjects clearly believe that cards (a) and (c) must be removed, and defend their view with considerable vigor. Yet these subjects clearly understand the conditions of the problem and have no false beliefs about what they are being asked to do.[10]

In defending his contention that ordinary intentional ascriptions gain their meaning against the background of a theory of intentional systems, Dennett offers a pair of arguments, one long and one short. The short one is the observation, attributed to Quine, that blatant or obvious inconsistency is the best evidence we can have that we are misdescribing a subject's beliefs. This fact is readily explained if belief ascription presupposes full rationality. The longer argument has much the same structure. In effect, Dennett maintains that his intentional system explication of ordinary belief and desire talk explains many of the facts about the way we use these locutions in describing and explaining the behavior of persons, animals and artifacts. All of this I cheerfully grant. I also grant that, until recently at least, Dennett's explication of ordinary intentional locutions was the best—indeed pretty near the only—game in town. None of this, however, persuades me to accept Dennett's explication. The reason is that I think there is a better explication of the way we use our workaday belief and desire locutions, an explication that handles all the facts Dennett's can handle without the paradoxical consequence that intentional descriptions of irrational beliefs are unstable or incoherent. The basic idea of this alternative explication is that, in using intentional locutions we are presupposing that the person or system to which they are applied is, in relevant ways, similar to ourselves. Thus inferential errors that we can imagine ourselves making—errors like those recounted in my previous section—can be described comfortably in intentional terms. It is only the sort of error or incoherence that we cannot imagine falling into ourselves that undermines intentional description. This is the reason that blatant inconsistency of the sort Quine has in mind is evidence that something has gone wrong in our intentional attributions. Plainly the alternative "similar-to-us" account of intentional locutions needs a much more detailed elaboration. I have made a beginning at this in Stich (1981) [838].[11]

IV

The second argument Dennett offers is one which he concedes he has left uncomfortably vague. So a fair bit of interpretation will be in order. By way of a label I will call this one *the argument from natural selection*. The closest Dennett comes to setting out the argument is in a passage where he is reflecting on whether we could adopt the intentional stance toward thoroughly exotic creatures encountered on another planet. His answer is that we could provided "we have reason to suppose that a process of natural selection has been in effect." But why would the mere existence of natural selection suffice to insure that the creatures would be good approximations to the thoroughly rational ideal embodied in the notion of an intentional system? Dennett offers no detailed answer, though he does provide us with a few hints, as have other writers who have sounded similar themes. On the most charitable interpretation I can come up with, these hints may be elaborated into the following argument.

1. Natural selection will favor (i.e., select for) inferential strategies which generally yield true beliefs. This is because, in general, true beliefs are more adaptive than false ones; they enable the organism to cope better with its environment. There are exceptions, of course. But on the whole and in the long run organisms will outcompete their conspecifics if their ratio of true beliefs to false ones is higher. So after an extended period of natural selection we can expect that the inferential strategies an organism uses will be ones which generally yield true beliefs.

2. An inferential strategy which generally yields true beliefs is a rational inferential strategy. Therefore,

3. Natural selection will favor rational inferential strategies.

Now since Dennett's Martians are, ex hypothesis, the product of an extended process of natural selection we can conclude that they use rational inferential strategies. And, closer to home, since human beings are the result of millions of years of natural selection we know that they too must use rational inferential strategies. Thus any research program which claims to have evidence for widespread and systematic irrationality among humans must be misinterpreting its results. It is my suspicion that a good number of the writers who have recently been urging a naturalized or evolutionary reinterpretation of epistemology have had something very like this argument hovering in penumbral consciousness. If so, then it is all the more important to focus critical scrutiny on the argument, for such scrutiny shows the argument to be very seriously flawed.

Consider the first step. Is it true that natural selection favors inferential strategies which generally yield true beliefs? The answer, I think, is clearly no. Perhaps the most vivid way to make the point is with a brief description of some intriguing experiments by John Garcia and his co-workers.[12] In one series of experiments Garcia's group fed rats distinctively flavored water or food, and then subjected them to substantial doses of radiation, enough to induce radiation sickness. After a single episode, the rats developed a strong aversion to the distinctively flavored food or water that had been used. Workers in other laboratories have demonstrated that the same phenomenon occurs even when the rat is exposed to radiation as much as twelve hours after eating or drinking. It has also been shown that the taste of the food is the object of the rats' aversion. The rats acquire no aversion to the cage in which the distinctive food was eaten, nor do they acquire an aversion to food pellets of a distinctive size. But if two substances are eaten in sequence prior to illness, novelty is a much more potent factor than recency in determination of the aversion. In short, the rat behaves as though it believes that anything which tastes like the distinctive tasting stuff it had eaten will cause it to become deathly ill. Moreover, it is clear that this belief, if that is what it is, is the result of an innate belief (or aversion) forming strategy which is surely the result of natural selection.

Consider now how often the inferential strategy which leads to the rat's belief will lead to a true belief. In the laboratory, of course, the inferential strategy is thoroughly unreliable. It is the radiation, not the food, which causes the rat's illness. But what about rats in their natural environment? I know of no studies of rat epidemiology which indicate the most common causes of acute illness among rats. I would suspect, however, that rats, like people, fall victim to all manner of acute afflictions caused by viruses and bacteria which are not transmitted through food—still less through distinctively flavored food. If this is right, if, to be more specific, more than half of the illnesses rats endure in the wild which lead to the development of Garcia aversions are not transmitted by distinctively flavored food, it follows that *most* of the beliefs produced by the innate inferential strategy Garcia discovered are *false* beliefs. So it is just not true that natural selection favors inferential strategies which generally yield true beliefs. It is important to note that this argument does not turn essentially on my conjecture about the percentage of rat illnesses caused by distinctive tasting food. The real point of my argument is that *if* my conjecture is correct, it would pose no puzzle for the student of natural selection. Natural selection might perfectly well opt for an inferential strategy which produces false beliefs more often than true ones. The sole concern of natural selection is with reproductive success and those features that foster it. When it comes to food poisoning, natural selection may well prefer an extremely cautious inferential strategy which is very often wrong, to a less cautious one which more often gets the right answer. It might be protested that the Garcia phenomenon does not really join the issue of irrational inference since the rats acquire an aversion, and aversions are not plausibly treated as beliefs. But this reply misses the essential point. Natural selection *could* perfectly well lead to inferential strategies which generally get the wrong answer, but are right when it counts most, just as it leads to aversions to foods most of which are harmless and nourishing. Often it is more adaptive to be safe than sorry.

Thus far my critique of the argument from natural selection has been aimed at the first step, the one which claims that natural selection favors inferential strategies that generally yield true beliefs. But even if we were to grant this dubious claim, the argument from natural selection would still be defective. For its second premise is false as well. That premise, recall, is that inferential strategies which generally yield the right answer are rational inferential strategies. In many cases this simply is not so. Perhaps the clearest examples of generally truth generating inferential strategies which are not rational are the cases in which a strategy is being invoked in a domain or setting significantly different from the one in which it presumably evolved. Once again an example from the study of animal behavior provides a striking illustration. Alcock recounts that a certain species of toad is capable of learning on a single trial to avoid eating a noxious species of millipede. However, the very same toad will continue to consume BBs that are rolled past it until it quite literally becomes a living bean-bag![13] With only a bit of anthropomorphism, we might describe the case as follows. On seeing a millipede of a species previously found to be noxious, the toad comes to believe (i.e., infers) that it is no good to eat. But BBs, with their bland flavor, produce no such belief. Each time a new BB is rolled by, the toad infers that it is good to eat. This belief, of course, is quite false, a fact which will become obvious the first time the BB-filled toad attempts to leap out of harm's way. But of course the inferential strategy which led to the belief *generally* yields true beliefs. Does this show that the strategy is normatively appropriate for the toad to use on the BBs? I am inclined to think that the answer is no.

For all its vividness, the toad example may not be the best one to make my point. For some would protest that they just don't know what counts as a rational inferential strategy for a toad, a protest with which I have considerable sympathy. But the moral I want to draw from the toad example is one which can be drawn also from many cases involving human inference. A common theme in the research on human inference is that people are inclined to overextend the domain of an inferential strategy, applying it to cases where it is normatively inappropriate. Nisbett and Wilson,[14] for example, suggest that many causal inferences are influenced by a primitive version of the representativeness heuristic.

People have strong a priori notions of the types of causes that ought to be linked to particular types of effects, and the simple "resemblance criterion" often figures heavily in such notions. Thus, people believe that great events ought to have great causes, complex events ought to have complex causes, and emotionally relevant events ought to have emotionally relevant causes. . . . The resemblance criterion is transparently operative in the magical thinking of prescientific cultures. [For example] Evans-Prichard . . . reported such Azande beliefs as the theory that fowl excrement was a cure for ringworm and the theory that burnt skull of red bush-monkey was an effective treatment for epilepsy. Westerners unacquainted with Azande ecology might be tempted to guess that such treatments were the product of trial and error or laborously accumulated folk wisdom. Unfortunately the truth is probably less flattering to Azande medical science. Fowl excrement resembles ringworm infection; the jerky, frenetic movements of the bush-monkey resemble the convulsive movements that occur during an epileptic seizure.[15]

Now it may well be that in a sufficiently primitive setting the primitive representativeness heuristic generally does get the right answer; it may have served our hunter-gatherer forebears in good stead. But it seems clear that the Azande are invoking the strategy in a domain where its applicability is, to say the least, normatively dubious. Nisbett and Ross go on to argue that the primitive representativeness heuristic plays a central role in psychoanalytic inference and in contemporary lay inference about the causes of disease, crime, success, etc. The normative inappropriateness of the heuristic in these settings is, I should think, beyond dispute.

The primitive representativeness heuristic is an extreme example of the overextension of an inferential strategy. For we have to go a long way back into our hunter-gatherer ancestry before coming upon life situations in which the heuristic is generally reliable and adaptive. But many of the other inferential failings recounted in the recent literature would seem to arise in a similar way. An inference pattern which generally gets the right answer in a limited domain is applied outside that domain, often to problems without precedent during the vast stretches of human and prehuman history when our cognitive apparatus evolved. Indeed, it is disquieting to reflect on how vast a gap there likely is between the inferences that are important to modern science and society and those that were important to our prehistoric forebears. As Einstein noted, "the most incomprehensible thing about the universe is that it is comprehensible."[16]

I have been arguing that inferential strategies which generally get the right answer may nonetheless be irrational or normatively inappropriate when applied outside the problem domain for which they were shaped by natural selection. If this is right, then the second premise of the argument from natural selection must be rejected. Before leaving this topic I want to digress briefly to raise a thornier issue about normatively appropriate inference. It seems beyond dispute that an inferential strategy like the primitive representativeness heuristic is out of place in modern inquiries about the causes of cancer or of reactor failures. But what about the use of these heuristics in their natural settings? Are they normatively appropriate in those domains to which natural selection has molded them and in which (let us assume) they generally do produce the right answer? If I understand Prof. Goldman's view correctly, he would answer with an unqualified affirmative. But I am less confident. At issue here is the deep and difficult question of just what we are saying of an inferential strategy when we judge that it is or is not normatively appropriate. This issue will loom large in the remaining pages of this paper.

Before leaving the argument from natural selection, we would do well to note one account of what it is for an inference strategy to be rational or normatively appropriate which had best be avoided. This is the reading which turns the conclusion of the argument from natural selection into a tautology by the simple expedient of defining *rational inferential strategy* as *inferential strategy favored by natural selection*. Quite apart from its prima facie implausibility, this curious account of rationality surely misses the point of psychological studies of reasoning. These studies are aimed at showing that people regularly

violate the normative canons of deductive and inductive logic, probability theory, decision theory, etc. They do not aim at showing that
people use inferential strategies which have not evolved by natural
selection!

V

The final argument I want to consider is one proposed by L. Jonathan
Cohen.[17] Cohen's argument grows out of an account of how we establish or validate normative theses about cognitive procedures—
how we justify claims about rational or irrational inference. On Cohen's view normative theses about cognitive procedures are justified
by what in ethics has come to be known as the method of *reflective
equilibrium*. The basic input to the method, the data if you will, are
intuitions, which Cohen characterizes as "immediate and untutored
inclination[s] . . . to judge that" something is the case (I, 1). In ethics
the relevant intuitions are judgments about how people ought or
ought not to behave. In the normative theory of reasoning they are
judgments about how people ought or ought not to reason.

According to Cohen, a normative theory of reasoning is simply an
idealized theory built on the data of people's individualized intuitions
about reasoning. As in science, we build our theory so as to capture
the bulk of the data in the simplest way possible. Our theory, in the
case at hand, will be an interlocking set of normative principles of
reasoning which should entail most individualized intuitions about
how we should reason in the domain in question. An idealized theory
need not aim at capturing all the relevant intuitions of all normal
adults. Scattered exceptions—intuitions that are not entailed by the
theory—can be tolerated in the same spirit that we tolerate exceptions
to the predictions of the ideal gas laws.

Cohen stresses that normative theories of reasoning are not theories about the data (that is, about intuitions) any more than physics
is a theory about observed meter readings, or ethics a theory about
intuitions of rightness and wrongness. Just what normative theories
are about is a question Cohen sidesteps. "Fortunately," he writes,

it is not necessary for present purposes to determine what exactly the study
of moral value, probability or deducibility has as its proper subject matter.
For example, an applied logician's proper aim may be to limn the formal
consequences of linguistic definitions. . . , the most general features of reality . . . or the structure of ideally rational beliefs systems. . . . But, whatever

the ontological concerns of applied logicians, they have to draw their evidential data from intuitions in concrete, individual cases; and the same is true for
investigations into the norms of everyday probabilistic reasoning. (I, 4)

But although a normative theory of reasoning is not a theory about
reasoning intuitions, it is perfectly possible, on Cohen's view, to construct an empirical theory which is concerned to describe or predict
the intuitive judgments which provide the data for the corresponding
normative theory. This second theory

will be a psychological theory, not a logical . . . one. It will describe a competence that human beings have—an ability, uniformly operative under ideal
conditions and often under others, to form intuitive judgements about particular instances of . . . right or wrong, deducibility or non-deducibility, probability or improbability. This theory will be just as idealized as the normative
theory. (I,4)

Having said this much, Cohen can now neatly complete his argument for the inevitable rationality of normal people. The essential
point is that the empirical theory of human reasoning, that is, the
psychological theory that aims to describe and predict intuitive judgments, exploits the same data as the normative theory of reasoning,
and exploits them in the same way. In both cases, the goal is to construct the simplest and most powerful set of principles that accounts
for the bulk of the data. Thus, once a normative theory is at hand,
the empirical theory of reasoning competence will be free for the asking, since it will be *identical* with the normative theory of reasoning!
Though the empirical theory of reasoning competence "is a contribution to the psychology of cognition," Cohen writes,

it is a by-product of the logical or philosophical analysis of norms rather than
something that experimentally oriented psychologists need to devote effort
to constructing. It is not only all the theory of competence that is needed in
its area. It is also all that is possible, since a different competence, if it actually
existed, would just generate evidence that called for a revision of the corresponding normative theory.

In other words, where you accept that a normative theory has to be based
ultimately on the data of human intuition, you are committed to the acceptance of human rationality as a matter of fact in that area, in the sense that it
must be correct to ascribe to normal human beings a cognitive competence—
however often faulted in performance—that corresponds point by point with
the normative theory. (I, 4)

It is important to see that Cohen's view does not entail that people
never reason badly. He can and does happily acknowledge that

people make inferential errors of many sorts and under many circumstances. But he insists that these errors are performance errors, reflecting nothing about the underlying, normatively unimpeachable competence. The account Cohen would give of inferential errors is analogous to the account a Chomskian would give about the errors a person might make in speaking or understanding his own language. We often utter sentences which are ungrammatical in our own dialect, but this is no reflection on our underlying linguistic competence. On the Chomskian view, our competence consists in a tacitly internalized set of rules which determines the strings of words that are grammatical in our language, and these rules generate no ungrammatical strings. Our utilization of these rules is subject to a whole host of potential misadventures which may lead us to utter ungrammatical sentences: there are slips of the tongue, failures of memory, lapses of attention, and no doubt many more. It is certainly possible to study these failures and thereby to learn something about the way the mind exploits its underlying competence. But while such studies might reveal interesting defects in performance, they could not reveal defects in competence. Analogously, we may expect all sorts of defects in inferential performance, due to inattention, memory limitations, or what have you. And a study of these failings may indicate something interesting about the way we exploit our underlying cognitive competence. But such a study could no more reveal an irrational or defective cognitive competence than a study of grammatical errors could reveal that the speaker's linguistic competence was defective.

This is all I shall have to say by way of setting out Cohen's clever argument. As I see it, the argument comes to grief in the account it offers of the justification of normative theses about cognitive procedures. Perhaps the clearest way to underscore the problem with Cohen's epistemological account is to pursue the analogy between grammar and the empirical or descriptive theory of reasoning competence. Both theories are based on the data of intuition and both are idealized. But on Cohen's account there is one striking and paradoxical dis-analogy. In grammar we expect different people to have different underlying competences which manifest themselves in significantly different linguistic intuitions. The linguistic competence of a Frenchman differs radically from the linguistic competence of an Englishman, and both differ radically from the linguistic competence of a Korean. Less radical, but still significant, are the differences between the competence of an Alabama sharecropper, an Oxford don, and a Shetland Island crofter. Yet on Cohen's account of the empirical theory of reasoning there is no mention of different people having different idealized competences. Rather, he seems to assume that in the domain of reasoning all people have exactly the same competence. But why should we not expect that cognitive competence will vary just as much as linguistic competence? The only answer I can find in Cohen's writing is a brief suggestion that cognitive competence may be *innate*. Yet surely this suggestion is entirely gratuitous. Whether or not individuals, social groups, or cultures differ in their cognitive competence is an *empirical* question, on all fours with the parallel question about linguistic competence. It is a question to be settled by the facts about intuitions and practice, not by a priori philosophical argument. And while the facts are certainly far from all being in, I am inclined to think that studies like those reviewed at the beginning of this paper, along with hundreds of others that might have been mentioned, make it extremely plausible that there are substantial individual differences in cognitive competence.

Now if this is right, if different people have quite different cognitive competences, then Cohen's account of the justification of a *normative* theory of reasoning faces some embarrassment. For recall that on his account a normative theory of reasoning is identical with a descriptive theory of cognitive competence; they are built on the same data and idealized in the same way. So if there are *many* cognitive competences abroad in our society and others, then there are *many* normative theories of cognition. But if there are many normative theories of cognition, which is the right one? Note that just here the analogy between linguistic competence and cognitive competence breaks down in an illuminating way. For although there are obviously great variations in linguistic competence, there is no such thing as a normative theory of linguistics (or at least none that deserves to be taken seriously). Thus there is no problem about which of the many linguistic competences abroad in the world corresponds to the normatively correct one.

The problem I have been posing for Cohen is analogous to a familiar problem in ethics. For there too there is good reason to suspect that the method of reflective equilibrium would yield different normative theories for different people, and we are left with the problem of saying which normative theory is the right one. One response to the problem in ethics, though to my mind an utterly unsatisfactory one, is a thoroughgoing relativism: my normative theory is the right one *for me*, yours is the right one *for you*. One way for Cohen to deal with the problem of the multiplicity of normative theories of cognition might be to adopt an analogous relativism. My inferential competence is right for me, yours is right for you. But this move is even more unpalatable for the normative theory of cognition than it is for ethics. We are not in the least inclined to say that any old inference is normatively acceptable for a subject merely because it accords with the rules which constitute his cognitive competence. If the inference is stupid or irrational, and if it accords with the subject's cognitive competence, then his competence is stupid or irrational too, in this quarter at least.

A second strategy for dealing with the multiplicity of normative theories might be to adopt a majoritarian view according to which it is the cognitive competence of the majority that is normatively correct. This is no more plausible than the relativist alternative, however. First, it is not at all clear that there is a majority cognitive competence, any more than there is a majority linguistic competence. It may well be that many significantly different competences coexist in the world, with the most common having no more than a meagre plurality. Moreover, even if there is a majority cognitive competence, there is little inclination to insist that it must be the normatively correct one. If, as seems very likely, most people disregard the impact of regression in estimating the likelihood of events, then most people infer badly![18]

The upshot of these reflections is that Cohen has simply told the wrong story about the justification of normative theories of cognition. Given the possibility of alternative cognitive competences, he has failed to tell us which one is normatively correct. Should he supplement his story along either relativist or majoritarian lines he would be stuck with the unhappy conclusion that a patently irrational inferential strategy might turn out to be the normatively correct one.[19]

By way of conclusion, let me note that there is a variation on Cohen's reflective equilibrium story which does a much better job at making sense of our normative judgments about reasoning, both in everyday life and in the psychology laboratory. It seems clear that we do criticize the reasoning of others, and we are not in the least swayed by the fact that the principles underlying a subject's faulty reasoning are a part of his—or most people's—cognitive competence. We are, however, swayed to find that the inference at hand is sanctioned or rejected by the cognitive competence of experts in the field of reasoning in question. Many well-educated people find statistical inferences involving regression to the mean to be highly counterintuitive, at least initially. But sensible people come to distrust their own intuition on the matter when they learn that principles requiring regressive inference are sanctioned by the reflective equilibrium of experts in statistical reasoning. In an earlier paper, Nisbett and I tried to parlay this observation into a general account of what it is for a normative principle of reasoning to be justified.[20] On our view, when we judge someone's inference to be normatively inappropriate, we are comparing it to (what we take to be) the applicable principles of inference sanctioned by expert reflective equilibrium. On this account, there is no puzzle or paradox implicit in the practice of psychologists who probe human irrationality. They are evaluating the inferential practice of their subjects by the sophisticated and evolving standard of expert competence. From this perspective, it is not at all that surprising that lay practice has been found to be markedly defective in many areas. We would expect the same, and for the same reason, if we examined lay competence in physics or in economics.

There is a hopeful moral embedded in this last observation. If, as Cohen suggests, cognitive competence is innate, then normatively inappropriate competence is ominous and inalterable. But if, as I have been urging, there is every reason to think that cognitive competence, like linguistic competence, is to a significant extent acquired and variable, then there is reason to hope that competence can be improved through education and practice, much as a child from Liverpool can acquire the crisp linguistic competence of an Oxford don. There is an important disanalogy, of course. Liverpudlean cadances are harmless and charming; normatively defective inference is neither. I am inclined to think it a singular virtue of recent studies of reasoning that they point to the areas where remedial education is most needed.

Notes

1. Wason and Johnson-Laird 1972 [139], Chs. 13–15; Wason 1977 [436]; Johnson-Laird and Wason 1970 [749].

2. Johnson-Laird, Legrenzi and Sonino-Legrenzi 1972 [749]. However, see also Griggs and Cox, 1982 [740].

3. Kahneman and Tversky 1982 [486].

4. Slovic, Fischoff and Lichtenstein 1977 [829].

5. Slovic and Fischoff 1978 [828].

6. Ross, Lepper and Hubbard 1975 [488].

7. Stich 1980 [836] and Stich 1981 [837].

8. Dennett 1981 [707], p. 42.

9. Dennett 1978 [562], p. 20.

10. For Dennett's attempt to blunt this point, cf. Dennett 1981 [707].

11. Dennett's view is often described as of a piece with Davidson's. But this is clearly mistaken. Davidson makes no use of the notion of an ideally rational system. Like me, he insists that a person must be cognitively *similar* to ourselves if we are to succeed in understanding his speech and ascribing beliefs to him. In particular, he maintains that "if I am right in attributing [a particular] belief to you, then you must have a pattern of beliefs much like mine." (Davidson 1979 [705], p. 295). Davidson goes on to argue that most of these beliefs must be *true*. This is a view that Dennett holds as well. But as we shall see in the next section, Dennett's defense of this doctrine turns on evolutionary considerations, while Davidson's does not. The least obscure argument Davidson offers for this conclusion goes like this: "There is nothing absurd in the idea of an omniscient interpreter" (ibid.). To interpret us, this omniscient interpreter must share the bulk of our beliefs. And since *ex hypothesis* all of his beliefs are true, it follows that the bulk of ours must be true as well. End of argument. It should be pretty clear, however, that this argument simply begs the question. Granting the point about belief similarity being necessary for interpretation, it is an open question whether an omniscient interpreter could interpret our utterances as meaning something in his language. He could do so only if the bulk of our beliefs are true. And that is just what the argument was supposed to establish.

12. Garcia, McGowan and Green 1972 [729].

13. Alcock 1975 [534].

14. Nisbett and Wilson 1977 [354].

15. Nisbett and Ross 1980 [89], pp. 115–116.

16. Quoted in Sinsheimer 1971 [827].

17. Cohen 1981 [190]. In the pages that follow, quotes from this paper will be identified by section numbers in parentheses in the text.

18. Cf. Nisbett and Ross 1980 [89], pp. 150ff.

19. We should note in passing that Cohen was not the first to introduce the competence-performance distinction into the debate about human rationality. Fodor 1981 [37] has an extended and illuminating discussion of the possibility that "the postulates of . . . logic are mentally represented by the organism, and this mental representation contributes (in appropriate ways) to the causation of its beliefs" (p. 120). Since the internally represented logic would be only one among many interacting causes of belief and behavior, "the evidence for attributing a logic to an organism would not be that the

organism believes whatever the logic entails. Rather, the appropriate form of argument is to show that the assumption that the organism internally represents the logic, when taken together with independently motivated theories of the character of the other interacting variables, yields the best explanation of the data about the organism's mental states and processes and/or the behaviors in which such processes eventuate." But if the facts turn out right, it would seem that the same sort of evidentiary considerations might also lead to the conclusion that the organism had internally represented a peculiar or normatively inappropriate "logic." This is not a possibility Fodor pursues, however, since he has been seduced by Dennett's argument from natural selection. Darwinian selection, he claims, "guarantees that organisms either know the elements of logic or become posthumous" (p. 121).

20. Stich and Nisbett 1980 [418].

16   Learning Inferential Rules

John H. Holland,
Keith J. Holyoak,
Richard E. Nisbett,
and Paul R. Thagard

In the last chapter we described how people use the law of large numbers and knowledge about variability in making generalizations. While modeling the world, they make observations that trigger the application of inductive inferential rules. As we noted in chapter 2, the function of inferential rules is not to model the environment directly but to generate empirical rules, adding these to the permanent base of general knowledge.

We hope to show in this chapter that statistical rule systems are not the only abstract inferential schemas that people possess, but that such schemas are common. As it happens, our belief that inferential rule systems exist is controversial. No one doubts, of course, that scientists, statisticians, and logicians possess such rules and can use them for analyzing formal propositions and for reasoning about scientific data. But some theorists hold that people do not use abstract inferential rules when reasoning about ordinary events but instead make inferences exclusively by means of domain-specific empirical rules. We wish to show that these theorists are mistaken and that laypeople do in fact possess inferential rules and use them for thinking about everyday events.

A second, related goal is to show that such inferential rules, in addition to being induced by people in the course of ordinary daily existence, can be taught. And at least some of them can be taught by purely abstract means, that is, by giving information about the rules themselves rather than by showing how they can be used to reason about particular concrete problems. Finally, we will suggest that

Reprinted from *Induction: Processes of Inference, Learning, and Discovery* by John H. Holland, Keith J. Holyoak, Richard E. Nisbett, and Paul R. Thagard (Cambridge, Mass.: MIT Press, 1986), pp 255–286, by permission of the publisher. Copyright © 1986, MIT Press.

inferential rules of the sort beloved by the logician, that is, the rules of formal logic, are not an important part of the layperson's repertoire and cannot readily be taught by purely abstract means. Instead, the rule systems that people actually use are what we call *pragmatic reasoning schemas*, that is, rule systems that are highly generalized and abstracted but nonetheless defined with respect to classes of goals and types of relationships, rather than being purely syntactic. Pragmatic reasoning schemas, unlike the rules of formal logic, can be easily taught in such a way that they are accessible for solving ordinary, everyday life problems.

Teaching Statistical Rules

Although we did not emphasize it, there were two different lines of evidence in the last chapter that indicated that subjects were solving problems using abstract statistical rules rather than more domain-specific empirical rules tied to particular types of events. The first is that when subjects were asked to justify their statistically correct answers, they often simply appealed to abstract statistical principles. Indeed, Piaget and Inhelder (1951/1975) [630] found that subjects as young as ten could supply generalized statistical justifications for particular inferences about the behavior of randomizing devices. Second, the cues that were shown to increase the likelihood of statistical reasoning are just the ones that would be expected to do so if subjects were using domain-independent statistical rules. These included manipulations of the salience of the central tendencies of distributions versus the dispersion of distributions, and manipulations of the apparent role of chance in producing the events in question. It is less ad hoc to say that people have generalized rules about uncertainty and apply them whenever they can code the uncertainty of the events in question than it is to say that subjects' rules for each empirical domain examined include rules that merely mimic the operation of statistical rules.

But we believe we have more solid evidence that people actually possess statistical rules in a highly abstract form and can apply them to ordinary events. This is the fact that the teaching of statistical rules in an abstract way, as it is normally done in statistics courses, for example, has an effect on the way people reason about problems in everyday life. Research by Fong, Krantz, and Nisbett (1986) [728] shows that the teaching of statistics affects the way people think about everyday problems far removed from the content of the typical statistics course. This work indicates that (a) purely abstract forms of statistical training affect reasoning about concrete events, and (b) even when statistical rules are learned in particular content domains they may be abstracted from those domains to a very great degree, sufficient to allow their application to quite different domains.

The Effects of Statistics Courses

In a series of studies Fong and colleagues (1986) [728] examined four groups of subjects differing widely in statistical training. The subjects were college students who either had or had not had statistical training in an elementary course, graduate students who had had one or more semesters of training, and Ph.D.-level scientists who had had several years of training. Subjects were presented with one of a pair of problems about meal quality in restaurants. In each a protagonist experienced a truly outstanding meal on the first visit to a restaurant but was disappointed on repeat visits. The subjects were asked to explain, in writing, why this might have happened. The explanation was classified as "statistical" if it suggested that meal quality on any single visit might not be a reliable indicator of the restaurant's overall quality (for example, "Very few restaurants have only excellent meals; odds are she was just lucky the first time"). Nonstatistical answers assumed that the initial good experience was a reliable indicator that the restaurant was truly outstanding, and attributed the later disappointment to a definite cause, such as a permanent or temporary change in the restaurant (for example, "Maybe the chef quit") or a change in the protagonist's expectation or mood. Explanations that were statistical were coded as to whether they merely referred vaguely to chance factors or whether they also articulated the notion that a single visit may be regarded as a small sample and hence as unreliable. Explanations thus were coded as falling into one of three categories: (1) nonstatistical, (2) poor statistical, and (3) good statistical. The frequencies in each of these categories were used to define two dependent variables: *frequency* of statistical answers, defined as the proportion of responses in categories 2 and 3, and *quality* of statistical answers, defined as the proportion of category 2 and 3 answers that were category 3.

It should be noted that the presence of nonstatistical statements in an answer did not by itself cause the answer to be coded as nonstatistical. On the contrary, answers were coded as statistical if there was any statistical statement at all. In order to be coded as a good statistical answer, however, the statistical portion had to contain a lucid conceptualization of the sample notion *and* express a preference for that over any nonstatistical answers that were offered. The consequence of this coding scheme is that the frequency measure is free of normative commitments: it simply expresses the proportion of subjects who made a statistical observation. The quality measure, on the other hand, reflects the investigators' views about the correct approach to the question.

The two versions of the restaurant problem differed. A probabilistic-cue version included a random mechanism for selection from the menu: the protagonist did not know how to read a Japanese menu and selected a meal by blindly dropping a pencil on the menu and observing where the point lay. The other version had no such cue. Within each group tested, half the subjects received the cue and half did not.

The effects of training on both dependent measures were dramatic, as may be seen in figure 16.1. College students without statistical training almost never gave an answer that was at all statistical unless the problem contained the probabilistic cue, in which case about half the answers were statistical. In contrast, more than 80 percent of the answers of Ph.D.-level scientists were statistical, whether or not there was a cue about randomness. The quality of the statistical answers also depended on the level of training. Only 10 percent of the statistical answers by untrained college students were rated as good, whereas almost 80 percent of the statistical answers by Ph.D.-level scientists were rated as good.

Although the presence of the randomness cue was very important in determining whether less-trained subjects would give statistical answers, it did not affect the quality of the statistical answers for subjects at any level of training. Apparently cues about randomness can trigger the use of statistical rules, but they do not necessarily produce good statistical answers. Such cues can only trigger rules at whatever level of sophistication the subject happens to possess.

Statistical training also influences inductive reasoning outside the classroom and laboratory. Fong and colleagues conducted a telephone "survey of opinions about sports." The subjects were males who were enrolled in an introductory statistics course and who admitted to being at least somewhat knowledgeable about sports. Some

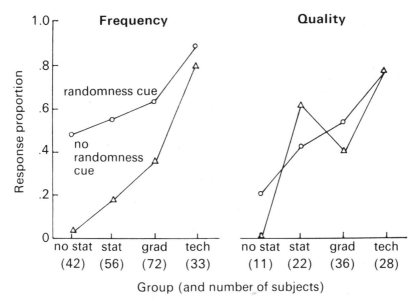

Figure 16.1
Frequency and quality of statistical answers to restaurant problem as a function of presence versus absence of probabilistic cue and level of statistical training (no stat = college students with no statistics; stat = college students with one or more statistics courses; grad = graduate students in psychology, most of whom had had two or more courses in statistics and methodology; tech = technical staff at a research laboratory). From Fong, Krantz, and Nisbett (1986 [727]).

subjects were randomly selected and "surveyed" during the first two weeks of the term they were enrolled in statistics, the others at or near the end of the term. In addition to filler questions on NCAA rules and NBA salaries, subjects were asked questions for which a statistical approach was relevant, as in the example below.

In general, the major league baseball player who wins Rookie of the Year does not perform as well in his second year. This is clear in major league baseball in the past ten years. In the American League, 8 rookies of the year have done worse in their second year; only 2 have done better. In the National League, the rookie of the year has done worse the second year 9 times out of 10. Why do you suppose the rookie of the year tends not to do as well his second year?

Most subjects answered this question in a purely nonstatistical way, invoking causal notions such as "too much press attention" and "slacking off." Some subjects answered the question statistically

("There are bound to be some rookies who have an exceptional season; it may not be due to any great talent advantage that one guy has over some of the others—he just got a particularly good year"). The statistics course markedly increased the percentage of statistical answers and also increased the quality of statistical answers to this question and to two of four others that were asked.

Abstract Rule Training and Concrete Example Training

It could be argued that statistics courses do not constitute fully abstract rule training, inasmuch as students are taught how to apply the rules to specific, concrete problems. To the degree that that is done, students may emerge not with fully abstract rules that can be applied across essentially the full range of problems for which a statistical approach is relevant, but with empirical rules for many domains that have a statistical flavor. In our view this is implausible, because most statistics courses with which we are familiar spend very little time teaching the use of the rules on content domains beyond IQ tests, agricultural plots, gambling devices, and so on.

But it is simple to rule out the possibility that subjects are learning merely domain-specific rules. This was done by Fong, Krantz, and Nisbett (1986) [727], who taught subjects about the law of large numbers in brief, fully abstract training sessions. The subjects were given one or both of two training packages. One covered formal aspects of the law of large numbers as a heuristic device in modeling problems. The abstract rule training consisted of definitions of population and sample distributions, a statement of the law of large numbers, and urn-problem illustrations showing that a population distribution is estimated more accurately, on the average, from larger samples. The examples training consisted of three problems (in the general style of the restaurant problem and similar to the subsequent test problems), each followed by a written solution that used the law of large numbers and emphasized the analogy between amount of evidence and size of sample.

There were four major conditions: a control group given no instruction, and three experimental groups—one given abstract rule training only, one given examples training only, and one given both types of training. The subjects were adults and high school students. The test consisted of fifteen problems. Five of these had clear probabilistic cues in the form of a randomizing device, five dealt with objective

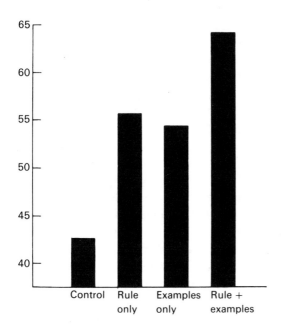

Figure 16.2
Percentage of statistical answers as a function of type of training. From Fong, Krantz, and Nisbett (1986 [727]).

attributes such as abilities or achievements, and five dealt with subjective judgments, such as are involved in the restaurant problem or the "college choice" problem described in chapter 8.

Training effects were marked for all three problem types, for both the frequency of statistical answers and the quality of statistical answers. Both abstract rule training and examples training produced very substantial effects. It may be seen in figure 16.2 that abstract training and examples training were about equally effective, and the combination of the two was substantially more effective than either alone.

A particularly important finding for present concerns is that examples training showed no domain-specificity effects. In the study just described, examples training was provided on objective-attribute problems only, yet these problems showed no more improvement due to training than did either probabilistic-cue problems or subjective-judgment problems. More important, in a companion study the investigators manipulated the type of problem on which training took place. Type of problem on which subjects were trained had no effect on performance. Subjects trained on subjective problems, for example, did no better on subjective problems than did subjects trained on either probabilistic or objective problems, and subjects trained on probabilistic-cue problems did no better on probabilistic-cue problems than did subjects trained on objective or subjective problems. These findings suggest that learning based on specific problem types is abstracted to a degree sufficient for use on widely different problem types.

The evidence thus indicates that statistical solutions to problems can be made more likely and their quality improved by purely abstract training as well as by training in how to model example problems in terms of the rules. In addition, training in a given domain generalizes to a very great degree. We interpret these results as indicating that people already possess some statistical rules in an abstract form. Purely abstract manipulations of the rules help people to solve problems because they already have substantial experience in solving problems by means of more primitive versions of them. Improvements in the rules thus can be "passed along" without further training in interpreting events in terms of the rules. Similarly, training in the use of the rules in a given domain produces improvements in a wide variety of other domains because people already possess rudimentary abstract versions of the rules and can readily generalize from the solutions applied to particular problems to improved versions of the rules in their abstract form.

Higher Education and Inductive Inferential Rules

One implication of the work of Fong and his colleagues is that different types of higher education ought to differ substantially in the degree to which they increase people's ability to reason using particular types of inductive rules. At one extreme are the social sciences, notably psychology, where the graduate curriculum contains a very heavy dose of formal inductive rules, in the form of statistics and methodology courses. At another extreme are various "hard science" fields such as chemistry and electrical engineering, which have little need to emphasize inferential rules for dealing with uncertainty, and nonscientific fields, such as law and the humanities.

A field such as medicine forms an interesting contrast. While training in medicine does not emphasize purely formal inductive rule training in the same way that social science training does, the prag-

matic content of medicine is inherently probabilistic. It deals with uncertain events, and thus training in it might be expected to convey
some appreciation of inductive rules.

Lehman, Lempert, and Nisbett (1986) [771] examined the effects of
graduate training in various fields on the use of inductive rules—both
statistical rules of the kind examined in chapter 8 and in the studies
just reported, and methodological rules such as rules for appropriate
control groups and rules for recognizing various artifacts in correlational studies. Subjects were tested over two very broad content domains. Some of the problems involved inductive reasoning about
scientific studies (both natural science studies and social science studies) and some concerned everyday life. An example of a "methodological" problem with everyday-life content is one that asked
whether the police chief of Indianapolis should be fired on the basis
of the increased crime rate observed during his tenure. A correct answer required recognizing that a decision should await comparison
with appropriate "controls," for example, crime rates in other Midwestern cities during the same time period. The subjects were graduate students in psychology, chemistry, law, and medicine at the
University of Michigan. They were tested either at the beginning of
their first year of study or at the beginning of their third.

The effects of the various types of graduate education were markedly different. The most dramatic effect was for the influence of psychology training. It had a strong effect on reasoning about material
both with scientific content and with everyday-life content. Medical
training had a weaker but still significant effect on both. Neither
chemistry nor law training produced any improvement in reasoning
about either type of problem.

The results of the Lehman, Lempert, and Nisbett study indicate
that formal education can have an effect on the way people reason
about uncertain events in everyday life. The results suggest that to
do so, however, a discipline must either teach about inductive rules
in a formal way or illustrate their use in the context of reasoning pragmatically about everyday-life content.

Domain Specificity and Encoding

The studies just discussed help to demonstrate that people have abstract statistical rules that can be applied to a wide range of events,
but they do not help us to understand the extreme domain specificity

of statistical rules discussed in chapter 8. Indeed, the studies tend to deepen the mystery of domain specificity. The studies by Fong and colleagues showed no domain specificity of training results, and those by Lehman and colleagues suggest that training in the fields both of psychology and of medicine transfers to a very wide range of everyday events.

Fong and Nisbett (1986) [728] reasoned that no domain specificity was found in their initial training studies because the domains employed were extremely broad and diverse, encompassing essentially all problems referring to events that could be described as "objectively codable abilities and achievements," "subjective judgments about the properties of a social object," and so on. They conjectured that if subjects were shown how to model problems in narrower content domains there might be some domain specificity of training effects, at least if the training effects were examined after a delay, when subjects would no longer have the training problems fresh in their memories for purposes of analogizing and generalizing their solutions to the target domain.

In order to examine this possibility, Fong and Nisbett (1986) [728] gave subjects example problems either in the domain of sports or in the domain of mental ability testing, showing them how to solve the problems using the law of large numbers. They then tested subjects in both domains. But for some subjects testing took place immediately after the training, while for others testing took place two weeks later. It was anticipated that showing subjects how to encode the events and relationships in a given domain in terms of the law of large numbers would confer a lasting ability to do so. When subjects were tested immediately on some other domain, they should be able to make substantial use of the training because they should be able to see the analogy between how to code events in the training domain and how to code events in the other domain. When subjects were tested after a substantial delay, however, they could not be expected to have sufficient memory of the training problems to be able to reason from them by analogy to the new domain. Thus there should be a significant reduction in the generalization of training to the new domain after a delay.

These anticipations were largely borne out, as may be seen in figure 16.3. For both sports problems and ability testing problems, there was no domain specificity of training effects immediately. Training on sports problems produced just as much improvement on ability prob-

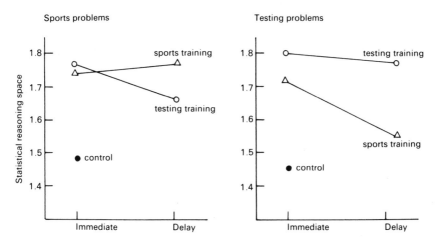

Figure 16.3.
Statistical reasoning as a function of domain of testing, domain of training, and immediate versus delayed testing. From Fong and Nisbett (1986 [728]).

lems as did training on ability problems, and vice versa. After a delay, however, matters were quite different. There was very substantial domain specificity, such that subjects trained on a different domain from that on which they were tested performed at a lower level than subjects trained on the same domain as that on which they were tested. Remarkably, there was no loss of training effects for subjects who were tested on the same domain on which they were trained. We have no ready explanation for the fact that there was no forgetting at all for this group, but it clearly suggests that encoding training can be extremely effective. Once subjects are taught in a brief training session how to think about the events in a given domain in terms of the law of large numbers, they may fully retain that ability, at least when the context is also reinstated, for a very substantial period of time.

The main results seem quite clear. They establish that there is no logical incompatibility between the extreme domain specificity of statistical reasoning reported in chapter 8 and the extreme lack of domain specificity of training effects. People are able to fully generalize the lessons of training to new domains so long as those lessons are fresh in memory. Once the lessons are no longer fresh, people cannot be expected to retain them in very great strength except in the domains in which they were taught.

We must add one more, broader caveat to the generally quite optimistic set of results we have been discussing. The law of large numbers is actually a very large and diverse set of rules, some of them nonintuitive or even counterintuitive, and it is applicable not merely to the kinds of relatively simple problems in the studies we have just reviewed, but to far more difficult problems as well. In addition, there are many other fundamental statistical principles that have relevance to everyday events, some of which are also complex or counterintuitive. Thus the literature shows that even people who are highly trained in statistics are sometimes no more likely than laypeople to apply particular statistical rules to particular problems (Kahneman, Slovic, and Tversky 1982 [68]; Kunda and Nisbett 1986 [768]; Tversky and Kahneman 1971 [475], 1983 [483]). Just which rules are most natural for people, which are most easily taught, and what are the best teaching techniques, are intriguing questions for the future.

Teaching Logical Rules

Do rules of deductive logic have the same properties as statistical rules? That is, do people possess logical rules in the same abstract form that they possess statistical rules, and are logical rules readily accessible for making inferences about everyday problems? In short, how do ordinary people reason about problems that the logician can solve by applying formal syntactic rules? One answer, since Aristotle, has been that ordinary people themselves use formal syntactic rules. According to both philosophers and psychologists (including Piaget and his followers) who are sympathetic to the syntactic view, these deductive rules are either known *a priori* or induced by everyone in the course of normal development because of their manifest utility in problem solving.

We will review evidence for an alternative view, based on the proposal that everyday reasoning typically relies on sets of inferential rules that constitute pragmatic reasoning schemas (Cheng and Holyoak 1985 [692]; Cheng, Holyoak, Nisbett, and Oliver 1986 [693]). First, however, we will critically examine earlier proposals.

Problems with the Syntactic View

It has always been known, of course, that people make errors when attempting to reason logically, but this fact usually has not been regarded as fatal to the syntactic view. Errors are often presumed to reflect vagaries in the interpretation of the material from which one reasons, including changes such as the addition or omission of premises (Henle 1962 [745]). For example, it has been pointed out that different conversational contexts invite different pragmatic assumptions (Fillenbaum 1975 [716], 1976 [717]; Geis and Zwicky 1971 [730]). The sentence "If you mow the lawn, I'll give you five dollars," for instance, clearly invites the inference "If you don't mow the lawn, I won't give you five dollars." Such an inference, although fallacious according to formal logic (it is functionally equivalent to the fallacy of Denying the Antecedent), is actually pragmatically valid within its context.

There is abundant evidence for such invited pragmatic inferences, but interpretive mistakes of that kind cannot account for typical patterns of errors produced by college students in a variety of deductive reasoning problems employing *arbitrary* symbols and relations. (See Evans 1982 [35] for a review.) The best known of these problems is Wason's (1966) [662] selection task. In this task subjects are informed that they will be shown cards that have numbers on one side and letters on the other, and are given a rule such as "If a card has an *A* on one side, then it has a 4 on the other." Subjects are then presented with four cards, which might show an *A*, a *B*, a 4, and a 7, and are asked to indicate all and only those cards that must be turned over to determine whether or not the rule holds. The correct answer in this example is to turn over the cards showing *A* and 7. More generally, the rule used in such problems is a conditional, "if p then q", and the relevant cases are p (because if p is the case it must be established that q is also the case) and *not-q* (because if it is not the case that q then it must be established that it is also not the case that p). When college students are presented with such problems in an abstract form, it is usually found that fewer than ten percent of them can produce the correct answer.

Each of the four alternatives in the selection task corresponds to the minor premise in one of the four possible inference patterns (two valid and two invalid) for the conditional. Selection of p corresponds to the minor premise in the valid rule of *modus ponens:*

If p then q

p
_____

Therefore, q.

Selection of *not-q* corresponds to the valid rule *modus tollens:*

If *p* then *q*

not-q

Therefore, *not-p.*

Selection of *not-p* corresponds to the fallacy of Denying the Antecedent:

If *p* then *q*

not-p

Therefore, *not-q.*

Selection of *q* corresponds to the fallacy of Affirming the Consequent:

If *p* then *q*

q

Therefore, *p.*

From a logical perspective it might seem that subjects in these experiments mistakenly interpret the rule as a biconditional (that is, *p if and only if q*), which requires that all four cards be turned over. In fact, however, this error is rare. Instead, most subjects select patterns that are irreconcilable with any logical interpretation, choosing, for example, *A* and 4 (that is, *p* and *q*). One of the errors in such an answer is omission of the card showing 7, indicating a failure to see the equivalence of a conditional statement and its contrapositive (that is, "If a card does not have a 4 on one side, then it does not have an *A* on the other"). Other errors include the fallacies of Affirming the Consequent (which corresponds to insistence on examining 4, which is unnecessary because the rule does not specify anything about the obverse of cards with a 4 on one side) and Denying the Antecedent (which corresponds to insistence on examining *B*, which also is unnecessary because the rule does not specify anything about cards that do not have an *A* on one side). Such errors suggest that typical college students do commit fallacies due to errors in the deductive process itself, at least with abstract materials.

Abstract Rules versus Specific Knowledge

Other research, however, has shown that subjects can solve problems that are formally identical to the selection task if they are presented in "realistic," "thematic" contexts. Johnson-Laird, Legrenzi, and Legrenzi (1972) [749], for example, took advantage of a now-defunct British postal rule requiring that sealed envelopes have more postage than unsealed envelopes. They asked their subjects to pretend that they were postal workers sorting letters and had to determine whether rules such as "If a letter is sealed, then it has a 5*d*. stamp on it" were violated. The problem was cast in the frame of a standard Wason selection task. The percentage of correct responses for this version was 81, whereas only 15 percent of the responses given by the same subjects to the "card" version were correct.

In contrast, younger subjects in more recent studies, unfamiliar with the old postal rule, turn out to perform no better on the envelope version of the task than they do on the card version (Griggs and Cox 1982 [740]; Golding 1981 [739]). This pattern of results has suggested to some that the source of facilitation in the experiment by Johnson-Laird and colleagues was prior experience with a rule, particularly prior experience with counterexamples. It has been argued that subjects familiar with the postal rule do well because the falsifying instance—a sealed but understamped letter—would be available immediately through the subjects' prior experience. Several theorists have generalized this interpretation, suggesting that people typically do not reason using the rules of formal logic at all, but instead rely on memory of specific experiences or content-specific empirical rules (D'Andrade 1982 [700]; Griggs and Cox 1982 [740]; Manktelow and Evans 1979 [784]; Reich and Ruth 1982 [812]). This is a position of extreme domain specificity, which holds that subjects do not possess general and abstract inferential rules at all, but instead possess only rules covering specific, concrete content domains and an ability to check for counterexamples in those domains to ensure that the rule obtains.

The syntactic view has not been abandoned by all theorists, however (Braine 1978 [683]; Braine, Reiser, and Rumain 1984 [684]; Rips 1983 [814]). Braine (1978) [683], for example, has proposed that there is a *natural* logic, different in its content from standard logic, but computationally complete and "mappable" onto a valid logical rule system. Natural logic is different from standard logic in that the connectives capture essential syntactic and semantic properties of the corresponding English words. Particular rules present in most standard logics—for example, *modus tollens*—are simply not represented in natural logic.

Work by Braine and his colleagues (1984) [684] shows that people who have not been tutored in logic can indeed solve purely arbitrary problems with great accuracy. For example, subjects can solve problems of the following form:

If there's a D or a J, then there's not a Q

There is a D

Is there a Q?

According to Braine and his colleagues, subjects solve this problem by means of sequential application of their inference schemas P7 and P3 (out of a total of 16 schemas):

P7   IF p_1 OR . . . p_n THEN q

       p_i
_____

       q

P3 p;

       False that p
_____

       INCOMPATIBLE

The fact that people are quite accurate in solving problems like those presented by Braine, Reiser, and Rumain poses problems for positions at the empirical extreme. Subjects cannot be plausibly held to have empirical rules, or memories for counterexamples, for problems involving Ds and Qs.

A quite different approach, which can be viewed as an attempt to merge the extreme positions represented by specific knowledge and abstract syntactic rules, has been taken by Johnson-Laird (1982 [749], 1983 [67]). He has proposed that people possess a set of procedures for modeling the relations in deductive reasoning problems so as to reach conclusions about possible states of affairs given the current model of relations among elements. In Johnson-Laird's theory, mental models are constructed using both general linguistic strategies for interpreting logical terms such as quantifiers, and specific knowledge retrieved from memory. The modeling procedures themselves are general and domain-independent.

Pragmatic Reasoning Schemas

The approach advocated by Cheng and her colleagues is based on a type of knowledge structure qualitatively different from those postulated by other theories of logical reasoning. This approach assumes that people often reason using neither formal syntactic rules nor memories of specific experiences, but rather pragmatic reasoning schemas, which are knowledge structures at an intermediate level of abstraction. Pragmatic reasoning schemas are highly abstract rule systems, inasmuch as they potentially apply to a wide range of content domains. Unlike syntactic rules, however, they are constrained by particular inferential goals and event relationships of certain broad types. Although pragmatic reasoning schemas are related to Johnson-Laird's (1983) [67] concepts of mental models, some important differences are evident. For example, whereas Johnson-Laird focuses on limitations in working-memory capacity as an explanation of reasoning errors, the schema approach explains errors (as defined by the dictates of formal logic) in terms of the ease of mapping concrete situations into pragmatic schemas, as well as the degree to which the evoked schemas generate inferences that in fact conform to standard logic.

Cheng and Holyoak (1985) [692] obtained several empirical findings that speak strongly for the existence of reasoning schemas. In one experiment using the selection paradigm, they compared the effect of direct experience to the effect of simply adding a rationale to rules that might otherwise seem arbitrary. Groups of subjects in Hong Kong and in Michigan were presented with both the envelope problem described earlier and another problem having to do with rule following. In the latter problem passengers at an airport were required to show a form, and it was necessary to check whether the rule "If the form says 'ENTERING' on one side, then the other side includes cholera among the list of diseases" was violated by each of four different cases corresponding to p, q, not-p, and not-q.

There was no reason to expect subjects in either location to have experience with the cholera rule. But because a version of the envelope rule had been in effect in Hong Kong until shortly before the experiment, subjects in Hong Kong were expected to have relevant specific experience to draw on. In addition, half the subjects in each location received brief rationales for the two rules. The stated rationale for the postal rule was that a sealed envelope defined first-class mail, for which the post office wished to receive more revenue; the rationale for the cholera rule was that the form listed diseases for which the passenger had been inoculated, and that a cholera inoculation was required to protect the entering passengers from the disease. It was anticipated that in both cases the rationale would trigger a

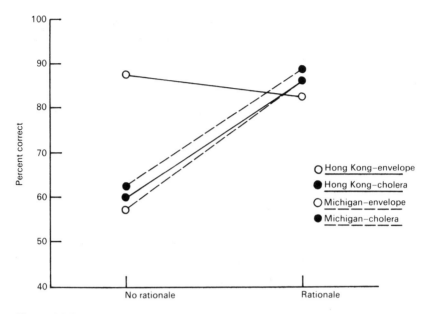

Figure 16.4
Percentage of subjects who solved the selection task correctly in each condition as a function of provision of a rationale. From Cheng and Holyoak (1985 [692]).

"permission schema," or set of rules having to do with circumstances under which action Y is required if action X is to be permitted (for example, higher postage must be paid if a letter is to be mailed first class).

The results of the experiment are depicted in figure 16.4. As expected, in the absence of a stated rationale only the Hong Kong subjects given the envelope problem performed particularly well. All groups, however, performed very well when an appropriate rationale was provided. For subjects lacking experience with a rule, the solution rate went from about 60 percent without the rationale to about 90 percent with the rationale.

This benefit conveyed by provision of a rationale is inexplicable according to either the domain-specificity view or the syntactic view. Except for the Hong Kong subjects given the envelope problem, subjects had no experience with the specific content in question and hence no memory for counterexamples to the rule. Thus improvement due to the rationale cannot be attributed to processes advocated by proponents of the domain-specificity view. On the other hand, improvement cannot be plausibly attributed to manipulation of the formal properties of the problems either, since the added rationale did not affect the logical structure of the problems.

These results are understandable, however, in terms of pragmatic reasoning schemas. The rules attached to such schemas are not abstract syntactic rules, but general rules or heuristics for solving problems of rather broad types. The schemas summarize habitually encountered relations among events of various kinds and rules for solving problems involving pragmatically important types of relations. Examples of pragmatic reasoning schemas include schemas for various types of regulations, such as "permissions," of which both the postal rule and the cholera rule are instances. Provision of a rationale for an otherwise arbitrary rule facilitated subjects' performance by supplying a cue that elicited a relevant reasoning schema for evaluating permissions.

The permission schema is particularly useful in performing the selection task because the rules that comprise it map well onto the rules of the logical conditional. The core of the permission schema is a rule of the form "If one is to do X" (for instance, buy liquor), "then one must satisfy precondition Y" (be over 21), together with an implicit or explicit justification for the regulation. Since satisfying precondition Y generally does not dictate doing X, the biconditional assumption is ruled out in this context. Moreover, the concept of permission stresses that one will not be allowed to do X if one violates precondition Y. Consequently, the contrapositive, "If one does not satisfy precondition Y, then one cannot do X," seems to be part of the permission schema, rather than derived by some indirect means such as the general logical rule of contraposition that states the equivalence of "If p then q" and "If not-q then not-p." Since an analysis of a problem in terms of a permission schema should dictate the same choices as would the conditional in formal logic, invocation of such a schema should especially facilitate performance on problems of the selection type.

In contrast, an arbitrary rule, being unrelated to typical life experiences, does not evoke any reasoning schemas. Subjects confronted with such a rule would therefore have to draw upon their knowledge of abstract reasoning principles to arrive at a correct solution. Only a small percentage of college students apparently knows the logical conditional well enough to use *modus tollens*. Instead, some might draw on some nonlogical strategy such as "matching" (that is, selecting the terms mentioned in the rule regardless of whether or not they are negated), as observed by Reich and Ruth (1982) [812] and Mank-telow and Evans (1979) [35], among others.

Cheng and Holyoak (1985) [692] obtained further evidence for the facilitative effect of a permission schema by presenting subjects with a selection problem based on an abstract description of a permission situation: "If one is to take action A, then one must first satisfy pre-condition P." Subjects were also given the arbitrary card problem. About 60 percent of the subjects solved the abstract permission prob-lem correctly when it was presented first, versus only about 20 per-cent who correctly solved the card version of the selection problem when it was presented first. The fact that a purely abstract description of a permission situation produces facilitation supports the schema hypothesis over the hypothesis that domain-specific knowledge is necessary to obtain high levels of performance.

Purely Formal versus Pragmatically Based Training

A series of training studies by Cheng, Holyoak, Nisbett, and Oliver (1986) [693] provides additional evidence differentiating the syntactic and pragmatic views. If people do not naturally reason using purely formal operations that are analogous to those of standard logic, and hence do not know how to map the terms in the abstract rules onto concrete cases, then it should be difficult or impossible to teach them effectively by purely abstract means. That is, it should be difficult to teach the rules in such a way that they actually are used in problems other than those that are presented during logic training. (It has long been known, of course, that teaching logic results in learning logic defined as manipulating the exact sorts of symbols presented in logic classes.) If, on the other hand, people typically do reason using purely abstract logical rules, then direct training in manipulating such rules according to standard logic might improve people's ability to reason in accord with logical requirements, just as purely abstract in-struction in statistical rules has been shown to have substantial effects on people's ability to reason in accord with statistical principles (Fong, Krantz, and Nisbett 1986 [728]).

Cheng and her colleagues argued that the pattern of results for training in the logic of the conditional would not be comparable to that found by Fong, Krantz, and Nisbett for training in the law of large numbers, because the full logic of the conditional has no coun-terpart in natural reasoning processes. They predicted instead that abstract training in logic would by itself have little or no impact on people's ability to reason about the Wason selection task, whether the task was presented in arbitrary form or in a form intended to evoke pragmatic reasoning schemas. They anticipated, however, that training in abstract logic would facilitate performance if it were coupled with training on how to model selection problems in terms that would facilitate the application of the conditional. Learning an abstract rule of logic and learning how to apply it to a particular type of problem may be separate requisites for correctly solving a reasoning problem by means of formal logic. If so, and if people typically do not naturally possess either requisite, then effective training for most people will require training both on the rule itself and on techniques for applying it. Only a small minority, who either are able to induce the relevant abstract rule from specific instances of it or are especially adept in applying newly learned rules, would benefit from training on either component alone.

Abstract Rule Training and Concrete Example Training

The first experiment by Cheng and colleagues was designed to assess the influence of a permission schema on performance in the selection task, as well as the usefulness of various training procedures based on abstract logic and/or examples of selection problems. Subjects who received abstract training read a seven-page booklet consisting of an exposition of conditional statements, followed by an inference exercise. The exposition consisted of an explanation of the equivalence between a conditional statement and its contrapositive, as well as an explanation of the two common fallacies of Affirming the Consequent and Denying the Antecedent. The contrapositive was explained in part by the use of a truth table, in part by Venn diagrams that used concentric circles to show the relations between a conditional statement and its contrapositive, and in part by an illustrative conditional statement, which expressed a realistic causal relation. Similarly, the fallacies were explained in part by diagrams and in part by alternative possible causes related to the illustrative statement.

Subjects who received examples training were requested to attempt to solve two selection problems. Neither problem bore any obvious surface similarities to the later test problems. Feedback was given about the subjects' success, and they were shown how to set up and solve the problem in terms dictated by the logic of the conditional. The correct answer for each example was explained in terms specific to the particular problem. Rule-plus-examples training consisted of the materials for the abstract condition followed by those for the examples condition. The only further addition was that for these subjects the explanation of the correct answer for each example was couched in terms of the abstract rules they had just learned.

The subjects were given a test that presented two types of problems involving a conditional rule—problems expressing an arbitrary relation and problems expressing a permission situation. (Other types of problems were also included, but these will not be discussed here.) Each problem took the form of a brief scenario, within which were embedded a conditional rule, a question asking the subject to determine the correctness of the rule, and a list of the four possible cases (p, not-p, q, and not-q) from which the subject was to select.

Two measures of performance were analyzed for each task— whether the subject made the correct selection (p and not-q) and whether the subject made any of the four possible kinds of errors. The four kinds of errors in the selection task were failing to select p, failing to select not-q, selecting q, and selecting not-p. These errors correspond respectively to errors on *modus ponens, modus tollens,* Affirming the Consequent, and Denying the Antecedent.

As expected, performance was much more accurate for the permission problems than for the arbitrary problems (66 percent versus 19 percent correct). Permission problems produced fewer errors of all four types than did arbitrary problems. It is particularly noteworthy that the permission problems yielded more accurate performance even for the choice of p, which corresponds to *modus ponens,* perhaps the most plausible of all the syntactic inference rules that Braine (1978) [683] posited as components of natural logic.

A comparison of the two permission problems provided a test of the domain-specificity hypothesis, which claims that only rules with which subjects have prior familiarity will yield good performance. One of the two rules was a "drinking age" rule ("If a customer is drinking an alcoholic beverage, then he or she must be over 21"), which was presumably quite familiar to the college subjects. The other rule was a version of the "cholera rule," which was presumably less familiar. Although the percentage of subjects making a correct selection was marginally higher for the more familiar rule (71 percent versus 61 percent), even the relatively unfamiliar rule produced a much lower error rate than did either arbitrary problem. Thus subjects were able to reason in accord with standard logic even for a

Table 16.1
Performance as a Function of Training Condition (after Cheng, Holyoak, Nisbett, and Oliver 1986 [693])

Training Condition	Percent Correct	Percent Errors of Each Type			
		p	*not-q*	*q*	*not-p*
Abstract plus examples	61	5	27	28	8
Abstract only	35	14	48	33	7
Examples only	38	10	45	37	12
Control	25	18	51	44	14

relatively unfamiliar rule if it evoked a permission schema. These results indicate that while specific experiences may play a role in reasoning, they cannot possibly provide a full account of reasoning performance.

The impact of the various training conditions, collapsed over type of selection problem, is indicated by the data in table 16.1. Abstract training coupled with examples training significantly decreased the frequencies of three types of errors—failure to select *p*, failure to select *not-q*, and erroneous selection of *q*. The frequency of correct selections increased from 25 percent for the control condition to 61 percent for the group given abstract training plus examples. Neither abstract training nor examples training alone decreased error frequencies significantly. This pattern suggests that knowledge of abstract rules of logic and the ability to apply them are two separate skills and that college students typically have not yet acquired either of them. Because the confidence intervals for pairwise differences between means were quite wide, however, the null hypothesis that neither abstract training nor examples training alone yielded any benefit cannot be accepted with confidence on the basis of this experiment alone.

The Effects of a Logic Course
The results of the above experiment indicated that training in standard logic, when coupled with training on examples of selection problems, leads to improved performance on subsequent selection problems. In contrast, logic training without such examples failed to significantly improve performance. An obvious possibility is that the experimental "microcourse" on the logic of the conditional was simply too minimal to convey much benefit. To assess this possibility,

Cheng and colleagues (1986) [693] performed a second experiment that examined the impact of a much broader and more prolonged abstract training condition, namely a one-semester undergraduate course in standard logic.

Two introductory logic courses, one at the Ann Arbor campus of the University of Michigan and one at the branch campus at Dearborn, provided subjects. Both courses covered topics in propositional logic, including *modus ponens*, *modus tollens*, Affirming the Consequent, and Denying the Antecedent, and the distinction between the conditional and the biconditional. In both courses the treatment of the valid and invalid inference patterns was primarily formal. While meaningful conditional sentences were introduced in lectures to illustrate the inference rules and fallacies, the emphasis was on formal logical analyses (truth-table analyses and construction of proofs). Neither course provided any exposure to the selection task or other psychological research on deductive reasoning.

A pretest was given in the first week of class before any discussion of the conditional had taken place; a post-test was given in the final week of the semester. To generate matched test materials, the selection problems used in the previous experiment were divided into two matched sets.

The results provided little comfort for the notion that formal instruction in logic is sufficient to improve reasoning performance as measured by the selection task. No significant improvement was obtained in the percentage of problems solved correctly; the mean improvement was a bare 3 percent. Indeed, the only apparent influence of a one-semester logic course was a small (10 percent) decrease in the tendency to make the error corresponding to Affirming the Consequent (that is, selecting the q alternative).

Training Based on a Pragmatic Schema
The ineffectiveness of abstract instruction in formal logic supports our contention that formal syntactic rules are not the vehicle for everyday reasoning. If this role is in fact played by pragmatic reasoning schemas, it should be possible to develop an effective training method that focuses on the elaboration of preexisting schemas. To test this possibility, Cheng and colleagues (1986) [693] performed a further experiment in which one group of college students was given training about *obligations*. Obligations are a type of regulation closely related to permissions. As the instructions pointed out, "Obligations can of-

ten be stated in an 'If . . . then' form. For example, the following regulation specifies an obligation: 'If a student is a psychology major, then the student must take an introductory psychology course.' More generally, if we call the initial situation *I* and the action *C*, an obligation has the form 'If *I* arises, then *C* must be done.' "

The obligation instructions went on to describe four rules related to the fulfillment of obligations. The rule for checking *p*, for example, was explained to subjects as follows: "If *I* occurs, then it is obligatory to do *C*. Clearly, if *I* arises, then failure to take the required action would constitute a violation of the obligation. To use our example, if a student is a psychology major, then that student must take an introductory psychology course." The four rules discussed were directly related to the rules governing the formal conditional: rule 1 is analogous to *modus ponens*, rule 2 rejects Denying the Antecedent, rule 3 rejects Affirming the Consequent, and rule 4 is analogous to *modus tollens*. The instructions were of a highly procedural nature, focusing on the conditions under which an obligation may or may not be violated. Except for the use of the single example about the psychology major, obligations were described only in abstract terms. No examples of selection problems were provided (unlike the "examples" conditions of the training study described earlier).

Other subjects were given training on the same checking procedures that obligation schema subjects were. They were shown how to reason about "contingencies" using precisely the same example about psychology majors. The training never made mention, however, of the notion of situations in which obligation arises, or indeed of any semantic interpretation at all.

Subjects who received instruction, as well as control subjects, were given a series of selection problems. Some of the problems contained conditional rules that could readily be interpreted as obligations, whereas others were relatively arbitrary.

The results are presented in table 16.2. It may be seen that, as usual, untrained control subjects solved more schema-interpretable problems than arbitrary problems. Even though both training packages presented the same formal checking procedures, the schema-based obligation training was more effective than the syntactic contingency training. Indeed, the nonsignificant trend was for the obligation training to be more effective even for the arbitrary problems. It is important to note that the syntactic contingency training had no effect at all on subjects' solutions to the semantically

Table 16.2
Percent Correct as a Function of Problem Type and Training Condition
(after Cheng, Holyoak, Nisbett, and Oliver 1986 [693]).

Problem Type	Training Condition			
	Control	Contingency	Obligation	$\overline{X}$
Arbitrary	27	45	55	42
Obligation	64	66	92	74
$\overline{X}$	46	55	73	

meaningful problems. This bolsters our view that pragmatic reasoning schemas are dominant wherever a semantic interpretation can be applied. Even when subjects have just been shown the exact checking procedures to be applied, they do not use them for the semantically meaningful problems. In our view, this is because a semantic interpretation will always lead to a search for reasoning schemas rather than for syntactic rules.

It should be noted that the obligation instruction used in this experiment forms an important contrast to the teaching of new empirical rules for physics and social psychology discussed in chapter 7. Whereas instruction in the latter case competes with rules the student already possesses, instruction in pragmatic reasoning schemas builds upon and supports prior knowledge. In our view, instruction in purely syntactic rule systems lies between the two extremes in that it neither competes with nor builds upon preexisting knowledge. On the other hand, because it is an alien type of rule system for understanding actual events in the world, it also will not add to the individual's effective repertoire of pragmatic rules.

Induction, Deduction, and Default Hierarchies

The results just reviewed provide support for the view that people typically reason using knowledge structures at a level intermediate between the extreme localism implied by the domain-specificity view and the ultra-generality implied by the formal view. Subjects reasoned in closer accord with standard logic when thinking about problems intended to evoke regulation schemas (permissions and obligations) than when thinking about purely arbitrary elements and relations. These results on problem types are incompatible with the domain-specificity view because experience with the precise rules referred to in the regulation problems was not necessary for successful performance. The results are incompatible with the formal view because all problem types were stated in syntactically equivalent forms. The results from the training studies are also incompatible with the formal view. An entire course in standard logic had no effect on the avoidance of error (save for a slight reduction in the fallacy of Affirming the Consequent). A brief training session, of a type shown to produce substantial effects on people's ability to reason in accord with the law of large numbers (Fong, Krantz, and Nisbett 1985 [728]), had no significant effect on subjects' ability to use *modus ponens* or *modus tollens* or to avoid the error of Affirming the Consequent or Denying the Antecedent. This was not simply because the training was inherently useless: when it was combined with examples training, subjects were able to make substantial use of the abstract training.

The near-total ineffectiveness of purely abstract training in logic contrasts starkly with the ready ease with which people seem able to apply a naturally acquired pragmatic reasoning schema. For example, after one semester's training in standard logic, students solved only 11 percent of the arbitrary problems correctly, whereas the same students solved 62 percent of the permission problems correctly before receiving any formal training. The generality of the benefit apparently conveyed by evocation of a permission schema is also striking. The permission problems yielded significantly fewer errors of all types, including not only the common error of failing to select *not-q* (equivalent to *modus tollens*) but also the much less frequent error of failing to select *p* (equivalent to *modus ponens*).

In contrast to the benefit conveyed by the evocation of a permission schema, a course in logic produced no significant reduction in either of these errors. The failure to reduce the frequency of errors for *modus ponens* cannot be attributed to a floor effect, since evocation of the permission schema did reduce the frequency of errors for the *p* alternative. This failure of abstract training to facilitate the use of *modus ponens* suggests that even this rule may not be a general rule of logic for at least a substantial fraction of subjects. Evidence that *modus ponens* can be overridden by a matching strategy (Manktelow and Evans 1979 [784]; Reich and Ruth 1982 [812]) also supports this hypothesis. If *modus ponens* is not a robust rule of natural logic, as our results suggest, it is difficult to imagine any formal deductive rule that is universally held and widely used for the solution of problems with meaningful content.

The primacy of pragmatic reasoning schemas received further support from the final training study performed by Cheng and colleagues (1986) [693], which demonstrated that brief instruction about the pragmatics of obligations greatly improved performance both on selection problems involving clear obligations and on problems involving relatively arbitrary rules. Instructional methods based on appropriate preexisting pragmatic knowledge appear to be far more effective than those based directly on syntactic rules.

A Default Hierarchy of Deductive Rules

The results we have reviewed speak strongly for the existence of pragmatic schemas at an intermediate level of abstraction, since the findings are inexplicable according to either the domain-specificity view or the formal view. Nonetheless, the findings need not be interpreted as evidence against the very possibility of the two extreme modes of reasoning. It is conceivable that these three modes coexist within a population and even within an individual. In fact, the results are consistent with this interpretation.

First, as in other reasoning studies, most of the subjects' inferences were in accordance with *modus ponens*, whereas very few were in accordance with *modus tollens*. Although *modus ponens* may not be universal, the results do not exclude the possibility that many people may in fact reason with this formal rule—or even that all people may use it under particularly favorable circumstances. The same individuals who use *ponens* as a formal rule may use a rule corresponding to *tollens* only within the context of certain intermediate-level schemas.

Second, familiarity with a rule may in itself sometimes facilitate performance, as suggested by the marginal difference in selection performance between the two permission problems used in the first experiment by Cheng and colleagues (1986) [693]. The presumably more familiar drinking-age rule yielded slightly better performance than did the cholera-inoculation rule. Familiarity may facilitate indirectly by evoking an appropriate schema more reliably, or it may do so more directly by providing relevant specific knowledge, as hypothesized by proponents of the domain-specificity view.

If multiple levels of concepts relevant to reasoning coexist, within a population as well as within an individual, how are the levels related to each other and what determines the level of abstraction attained? Our pragmatic approach to induction suggests a possible answer. As we have emphasized throughout, the process of induction from experience across many different domains results in a default hierarchy of rules. Rules are used to make predictions about regularities in environmental inputs to the cognitive system. Successive levels in the default hierarchy are related in that the more abstract level comprises a set of default categories and rules, relative to which the more specific level comprises a set of exception categories and rules. The default rules are generally predictive and are consequently followed in most circumstances, except when they are overridden by more specific exception rules.

Basic inductive processes, such as generalization and specialization, are applied to environmental inputs to produce a default hierarchy that has predictive utility in achieving the learner's problem-directed goals. If induction proceeds in a bottom-up, experience-driven manner, then successively more abstract concepts and associated rule schemas will be formed by generalization on the basis of constancies observed in inputs. Increasingly abstract default levels will emerge as long as concepts capturing significant regularities with predictive utility can be formed.

Let us consider how induction might proceed in the domains relevant to conditional logic. At the most specific level, experience with particular contingencies between events (such as the relationship between touching a stove and feeling pain, or between a request for assistance and help from a parent) will accrue to the learner. The concepts and rules induced in the process of dealing with specific contingency situations will be of the kind assumed by the domain-specificity hypothesis. At this point the person will be able to reason effectively in familiar situations and in those highly similar to them, but not elsewhere.

As experience with a range of contingency situations accrues, people will, through the operation of generalization mechanisms, induce a more abstract set of default concepts and rules. Many important subtypes of contingency situations will emerge, involving such concepts as causation, regulation, and set inclusion. This is the level at which pragmatic reasoning schemas emerge. Each schema will consist of a cluster of rules for dealing with a particular type of contingency situation. Because the concepts at this level are quite abstract, rules for dealing with situation types as general as "deterministic causation," for example, will be applicable to novel situations with little superficial resemblance to those from which the concepts were originally induced.

Kelley's (1972 [756], 1973 [757]) *causal schemas*, it should be noted, are excellent examples of the kind of constructs we wish to include under the rubric of pragmatic reasoning schemas. Kelley proposed that people have very general rules for dealing with causality that are attached to particular kinds of causal relationships. People have, for example, a schema for reasoning about relationships that they take to involve a single determining cause, that is, those in which only a single cause can produce the effect and if present it invariably does so. They also have a schema for reasoning about multiple-cause, probabilistic relationships, namely, those in which many factors can produce the effect but the presence of any one of the factors does not entail certainty that the effect will occur. These causal schemas exist at a purely abstract level, independent of any content domain.

Eventually, constancies across various types of reasoning schemas may, through the same inductive mechanisms, produce yet more abstract concepts and rules at the level of a natural formal logic. The results we have reviewed suggest that this level of abstraction in conditional reasoning is seldom attained; and at any rate, rules at that level are probably only rarely applied to semantically meaningful material.

Why Formal Deductive Rules Are Difficult to Induce

In view of our negative conclusion regarding the prevalence of a natural logic based on syntactic rules, an obvious question arises: Why are such rules so difficult to induce? Or at least, why are they seldom used for reasoning about real events? Logicians through the centuries have assumed the existence, and the everyday use, of a natural repertoire of purely abstract logical rules, as have psychologists such as Piaget. We contend that although Piaget was right in believing that people develop and heavily use a schema corresponding to the inductive rule system embodied in the law of large numbers, he was wrong in believing that they make much use of formal operations of deductive logic.

The reason for the difficulty in inducing rules for deductive logic appears to be that too few reliable, useful constancies in deductive rules hold at such abstract levels. In particular, the material conditional—the abstract formal conditional taught in elementary logic courses—has limited pragmatic value. The various pragmatic reasoning schemas differ from each other in many important ways. For example, in a causal statement of the form "If ⟨cause⟩, then ⟨effect⟩," the cause temporally precedes the effect. In the corresponding form of a permission statement, "If ⟨action⟩, then ⟨permission required⟩," the action typically *follows* the necessary permission. The individuating aspects of pragmatic reasoning schemas are far more important to successful problem solving than their commonalities. In order for the conditional to be employed in assessing causal claims, for example, extensive interpretation of problems in terms of causal direction, number of possible causes, certainty of effects given causes, and so on, is required. For most lay purposes the formal conditional therefore may not be an economical default rule.

Of the various syntactic rules associated with the formal conditional, virtually none have general utility. The formally valid contrapositive transformation cannot by itself solve many pragmatic problems that are expressible in its terms, because substantial interpretation concerning causality and other matters is required before it can be applied. Moreover, the "fallacies" of Denying the Antecedent and Affirming the Consequent often lead to pragmatically useful inferences in many contexts (Fillenbaum 1975 [716], 1976 [717]; Geis and Zwicky 1971 [730]). For example, abduction of a hypothesis A to explain B using the rule "If A then B" is formally equivalent to the deductive fallacy of Affirming the Consequent but can be an inductively important form of inference.

Not only is contraposition lacking in positive utility, in some important cases it actually fails. Lewis (1973) [610] points out that contraposition fails for counterfactual conditionals, in which the antecedent is known to be false. For example, it may be true that if the power hadn't failed, dinner would have been on time; but it does not follow that if dinner had not been on time, then the power would have failed (Ginsberg 1985 [736]). Our ability to determine the truth of counterfactual conditionals depends on special knowledge about causality in the world, of the sort that pragmatic reasoning schemas can encapsulate. It thus seems that only *modus ponens* constitutes a plausibly pragmatic abstract rule of inference, although the results of Cheng and colleagues (1986) [693] suggest that even *modus ponens* may not be available as a fully abstract rule for purposes of everyday reasoning. It may be that rather than inducing an isolated abstract rule, many people maintain a more specific rule analogous to *modus ponens* within each of a number of pragmatic reasoning schemas.

In contrast to people's apparent failure to induce some abstract deductive rules, we have seen evidence that they do induce some abstract *inductive* rules, such as simple versions of the law of large numbers. This difference has a ready explanation within the present framework. Unlike deductive rules such as *modus tollens*, the law of large numbers is an excellent default rule (or set of rules) that does not require extensive domain-specific interpretation in order to be made applicable. Given (codable) uncertainty, the rule system in its totality has potential relevance. Consequently, everyday learning conditions will be favorable to induction of the law of large numbers at the highest level of generality and abstraction.

We are led, then, to the surprising possibility that the mechanisms of induction may result in the induction of various abstract inductive rules, but not certain abstract deductive rules, for the good reason that many abstract inductive rules are more obviously useful than some of their deductive counterparts in formal logic.

Implications for Education

It is interesting to relate the present findings to the old debate at the turn of the century about faculty psychology. The defense offered for the classical education consisting of Latin, mathematics, and memorization was that pursuit of these disciplines caused the mental faculties to improve. They served, in effect, to exercise the muscles of the mind. The consequence was a smarter person, with better faculties, just as the consequence of physical exercise is a stronger person, with bigger muscles. This view was derided by early psychologists, who argued that there is little transfer of training across tasks unless they share a large proportion of identical elements.

One set of results that we have presented constitutes an important counterweight to the generally correct view of those early psychologists. Training in statistics has a demonstrable effect on the way people reason about a vast range of events in everyday life. Thus formal training of that particular type of rule system does indeed make people smarter in a pragmatic sense. (At least it does if one shares our view that statistical considerations are normally helpful.)

Another set of results we have presented constitutes a reaffirmation of the early psychologists' critique of faculty psychology. Teaching people formal logic does not seem to make them smarter in the sense of increasing the scope of problems to which they can apply the material conditional. Our interpretation of the results also gives a firmer foundation to the critique: Rule systems that are foreign to the rules governing everyday pragmatic reasoning cannot readily be made to influence such reasoning. There are plenty of justifications for teaching formal logic to special groups such as philosophy students and computer programmers, but we should not expect much of an impact on reasoning in everyday life.

Another aspect of the experimental results suggests an important respect in which education does improve logic in everyday life. This work gives support to the view that various pragmatic reasoning schemas can be taught, and that unlike the teaching of logic and some types of empirical rules, such instruction may amount to "swimming downstream" educationally. Teaching causal schemas and methodological principles, such as the need for control conditions and the need to accommodate the vagaries of correlational evidence, is the sort of thing that formal education probably does rather well.

Our analysis of these results also suggests several respects in which education could be improved. Perhaps the most fundamental suggestion is that one should have a clear idea about the nature of the rule system that one is teaching. Is it one that is "graceful" in the sense that it is likely to build upon, rather than be irrelevant to or even compete with, rule systems that the student already possesses? If the rule system is graceful in that sense, then probably one can expect improvements in it to be carried through to reasoning in everyday life. If the rule system is alien, as we believe most purely syntactic systems to be, then the justification for teaching the system has to be on grounds other than pragmatic reasoning improvements. In addition, there is probably little point in trying to dress up education in such rules in the clothing of everyday-life examples, as many teachers of logic try to do. Formal logic is probably just going to be a rule system that cannot be made to have much impact on pragmatic reasoning.

A second implication is that the effects of education in those rules that do have ready impact on everyday reasoning could probably be much enhanced by just the kind of dressing up that has little impact in logic courses. Statistics and methodology courses might be made to have substantially greater impact on everyday reasoning if teachers were to take the trouble to teach their students how to reason about various kinds of everyday domains using the rules. Although it has been shown that abstract training can be effective in itself, it has also been shown that its effectiveness can be enhanced by—indeed its effectiveness often may depend on—teaching students how to model particular events in terms of the rule system. Statistics and methodology courses have an important place in the liberal arts curriculum quite independent of any utility they have for scientific reasoning. The teachers of those courses ought to capitalize on the new-found justification for their role by thinking of inventive ways to extend the scope of the rules they teach.

Most of the new teaching techniques would make use of analogies between scientific problems and everyday problems, and show that a given rule holds for similar reasons in both cases. It is to the topic of analogy, and how it can best be employed in transferring knowledge from one domain to another, that we now turn.

17

A Pragmatic Account of Cognitive Evaluation

Stephen P. Stich

The last two chapters have been motivated by concerns about the evaluation of alternative cognitive systems. We began chapter 4 by asking just what it was for a system of cognitive processes to be a good one or for one such system to be better than another. And we have now come to reject two broad categories of answers—those associated with the tradition of analytic epistemology and those that tie cognitive evaluation to the generation of true beliefs. Though the arguments of chapters 4 and 5 are largely negative in tone, they also contain the seeds of a much more promising proposal on how to go about evaluating cognitive systems, a proposal that is in the spirit of pragmatism. My goals in this chapter are to sketch this pragmatic alternative, to defend it against some of the more obvious complaints that might be lodged against it, and to explore some of its implications. In saying that I propose to *sketch* a pragmatist account of cognitive evaluation, I choose my words carefully. For the story I have to tell in the next section is very much a preliminary sketch, leaving many questions unanswered and much work to be done. Some further details will be added in the sections to follow, in the course of answering objections and putting the theory to work. But even when the chapter and the book have come to an end, there will still be much to say about how the details of a pragmatist account should be developed. I'll note a number of these lacunae in passing and say a bit about why I have chosen to leave them as open questions. In general, of course, the reason is simply that I don't know what to say.

Reprinted from *The Fragmentation of Reason*, by Stephen P. Stich (Cambridge, Mass.: MIT Press, 1990), pp. 129–158, by permission of the publisher. Copyright © 1990, MIT Press.

That is one of the reasons I've chosen to describe the book as a *Preface* to a Pragmatic Account of Cognitive Evaluation.

Toward Pragmatism

Let me begin with a brief reminder of just why it was that the analytic and truth-generating accounts of cognitive assessment came to grief. In each case, I think, there is a lesson to be learned about how a more successful account can be developed. In chapter 4, we rejected the research program that proposes to choose among competing accounts of cognitive assessment by determining which of them best accords with commonsense concepts or practices of cognitive evaluation—the concepts and practices "embedded in everyday thought and language." At bottom, the argument against this analytic program was that, on reflection, being sanctioned by those concepts and practices is of no particular value to most of us. For even if it should turn out that our own evaluative notions are reasonably coherent, systematic, and stable, they mark only one spot in a rich and varied space of possible (and probably actual) alternatives. If the principal reason that our evaluative epistemic concepts, concepts like rationality and justification, stand out from the crowd is that they happen to be the evaluative notions passed on by our language and culture, it's hard to see why anyone but an epistemic chauvinist would much care whether his cognitive processes were sanctioned by those notions. Yet if the appeal of local, culturally inherited concepts won't lead a clear headed nonchauvinist to prefer one system of cognitive processes over another, what will?

A natural suggestion is that rather than looking at how high alternative systems of cognitive processes rank on some evaluative standard embedded in our language, we attend instead to the *consequences* of employing one alternative or the other—more specifically, to the likelihood that use of one system or the other will lead to something we value. Just as I don't much care whether the cognitive system I use does better than some proposed alternative on a standard that might be extracted from venerable texts, so too I don't much care whether it does better on a standard that may happen to have been bequeathed by my culture. But I do care whether my cognitive system does a better job than a proposed alternative at bringing about consequences that I value. Nor do I take myself to be at all unusual here.

For most people who see the issue clearly, what will really be important in choosing among cognitive systems will be the consequences to which they lead. So the moral I would extract from the failure of the analytic strategy is that our account of cognitive virtue should be a *consequentialist* account.

But now what sort of consequences are going to be relevant for the evaluation of cognitive strategies? Truth, or true beliefs, is the obvious answer, since truth is widely held to be the appropriate goal of cognition. However, the moral I would draw from the arguments of chapter 5 is that, despite being both venerable and intuitively plausible, for most of us this is exactly the wrong answer. It is the wrong answer because in order to avoid the "who cares" complaint that scuttles the analytic program, a consequentialist account must take as the relevant consequences something that people actually value. And the burden of the argument in chapter 5 is that for most of us true belief just won't do, once we see how limited and idiosyncratic the notion of true belief is. Without some reason for thinking that true beliefs stand us in better stead than TRUE* ones, TRUE** ones, and all the rest, it is hard to see why anyone would care whether his beliefs are true rather than, say, TRUE****. Moreover, if you don't care whether your beliefs are true rather than TRUE****, if you attach no greater value to having true beliefs than to having TRUE***** ones, you're not likely to care whether your cognitive processes lead to true beliefs rather than TRUE***** ones.

At this juncture one might begin to worry that we have painted ourselves into a corner. If our account of cognitive evaluation is going to be a consequentialist account, and if truth is not the relevant consequence, what is? What else could possibly be viewed as a value that is relevant to the assessment of cognition?

The first step toward the answer I would urge is to adopt a perspective on cognition that grows out of the pragmatist tradition. Cognitive processes, pragmatists will insist, should not be thought of primarily as devices for generating truths. Rather they should be thought of as something akin to tools or technologies or practices that can be used more or less successfully in achieving a variety of goals. Viewing cognitive processes as akin to technologies suggests an obvious answer to the question of what goals or values we might appeal to in assessing them. The consequences that may be considered in deciding whether to adopt a given technological innovation are as rich and varied as the things that people find intrinsically valuable. Some of these things, like health, happiness, and the well-being of one's children, we are probably biologically predisposed to value, and thus they are likely to be valued by large numbers of people. Other things may be valued only in a more limited cultural environment; and still others may be valued by only a few idiosyncratic individuals. If, as I am urging, we view systems of cognitive processes as analogous to tools or technologies, then they too are to be evaluated by appeal to the rich and varied class of things that people take to be intrinsically valuable.

Here, then, is a first pass at a pragmatic account of cognitive evaluation. In evaluating systems of cognitive processes, the system to be preferred is the one that would be most likely to achieve those things that are intrinsically valued by the person whose interests are relevant to the purposes of the evaluation. In most cases, the relevant person will be the one who is or might be using the system. So, for example, if the issue at hand is the evaluation of Smith's system of cognitive processes in comparison with some actual or hypothetical alternative, the system that comes out higher on the pragmatist account of cognitive evaluation is the one that is most likely to lead to the things that Smith finds intrinsically valuable. In contrast with the analytic and truth-generating accounts, there is no mystery about why Smith should care about the outcome of this evaluation.[1]

This, as advertised, is only a sketch of the sort of pragmatic account of cognitive evaluation that I would recommend. In drawing the sketch, I have helped myself to unanalyzed notions, invoked undefended assumptions, and tucked some substantive problems under the rug. Moreover, at this point I have neither analyses nor defenses nor solutions to offer. But I will say a little about each of these shortcomings and about work that still needs to be done.

Perhaps the most obviously problematic notion that I am invoking is the idea of a person intrinsically valuing something. The textbook story about intrinsic valuing is that intrinsically valued things are the things a person values for their own sake, not because he believes they will lead to other things. And any well-trained undergraduate philosophy major should be able to come up with a blue book full of quibbles with that story.[2] The textbook story about valuing—about what it is for a person to value something—is near enough the Louis Armstrong story: "If you gotta ask, you ain't ever gonna get to know." Plainly, at some point in the elaboration of a pragmatic theory of cognitive evaluation, a careful and empirically well-grounded examination of the concepts of valuing and intrinsic valuing will be in order. And I would not be surprised if, in the light of such an examination, the pragmatic story itself may be seen to need some substantial reworking.[3] Still, I am inclined to think that for many purposes the intuitive notion of valuing and the textbook account of intrinsic valuing are solid enough to work with. Neither the discussion of objections to pragmatism in the following two sections nor the applications of the pragmatic account in the section after that are much hampered by the lack of a detailed account of the nature of intrinsic valuing.

In discussing what people may intrinsically value, I have persistently presupposed an exuberant pluralism. People, I have claimed, can and do intrinsically value a great diversity of things, with some of these values being widely shared while others are local or idiosyncratic. There is, of course, a long philosophical tradition that takes the opposite view. Monists about what is intrinsically valued maintain that there is only one thing (typically happiness, pleasure, or some similar commodity) that anyone could possibly value intrinsically. This is, by my lights, a wildly implausible view supported by notoriously unpersuasive arguments. But in the present context there is no need to defend my value-pluralism, since this sort of pluralism only makes things more difficult for the brand of epistemic pragmatism I advocate. As we'll see in the next section, value-pluralism entails that the pragmatic account of cognitive evaluation is relativistic in a way that truth-generating accounts are not. And since relativism is widely viewed as a liability, I am doing myself no favor by assuming value-pluralism.

Actually, the fact that value-pluralism engenders relativism is not much of a concern for me since, as I'll argue later, relativism in cognitive evaluation is itself nothing to worry about. A more unsettling fact about value-pluralism is that if it is true, it may considerably complicate the pragmatist's calculation of consequences. To see the point, let's go back to the analogy between cognitive systems, on the one hand, and technologies, on the other. How would someone with consequentialist leanings go about assessing the relative merits of a pair of technological options. Perhaps the simplest idea is to use a sort of "cost-benefit analysis" that is a straightforward generalization of the basic utilitarian strategy. For each option we construct a list of possible outcomes and try to determine the probability that the option in question will lead to each of those outcomes. We then must make some assessment of the value of each outcome and express that value as a cardinal number. Having done all this, we can determine the "expected value" of an option by multiplying the value of each outcome by the probability that the option will lead to that outcome and then summing the numbers that result. The option to be preferred is the one with the greatest expected value.[4]

It has long been recognized that one of the difficulties facing a policy maker who would assess technologies in this way is the fact that the "outcomes" whose values must be assessed are typically complex states of affairs whose components may be very hard to compare. For example, one possible outcome of a given technological option might be the state of affairs in which a thousand new jobs will be generated in an economically depressed area. Another possible outcome might be a state of affairs that is similar to the first except that, in addition to creating the new jobs, one worker a year will be killed in an industrial accident. Obviously, the value assigned to the second outcome should be lower than the value assigned to the first. But how much lower? To answer the question requires that we have some fairly specific quantitative assessment of the comparative value of lives and economic benefits. And such assessments are notoriously hard to make.

Suppose, now, that we take this "expected value" approach to technology assessment as our model in pragmatic cognitive evaluation. To assess the comparative merits of a pair of cognitive systems that a person might exploit requires that we compute the expected value of adopting each system. To do that, we must try to determine the probability of each option leading to various possible outcomes and then multiply those probabilities by cardinal number indices of the values we have assigned to the outcomes. The consequences that are important for a pragmatic evaluation will be things that the person in question takes to be intrinsically valuable. And if value-pluralism is true, the outcomes to which numbers must be assigned will often be conjunctive states of affairs combining various different intrinsically valued elements. Thus, in making the assignments we must find some way of weighing a person's intrinsic values against one another. And often that will be no easy task.

The simple expected value approach to technology assessment is, of course, not the only one that has been proposed. The assumptions—about coherently ordered values and discoverable probabilities—needed to make this approach work are very strong ones. And in many cases, they seem hopelessly unrealistic. These difficulties have given rise to a large, sophisticated literature exploring alternative decision strategies, many of them clearly consequentialist in spirit, which relax some of the implausible assumptions of the expected value approach.[5] The existence of these alternative approaches poses something of a problem for my rough-and-ready account of how an epistemic pragmatist would evaluate competing cognitive systems. For according to that account, the cognitive system to be preferred is the one best suited to the attainment of what we intrinsically value. But it now appears that there are various rather different ways of unpacking this idea and no overriding reason why the pragmatist should take the simple expected value approach as his model rather than one of the alternatives.

Clearly this is another area where the epistemic pragmatist has more work to do. And much of this work will have to be done in collaboration with psychologists, anthropologists, economists, and others who are trying to get an empirically plausible account of the nature of human value systems. This sort of integration of empirical and normative investigations is a hallmark of the pragmatic tradition in epistemology. We'll see some further examples of it below.

Pragmatism and Relativism

It is a virtue of the sort of pragmatic evaluation of cognitive processes sketched in the previous section that it provides an obvious answer to the question of why we should care how such an evaluation turns out. Though it's hard to see why anyone but an epistemic chauvinist would be much concerned about rationality or truth, we can count on people caring about the pragmatic evaluation of their cognitive processes because that evaluation is tied to goals that they themselves take to be intrinsically valuable. Offsetting this positive point about pragmatic evaluation, however, are a number of *prima facie* deficits. Among these, the one that many people seem to find the most worrisome is that pragmatic evaluation is blatantly and floridly relativistic. What I propose to do in the current section is first to explain the various ways in which a pragmatic account of cognitive evaluation may give rise to relativism. I will then go on to ask a question that has, in my experience, been asked all too infrequently: What's so bad about epistemic relativism? I will propose a pair of answers that, I think, together account for much of the disquiet that people feel about relativism. I'll then go on to argue that this disquiet is largely unjustified, since the first of the alleged nasty consequences of relativism is not a consequence at all, while the second is nothing much to worry about.

How Pragmatism Leads to Relativism

Before setting out the various ways in which pragmatism gives rise to relativism, we'd do well to get a bit clearer on just what relativism, as I use the notion, comes to. And to do that, we'll have to back up a bit and remind ourselves of some terminology set out in chapter 1. In that chapter, I introduced the label *normative cognitive pluralism* for the thesis that there is no uniquely good system of cognitive processes—no single system that people ought to use. Rather, the normative cognitive pluralist insists, there may be various systems of cognitive processes that are significantly different from each other, though they are all equally good. One way in which this situation might arise—a thoroughly nonrelativistic way—would be for our account of what it is for a cognitive system to be a good one to turn on intrinsic (perhaps formal) features of the system. If the story about cognitive virtue were told in the right way, it might happen that two or more substantially different systems each have the specified intrinsic virtues to just the same extent and thus come out tied for first.

There is also a very different way in which the situation envisioned by the normative cognitive pluralist might arise. Suppose that our account of what makes one system of cognitive processes better than another involves relational features of the systems being evaluated, where one of the elements in the relation is the person or group using the system, or some property of that person or group. If systems of cognitive processes are evaluated in this user-relative way, then in general it will not make sense to ask whether one system is better than another (full stop). Rather, we must ask whether one system is better than another for a given person or group; and it may well turn out that one system is best for one person or group, while another system is best for another person or group. I take this possibility to be the hallmark of relativism in the assessment of cognitive processes. An account of cognitive evaluation is relativistic if the assessments of cognitive systems it offers are sensitive to facts about the person or group using the system.[6]

Given this characterization of relativism, a pragmatic account of cognitive evaluation is going to be relativistic for two quite different reasons. The most obvious source of relativism is the plurality of values to which a pragmatic assessment must be sensitive. A somewhat less obvious source is the consequentialist character of pragmatic evaluation. Let me take these up in turn.

The pragmatic account urges that we assess cognitive systems by their likelihood of leading to what their users value. If, as I have been supposing, people can and do intrinsically value a wide variety of things, with considerable variation from person to person and culture to culture, then pragmatic assessments of cognitive systems will be sensitive to highly variable facts about the users of those systems. Moreover, given the diversity of goals and values, it is all but certain that different systems of cognitive processes will be pragmatically preferable for different people. Indeed, pragmatic assessment will even distinguish between people who share the same values but who differ in the relative importance they attach to them.

While it is no surprise that pragmatic evaluations must be relativized to people's varying values, it is perhaps less obvious that pragmatic assessment is also relativistic for a quite different reason. Epistemic pragmatism urges a consequentialist account of inferential virtue—the goodness or badness of a system of cognitive processes depends on the likelihood of the system leading to certain consequences. And consequentialist evaluations will typically be relativistic, since the likelihood of a given system leading to a certain consequence will generally depend on the environment in which the system is operating. If we keep the goals constant, the probability that a given system of cognitive processes will lead to those goals is going to depend, to a significant extent, on the circumstances of the person using the system.

Though not often emphasized, this sort of relativism is as much a feature of truth-generating accounts of inferential virtue as it is of pragmatic accounts. Whether a given system of cognitive processes is likely to produce truths depends on the environment of the person using the system.[7] Perhaps the easiest way to see the point is to invoke a variation on the Cartesian evil demon theme. Imagine a pair of people who suddenly fall victim to such a demon and are from that time forward provided with systematically misleading or deceptive perceptual data. Let's further suppose that one of the victims has been using cognitive processes quite like our own and that these have done a pretty good job of generating truths and avoiding falsehoods, while the other victim's cognitive processes have been (by our lights) quite mad, and have produced far more falsehoods and far fewer truths. In their new demon-infested environment, however, the sane system of cognitive processes—the one like ours—will yield a growing fabric of false beliefs. The other system, by contrast, may now do a much better job at generating truths and avoiding falsehoods, since what the evil demon is doing is providing his victims with radically misleading evidence—evidence that only a lunatic would take to be evidence for what actually is the case. So on a truth-generating, consequentialist account of cognitive evaluation, our system would be preferable in one environment, while the mad system would be preferable in another environment. And clearly an entirely parallel tale could be told if the goal being sought were not truth but some other more pragmatic commodity.

We have just seen that consequentialism in cognitive evaluation is capable of bringing relativism in its wake. But my invocation of evil demons to make the point might suggest that this is a very peripheral phenomenon, one not worth worrying about except in Cartesian nightmares. I think that would be a serious mistake. For whether it is truth we want our cognitive processes to produce, or whether we have other goals whose desirability is less problematic, the chances of success are going to depend on features of the environment that are much less exotic than infestation by evil demons. Consider, for example, the effects of the commonsense world view prevailing in the culture that surrounds a person in his formative years—the fabric of socially shared beliefs, concepts, and distinctions (both explicit and tacit) about matters physical and metaphysical, cosmological, theological, psychological, and social. It is plausible to speculate that most people internalize a fair amount of this socially shared Weltanschauung very uncritically and very early on, in the course of language acquisition and acculturation.[8] But now consider how a consequentialist account of cognitive evaluation would assess the cognitive processes underlying the assimilation of a world view. If such matters as theology, folk geography, folk cosmology, and folk medicine are included in the domain of these assimilative processes, then plainly the consequentialist's assessment is going to vary significantly with the surroundings in which the assimilative processes are working. The folk wisdom my children acquired on these topics contains vastly more that is true and (for some purposes at least) vastly more that is useful than the folk wisdom acquired by Thales's children. Indeed, from the perspective of a consequentialist whose single goal is truth, Thales's children might have been better served by a system of assimilative processes that systematically distorted the socially provided input in the direction of a world view more like our own. Given other goals, of course, processes of world view assimilation that systematically distort the input might serve their users less well. If Thales's children had ended up with the folk wisdom of contemporary California kids, they might have become great leaders; but it is more likely that they would have been social outcasts, taken to be mad. The moral here is that if the output of a cognitive process depends heavily on the social environment in which it is functioning, then consequentialist evaluations of that process are typically going to be highly environment-relative.

Nor is this the only way in which consequentialist accounts of cognitive virtue give rise to relativism. Suppose for a moment that the members of a given group—the community of scientists, perhaps—each has as a high priority goal the group's discovering and coming to accept important truths of nature. Suppose, further, that within the group there is considerable variability in the amount of evidence it takes to dislodge conviction in an accepted theory and launch off along some new line of inquiry. The cognitive processes of investigators at one end of the spectrum lead them to hang on to prevailing theories or paradigms until the evidence against them is overwhelming, while the cognitive processes of investigators at the other end of the spectrum may lead them to reject the prevailing doctrines and commit themselves to new ideas while the preponderance of evidence still clearly favors the established view. And between these two extremes, there is a variety of intermediate positions. Given that the shared goal of the community is the discovery and acceptance of important scientific truths, which of these cognitive processes should a scientist have; which is the best? The answer is that there may be no answer—that the question itself is badly posed. For the question presupposes that there is a single optimal spot along the spectrum described, a cognitive system such that if everyone in the scientific community were to share it, the community would stand the best chance of achieving its goal. However, as Philip Kitcher has shown, there are many circumstances in which this presupposition is simply untenable.[9] In these circumstances the probability of achieving the community's goal is maximized by a mixed strategy in which some investigators are very conservative in giving up received doctrines, while others do so much more readily. This is not the place to recount the sophisticated mathematical models that support Kitcher's conclusion. However, the point should be intuitively plausible even without a detailed proof. If we assume that investigators typically invest their energy attempting to elaborate and support the theory they accept, then it will often be best to have the community's allegiance divided, with the bulk of the effort going into the established (and presumably the best-supported) theory, while some effort is devoted to exploring new ideas and long shots. Moreover, when the established theory is seriously threatened, it will often be best to have some substantial number of residual defenders trying to shore it up, rather than to have everyone jump ship more or less simultaneously.

What makes all this important for our purposes is that it points to another potential source of relativism in consequentialist accounts of cognitive assessment. Consider the situation of a single investigator in the inquiring community. Should she be conservative in her attitude toward the received theory, or would it be better if she were more of a radical, more willing to reject the community's favored theory? The answer, of course, is that it depends on what the rest of the community is doing. If the community is already oversupplied with conservatives, then their shared goal would be best served if her cognitive processes tend in the radical direction. While if radicals abound, she ought to be a conservative. What is more, exactly the same conclusion follows if, instead of assuming that our investigator values the communal discovery of truth, we suppose instead that her goal is getting tenure, developing a new and useful technology, or winning a Nobel Prize. The likelihood that one's cognitive processes will lead to these goals will often be partly determined by what others in one's community are doing, since the expected payoff of exploring unpromising domains will often decline if one has too much company. Whether it is truth or fame or technological prowess we want, there is no saying which cognitive system is best (full stop); the evaluation of a system must be relativized to the setting in which it is used.[10]

Though I won't attempt an exhaustive inquiry into the various ways in which consequentialism in cognitive evaluation gives rise to relativism, I am inclined to think that the few illustrations I've provided are just the very small tip of a very large iceberg. Whether the goal is truth or some cluster of things whose desirability is easier to understand, it is my bet that a consequentialist evaluation of cognitive processes is going to be acutely sensitive to the cultural, technological, and epistemic setting in which the processes are to function. The likelihood that one system of cognitive processes will do a better job than another at securing just about any plausible goal will, I suspect, depend on such factors as the existence of a system of writing, the existence and the structure of disciplinary communities, and the relation of those communities to the political and economic arrangements of the wider society. It will also often depend on the level of conceptual, mathematical, scientific, and technological sophistication that has been achieved. It's not implausible to suppose that there are strategies of thought that will lead to a dead end in a community where geometry is unknown, others that will lead to a dead end without the calculus, or probability theory, or powerful computers, and still others that will be pragmatically powerful only in environments where the distinction between velocity and acceleration has been clearly drawn, where the basic idea of evolution by natural selection is widely accepted, or where the expectation that things have final causes has been rejected. If these conjectures are right, it follows that pragmatic accounts of cognitive or epistemic evaluation will have a certain post-Hegelian historicist flavor. There will be no one ideal method of inquiry, no cognitive system that excels in all historical settings. Rather, we can expect that the assessment of a cognitive system will vary as its historical setting varies and that, just as with technologies (and indeed with genes), it will sometimes happen that a successful system will undermine its own success by changing the environment in such a way that competing systems will now be more successful. There are people, and I am one of them, who find something refreshing, even liberating, in the thought that there may be no final, ultimate, best way of going about the business of cognition. But, among philosophers at least, the sort of relativism that a pragmatic epistemology engenders is more often a source of dread than of celebration. So the next item on my agenda will be to explore why it is that many people find relativism so ominous a view, and to see what can be said to quiet these qualms.

Is Epistemic Relativism Really Worrisome?

It is an easy matter to find evidence for the widespread abhorrence of relativism among contemporary philosophers. Indeed, it sometimes seems that many of my philosophical acquaintances can barely bring themselves to utter the word without embedding it in an epithet. "The specter of relativism" is a phrase that comes naturally to many. It is, however, a much more difficult matter to find any serious effort to justify this negative attitude—to show that relativism is a bad thing, or that it would lead to ominous consequences. What I propose to do in this section is to sketch the two lines of argument that have most often emerged in conversation when I have asked philosophers to support the view that epistemic relativism is an ominous or unwelcome doctrine. In the first case my reply will be that the danger is imaginary—that it rests on a misunderstanding of what relativists, particularly pragmatic relativists, claim. The second argument will require a longer discussion. For, in that case, I think the accusation leveled against relativism can likely be made to stick. However, if the arguments elaborated in the previous chapter are successful, only those whose intrinsic values are epistemically chauvinistic should find the accusation worrisome. Perhaps there are other, more plausible reasons to find epistemic relativism worrisome. But if so, I don't know what they are.

The first charge against relativism, and the easiest to dispatch, is that it is nihilistic, that it simply gives up on the project of distinguishing good cognition from bad and embraces a Feyerabendian cognitive libertinism—the doctrine that "anything goes." I am not at all certain that Feyerabend would really endorse the view that there is no distinction between good and bad ways of going about the business of cognition, or that he would be serious about it if he did.[11] But however this may be, it is quite clear that the "anything goes" slogan is singularly inappropriate for epistemic pragmatism or the relativism it engenders. Pragmatism does not give up on the project of assessing cognitive processes. Quite the contrary. Epistemic pragmatism offers an account of cognitive evaluation that is both demanding and designed to produce assessments that people will care about. For a given cognitive agent in a given historical setting, it will typically be the case that a pragmatic evaluation will rank one cognitive system higher than another. Occasionally perhaps a pair of cognitive systems may come out ranked equally. But it will near enough never be the case that pragmatism ranks all contenders on a par.

It is sometimes supposed that epistemic relativists must be wimps when it comes to evaluating the cognitive doings of other people or other cultures—that they must condone whatever they find. But clearly no such consequence follows from pragmatism. The fact that a given system of cognitive processes prevails in a culture does not even begin to show that that system is the best one for that culture. The pragmatist is perfectly prepared to find that people in some other culture would be doing a better job of cognition if they were to replace their own cognitive processes with ours. But he is also prepared to find that people in another culture are doing quite a good job of cognition, given their goals and circumstances, even though their system of cognitive processes would be a disaster for us. (Indeed, in the assessment of the cognitive practices of premodern science, I'd not be surprised if this turned out to be just the right thing to say.) Pragmatism in the assessment of cognition is no more nihilistic than pragmatism in the assessment of alternative technologies. In both cases, the evaluations proposed are going to depend on the goals of the users and on the situations in which they find themselves. But in neither case does pragmatism entail that anything goes.

A second complaint against relativism in epistemology is that it threatens the connection between cognitive inquiry and truth. To see the point, it helps to go back to Descartes and the very beginnings of modern epistemology. In the *Meditations*, Descartes sketches the method of clear and distinct ideas that, he urges, is the correct strategy of inquiry—the right way to go about the business of cognition. Having set out the method, Descartes goes on to ask what guarantee it provides. Why should we suppose that if we use the method diligently, we must ultimately arrive at the truth? Descartes's answer, which appeals to the goodness of God, runs roughly as follows. *If this, the best of methods, were to fail, then we might end up with false beliefs despite doing the best we could. But having done the best we could, our error would not be our fault; it would be God's. Moreover, if God built the world in such a way that we could not help being deceived despite doing the best we could, then God is a deceiver. And that we know to be impossible, since it is incompatible with His goodness.*

This answer is notoriously unconvincing. But if Descartes's answer was a nonstarter, his question certainly was not. Epistemologists from his time onward have been preoccupied with the relation between good thinking or good methods of inquiry, on the one hand, and truth, on the other. What reason do we have to believe that if we do a good job of cognition, the beliefs we end up with will be any closer to the truth than they would be if we reasoned poorly? The last four centuries have seen no shortage of attempts to answer this question. They have also seen more than a few skeptical arguments aimed at showing that an answer is impossible. And it is just here that relativism enters the picture. For it might well be thought that if epistemic relativism can be sustained, then the skeptics will have won the day.

A first pass at an argument to this effect might run something like this:

Suppose the epistemic relativist is right. Then there may be a pair of people whose cognitive systems are very different from one another, though the systems are equally (and even optimally) good. But if their cognitive systems are really very different from one another, we can expect that, on being exposed to essentially the same data, they will generally end up with very different sets of beliefs. When this happens, it can't be the case that both sets are true; at least one set of beliefs must be substantially mistaken. Since at least one of our hypothetical people will end up with false beliefs, and since ex hypothesis *they are both using optimally good cognitive systems, it can't be the case that good cognition guarantees truth. Indeed, it can't even be the case that good cognition has a high probability of producing the truth. For our story might just as well have been told with fifty people as with two. If relativism is right, these fifty people could have fifty different cognitive systems, all equally good. But, at most, one is going to end up with the truth.*

Now, as it stands, this argument is hardly ironclad. One possible objection turns on the assumption that alternative sets of beliefs generated by alternative cognitive systems cannot both be true. This assumption would surely be defensible if there were some reason to think that the alternative belief sets must be logically incompatible with one another. But nothing the relativist says commits him to that. Perhaps alternative cognitive systems produce alternative beliefs that are not logically incompatible but rather logically "incommensurable" in some way. One might, for example, imagine them stored in alternative dialects of mentalese whose concepts and constructions, and the mental sentences built from them, are not intertranslatable.

Confronted with this objection, those who are tempted by the argument sketched above have a number of options. One option would be to accept the objection and modify the conclusion the argument aims to establish. Rather than showing that relativism severs the connection between good thinking and truth, what the argument shows is that relativism severs the link between good thinking and the whole truth. If two people can each exploit good cognitive processes in a given environment and end up with very different sets of beliefs, then even if both sets are true it is still the case that neither person can get at the whole truth. So relativism seems to lead us to a doctrine of separate truths. The users of alternative, equally good cognitive systems each have a perspective on reality from which the other is excluded. But, for two reasons, this seems a less-than-promising path for those who would argue that epistemic relativism is a bad thing. First, it requires that we make some sense of the idea that mental sentences or cognitive states can have truth conditions and truth values despite being "incommensurable" with our own beliefs. Second, even if some sense can be made of the idea of beliefs that are true but incommensurable, it's far from clear why this new accusation is a problem for relativism. Many theorists are anxious to show that good reasoning will get us closer to the truth. But not even Descartes thought that by pursuing proper strategies of reasoning we could come to know *everything* that is true.

A second option, for those who would press the complaint against relativism, and by my lights a far more promising one, would be to challenge the suggestion that incommensurable systems of belief could possibly both be true. Those who pursue this line can grant that there may be systems of belieflike cognitive states that are incommensurable with our beliefs—systems of mental sentences perhaps that are built from significantly different concepts and constructions. But, they would insist, the very fact that they are incommensurable entails that these cognitive states have no truth conditions, and thus they are neither true nor false. It would, of course, require a fair bit of additional argument to shore up this response and show just why it is that systems of cognitive states incommensurable with our own have no truth conditions. But I am inclined to think that a plausible case might be made along these lines. Indeed, our discussion of truth in the previous chapter provides a good beginning, since we saw there that one of the more promising and well-articulated accounts of what it is for a mental state to have a truth condition entails that there will be a large space of belieflike cognitive states which do not have truth conditions. We also saw why any plausible alternative account of the interpretation function is likely to lead to the same conclusion. So I am prepared to concede, for argument's sake at least, that some suitably elaborated version of the argument displayed above does in fact go through, and thus that if epistemic relativism is right, there is no hope of showing that good reasoning leads to the truth.

But my mention of the results of the previous chapter will perhaps suggest why I am unfazed by this complaint. A central thesis of that chapter is that there is an enormous space of head-world relationships among which the one picked out by the socially transmitted, intuitively sanctioned notion of truth has no unique advantages. Apart from epistemic chauvinists, it is hard to see why any clear-headed person would care whether her beliefs were true—why she would prefer true beliefs to TRUE* ones, TRUE** ones, and so on. It is harder still to see why a clearheaded person would prefer cognitive processes that typically yield true beliefs over cognitive processes that are pragmatically sanctioned. For the latter, in contrast with the former, have an obvious connection with what the person wants and values. So to the complaint that relativism would sever the connection between good cognition and truth, my answer is as follows. Perhaps that's right; perhaps it would. But this is no reason to *worry* about relativism unless we have some reason to want our beliefs to be true, some reason to care whether they are true rather than TRUE*, TRUE**, and so on. Without some reason to prefer truth to the infinite variety of alternative head-world relationships, we should be no more concerned about the fact that good reasoning may not lead to truth than we are about the fact that good reasoning may not lead to TRUTH*****—or, for that matter, about the fact that good reasoning may not lead to beliefs sanctioned by some ancient text.

The epistemological tradition that begins with Descartes is built on the unquestioned assumption that there is some unique, special, intrinsically desirable relationship—the truth relationship—in which cognitive states should stand to nature. Much of the work in that tradition is fueled by the fear that this relation may be in jeopardy. But on my view—and here I think I echo a central thesis in the history of pragmatism—the entire Cartesian project is ill conceived. There is no unique, intrinsically desirable head-world relationship to which all cognitive agents should aspire. And since there is no universally desirable endpoint of cognitive activity, there is no point in fretting over the fact that if relativism is right, good thinking won't get us there.[12]

Pragmatism and Circularity

The previous section was motivated by the worry that the relativism implicit in my pragmatic account of cognitive evaluation might count as a deficit for that account. My response was that, though pragmatism does indeed lead to a kind of epistemic relativism, for most of us this relativism should be no cause for concern. In this section I want to consider another putative deficit that might be thought to encumber a pragmatic epistemology. In this case, the charge is circularity. But, I shall argue, when we see just what this accusation comes to, it turns out that in this case too the alleged defect is not worth worrying about. Since pragmatic accounts of cognitive evaluation have not been center stage in the philosophical literature, the charge that they are somehow viciously circular has not been debated in any detail. However, that charge has been repeatedly leveled at various truth-linked accounts of cognitive evaluation, and in ways that invite straightforward extension to pragmatic accounts. So I will begin my discussion of the circularity objection by reworking what I take to be the most cogent version of the complaint, taking pragmatic rather than truth-linked theories as the target.[13] That done, I will set out a series of replies, most of which are themselves adapted from parallel moves that have been made in defense of truth-linked accounts.[14] Taken together, these replies should suffice to show that the putative circularity does pragmatism no damage.

The best of the arguments alleging that truth-linked accounts of cognitive evaluation involve some sort of vicious circularity focus on the situation that arises when we attempt to apply these accounts. So in building the parallel case against epistemic pragmatism, let's consider where circularity might be thought to lurk in the application of the theory. According to the pragmatic account, one system of cognitive processes is better than another if it is more likely to achieve those things that are intrinsically valued by the relevant person. Let us suppose that in a given instance I am the relevant person, and I am trying the determine whether my own system of cognitive processes is better than some alternative system that has been proposed. In order to do that, I must study both systems and attempt to determine the likelihood of various consequences that might follow if I used one system or the other. But, of course, in order to do this I must do some thinking; I must *use* my cognitive system. And, the critic protests, it is just here that we confront a vicious circularity. For suppose that as a result of my inquiry I conclude that my own system of cognitive processes is indeed better than the proposed alternative. In coming to that conclusion, I have used the very system whose superiority I claim to have established. Moreover, it may well be the case that had I used some other system of cognitive processes (perhaps even the system whose merits I am comparing with mine), I might have ended up with just the opposite conclusion; I might have concluded that the proposed alternative is better than mine. Since in establishing the superiority of my own system of reasoning I have made essential use of that very system, the critic concludes that my effort has been viciously circular. I am trying, in vain, to pull myself up by my own bootstraps.

The argument just sketched is a variation on a venerable and very influential theme in the history of philosophy. Similar arguments can be found in writers as diverse as Sextus Empiricus, Montaigne, and Roderick Firth.[15] But despite its long history and its enormous influence, I find the argument singularly unpersuasive. Whether aimed at truth-linked or pragmatic accounts, it is very hard to see why the sort of circularity on which the argument turns is anything other than benign. To make the point, I'll assemble a number of replies.

First, it is important to recognize that the outcome in the story imagined by the critic is not the only possible outcome. In the critic's story, I use my cognitive system to reach the conclusion that it is itself better than some proposed alternative. However, it is entirely possible that the inquiry could come out just the other way and that, while using my cognitive system, I might reach the conclusion that the alternative system is in fact the better one. Were this to happen, I might contrive to rerun the inquiry using the proposed alternative (perhaps after doing a bit of cognitive retooling) and discover that, that way too, the alternative comes out best. This would be a prime example of the sort of "bootstrapping" imagined by those who view the project of cognitive assessment as part of a larger project whose goal is cognitive improvement. And plainly there is no vicious circularity lurking in this scenario. Similarly, there will be no hint of unwelcome circularity if the assessment is run by both my system and the alternative, and they both end up with the conclusion that mine is better. The only case in which there is even a *prima facie* danger of begging the question is the one in which my system ends up with the conclusion that it is better, and the alternative ends up with the opposite conclusion. But obviously not all attempts at pragmatic cognitive assessment need turn out this way, nor is there any reason to think that such cases are going to be particularly common. So my first reply is that the circularity the critic fears will not be found in all attempts to apply a pragmatic account of cognitive evaluation. It may turn out to be quite rare.

My second reply is that, even in the *prima facie* problematic cases, there is no formal fallacy being committed. For an argument to beg the question, or be viciously circular, it must take as one of its premises the very conclusion that it purports to establish. But the pragmatic cognitive assessment imagined by the critic involves no such formal begging the question. The conclusion of that assessment is that my cognitive system is more likely than the alternative to achieve those things that I intrinsically value. To establish that conclusion, I will need to detail the workings of the two systems and to explore how they are likely to interact with my physical and social environment. But at no point in this inquiry am I going to assert the conclusion as a premise. To see this more clearly, it may help to compare the pragmatic assessment of a pair of cognitive systems with the pragmatic assessment of a pair of noncognitive tools. In both cases I am trying to determine which alternative is more likely to achieve what I value. And in both cases, of course, I must use my cognitive system in the process of coming up with an answer. But in assessing tools, there is plainly no need to invoke a premise about the efficacy of the cognitive system I am using. Nor is there any need to do so in assessing cognitive systems.

At this point, the critic may protest that, while the conclusion is not explicitly asserted in arguments for the superiority of our own cognitive system, it is tacitly presupposed. To make this objection stick, however, the critic will have to tell us a lot more about his notion of presupposition and about the principles that determine which propositions are presupposed by a given argument. This promises to be no easy matter, since the principle that seems to underwrite the critic's charge of tacit circularity quickly leads to absurdity. To see this, consider the case at hand in a bit more detail. We are supposing we have before us an empirical argument to the conclusion that our cognitive system is pragmatically better than a proposed alternative. (Let's call the alternative System A, and the conclusion Proposition A.) It is claimed that because we are using our cognitive system in constructing and assessing the argument, the argument must tacitly

presuppose Proposition A. But, of course, we use our cognitive system in all our reasoning. So if the mere fact that we use our cognitive
system in constructing and assessing an argument entails that the
argument presupposes Proposition A, then all our arguments presuppose Proposition A, even those that have nothing to do with the
comparative merits of cognitive systems. Moreover, since proposition
A is hardly unique, this is just the beginning of the critic's list of
ubiquitous presuppositions. Consider the claim (call it Proposition B)
that our cognitive system is better than some other alternative, System B. Presumably, the critic would claim that in using our cognitive
system to construct arguments for Proposition B, we tacitly presuppose Proposition B. But, once again, if the mere fact that we use our
cognitive system in constructing an argument entails that the argument presupposes Proposition B, then all our arguments presuppose
Proposition B. And so on, for Proposition C, Proposition D, and indefinitely many more. Yet surely there is something more than a bit
absurd about any view entailing that all our arguments have infinitely
many presuppositions. To summarize, my second reply runs as follows: In applying the pragmatic account there will be no explicit circularity, and the critic who insists that there is a tacit circularity owes us
some account of the notion of presupposition that does not lead to
absurd consequences.

For argument's sake, let's ignore the problems with the notion of
presupposition and grant that in some cases there will be a tacit circularity in applying the pragmatic account of cognitive evaluation.
Against the background of these concessions, my third reply is that
this circularity is no special problem for the pragmatic account, since
an entirely parallel circularity will beset attempts to apply any other
account of cognitive evaluation. What motivates the charge of circularity in applying the pragmatic account is simply that we are using
our cognitive system in the process of showing that it is pragmatically
better than some proposed alternative. But now suppose that we reject the pragmatic account in favor of some different account that says
system A is better than system B if and only if A has property P and
B doesn't. For any P that is even remotely plausible, we are going to
have to use our cognitive system in order to determine whether our
system has it and the alternative does not. And if that use of our
cognitive system is all it takes to convict an account of cognitive evaluation of circularity, then any remotely plausible alternative to pragmatism is going to be circular, too. So the "circularity problem" gives

us no reason to reject the pragmatic account in favor of some other account of cognitive evaluation.

The fact that the circularity argument is equally threatening to all accounts of cognitive evaluation should be no surprise, since the historical prototypes for the argument were skeptical in intent, aimed at undermining all efforts to show that our beliefs are justified. Taking a cue from that skeptical heritage, the critic might respond to my third reply by granting the broad applicability of the circularity argument and urging that in fact all accounts of cognitive evaluation are circular. To this move, I offer a fourth, and last, reply. Suppose we agree with the critic that pragmatism, along with all other accounts of cognitive evaluation, are "tacitly circular" when we attempt to apply them. Why is this circularity supposed to be a defect? The critic's answer, presumably, is that we should want something more from an account of cognitive evaluation; we should want an account that can be applied without this sort of circularity. But let's think a bit more carefully about this. The "tacit circularity" arises simply in virtue of the fact that we use our cognitive system in assessing cognitive systems. So according to the critic, what we should want is an account of cognitive evaluation that can be applied without any cognitive activity at all. Surely, at this juncture, the right reply to make is that this is a perfectly preposterous thing to want. The "defect" that the critic has discovered in the pragmatic account (and all the others) is simply that we can't apply it without thinking. And that, I submit, is not a defect that any sensible person should worry about.

Interpreting Psychological Studies of Reasoning: Pragmatism Applied

The reader who is favored with an unusually robust memory may recall that my concern with the evaluation of alternative strategies of cognitive processing was originally provoked by some striking experimental findings and by a question about how those findings were to be interpreted. The findings indicated that in quite ordinary and unthreatening environments, many normal subjects exhibited curious and unexpected patterns of reasoning—patterns which inclined some experimenters to conclude that the subjects were reasoning very poorly. The question was raised by critics who acknowledged the findings but challenged the experimenters' conclusion: Are the subjects really doing a bad job at the business of reasoning? This question leads very quickly to some more general ones: What is it to reason well or poorly? What constitutes doing a good job at the business of cognition? Much of the work of chapters 4, 5, and 6 has been devoted to undermining some widely endorsed answers to these questions and to laying the groundwork for a pragmatic alternative. It seems appropriate to end the volume by exploring how the pragmatic account of cognitive evaluation that I have endorsed might be used in answering the questions that have been raised about the implications of the experimental findings. What does the pragmatic account say about those troubling results in the psychological study of cognition? Is it the case that people are indeed reasoning badly when they exhibit belief perseverance, neglect base rates, make judgments on the basis of biased samples, or exploit one of the other suspect patterns of reasoning?

Perhaps the least controversial lesson to be drawn from the arguments of chapters 4 and 5 is that this last question is in need of some serious glossing before we try to answer it. In asking whether a pattern of reasoning, or the system of cognitive processes that underlies it, is good or bad, there are lots of things the questioner might have in mind. She might, for example, be asking whether the cognitive processes in question are rational, or whether they are the sort that give rise to justified beliefs, where the concepts of rationality or justification are presumed to be implicit in our ordinary thought and language. If this is the question being asked, then there is an obvious way to go about trying to answer it. The first step is to analyze or explicate the concepts of rationality or justification embedded in everyday thinking. The next step is to do some psychology in order to discover in sufficient detail just what the cognitive processes at hand are like. The final step is to determine whether the cognitive processes that have been described fall within the extension of the concept that has been explicated. None of this is likely to be easy, of course, and it may even prove to be impossible. For, as we noted in chapter 4, there is no guarantee that the concepts of rationality or justification underlying ordinary usage are sufficiently coherent and well behaved to sustain a usable explication. Moreover, even if things go well on this score, there is a serious worry about why anyone should much care how the whole project comes out, since, absent some further argument, the local evaluative concepts that drive the project have no more going for them than local notions of etiquette.

But my current purpose is not to refight the battle over "analytic epis-temology." Rather, it is to stress that questions about the goodness or badness of cognitive systems admit of a variety of interpretations. To tackle such questions without first thinking long and hard about how we propose to understand them is an open invitation to confu-sion. It is a mug's game to ask whether someone is reasoning well without some clear idea of what it is we really want to know and how we might go about finding out.

It's been my contention that questions about the evaluation of cog-nitive processes are most productively understood as pragmatic ques-tions—that in most cases what we really want to know is how well the cognitive systems at issue will do at achieving what the people using them value. But most of what I have said about the pragmatic assessment of cognitive systems has focused on the comparative as-sessment of two or more systems, and this comparative account does not directly address the question of whether a given system is a good one, or whether people using that system are reasoning well. So let us ponder how the comparative pragmatic account might serve as the basis of a plausible pragmatic interpretation for those noncompara-tive evaluative questions.

One thought that might seem tempting is to count a particular cog-nitive system as a good one (for a specified person, in a specified context) if it is at least as good, from the pragmatic point of view, as any logically possible alternative. But, for a pair of closely related reasons, I am more than a bit dubious about this proposal. The first reason is that if we take it literally, the proposal seems to stack the deck in favor of a negative evaluation of our own cognitive system. No matter how pragmatically successful our cognitive system might turn out to be, it is hard to believe there isn't some logically possible alternative that won't do a bit better. Moreover, and this is the second reason, when we set out to evaluate a cognitive system—our own or someone else's—it is not clear that we are really very interested in knowing whether it reaches the ideal standard of being at least as successful as any logically possible alternative. For, given almost any plausible set of values that might be plugged into a pragmatic evalua-tion, that standard is likely to be vastly beyond anything that could even be approached by a creature with a brain like ours. And it is implausible to suppose that in debating whether people are reasoning well, what we are concerned about is whether they are living up to a standard that beings like us cannot even remotely approach. Since the point is an important one, and since the gap between our biological capacities and the idealized standard of what is logically possible all too often goes unappreciated, I think we would do well to consider a number of examples.

The first is drawn from Cherniak's fascinating work on the epistemological implications of complexity theory, a branch of computer science concerned with assessing the computational feasibility of various classes of algorithms.[16] Among the surprising results in this area is the demonstration that many quite familiar algorithms—including some that would likely be of considerable pragmatic utility to any cognitive system that could compute them easily—require immensely more computational power than could be packed into a human skull. Consider, for example, the *prima facie* pragmatically desirable project of testing one's beliefs from time to time for truth-functional consistency. One familiar way to do this is to use the truth table method. But, it turns out, this is not only unfeasible for a human brain, it is unfeasible even for what we might suppose to be the ideal, physically buildable computer. Here is how Cherniak makes the point:

> Suppose that each line of the truth table for the conjunction of all [of a person's] beliefs could be checked in the time a light ray takes to traverse the diameter of a proton, an appropriate "supercycle" time, and suppose that the computer was permitted to run for twenty billion years, the estimated time from the "big-bang" dawn of the universe to the present. A belief system containing only one hundred and thirty-eight logically independent propositions would overwhelm the time resources of this supermachine.[17]

Cherniak goes on to note that, while it is not easy to estimate the number of atomic propositions in a typical human belief system, the number must be vastly in excess of 138. It follows that, whatever its practical benefits might be, the proposed consistency-checking algorithm is not something a human brain could even approach.[18] Thus, it would seem perverse, to put it mildly, to insist that a person's cognitive system is doing a bad job of reasoning because it fails to periodically execute the algorithm and check on the consistency of the person's beliefs.

For a second illustration, consider the phenomenon of belief perseverance, in which a belief persists despite the fact that the subject no longer accepts the evidence from which the belief has been inferred.[19] Though the details would no doubt be a long story, and not an easy one to tell, it is *prima facie* plausible to suppose that (in most settings and for most values) belief perseverance will occasionally get you in pragmatic trouble. Thus, some logically possible cognitive system that does not exhibit perseverance will be pragmatically preferable to systems like ours that do. But, as Harman has noted, to build such a nonperseverating system would require placing extraordinary demands on memory, since the system would have to remember all of the evidence (including, presumably, all of the perceptual beliefs) on which each of its beliefs is based.[20] Plainly, our brains do not work in this way. And, though we do not know enough about the mechanisms of human memory to give a conclusive argument for the point, I would not be much surprised if it turned out that for a brain built like ours to store that much information, it would have to be the size of a bathtub, or perhaps a battleship. Suppose this is right. Are we then prepared to say that our own cognitive system is reasoning badly in this domain, because there are logically possible alternatives that would not exhibit belief perseverance and that would thus do a pragmatically better job? Plainly, that would be very odd.

For my final illustration, I once again borrow from Cherniak, this time his work on memory compartmentalization.[21] To begin, consider a pair of anecdotes that Cherniak recounts.

At least a decade before Fleming's discovery of penicillin, many microbiologists were aware that molds cause clear spots in bacteria cultures, and they knew that such a bare spot indicates no bacterial growth. Yet they did not consider the possibility that molds release an antibacterial agent.[22]

Smith believes an open flame can ignite gasoline . . . , and Smith believes the match he now holds has an open flame . . . , and Smith is not suicidal. Yet Smith decides to see whether a gas tank is empty by looking inside while holding the match nearby for illumination. Similar stories appear often in newspapers; this is approximately how one of Faulkner's characters, Eck Snopes, dies in *The Town*.[23]

The point Cherniak is illustrating with these examples is that it is "part of the human condition" that we "fail to 'make the connections' sometimes in a web of interconnected beliefs."[24] The explanation for this failure, Cherniak suggests, is that human long-term memory is organized into separate files or compartments and that typically only a small number of these compartments are actively searched in the course of dealing with a given cognitive problem. When a salient bit of information is stored in a memory compartment that has not been searched, the subject will not retrieve it and will fail to "make the connection." Moreover, Cherniak argues, the fact that human memory is organized into separately searchable compartments "is not just an accident of human psychology."[25] For, given the large size of the typical adult memory, the fact that memory search takes time, and the fact that there are serious time constraints on much of our cognitive activity, particularly when it involves practical matters, it would often be unfeasible, indeed fatal, to attempt an exhaustive search of memory. Compartmentalization makes it possible for the system to search quickly through those files that promise to be most relevant, though as Cherniak's two anecdotes show, there will sometimes be a pragmatic price to be paid for this efficiency. It is, of course, easy to imagine a logically possible cognitive system whose pragmatic performance is better than ours, because its search speed is so fast that it doesn't need to compartmentalize its memory. But, once again, it seems perverse to conclude that our system is doing a bad job at the business of cognition simply because such an alternative system is logically possible.

The point I have been belaboring with these examples is that in many areas there is going to be an enormous gap between what brains like ours can do and what would be done by the best logically possible cognitive systems. The conclusion I would draw is that in looking for a plausible pragmatic interpretation of what we want to know when we ask whether a person's cognitive system is a good one, it won't do to insist that the system be at least as good (or even almost as good) as any logical possible alternative. But if that's not the question we're asking, what is?

In all three of the examples, the pragmatically superior cognitive system was for one reason or another completely unfeasible for us. It was not something that creatures with brains like ours could hope to approach. And because the best alternative was not something we could even get close to, it seemed inappropriate to conclude that people are doing a bad job of reasoning simply because such an alternative is logically possible. This suggests that when we ask whether subjects are reasoning well, perhaps what we really want to know is whether their cognitive system is at least as good as any *feasible* alternative, where an alternative is feasible if it can be used by people operating within some appropriate set of constraints. This is, I think, a step in the right direction. But it leaves us with the problem of saying just which constraints we are going to count as appropriate. And here there is a danger of going too far in the constraints we take into account.

That danger was driven home to me by a conversation with Donald Norman in which (perhaps just as the devil's advocate) he defended the view that there is no such thing as bad or irrational reasoning. He was, of course, perfectly prepared to concede that in some cases we can describe patterns of reasoning that are better than the ones subjects actually exhibit. But, he insisted, these alternatives are irrelevant since they are not alternatives that the subjects could have used. In some cases, the subjects couldn't use them because they had never learned them; in other cases, they couldn't use them because they didn't remember them; in still other cases, there may have been environmental or internal stimuli that caused the subjects' cognitive systems to react as they did. In all of these cases, the subjects are reasoning and behaving within a rich structure of historical, psychological, and environmental constraints. And, Norman argued, when all of those constraints are taken into account, the subjects are doing as well as they can.

There is one point in Norman's argument that I think we should be prepared to concede. Given all the constraints under which subjects are operating, it may well be that their cognitive processes are completely determined. So, if we take all of those constraints as given, the subjects could do no better (and no worse). But the moral I would draw here is quite different from the one Norman proposed. Rather than concluding that bad reasoning is impossible, I think the right conclusion is that when we ask whether a subject has reasoned well, we do not take all of these constraints to be relevant to our question. What we really want to know is whether there are pragmatically superior cognitive systems that are feasible in the sense that the subject might have used them if some, but not all, of the constraints that actually obtained had been relaxed. This gets us back to the question of which constraints are appropriate.

One way to tackle this questions would be to hunt for a single set of constraints, and thus a general notion of feasibility, that will capture our intentions whenever we raise questions about the quality of a person's reasoning. But I think it is clear that this approach is doomed to failure for the very simple reason that there is no single set of intentions lying behind all questions about the goodness or badness of a person's reasoning. Rather, I suggest, there are many different reasons why we might ask whether a person's cognitive system is a good one. The question may be raised as part of different projects with different goals, and when asking the question there may be many different things we want to know. These varying projects impose a variety of interpretations on the notion of feasible alternatives for a given cognitive system, and thus the question, Which constraints are appropriate? admits of no general answer. My proposal (and here again I am following in the footsteps of the pragmatists) is that in deciding which constraints are relevant, or which alternative cognitive systems we will count as feasible, we must look to our purposes in asking the question. Or, as William James might put it, we must ask what the "cash value" of the question is—what actions might we take as the result of one answer or another. A consequence of this proposal is that there is yet another sort of relativism lurking in our questions about the goodness or badness of reasoning, a relativism that turns on the purpose of the inquiry. Another consequence is that to the extent that we do not have a clear purpose in asking whether people are reasoning well or poorly, the question itself is obscure and ill defined. I think there is good reason to suppose that much debate over the normative standing of one or another experimentally observed inferential strategy has been carried on without any well-focused idea about the purpose of the inquiry and thus without any clear understanding of what was being debated.[26]

Among the various purposes one might have in asking whether people's reasoning in a given domain is good or bad, there is at least one that is of obvious relevance to traditional epistemological concerns. From Bacon and Descartes to Mill and Goldman, epistemologists have aspired not simply to evaluate reasoning but to improve it. This same goal looms large for a number of the psychologists whose studies of reasoning have proved so unsettling. So let us stipulate that for present purposes the cash value of questions about the quality of reasoning is to be found in the steps we might subsequently take to help people reason better. Against this background, finally, we can ask how studies in the psychology of reasoning should be interpreted. Are the psychologists who see these studies as having "bleak implication for human reasoning" right? Do the studies indicate that the subjects are reasoning badly? The answer I propose to defend is that in just about every case the critique of ordinary inference has been premature. When the question is unpacked along the lines I have suggested, it is *far* from clear that the subjects are doing a bad job at the business of reasoning.

In order to sustain the charge that subjects in a given experiment are reasoning badly, we must show that there is some alternative to the cognitive system that the subjects are currently using that is both pragmatically superior and feasible. When our goal is to help people do a better job of reasoning, a feasible alternative will be one that we could actually get people to employ. So, given current purposes, a feasible alternative cognitive system is one we have some effective method or technology for imparting. And for the time being at least, educational strategies of various sorts are the only candidates we need to take seriously. What we need to ask, then, is whether there are teachable strategies that are pragmatically superior to the ones subjects currently use. To answer this question in detail will, of course, require careful empirical exploration of the effects that can be achieved by various educational strategies. And, as it happens, some of the researchers who earlier uncovered curious patterns of reasoning have, in more recent work, turned their attention to the question of what reasoning strategies can and cannot be taught with various techniques.

To date, the results of those studies have been tentative and controversial, and the studies themselves have examined only a handful of teaching strategies. But even before considering those results, we should note that in some cases those who drew bleak implications from experiments on reasoning were obviously too hasty. Studies of belief perseverance are a good example here. The experimental results make it clear that people do perseverate and that the phenomenon is widespread and robust. But if the goal is amelioration then, as our recent reflections have shown, these findings by themselves are not adequate to establish that people are reasoning poorly. To support that conclusion, we must also show that there are pragmatically superior feasible alternatives—alternatives that can be taught and learned. As Harman has argued, an alternative cognitive system that keeps track of *all* its evidence for *all* of its beliefs is almost certainly not one that could be learned, because it imposes such extraordinary demands on memory. So, even if it is granted that nonperseverating systems would be pragmatically superior to ours, it still does not follow that we are reasoning badly when we hold on to a belief after rejecting the evidence on which the belief is based. Of course, it need not be the case that a cognitive system must avoid belief perseverance altogether in order to be better than ours. It may be that a modest reduction in perseverance has a significant pragmatic payoff and that we can learn how to reduce perseverance to a certain degree. But so far as I know, the feasibility of such alternatives has not yet been

explored. Thus it is an open question whether people who perseverate are reasoning badly. Much the same conclusion follows about
people who fail to eliminate all inconsistencies in their beliefs and
about people who fail to use all the relevant information they have
available.

Recent research on teaching strategies of reasoning suggests that
even after a course devoted to the topic, people are generally very
bad at using purely formal or syntactic principles of inference of the
sort that are usually encountered in traditional formal logic. However, it is much easier to get people to use various strategies of statistical reasoning, including in particular those that exploit the "law of
large numbers." [27] With a relatively modest amount of instruction, it
seems that people can be gotten to grasp the notion that, in populations that are not likely to be homogeneous, predictions based on a
small sample are likely to be much less reliable than predictions based
on a larger sample. Moreover, what people learn is typically utilized
in dealing with topics and tasks quite different from those on which
they are trained. Thus, there are feasible alternatives to those cognitive systems which readily generalize from small samples in nonho-
mogeneous populations. But, of course, this result by itself is not
sufficient to show that people whose reasoning regularly flouts the
law of large numbers are doing a bad job of reasoning. We must also
show that one or another of the alternatives they might learn would
be pragmatically superior. And to do this, we must know enough
about their values and about the environments in which they operate
to show that if they were to adopt one of the learnable alternative
systems, it would serve them in better stead. There is no shortage of
anecdotes in the literature illustrating how reasoning that ignores the
law of large numbers can lead to frustration—or worse. But there is a
considerable gap between such anecdotes and a systematic demonstration that an alternative cognitive system is pragmatically superior
for a given person or group. Thus, I submit, even in these cases a
bleak assessment of ordinary reasoning would be premature.

This cautious conclusion should not, however, be mistaken for an
endorsement of commonsense reasoning, nor should it give much
encouragement to those Panglossian optimists who think that in matters cognitive we live in (or near) the best of all possible worlds. For
even if current membership is sparse in the set of alternative cognitive
systems that are both feasible and known to be pragmatically superior, there is no reason to think that this situation will not change

dramatically as we learn more about what makes cognitive systems useful and develop more powerful technologies for modifying the systems that nature and culture have provided. Cognition, for the pragmatist, is an activity that plays a central role in the pursuit of a variety of ends. Viewed from this perspective, it is no more likely that there is a best way of going about the business of cognition than that there is a best means of transportation, or of communication. A pragmatic epistemology encourages the hope that human cognitive systems may improve without limit, as we learn more about how to expand their capacities and as our physical, social, and technological environments present us with new opportunities and new challenges. Nor should we assume that all the improvements in human reasoning must follow the same path. From the pragmatist perspective it's to be expected that quite different strategies for improving cognitive processing may prove preferable for different people with different goals, different technologies, or different environments. Just as there are many good ways to prepare food, or raise children, or organize a society, so too there may be many good ways to go about the business of cognition.

Notes

1. This would be a good place to record one of my more significant intellectual debts. The sort of epistemic pragmatism I advocate is species of what Rescher (1977) [108] calls "methodological pragmatism," and my thinking about these matters has been influenced in many ways by Rescher's rich and lucid book. There are many points on which Rescher and I disagree. We could hardly be further apart in our views about the importance of truth and the prospects for showing that pragmatically sanctioned cognitive strategies will lead to truth. But whether one agrees with Rescher or disagrees, his book is essential reading for anyone interested in a pragmatic epistemology.

2. Historically, of course, pragmatists have been very suspicious of the distinction between intrinsic and instrumental values.

3. One particularly worrisome challenge to the framework of the pragmatic account is the claim that people typically do not have stable or determinate values. For a discussion of some of the literature supporting this conclusion, see Slovic 1990, in Osherson and Smith 1990 [625].

4. For further details see Stich (1982b) [839].

5. For lucid discussions see Schick (1984) [647] and Levi (1986) [607].

6. This use of 'relativism' differs from the use in Stich (1984) [248], where I did not distinguish relativism from nonrelativistic sorts of pluralism. Thanks

are due to Francis Snare for helping me to think more clearly about the distinction between relativism and pluralism.

7. One writer in the reliabilist tradition who has been particularly sensitive to the fact that the environment in which a cognitive system operates will effect how well it does in producing truths is Goldman (1986) [49]. See the discussion of his notion of "normal worlds" in 4.6.3.

8. See, for example, Carey (1985) [552].

9. Kitcher 1992 [528].

10. It's worth noting that the situation is analogous, in important ways, to the case of the hawk and dove genes, discussed in 3.6.

11. For the reader who wants to judge for him- or herself, the place to start is Feyerabend (1978) [568] or (1978) [569].

12. For some insightful observations on the pragmatists' rejection of the view that there is a single desirable way in which beliefs should relate to the world, see Rorty (1982) [640].

13. For some discussion of the circularity objection as it applies to pragmatism, see Rescher (1977) [108], chaps. 2, 3, 7.

14. There is an excellent discussion of the circularity objection aimed at truth-linked theories in Goldman (1986) [49], pp. 116–21. I've borrowed substantially from that discussion, particularly in my second and third replies.

15. Sextus Empiricus (1933) [653], pp. 163–64; Montaigne (1933) [619], p. 544; Firth (1981) [390], p. 19.

16. Cherniak (1986) [19], chap. 4.

17. Ibid, p. 93.

18. Cherniak notes that more efficient algorithms are known. But even these "still require as much time in the worst cases" (93).

19. See 1.2.1.4.

20. Harman (1986) [60], pp. 37–42.

21. Cherniak (1983) [361]; (1986) [19], chap. 3.

22. Cherniak (1986) [19], p. 50.

23. Ibid., p. 57.

24. Ibid., p. 50.

25. Ibid., p. 61.

26. See, for example, Cohen (1979) [465], (1980) [466], (1981) [190], (1982) [468]; Kahneman and Tversky (1973) [474], (1979) [486].

27. Cheng and Holyoak (1985) [692]; Fong, Krantz, and Nisbett (1986) [728]; Cheng et al. (1986) [693]; Nisbett et al. (1987) [796]. For a useful review, see Holland et al. (1986) [64], chap. 9.

Bibliography

Frederick F. Schmitt and
James Spellman

This is a selected bibliography of naturalistic epistemology. The deluge of new books and articles on the subject since the first edition of this anthology has forced us to abandon the aim of completeness. We have concentrated on work by philosophers, and we have omitted relevant work in psychology, cognitive science, neuroscience, artificial intelligence, and science studies, as well work in the philosophy of these fields and in the philosophy of mind, logic, mathematics, and language, including naturalistic epistemology in these areas. We have minimized the number of comments and papers in the proceedings of conferences and associations. Work on the naturalistic epistemology of Robert Nozick is omitted because there is an excellent bibliography in Luper-Foy 1987 [80]. Work on the history of naturalistic epistemology, including secondary literature on Hume, Reid, Peirce, Dewey, Popper, Piaget, and Quine is also omitted. We omit work on feminist epistemology that is not expressly naturalistic and refer readers to the bibliography in the APA's *Newsletter on Feminism and Philosophy*, Fall 1990. Finally, we omit work on social epistemology that is not also expressly naturalistic, and we refer readers to Schmitt forthcoming [120] for an extensive bibliography of social epistemology.

Books

1. Alston, W. 1989. *Epistemic Justification: Essays in the Theory of Knowledge*, Ithaca: Cornell University Press.

2. Antony, L. and Witt, C., eds. 1992. *A Mind of One's Own: Feminist Essays on Reason and Objectivity*, Boulder: Westview Press.

3. Armstrong, D. M. 1973. *Belief, Truth and Knowledge*, London: Cambridge University Press.

4. Asquith, P. D. and Giere, R. N., eds. 1982. *PSA 1980*, 2, East Lansing: Philosophy of Science Association.

5. Audi, R. 1988. *Belief, Justification, and Knowledge*, Belmont, Cal.: Wadsworth.

6. Barrett, R., ed. 1990. *Perspectives on Quine*, Cambridge: Blackwell.

7. Berkowitz, L. 1977. *Advances in Experimental Social Psychology* X, New York: Academic Press.

8. Bieri, P., ed. 1987. *Analytische Philosophie der Erkenntnis*, Frankfurt: Athenaeum.

9. Bieri, P., Horstmann, R.-P., and Kruger, L., eds. 1979. *Transcendental Arguments and Science*, Dordrecht: Reidel.

10. Bloor, D. 1976. *Knowledge and Social Imagery*, London: Routledge and Kegan Paul.

11. Bogdan, R., ed. 1984. *Profile: D. M. Armstrong*, Dordrecht: Reidel.

12. Bogdan, R., ed. 1985. *Belief*, Oxford: Oxford University Press.

13. Bogdan, R., ed. 1991. *Mind and Common Sense*, Cambridge: Cambridge University Press.

14. BonJour, L. 1985. *The Structure of Empirical Knowledge*, Cambridge, Mass.: Harvard University Press.

15. Brand, M. and Harnish, R., eds. 1986. *The Representation of Knowledge and Belief*, Tucson: University of Arizona Press.

16. Buchler, J., ed. 1955. *Philosophical Writings of Peirce*, New York: Dover.

17. Butterworth, G., ed. 1982. *Infancy and Epistemology*, New York: St. Martin's Press.

18. Carroll, J. S. and Payne, J. W., eds. 1976. *Cognition and Social Behavior*, Hillsdale, N.J.: Lawrence Erlbaum Associates.

19. Cherniak, C. 1986. *Minimal Rationality*, Cambridge, Mass.: MIT Press. A Bradford Book.

20. Chisholm, R. M. and Swartz, R., eds. 1973. *Empirical Knowledge*. Englewood Cliffs, N.J.: Prentice-Hall.

21. Churchland, P. S. 1986. *Neurophilosophy: Toward a Unified Science of the Mind/Brain*, Cambridge, Mass.: MIT Press. A Bradford Book.

22. Churchland, P. M. 1979. *Scientific Realism and the Plasticity of Mind*, Cambridge: Cambridge University Press.

23. Churchland, P. M. 1989. *A Neurocomputational Perspective: The Nature of Mind and the Structure of Science*, Cambridge, Mass.: MIT Press. A Bradford Book.

24. Clarke, D. S. 1988. *Rational Acceptance and Purpose: Outline of a Pragmatic Epistemology*, Savage, Md.: Rowman and Littlefield.

25. Clay, M. and Lehrer, K., eds. 1989. *Knowledge and Skepticism*. Boulder: Westview.

26. Code, L. 1987. *Epistemic Responsibility*, Hanover, N.H.: University of New England Press.

27. Cohen, R., ed. 1984. *Methodology, Metaphysics, and the History of Science*, Dordrecht: Reidel.

28. Dancy, J. 1985. *Contemporary Epistemology*, Oxford: Oxford University Press.

29. Davidson, D. 1980. *Essays on Actions and Events*, New York: Oxford University Press.

30. Davis, S., ed. *Causal Theories of Mind: Action, Knowledge, Memory, Perception, and Reference*, New York: De Gruyter.

31. Dretske, F. I. 1969. *Seeing and Knowing*, Chicago: University of Chicago Press.

32. Dretske, F. I. 1981. *Knowledge and the Flow of Information*, Cambridge, Mass.: MIT Press. A Bradford Book.

33. Duran, J. 1989. *Epistemics*, Washington, D.C.: University Press of America.

34. Duran, J. 1990. *Toward a Feminist Epistemology*, Savage, Md.: Rowman and Littlefield.

35. Evans, J. St.B. T. 1983. *Thinking and Reasoning*, London: Routledge and Kegan Paul.

36. Fishbein, M., ed. 1977. *Progress in Social Psychology*, Hillsdale, N.J.: Lawrence Erlbaum Associates.

37. Fodor, J. 1981. *Representations: Philosophical Essays on the Foundations of Cognitive Science*, Cambridge, Mass.: MIT Press. A Bradford Book.

38. Fodor, J. 1983. *The Modularity of Mind*, Cambridge, Mass.: MIT Press.

39. Foley, R. 1987. *A Theory of Epistemic Rationality*, Cambridge, Mass.: Harvard University Press.

40. Foss, B. M. 1966. *New Horizons in Psychology*, Hammondsworth: Penguin.

41. Foster, L. and Swanson, S. W. eds. 1970. *Experience and Theory*, Amherst, Mass.: University of Massachusetts Press.

42. French, P., Uehling, T., Jr., and Wettstein, H., eds. 1979. *Midwest Studies in Philosophy* IV: *Contemporary Perspectives in the Philosophy of Language*, Minneapolis: University of Minnesota Press.

43. French, P., Uehling, T., Jr., and Wettstein, H., eds., and Feleppa, Robert, assoc. ed. 1980. *Midwest Studies in Philosophy* V: *Studies in Epistemology*, Minneapolis: University of Minnesota Press.

44. French, P., Uehling, T., Jr., and Wettstein, H., eds. 1981. *Midwest Studies in Philosophy* VI: *Analytic Philosophy*, Minneapolis: University of Minnesota Press.

45. French, P., Uehling, T., Jr., and Wettstein, H., eds. 1984. *Midwest Studies in Philosophy* IX, Minneapolis: University of Minnesota Press.

46. Garver, N. and Hare, P., eds. 1986. *Naturalism and Rationality*, Buffalo: Prometheus.

47. Giere, R. 1988. *Explaining Science: A Cognitive Approach*, Chicago: University of Chicago Press.

48. Goldman, A. H. 1988. *Empirical Knowledge*, Berkeley: University of California Press.

49. Goldman, A. I. 1986. *Epistemology and Cognition*. Cambridge, Mass.: Harvard University Press.

50. Goldman, A. I. 1992. *Liaisons: Philosophy Meets the Cognitive and Social Sciences*, Cambridge, Mass.: MIT Press. A Bradford Book.

51. Goldman, A. I. 1993. *Philosophical Applications of Cognitive Science*, Boulder: Westview.

52. Goldman, A. I. and Kim, J., eds. 1978. *Values and Morals: Essays in Honor of William Frankena, Charles Stevenson, and Richard Brandt*, Dordrecht: Reidel.

53. Goodman, N. 1955/1965. *Fact, Fiction and Forecast*, Indianapolis: Bobbs-Merrill.

54. Griffiths, M. 1988. *Feminist Perspectives in Philosophy*, Bloomington: Indiana University Press.

55. Gulber, H. et al., eds. 1957. *Contemporary Approaches to Cognition*, Cambridge, Mass.: Harvard University Press.

56. Guttenplan, S., ed. 1975. *Mind and Language*, Oxford: Clarendon Press.

57. Hahlweg, K. 1989. *Issues in Evolutionary Epistemology*, Albany: SUNY Press.

58. Hanson, N. R. 1958. *Patterns of Discovery*, London: Cambridge University Press.

59. Harman, G. 1973. *Thought*, Princeton: Princeton University Press.

60. Harman, G. 1986. *Change in View: Principles of Reasoned Revision*, Cambridge, Mass.: MIT Press. A Bradford Book.

61. Hatfield, G. 1991. *The Natural and the Normative: Theories of Spatial Perception from Kant to Helmholtz*, Cambridge, Mass.: MIT Press. A Bradford Book.

62. Heil, J. forthcoming. *Rationality, Morality, and Self-Interest*, Savage, Md.: Rowman and Littlefield.

63. Hoffman, R. R. and Palermo, D. S., eds. 1992. *Cognition and the Symbolic Processes: Applied and Ecological Perspectives*, Hillsdale, N.J.: Lawrence Erlbaum Associates.

64. Holland, J., Holyoak, K., Nisbett, R., and Thagard, P. 1986. *Induction: Processes of Inference, Learning, and Discovery*, Cambridge: MIT Press.

65. Hookway, C., ed. 1984. *Minds, Machines and Evolution*, Cambridge: Cambridge University Press.

66. Hronszky, I., Feher, M., and Dajka, B. 1984. *Scientific Knowledge Socialized*. Dordrecht: Kluwer.

67. Johnson-Laird, Philip N. 1983. *Mental Models*, Cambridge: Cambridge University Press.

68. Kahneman, D., Slovic, P., and Tversky, A. 1982. *Judgment under Uncertainty: Heuristics and Biases*, Cambridge: Cambridge University Press.

69. Kalechofsky, R. 1987. *The Persistence of Error: Essays in Developmental Epistemology*, Lanham, Md.: University Press of America.

70. Kitcher, P. 1983. *The Nature of Mathematical Knowledge*, New York: Oxford University Press.

71. Kitcher, P. 1993. *The Advancement of Science*, Oxford: Oxford University Press.

72. Kleinmuntz, B., ed. 1968. *Formal Representation of Human Judgment*, New York: Wiley.

73. Kornblith, H. ed. 1985. *Naturalizing Epistemology*, 1st ed., Cambridge, Mass.: MIT Press. A Bradford Book.

74. Kornblith, H. 1993. *Inductive Inference and Its Natural Ground: An Essay in Naturalistic Epistemology*, Cambridge, Mass.: MIT Press. A Bradford Book.

75. Kuhn, T. 1962. *The Structure of Scientific Revolutions*. Chicago: University of Chicago Press.

76. Kvanvig, J. L. 1991. *The Intellectual Virtues and the Life of the Mind: On the Place of the Virtues in Contemporary Epistemology*, Savage, Md.: Rowman and Littlefield.

77. Lehrer, K. 1974. *Knowledge*, Oxford: Oxford University Press.

78. Lehrer, K. 1990. *Theory of Knowledge*, Boulder: Westview.

79. LePore, E., ed. 1986. *Truth and Interpretation*, Oxford: Basil Blackwell.

80. Luper-Foy, S. 1987. *The Possibility of Knowledge*, Totowa, N.J.: Rowman and Littlefield.

81. Lycan, W. 1988. *Judgement and Justification*, Cambridge: Cambridge University Press.

82. McDowell, J. and Pettit, P., eds. 1986. *Subject, Thought and Context*, Oxford: Oxford University Press.

83. McLaughlin, B. 1991. *Dretske and His Critics*, Oxford: Blackwell.

84. Mellor, D. H., ed. 1980. *Prospects for Pragmatism: Essays in Honor of F. P. Ramsey*, New York: Cambridge University Press.

85. Midgley, M. 1991. *Wisdom, Information and Wonder: What Is Knowledge For?*, Oxford: Oxford University Press.

86. Mischel, T. 1971. *Cognitive Development and Epistemology.* New York: Academic Press.

87. Morton, A. 1977. *A Guide Through the Theory of Knowledge*, Encino, Calif.: Dickerson.

88. Nelson, L. H. 1990. *Who Knows: From Quine to a Feminist Empiricism*, Philadelphia: Temple University Press.

89. Nisbett, R. and Ross, L. 1980. *Human Inference: Strategies and Shortcomings of Social Judgment*, Englewood Cliffs, N.J.: Prentice-Hall.

90. Nozick, R. 1981. *Philosophical Explanations*, Cambridge, Mass.: Harvard University Press.

91. O'Connor, D. J. and Carr, B. 1982. *Introduction to the Theory of Knowledge*, Minneapolis: University of Minnesota Press.

92. Pappas, G. S., ed. 1979. *Justification and Knowledge: New Studies in Epistemology*, Dordrecht: Reidel.

93. Pappas, G. S. and Swain, M., eds. 1978. *Essays on Knowledge and Justification*, Ithaca: Cornell University Press.

94. Piaget, J. 1970. *Genetic Epistemology*, trans. E. Duckworth, New York: Columbia University Press.

95. Piaget, J. 1972. *The Principles of Genetic Epistemology*, trans. W. Mays, New York: Basic Books.

96. Plantinga, A. 1992. *Warrant: The Current Debate*, Oxford: Oxford University Press.

97. Plantinga, A. 1992. *Warrant and Proper Function*, Oxford: Oxford University Press.

98. Pollock, J. 1986. *Contemporary Theories of Knowledge*, Totowa, N.J.: Rowman and Littlefield.

99. Quine, W. V. 1953. *From a Logical Point of View*, Cambridge, Mass.: Harvard University Press.

100. Quine, W. V. 1960. *Word and Object*, Cambridge, Mass.: MIT Press.

101. Quine, W. V. 1969. *Ontological Relativity and Other Essays*, New York: Columbia University Press.

102. Quine, W. V. 1970. *Philosophy of Logic*, Englewood Cliffs, N.J.: Prentice-Hall.

103. Quine, W. V. 1973. *The Roots of Reference*, LaSalle, IL.: Open Court.

104. Quine, W. V. 1976. *The Ways of Paradox and Other Essays*, Cambridge, Mass.: Harvard University Press.

105. Quine, W. V. 1981. *Theories and Things,* Cambridge, Mass.: Harvard University Press.

106. Quine, W. V. and Ullian, J. S. 1978. *The Web of Belief,* 2nd ed., New York: Random House.

107. Radnitzky, G. and Bartley, W. W. III, eds. 1987. *Evolutionary Epistemology, Theory of Rationality and the Sociology of Knowledge,* LaSalle, Ill.: Open Court.

108. Rescher, N. 1977. *Methodological Pragmatism,* New York: New York University Press.

109. Rescher, N. 1980. *Induction,* Oxford: Basil Blackwell.

110. Rescher, N. 1985. *Reason and Rationality in Natural Science,* Lanham, Md.: University Press of America.

111. Rescher, N., ed. 1990. *Evolution, Cognition and Realism,* Lanham, Md.: University Press of America.

112. Rescher, N. 1990. *A Useful Inheritance: Evolutionary Aspects of the Theory of Knowledge,* Savage, Md.: Rowman and Littlefield.

113. Ringle, M. 1979. *Philosophical Perspectives in Artificial Intelligence,* New York: Humanities Press.

114. Rorty, R. 1979. *Philosophy and the Mirror of Nature,* Princeton: Princeton University Press.

115. Ross, G. and Roth, M. 1990. *Doubting: Contemporary Perspectives on Skepticism,* Lancaster, Pa.: Franklin and Marshall.

116. Savage, C. W., ed. 1978. *Minnesota Studies in the Philosophy of Science IX: Perception and Cognition: Issues in the Foundations of Psychology,* Minneapolis: University of Minnesota.

117. Sayre, K. 1976. *Cybernetics and the Philosophy of Mind,* New York: Humanities Press.

118. Schilpp, P., ed. 1974. *The Philosophy of Karl Popper,* LaSalle, Ill.: Open Court.

119. Schmitt, F. F. 1992. *Knowledge and Belief,* London: Routledge.

120. Schmitt, F. F., ed. forthcoming. *Socializing Epistemology,* Savage, Md.: Rowman and Littlefield.

121. Sieg, W., ed. 1990. *Acting and Reflecting: The Interdisciplinary Turn in Philosophy,* Norwell, Mass.: Kluwer.

122. Sellars, W. 1963. *Science, Perception and Reality,* New York: Humanities.

123. Shimony, A. and Nails, D. eds. 1987. *Naturalistic Epistemology: A Symposium of Two Decades,* Dordrecht: Reidel. Collection.

124. Shope, R. K. 1983. *The Analysis of Knowing: A Decade of Research,* Princeton: Princeton University Press.

125. Sosa, E. 1991. *Knowledge in Perspective,* Cambridge: Cambridge University Press.

126. Stemmer, N. 1984. *The Roots of Knowledge,* New York: St. Martin's Press.

127. Stich, S. P., ed. 1975. *Innate Ideas,* Berkeley: University of California Press.

128. Stich, S. P. 1990. *The Fragmentation of Reason,* Cambridge, Mass.: MIT Press. A Bradford Book.

129. Strawson, P. F. 1985. *Skepticism and Naturalism: Some Varieties,* New York: Columbia University Press.

130. Stroud, B. 1984. *The Significance of Philosophical Scepticism,* Oxford: Oxford University Press.

131. Swain, M. 1981. *Reasons and Knowledge,* Ithaca: Cornell University Press.

132. Swartz, R., ed. 1965. *Perceiving, Sensing and Knowing,* Berkeley: University of California Press.

133. Talbott, W. 1990. *The Reliability of the Cognitive Mechanism: A Mechanist Account of Empirical Justification,* New York: Garland.

134. Thagard, P. 1988. *Computational Philosophy of Science,* Cambridge, Mass.: MIT Press. A Bradford Book.

135. Tomberlin, J., ed. 1988. *Philosophical Perspectives* 2, Atascadero, Calif.: Ridgeview.

136. Villanueva, E. 1990. *Information, Semantics and Epistemology.* Oxford: Basil Blackwell.

137. Vuyk, R. 1981. *Overview and Critique of Piaget's Genetic Epistemology 1965–1980,* 2 vols, New York: Academic Press.

138. Wagner, S. J. and Warner, R., eds. 1992. *Naturalism: A Critical Reappraisal,* South Bend: Notre Dame Press.

139. Wason, P. C. and Johnson-Laird, P. N. 1972. *The Psychology of Reasoning: Structure and Content,* London: Batsford.

140. Will, F. L. 1974. *Induction and Justification,* Ithaca: Cornell University Press.

141. Will, F. L. 1988. *Beyond Deduction: Ampliative Aspects of Philosophical Reflection,* London: Routledge.

142. Williams, M. 1977. *Groundless Belief,* New Haven: Yale University Press.

143. Williams, M. 1992. *Unnatural Doubts: Epistemological Realism and the Basis of Scepticism,* Cambridge: Blackwell.

144. Wuketits, F., ed. *Concepts and Approaches in Evolutionary Epistemology,* Dordrecht, Reidel.

Articles, by Topic

Epistemology and Cognitive Science

Replacing Epistemology with Cognitive Science

145. Almeder, R. 1990. "On Naturalizing Epistemology," *American Philosophical Quarterly*, 27, 263–279.

146. Amundson, R. 1983. "The Epistemological Status of a Naturalized Epistemology," *Inquiry*, 26, 33–344.

147. Bieri, P. 1987. "Naturalisierte Erkenntnistheorie." In Bieri 1987 [8].

148. Churchland, P. S. 1987. "Epistemology in the Age of Neuroscience," *Journal of Philosophy*, 84, 544–553.

149. Duran, J. 1984. "Descriptive Epistemology," *Metaphilosophy*, 15, 185–195.

150. Gibson, R. 1987. "Quine on Naturalism and Epistemology," *Erkenntnis*, 27, 57–78.

151. Gibson, R. 1989. "Stroud on Naturalized Epistemology," *Metaphilosophy*, 20, 1–11.

152. Kim, J. 1988. "What is Naturalized Epistemology?" In this anthology.

153. Koppelberg, D. 1990. "Why and How To Naturalize Epistemology." In Barrett 1990 [6].

154. Kornblith, H. 1985. "What is Naturalistic Epistemology?" In Kornblith 1985 [73].

155. Lauener, H. 1990. "Holism and Naturalized Epistemology Confronted with the Problem of Truth." In Barrett 1990 [6].

156. McCauley, R. 1988. "Epistemology in an Age of Cognitive Science," *Philosophical Psychology*, 1, 147–149.

157. O'Gorman, A. 1984. "Quine's Epistemological Naturalism," *Philosophical Studies*, 30, 205–219.

158. Parsons, C. 1990. "Genetic Explanation in *The Roots of Reference*." In Barrett 1990 [6].

159. Peirce, C. S. 1955. "The Fixation of Belief." In Justus Buchler 1955 [16].

160. Putnam, H. 1982. "Why Reason Cannot Be Naturalized," *Synthese*, 52, 3–23.

161. Quine, W. V. 1953. "Two Dogmas of Empiricism." In Quine 1953 [99].

162. Quine, W. V. 1969. "Epistemology Naturalized." In this anthology.

163. Quine, W. V. 1969. "Natural Kinds." In this anthology.

164. Quine, W. V. 1970. "Grades of Theoreticity." In Foster and Swanson 1970 [41].

165. Quine, W. V. 1975. "The Nature of Natural Knowledge." In Guttenplan 1975 [56].

166. Quine, W. V. 1976. "The Limits of Knowledge." In Quine 1976 [104].

167. Quine, W. V. 1981. "Reply to Stroud." In French et al. 1981 [44].

168. Ricketts, T. G. 1982. "Rationality, Translation, and Epistemology Naturalized," *The Journal of Philosophy* 79, 117–136.

169. Roth, P. 1983. "Siegel on Naturalized Epistemology and Natural Science," *Philosophy of Science*, 50, 482–493.

170. Sagal, P. 1987. "Naturalistic Epistemology and the Harakiri of Philosophy." In Shimony and Nails 1987 [123].

171. Shatz, D. 1992. "Remarks on Naturalism." In Wagner and Warner 1992 [138].

172. Sheehan, P. 1973. "Quine on Revision: A Critique," *Australasian Journal of Philosophy*, 51, 95–104.

173. Siegel, H. 1980. "Justification, Discovery, and the Naturalizing of Epistemology," *Philosophy of Science*, 47, 297–321.

174. Siegel, H. forthcoming. "Empirical Psychology, Naturalized Epistemology, and First Philosophy," *Philosophy of Science*.

175. Solomon, M. 1989. "Quine's Point of View," *Journal of Philosophy*, 86, 113–136.

176. Sosa, E. 1983. "Nature Unmirrored, Epistemology Naturalized." In Sosa 1991 [125].

177. Stroud, B. 1979. "The Significance of Scepticism." In Bieri et al. 1979 [9].

178. Varela, F. 1986. "Experimental Epistemology: Background and Future," *Eidos*, 5, 143–161.

The Relevance of Cognitive Science to Epistemology

179. Adler, J. 1989. "Epistemics and the Total Evidence Requirement," *Philosophia*, 19, 227–243.

180. Annis, D. 1982. "Epistemology Naturalized," *Metaphilosophy*, 13, 201–208.

181. Antony, L. 1987. "Naturalistic Epistemology and the Study of Language." In Shimony and Nails 1987 [123].

182. Antony, L. 1992. "Quine as a Feminist: The Radical Import of Naturalized Epistemology." In Antony and Witt 1992 [2].

183. Boden, M. 1990. "Interdisciplinary Epistemology," *Synthese*, 85, 185–197.

184. Brown, H. 1988. "Normative Epistemology and Naturalized Epistemology," *Inquiry*, 31, 53–78.

185. Brown, H. 1991. "Epistemic Concepts: A Naturalistic Approach," *Inquiry*, 34, 323–351.

186. Campbell, D. 1959. "Methodological Suggestions from a Comparative Psychology of Knowledge Processes," *Inquiry*, 2, 152–182.

187. Campbell, D. 1987. "Neurological Embodiments of Belief and the Gaps in the Fit of Phenomena to Noumena." In Shimony and Nails 1987 [123].

188. Cherniak, C. 1981. "Minimal Rationality," *Mind*, 90, 161–183.

189. Cherniak, C. 1986. "Limits for Knowledge," *Philosophical Studies*, 49, 1–18.

190. Cohen, L. J. 1981. "Can Human Irrationality Be Experimentally Demonstrated?" *The Behavioral and Brain Sciences*, 4, 317–331. Open Peer Commentary, 4, 331–359. Author's Response: "Are There Any A Priori Constraints on the Study of Rationality?" 4, 359–367. Continuing Commentary, 6, 487–510. Author's Response: "The Controversy about Rationality," 6, 510–515.

191. Conee, E. and Feldman, R. 1983. "Stich and Nisbett on Justifying Inference Rules," *Philosophy of Science*, 50, 326–331.

192. Corlett, J. A. 1991. "Some Connections between Epistemology and Cognitive Psychology," *New Ideas in Psychology*, 9, 285–306.

193. Dascal, M. 1986. "Artificial Intelligence as Epistemology?" In Villanueva 1990 [136].

194. Doppelt, G. 1990. "The Naturalist Conception of Methodological Standards in Science," *Philosophy of Science*, 57, 1–19.

195. Duran, J. 1988. "Reductionism and the Naturalization of Epistemology," *Dialectica*, 42, 295–306.

196. Feldman, R. 1989. "Goldman on Epistemology and Cognitive Science," *Philosophia*, 19, 197–207.

197. Flew, A. 1987. "Must Naturalism Discredit Naturalism?" In Radnitzky and Bartley 1987 [107].

198. Fodor, J. 1984. "Observation Reconsidered," *Philosophy of Science*, 51, 23–42.

199. Fuller, S. 1991. "Naturalized Epistemology Sublimated: Rapprochement without the Ruts," *Studies in the History and Philosophy of Science*, 22, 277–293.

200. Giere, R. N. 1985. "Philosophy of Science Naturalized," *Philosophy of Science*, 52, 331–56.

201. Goldman, A. H. 1981. "Epistemology and the Psychology of Perception," *American Philosophical Quarterly*, 18, 43–51.

202. Goldman, A. H. 1982. "Epistemic Foundationalism and the Replaceability of Ordinary Language," *The Journal of Philosophy* 79, 136–154.

203. Goldman, A. I. 1978. "Epistemics: The Regulative Theory of Cognition," *Journal of Philosophy*, 75, 509–523.

204. Goldman, A. I. 1978. "Epistemology and the Psychology of Belief," *Monist*, 61, 525–535.

205. Goldman, A. I. 1979. "Varieties of Cognitive Appraisal," *Nous* 13, 23–38.

206. Goldman, A. I. 1983. "Epistemology and the Theory of Problem Solving," *Synthese*, 55, 21–48.

207. Goldman, A. I. 1985. "The Relation between Epistemology and Psychology," *Synthese*, 64, 29–68.

208. Goldman, A. I. 1986. "Epistemology and the New Connectionism." In Garver and Hare 1986 [46].

209. Goldman, A. I. 1992b. "Epistemic Folkways and Scientific Epistemology." In Goldman 1992 [50].

210. Greif, G. 1987. "Piaget's Genetic Epistemology and the Problem of Truth," *Dialogue*, 26, 501–512.

211. Haack, S. 1975. "The Relevance of Psychology to Epistemology," *Metaphilosophy*, 6, 161–176.

212. Halstead, R. 1979. "The Relevance of Psychology to Educational Epistemology," *Philosophy of Education 1979*, 65–76.

213. Hoffman, R. and Nead, J. 1983. "General Contextualism, Ecological Science and Cognitive Research," *Journal of Mind and Behavior*, 4, 507–560.

214. Kelly, K. 1990. "Effective Epistemology, Psychology, and Artificial Intelligence." In Sieg 1990 [121].

215. Ketchum, R. 1991. "The Paradox of Epistemology: A Defense of Naturalism," *Philosophical Studies*, 62, 45–66.

216. Kitchener, R. F. 1980. "Genetic Epistemology, Normative Epistemology, and Psychologism," *Synthese*, 45, 257–280.

217. Kitcher, P. 1992. "The Naturalists Return," *Philosophical Review*, 101, 53–114.

218. Kornblith, H. 1982. "The Psychological Turn," *Australasian Journal of Philosophy*, 60, 230–253.

219. Kornblith, H. 1993. "Epistemic Normativity," *Synthese*, 94, 357–376.

220. Kosso, P. 1991. "Empirical Epistemology and Philosophy of Science," *Metaphilosophy*, 22, 349–363.

221. Laudan, L. 1987. "Progress or Rationality? The Prospects for Normative Naturalism," *American Philosophical Quarterly*, 24, 19–31.

222. Laudan, L. 1987. "Relativism, Naturalism, and Reticulation," *Synthese*, 71, 221–34.

223. Laudan, L. 1990. "Normative Naturalism," *Philosophy of Science*, 57, 44–59.

224. Levine, J. 1987. "Quine on Psychology." In Shimony and Nails 1987 [123].

225. Levine, M. 1989. "Alvin I. Goldman's *Epistemology and Cognition:* An Introduction," *Philosophia*, 19, 209–225.

226. Loptson, P. and Kelly, J. 1984. "Genetic Epistemology and Philosophical Epistemology," *Philosophy of the Social Sciences*, 14, 377–384.

227. McGinn, C. 1986. "Radical Interpretation and Epistemology." In LePore 1986 [79].

228. Maffie, J. 1990. "Recent Work on Naturalized Epistemology," *American Philosophical Quarterly*, 27, 281–293.

229. Maffie, J. 1990. "Naturalism and the Normativity of Epistemology," *Philosophical Studies*, 59, 333–349.

230. Maffie, J. forthcoming. "Naturalism and the Unity of Science and Epistemology."

231. Maffie, J. forthcoming. "Realism, Constructivism, and the Roots of Epistemology."

232. Meyers, R. 1986. "Naturalizing Epistemic Terms." In Garver and Hare 1986 [46].

233. Montgomery, R. 1989. "Does Epistemology Reduce to Cognitive Psychology?" *Philosophia*, 19, 245–263.

234. Page, R. 1979. "Epistemology, Psychology, and Two Views of Indoctrination," *Philosophy of Education 1979*, 77–86.

235. Reed, E. S. 1987. "Why Ideas Are Not in the Mind: An Introduction to Ecological Epistemology." In Shimony and Nails 1987 [123].

236. Rosenberg, A. 1990. "Normative Naturalism and the Role of Philosophy," *Philosophy of Science*, 57, 34–43.

237. Schmitt, F. F. 1991. "How Is Psychology Relevant to Epistemology?" *New Ideas in Psychology*, 9, 315–320.

238. Shames, M. 1991. "On the Transdisciplinary Nature of the Epistemology of Discovery," *Zygon*, 26, 343–357.

239. Siegel, H. 1979. "Can Psychology be Relevant to Epistemology?" *Philosophy of Education 1979*, 55–64.

240. Siegel, H. 1983. "Psychology, Epistemology, and Critical Thinking," *Proceedings of the 39th Annual Meeting of the Philosophy of Education Association*, 197–200.

241. Siegel, H. 1989. "Philosophy of Science Naturalized? Some Problems with Giere's Naturalism," *Studies in History and Philosophy of Science*, 20, 365–375.

242. Siegel, H. 1990. "Laudan's Normative Naturalism," *Studies in History and Philosophy of Science,* 21, 295–313.

243. Siegel, H. 1993. "Naturalized Philosophy of Science and Natural Science Education," *Science and Education,* 2.

244. Siegel, H. forthcoming. "Naturalism, Instrumental Rationality, and the Normativity of Epistemology."

245. Smokler, H. 1990. "Are Theories of Rationality Empirically Testable?" *Synthese,* 82, 297–306.

246. Sober, E. 1978. "Psychologism," *Journal for the Theory of Social Behavior,* 8, 165–191.

247. Solomon, M. 1992. "Scientific Rationality and Human Reasoning," *Philosophy of Science,* 439–455.

248. Stich, S. 1984. "Relativism, Rationality, and the Limits of Intentional Description," *Pacific Philosophical Quarterly,* 65, 211–235.

249. Stich, S. and Nisbett, R. 1980. "Justification and the Psychology of Human Reasoning," *Philosophy of Science,* 47, 188–202.

250. Tennant, N. 1983. "In Defense of Evolutionary Epistemology," *Theoria,* 49, 32–48.

251. Thagard, P. and Nisbett, R. 1983. "Rationality and Charity," *Philosophy of Science,* 50, 250–267.

252. van Fraassen, B. forthcoming. "Against Naturalistic Epistemology," manuscript.

253. Vollmer, G. 1987. "On Supposed Circularities in an Empirically Oriented Epistemology." In Radnitzky and Bartley 1987 [107].

The Relevance of Epistemology to Psychology

254. Davidson, D. 1980. "Psychology as Philosophy." In Davidson 1980 [29].

255. Harman, G. 1976. "Inferential Justification," *The Journal of Philosophy,* 73, 570–571.

256. Harman, G. 1978. "Using Intuitions about Reasoning to Study Reasoning: A Reply to Williams," *The Journal of Philosophy,* 75, 433–438.

257. Harman, G. 1980. "Reasoning and Evidence One Does Not Possess." In French et al. 1980 [43].

258. Heil, J. 1986. "Does Psychology Presuppose Rationality?" *Journal for the Theory of Social Behavior,* 16, 77–87.

259. Lycan, W. G. 1977. "Evidence One Does Not Possess," *Australasian Journal of Philosophy,* 55, 114–126.

260. Williams, M. 1978. "Inference, Justification and the Analysis of Knowledge," *The Journal of Philosophy,* 75, 249–263.

Knowledge

Causal Theories

261. Barker, J. 1972. "Knowledge and Causation," *Southern Journal of Philosophy*, 10, 313–321.

262. Carrier, L. S. 1976. "The Causal Theory of Knowledge," *Philosophia*, 6, 237–258.

263. Coder, D. 1974. "Naturalizing the Gettier Argument," *Philosophical Studies*, 26, 111–118.

264. Collier, K. 1974. "Contra the Causal Theory of Knowing," *Philosophical Studies*, 24, 350–351.

265. Dretske, F. and Enc, B. 1984. "Causal Theories of Knowledge." In French et al. 1984 [45].

266. Goldman, A. I. 1967. "A Causal Theory of Knowing," *Journal of Philosophy*, 64, 357–372.

267. Goldstick, D. 1972. "A Contribution Towards the Development of the Causal Theory of Knowledge," *Australasian Journal of Philosophy*, 50, 238–248.

268. Hanson, P. 1978. "Prospects for a Causal Theory of Knowledge," *Canadian Journal of Philosophy*, 8, 457–474.

269. Harman, G. 1970. "Knowledge, Reasons, and Causes, *The Journal of Philosophy*, 67, 841–855.

270. Klein, P. D. 1976. "Knowledge, Causality and Defeasibility," *The Journal of Philosophy* 73, 792–812.

271. Lehrer, K. 1971. "How Reasons Give Us Knowledge, or the Case of the Gypsy Lawyer," *The Journal of Philosophy*, 68, 311–313.

272. Loeb, L. 1974. "On a Heady Attempt to Befiend Causal Theories of Knowledge," *Philosophical Studies*, 29, 331–336.

273. Luper-Foy, S. 1987. "The Causal Indicator Analysis of Knowledge," *Philosophy and Phenomenological Research*, 47, 563–587.

274. Skyrms, B. 1967. "The Explication of 'X Knows That p'," *The Journal of Philosophy*, 64, 373–389.

275. Swain, M. 1972. "Knowledge, Causality and Justification," *The Journal of Philosophy*, 69, 291–300.

276. Swain, M. 1978. "Reasons, Causes, and Knowledge," *The Journal of Philosophy*, 75, 229–248.

277. Swain, M. 1978. "Some Revisions of Knowledge, Causality and Justification." In Pappas and Swain 1978 [93].

Nonaccidentality Theories

278. Engel, M. 1992. "Is Epistemic Luck Compatible with Knowledge?" *Southern Journal of Philosophy*, 30, 59–75.

279. Ravitch, H. 1976. "Knowledge and the Principle of Luck," *Philosophical Studies*, 30, 347–349.

280. Unger, P. 1968. "An Analysis of Factual Knowledge," *The Journal of Philosophy*, 65, 157–170.

Nomic Regularity Theories

281. Adams, F. and Kline, D. 1987. "Nomic Reliabilism: Weak Reliability Is Not Enough," *Southern Journal of Philosophy*, 25, 433–443.

282. Lycan, W. G. 1984. "Armstrong's Theory of Knowing." In Bogdan 1984 [11].

283. Olen, J. 1977. "Knowledge, Probability and Nomic Connections," *Southern Journal of Philosophy*, 15, 521–526.

Counterfactual Dependency Theories

284. Clarke, D. S. 1990. "Two Uses of 'Know'," *Analysis*, 50, 188–190.

285. Clarke, D. S. 1991. "Knowledge, Information Exchange, and Responsibility," *Southern Journal of Philosophy*, 29, 445–463.

286. Dretske, F. I. 1970. "Epistemic Operators," *The Journal of Philosophy*, 67, 1007–1023.

287. Dretske, F. I. 1971. "Conclusive Reasons," *Australasian Journal of Philosophy*, 49, 1–22.

288. Dretske, F. I. 1981. "The Pragmatic Dimension of Knowledge," *Philosophical Studies*, 40, 363–378.

289. Luper-Foy, S. 1984. "The Epistemic Predicament: Knowledge, Nozickian Tracking, and Scepticism," *Australasian Journal of Philosophy*, 62, 26–49.

290. McGinn, C. 1984. "The Concept of Knowledge." In French et al. 1984.[45].

291. Shatz, D. 1981. "Reliability and Relevant Alternatives," *Philosophical Studies*, 39, 393–408.

292. Yourgrau, P. 1983. "Knowledge and Relevant Alternatives," *Synthese*, 55, 175–190.

Reliability Theories

293. Audi, R. 1980. "Defeated Knowledge, Reliability, and Justification." In French et al. 1980 [43].

294. BonJour, L. 1980. "Externalist Theories of Empirical Knowledge." In French et al. 1980 [43].

295. Dretske, F. 1991. "Two Conceptions of Knowledge: Rational vs. Reliable Belief," *Grazer Philosophische Studien*, 40, 15–30.

296. Elgin, C. 1988. "The Epistemic Efficacy of Stupidity," *Synthese*, 74, 297–311.

297. Grandy, R. E. 1980. "Ramsey, Reliability, and Knowledge." In Mellor 1980 [84].

298. Schmitt, F. F. 1983. "Knowledge, Justification, and Reliability," *Synthese*, 55, 209–229.

299. Sosa, E. 1991. "Knowledge and Intellectual Virtue." In Sosa 1991 [125].

300. White, J. L. 1989. "Externalist Epistemologies, Reliability, and the Context Relativity of Knowledge," *Southern Journal of Philosophy*, 27, 459–472.

Informational Theories

301. Dretske, F. I. 1980. "The Intentionality of Cognitive States." In French et al. 1980 [43].

302. Dretske, F. I. 1983. "The Epistemology of Belief," *Synthese*, 55, 3–19.

303. Dretske, F. I. 1983. "Precis of *Knowledge and the Flow of Information*." In this anthology. Open Peer Commentary, *Behavioral and Brain Sciences*, 6, 63–82. Author's Response: "Why Information?" 6, 82–89.

304. Dretske, F. I. 1985. "Misrepresentation." In Bogdan 1985 [12].

305. Foley, R. 1987. "Dretske's 'Information-Theoretic' Account of Knowledge," *Synthese*, 70, 159–184.

306. Gjelsvik, O. 1991. "Dretske on Knowledge and Content," *Synthese*, 86, 425–441.

307. Grandy, R. 1987. "Information-Based Epistemology, Ecological Epistemology and Epistemology Naturalized," *Synthese*, 70, 191–203.

308. Maloney, J. C. 1985. "Dretske on Knowledge and Information," *Analysis*, 43, 25–28.

309. Morillo, C. R. 1984. "Epistemic Luck, Naturalistic Epistemology and the Ecology of Knowledge: On What the Frog Should Have Told Dretske," *Philosophical Studies*, 46, 109–130.

310. Morris, W. E. 1990. "Knowledge and the Regularity Theory of Information," *Synthese*, 82, 375–398.

311. Sanford, D. 1991. "Proper Knowledge." In McLaughlin 1991 [83].

312. Savitt, S. 1987. "Absolute Informational Content," *Synthese*, 70, 185–190.

313. Sayre, K. 1979. "The Simulation of Epistemic Acts." In Ringle 1979 [113].

314. Yourgrau, P. 1987. "Information Retrieval and Cognitive Accessibility," *Synthese*, 70. 229–246.

Proper Function Theories

315. Feldman, R. 1993. "Proper Functionalism," *Nous*, 27, 34–50.

316. Millikan, R. G. 1984. "Naturalist Reflections on Knowledge," *Pacific Philosophical Quarterly*, 65, 315–334.

317. Plantinga, A. 1988. "Positive Epistemic Status and Proper Function." In Tomberlin 1988 [135].

Skepticism and Naturalistic Theories of Knowledge

318. Bell, M. and McGinn, M. 1990. "Naturalism and Scepticism," *Philosophy*, 65, 399–418.

319. Bogen, J. 1985. "Traditional Epistemology and Naturalistic Replies to Its Skeptical Critics," *Synthese*, 64, 195–224.

320. Boyd, R. 1980. "Scientific Realism and Naturalized Epistemology." In Asquith and Giere 1982 [4].

321. Burge, T. 1986. "Cartesian Error and the Objectivity of Perception." In McDowell and Pettit 1986 [82].

322. Cohen, S. 1991. "Skepticism, Relevance, and Relativity." In McLaughlin 1991 [83].

323. deVries, W. 1990. "Burgeoning Skepticism," *Erkenntnis*, 33, 141–164.

324. Fumerton, R. 1990. "Metaepistemology and Skepticism." In Ross and Roth 1990 [115].

325. Hetherington, S. C. 1992. "Nozick and Sceptical Realism," *Philosophical Papers*, 21, 33–44.

326. Lammenranta, M. 1992. "Scepticism and Goldman's Naturalism," *Ratio*, 5, 38–45.

327. Luper-Foy, S. 1987. "The Possibility of Scepticism." In Luper-Foy 1987 [80].

328. Schreck, P. 1989. "Cartesian Scepticism and Relevant Alternatives," *Eidos*, 8, 125–137.

329. Sosa, E. 1988. "Beyond Scepticism, to the Best of Our Knowledge," *Mind*, 97, 153–188.

330. Sosa, E. 1989. "The Skeptic's Appeal." In Clay and Lehrer 1989 [25].

331. Stine, G. 1976. "Skepticism, Relevant Alternatives and Deductive Closure," *Philosophical Studies*, 29, 249–260.

332. Stroud, B. 1989. "Understanding Human Knowledge in General." In Clay and Lehrer 1989 [25].

333. Van Cleve, J. 1984. "Reliability, Justification, and the Problem of Induction." In French et al. 1984 [45].

334. Winblad, D. 1989. "Skepticism and Naturalized Epistemology," *Philosophia*, 19, 99–113.

335. Woods, M. 1980. "Scepticism and Natural Knowledge," *Proceedings of the Aristotelian Society*, 80, 231–248.

Perceptual Knowledge

336. Alston, W. 1990. "Externalist Theories of Perception," *Philosophy and Phenomenological Research*, 50 supp., 73–97.

337. Dretske, F. I. 1978. "The Role of the Percept in Visual Cognition." In Savage 1978 [116].

338. Fodor, J. 1984. "Observation Reconsidered," *Philosophy of Science*, 51, 23–43.

339. Goldman, A. I. 1976. "Discrimination and Perceptual Knowledge," *Journal of Philosophy*, 73, 771–791.

340. Goldman, A. I. 1977. "Perceptual Objects," *Synthese*, 35, 257–284.

341. Grice, H. P. 1965. "The Causal Theory of Perception." In Swartz 1965 [132].

342. Heffner, J. 1987. "Causal Relations in Visual Perception." In Shimony and Nails 1987 [123].

343. Kim, J. 1977. "Perception and Reference Without Causality," *The Journal of Philosophy*, 74, 606–620.

344. Pears, D. F. 1976. "The Causal Conditions of Perception," *Synthese*, 33, 25–40.

345. Robinson, W. 1982. "Causation, Sensations and Knowledge," *Mind*, 91, 524–540.

346. Siegfried, H. 1988. "Against Naturalizing Preconceptual Experience," *Philosophy and Phenomenological Research*, 48, 505–518.

Introspective Knowledge

347. Alston, W. P. 1971. "Varieties of Privileged Access." *American Philosophical Quarterly* 8, 223–241.

348. Burge, T. 1988. "Individualism and Self-Knowledge," *Journal of Philosophy*, 85, 649–663.

349. Byrne, R. 1983. "Protocol Analysis in Problem Solving." In Evans 1983 [35].

350. Davidson, D. 1984. "First Person Authority," *Dialectica*, 38, 101–112.

351. Ericson, K. A., and Simon, H. A. 1980. "Verbal Reports as Data." *Psychological Review*, 87, 215–251.

352. Johnson-Laird, P. N., and Wason, P. C. 1970. "A Theoretical Analysis of Insight into a Reasoning Task" and "Postscript- 1977." In Wason and Johnson-Laird 1972 [139].

353. Kornblith, H. 1989. "Introspection and Misdirection," *Australasian Journal of Philosophy*, 67, 410–422.

354. Nisbett, R. E. and Wilson, T. D. 1977. "Telling More Than We Can Know: Verbal Reports on Mental Processes." *Psychological Review* 84, 231–259.

355. Wilson, T. D. and Nisbett, R. E. 1978. "The Accuracy of Verbal Reports about the Effects of Stimuli on Evaluations and Behavior," *Social Psychology*, 41, 118–131.

Inferential Knowledge

356. Bogdan, R. 1985. "Cognition and Epistemic Closure," *American Philosophical Quarterly*, 22, 55–64.

357. Goldman, A. I. 1973. "Discrimination and Inferential Knowledge," unpublished manuscript.

358. Thagard, P. 1984. "Frames, Knowledge, and Inference," *Synthese*, 61, 233–259.

359. Warfield, T. 1991. "Deductive Closure and Relevant Alternatives," *Southwestern Philosophical Studies*, 13, 104–116.

360. White, J. 1991. "Knowledge and Deductive Closure," *Synthese*, 86, 409–423.

Memory Knowledge

361. Cherniak, C. 1983. "Rationality and the Structure of Human Memory," *Synthese*, 57, 163–186.

362. Dretske, F. I. and Yourgrau, P. 1983. "Lost Knowledge," *Journal of Philosophy*, 80, 356–367.

363. Martin, C. B. and Deutscher, Max. 1966. "Remembering," *Philosophical Review*, 75, 161–196.

364. Pappas, G. 1987. "Suddenly He Knows." In Luper-Foy 1987 [80].

Innate Knowledge

365. Goldman, A. I. 1975. "Innate Knowledge." In Stich 1975 [127].

A Priori Knowledge

366. Casullo, A. 1988. "Revisability, Reliabilism, and A Priori Knowledge," *Philosophy and Phenomenological Research*, 49, 187–213.

367. Kitcher, P. 1980. "A Priori Knowledge." In this anthology.

368. Quine, W. V. 1953. "Two Dogmas of Empiricism." In Quine 1953 [99].

369. Sober, E. 1981. "Revisability, A Priori Truth, and Evolution," *Australasian Journal of Philosophy*, 59, 68–85.

370. Summerfield, D. 1991. "Modest A Priori Knowledge," *Philosophy and Phenomenological Research*, 51, 39–66.

371. Thompson, M. 1981. "Epistemic Priority, Analytic Truth, and Naturalized Epistemology," *American Philosophical Quarterly*, 18, 1–12.

372. Unger, P. 1967. "Experience and Factual Knowledge." *Journal of Philosophy*, 64, 152–173.

Justified Belief

Justification and Causation

373. Audi, R. 1983. "The Causal Structure of Indirect Justification." *Journal of Philosophy*, 80, 398–415.

374. Duran, J. 1988. "Causal Reference and Epistemic Justification," *Philosophy of Science*, 55, 272–279.

375. Kornblith, H. 1980. "Beyond Foundationalism and the Coherence Theory." In this anthology.

376. Kornblith, H. 1982. "The Psychological Turn." *Australasian Journal of Philosophy*, 60, 238–243.

377. Pappas, G. S. 1979. "Basing Relations." In Pappas 1979 [93].

378. Swain, M. 1979. "Justification and the Basis of Belief." In Pappas 1979 [93].

Reliability Theories

379. Almeder, R. and Hoff, F. 1989. "Reliabilism and Goldman's Theory of Justification," *Philosophia*, 19, 165–187.

380. Alston, W. 1988. "An Internalist Externalism," *Synthese*, 74, 265–283.

381. Alston, W. 1989. "Goldman on Epistemic Justification," *Philosophia*, 19, 115–131.

382. Audi, R. 1988. "Justification, Truth, and Reliability," *Philosophy and Phenomenological Research*, 49, 1–29.

383. Bach, K. 1985. "A Rationale for Reliabilism," *Monist*, 68, 246–263.

384. Bach, K. 1992. "Truth, Justification, and the American Way," *Pacific Philosophical Quarterly*, 73, 16–30.

385. Clarke, M. 1986. "Reliability and Two Kinds of Epistemic Justification." In Garver and Hare 1986 [46].

386. Cohen, S. 1984. "Justification and Truth," *Philosophical Studies*, 46, 279–295.

387. Conee, E. 1992. "The Truth Connection," *Philosophy and Phenomenological Research*.

388. Duran, J. 1988. "Reliabilism, Foundationalism and Naturalized Epistemic Justification Theory," *Metaphilosophy*, 19, 113–127.

389. Feldman, R. 1985. "Reliability and Justification," *Monist*, 68, 159–174.

390. Firth, R. 1981. "Epistemic Merit, Intrinsic and Instrumental," *Proceedings and Addresses of the American Philosophical Association*, 55, 5–23.

391. Foley, R. 1985. "What Is Wrong with Reliabilism?" *Monist*, 68, 188–202.

392. Freed, R. B. 1988. "Reliability, Reasons, and Belief Contexts," *Canadian Journal of Philosophy*, 18, 681–696.

393. Friedman, M. 1979. "Truth and Confirmation." In this anthology.

394. Fumerton, R. 1988. "Foundationalism, Conceptual Regress, and Reliabilism," *Analysis*, 178–184.

395. Gleb, G. 1990. "The Trouble with Goldman's Reliabilism," *Australasian Journal of Philosophy*, 68, 382–394.

396. Ginet, C. 1985. "*Contra* Reliabilism," *Monist*, 68, 175–187.

397. Goldman, A. I. 1979. "What is Justified Belief?" In this anthology.

398. Goldman, A. I. 1988. "Strong and Weak Justification." In Tomberlin 1988 [135].

399. Goldstick, D. 1992. "Cognitive Reason," *Philosophy and Phenomenological Research*, 52, 117–124.

400. Heil, J. 1982. "Foundationalism and Epistemic Rationality," *Philosophical Studies*, 42, 179–188.

401. Heil, J. 1984. "Reliability and Epistemic Merit," *Australiasian Journal of Philosophy*, 62, 327–338.

402. Kapitan, T. 1985. "Reliability and Indirect Justification," *Monist*, 68, 277–287.

403. Kvanvig, J. 1986. "How To Be a Reliabilist," *American Philosophical Quarterly*, 23, 189–198.

404. Luper-Foy, S. 1985. "The Reliabilist Theory of Rational Belief," *Monist* 68, 203–225.

405. Moser, P. 1989. "Reliabilism and Relevant Worlds," *Philosophia*, 19, 155–164.

406. Pappas, G. 1983. "Ongoing Knowledge." *Synthese*, 55, 253–267.

407. Pollock, J. 1984. "Reliability and Justified Belief," *Canadian Journal of Philosophy*, 14, 103–114.

408. Schmitt, F. F. 1984. "Reliability, Objectivity and the Background of Justification," *Australasian Journal of Philosophy*, 62, 1–15.

409. Shatz, D. 1983. "Foundationalism, Coherentism, and the Levels Gambit," *Synthese*, 55, 97–118.

410. Shope, R. 1989. "Justification, Reliability and Knowledge," *Philosophia*, 19, 133–154.

411. Sosa, E. 1991. "Methodology and Apt Belief." In Sosa 1991 [125].

412. Sosa, E. 1991. "Reliability and Intellectual Virtue." In Sosa 1991 [125].

413. Swain, M. 1981. "Justification and Reliable Belief," *Philosophical Studies*, 40, 389–407.

414. Swain, M. 1985. "Justification, Reasons, and Reliability," *Synthese*, 64, 69–92.

415. Swank, C. 1988. "A New and Unimproved Version of Reliabilism," *Analysis*, 48: 176–177.

416. Thagard, P. 1989. "Connectionism and Epistemology: Goldman on Winner-Take-All Networks," *Philosophia* 19, 189–196.

Psychologism

417. Sober, E. 1978. "Psychologism," *Journal for the Theory of Social Behavior* 8, 165–191.

418. Stich, S. P., and Nisbett, R. E. 1980. "Justification and the Psychology of Human Reasoning," *Philosophy of Science*, 47, 188–202.

Epistemic Conservatism

419. Adler, J. 1990. "Conservatism and Tacit Confirmation," *Mind*, 99, 559–570.

420. Foley, R. 1983. "Epistemic Conservatism," *Philosophical Studies*, 41, 165–182.

421. Goldstick, D. 1971. "Methodological Conservatism," *American Philosophical Quarterly*, 8, 186–191.

422. Kaplan, M., and Sklar, L. 1976. "Rationality and Truth," *Philosophical Studies*, 30, 197–201.

423. Kvanvig, J. 1989. "Conservatism and Its Virtues," *Synthese*, 79, 143–163.

424. Lycan, W. 1985. "Conservation and the Data Base." In Rescher 1985 [110].

425. Sklar, L. 1975. "Methodological Conservatism," *Philosophical Studies*, 84, 374–400.

Justification and Epistemic Responsibility

426. Code. L. 1984. "Toward a 'Responsibilist" Epistemology," *Philosophy and Phenomenological Research*, 45, 29–50.

427. Code, L. 1988. "Experience, Knowledge and Responsibility." In Griffiths 1988 [54].

428. Code, L. 1989. "Responsibilism: A New Epistemological Focus." In V. Cauchy, ed., *Philosophy and Culture: Proceedings of the XVII World Congress of Philosophy*, vol. 2, Montreal: Ed Montmorency.

429. Kornblith, H. 1983. "Justified Belief and Epistemically Responsible Action," *Philosophical Review*, 92, 33–48.

Externalism and Internalism

430. Adams, F. 1986. "The Function of Epistemic Justification," *Canadian Journal of Philosophy*, 16, 465–492.

431. Alston, W. 1989. "Internalism and Externalism in Epistemology." In Alston 1989 [1].

432. Audi, R. 1989. "Causalist Internalism," *American Philosophical Quarterly*, 26, 309–320.

433. Duran, J. 1992. "Delightful, Delovely and Externalist," *Critica*, 70, 65–81.

434. Davidson, D. 1991. "Epistemology Externalized," *Dialectica*, 45, 191–202.

435. Fumerton, R. 1988. "The Internalism/Externalism Controversy." In Tomberlin 1988 [135].

436. Goldman, A. I. 1980. The Internalist Conception of Justification." In French et al. 1980 [43].

437. Greco, J. 1990. "Internalism and Epistemically Responsible Belief," *Synthese*, 85, 245–277.

438. Hetherington, S. C. 1990. "Epistemic Internalism's Dilemma," *American Philosophical Quarterly*, 27, 245–251.

439. Kornblith, H. 1985. "Ever Since Descartes," *Monist*, 68, 264–276.

440. Kornblith, H. 1988. "How Internal Can You Get?" *Synthese*, 74, 313–327.

441. Luper-Foy, S. 1988. "The Knower, Inside and Out," *Synthese*, 74, 349–367.

442. Pollock, J. 1987. "Epistemic Norms," *Synthese*, 71, 61–96.

443. Schmitt, F. F. forthcoming. "Epistemic Perspectivism." In Heil forthcoming [62].

Rational Judgment

Rational Belief and Belief Revision

444. Brueckner, A. 1989. "Harman's Naturalistic Study of Reasoning," *Metaphilosophy*, 20, 356–370.

445. Bruner, J. S. 1957. "On Going Beyond the Information Given." In Gulber et al. 1957 [55].

446. Cam, P. 1988. "Modularity, Rationality, and Higher Cognition," *Philosophical Studies*, 53, 279–294.

447. Cherniak, C. 1981. "Feasible Inferences," *Philosophy of Science*, 48, 248–268.

448. Foss, J. 1988. "Testability Naturalized with Help from Peirce." In V. Cauchy, ed., *Philosophy and Culture: Proceedings of the XVII World Congress of Philosophy*, vol. 2, Montreal: Ed Montmorency.

449. Harman, G. 1984. "Positive vs. Negative Undermining in Belief Revision." In this anthology.

450. Kornblith, H. 1986. "Naturalizing Rationality." In Garver and Hare 1986 [46].

451. Pollock, J. 1988. "Interest-Driven Reasoning," *Synthese*, 74, 369–390.

452. Stabler, E. P. 1984. "Rationality in Naturalized Epistemology," *Philosophy of Science*, 51, 64–78.

453. Stich, S. P. 1985. "Could Man Be an Irrational Animal?" In this anthology.

454. Wason, P. C. 1966. "Reasoning." In Foss 1966 [40].

455. Weirich, P. 1986. "A Naturalistic Approach to Rational Deliberation." In Garver and Hare 1986 [46].

Problem Solving

456. Goldman, A. I. 1983. "Epistemology and the Theory of Problem Solving," *Synthese*, 55, 21–48.

457. Richardson, J. T. E. 1983. "Mental Imagery in Thinking and Problem Solving." In Evans 1983 [35].

Deductive Inference

458. Bogdan, R. 1985. "Cognition and Epistemic Closure," *American Philosophical Quarterly*, 22, 55–63.

459. Cherniak, C. 1984. "Prototypicality and Deductive Reasoning," *Journal of Verbal Learning and Verbal Behavior*, 23, 625–642.

460. Harman, G. 1984b. "Logic and Reasoning," *Synthese*, 60, 107–127.

461. Johnson-Laird, Philip N. 1983. "Thinking as a Skill." In Evans 1983 [35].

462. Johnson-Laird, P. N., Legrenzi, P., and Sonino Legrenzi, M. 1972. "Reasoning and a Sense of Reality." *British Journal of Psychology*, 63, 395–400.

463. Wason, Peter C. 1977. "Self-Contradictions." In Johnson-Laird and Wason 1977 [139].

464. Wason, Peter C. 1983. "Realism and Rationality in the Selection Task." In Evans 1983 [35].

Statistical Inference

Heuristics for Probability Judgments
465. Cohen, L. J. 1979. "On the Psychology of Prediction: Whose Is the Fallacy?" *Cognition*, 7, 385–407.

466. Cohen, L. J. 1980. "Whose Is the Fallacy? A Rejoinder to Daniel Kahneman and Amos Tversky," *Cognition*, 8, 89–92.

467. Cohen, L. J. 1981. "Can Human Irrationality Be Experimentally Demonstrated?" *Behavioral and Brain Sciences*, 4, 317–331.

468. Cohen, L. J. 1982. "Are People Programmed to Commit Fallacies? Further Thoughts about the Interpretation of Experimental Data on Probability Judgment," *Journal for the Theory of Social Behavior*, 12, 251–274.

469. Edwards, W. 1968. "Conservatism in Human Information Processing." In Kleinmuntz 1968 [72].

470. Kahneman, D., and Tversky, A. 1982. "On the Study of Statistical Intuitions," *Cognition*, 11, 123–141.

471. Nisbett, R. E., Krantz, D. H., Kunda, Z. 1983. "The Use of Statistical Heuristic in Everyday Inductive Reasoning," *Psychological Review*, 90, 339–363.

472. Tversky, A. and Kahneman, D. 1974. "Judgment under Uncertainty: Heuristics and Biases," *Science*, 185, 1124–1131.

Representativeness
473. Kahneman, D. and Tversky, A. 1972. "Subjective Probability: A Judgment of Representativeness," *Cognitive Psychology*, 3, 430–454.

474. Kahneman, D. and Tversky, A. 1973. "On the Psychology of Prediction," *Psychological Review*, 80, 237–251.

475. Tversky, A. and Kahneman, D. 1971. "Belief in the Law of Small Numbers," *Psychological Bulletin*, 2, 105–110.

476. Tversky, A. and Kahneman, D. 1982. "Judgments of and by Representativeness." In Kahneman et al. 1982 [68].

Availability
477. Kahneman, D. and Tversky, A. 1982. "The Simulation Heuristic." In Kahneman et al. 1982 [68].

478. Tversky, A. and Kahneman, D. 1973. "Availability: A Heuristic for Judging Frequency and Probability," *Cognitive Psychology* 4, 207–232.

Reasoning about Control and Covariation
479. Einhorn, H. J. 1982. "Learning from Experience and Suboptimal Rules in Decision Making." In Kahneman et al. 1982 [68].

Causal Reasoning
480. Nisbett, R. E., Borgida, E., Crandell, R., and Reed, H. 1976. "Popular Induction: Information Is Not Necessarily Informative." In Carroll and Payne 1976 [18].

481. Ross, L. 1977. "The Intuitive Psychologist and His Shortcomings: Distortions in the Attribution Process." In Berkowitz 1977 [7].

482. Tversky, A. and Kahneman, D. 1977 "Causal Schemata in Judgments under Uncertainty." In Fishbein 1977 [36].

483. Tversky, A. and Kahneman, D. 1982. "Evidential Impact of Base Rates." In Kahneman et al. 1982 [68].

Corrective Procedures
484. Dawes, R. M. 1979. "The Robust Beauty of Improper Linear Models in Decision Making," *American Psychologist*, 34, 571–582.

485. Fischhoff, B. 1982. "Debiasing." In Kahneman et al. 1982 [68].

486. Kahneman, D. and Tversky, A. 1982. "Intuitive Predictions: Biases and Corrective Procedures." In Kahneman et al. 1982 [68].

487. Nisbett, R. E., Krantz, D. H., Jepson, C., and Fong, G. H. 1982. "Improving Inductive Inference." In Kahneman et al. 1982 [68].

488. Ross, L., Lepper, M. R., and Hubbard, M. 1975. "Perseverance in Self-Perception and Social Perception: Biased Attributional Processes in the Debriefing Paradigm," *Journal of Personality and Social Psychology*, 32, 880–892.

Biological Epistemology

489. Bechtel, W. 1990. "Toward Making Evolutionary Epistemology into a Truly Naturalized Epistemology." In Rescher 1990 [112].

490. Bradie, M. 1986. "Assessing Evolutionary Epistemology," *Biology and Philosophy*, 1, 401–459.

491. Bradie, M. 1989. "Evolutionary Epistemology as Naturalized Epistemology." In Hahlweg 1989 [57].

492. Brown, J. R. 1985. "Rescher's Evolutionary Epistemology," *Philosophia*, 15, 287–300.

493. Clark, A. 1984. "Evolutionary Epistemology and Ontological Realism," *Philosophical Quarterly*, 34, 482–490.

494. Clark, A. 1986. "Evolutionary Epistemology and the Scientific Method," *Philosophica*, 37, 151–162.

495. Clarke, M. 1990. "Epistemic Norms and Evolutionary Success," *Synthese*, 85, 231–244.

496. Clendinnen, F. 1989. "Evolutionary Epistemology and the Justification of Belief." In Hahlweg 1989 [57].

497. Dretske, F. 1989. "The Need to Know." In Clay and Lehrer 1989 [25].

498. Feldman, R. 1988. "Rationality, Reliability, and Natural Selection," *Philosophy of Science*, 55, 218–227.

499. Fetzer, J. 1990. "Evolution, Rationality, and Testability," *Synthese*, 82, 423–439.

500. Holland, A. 1984. "On What Makes an Epistemology Evolutionary, Part I," *Aristotelian Society Supplement*, 58, 177–192.

501. Hookway, C. 1984b. "Naturalism, Fallibilism and Evolutionary Epistemology." In Hookway 1984 [65].

502. Leeds, A. 1984. "Sociobiology, Epistemology, and Human Nature." In Cohen 1984 [27].

503. Lycan, W. 1985. "Epistemic Value." *Synthese* 64, 137–164.

504. Munevar, G. 1988. "Evolution and Justification," *Monist*, 71, 339–357.

505. O'Hear, A. 1984. "On What Makes an Epistemology Evolutionary, Part II," *Aristotelian Society Supplement*, 58, 193–218.

506. O'Hear, A. 1989. "Evolution, Knowledge, and Self-Consciousness," *Inquiry*, 32, 127–150.

507. Olding, A. 1983. "Biology and Knowledge," *Theoria*, 49, 1–22.

508. Smith, C. 1989. "Evolution, Epistemology and Visual Science." In Hahlweg 1989 [57].

509. Sober, E. 1981. "The Evolution of Rationality," *Synthese*, 46, 95–120.

Developmental Epistemology

510. Brewer, W. F. and Samarapungavan, A. 1991. "Children's Theories vs. Scientific Theories: Differences in Reasoning or Differences in Knowledge?" In Hoffman and Palermo 1991 [63].

511. Hamlym, D. W. 1971. "Epistemology and Conceptual Development." In Mischel 1971 [86].

512. Haroutunian, S. 1985. "Can Jean Piaget Explain the Possibility of Knowledge?" *Synthese*, 65, 65–86.

513. Kaplan, Bernard. 1971. "Genetic Psychology, Genetic Epistemology, and Theory of Knowledge." In Mischel 1971 [86].

514. Kitchener, R. F. 1980a. "Piaget's Genetic Epistemology," *International Philosophical Quarterly*, 20, 377–405.

515. Kitchener, R. F. 1980b. "Genetic Epistemology, Normative Epistemology, and Psychologism," *Synthese*, 45, 257–280.

516. Kitchener, R. F. 1981. "The Nature and Scope of Genetic Epistemology," *Philosophy of Science*, 48, 400–415.

517. Kitchener, R. F. 1987. "Is Genetic Epistemology Possible?" *British Journal for the Philosophy of Science*, 38, 283–299.

518. Siegel, H. 1978. "Piaget's Conception of Epistemology," *Educational Theory*, 28, 16–22.

519. Smith, L. 1984. "Genetic Epistemology and the Child's Understanding of Logic," *Philosophy of the Social Sciences*, 14, 367–376.

520. Toulmin, S. 1977. "Epistemology and Developmental Psychology," *Nous*, 11, 51–53.

Social Epistemology

521. Bogdan, R. 1991. "Common Sense Naturalized: The Practical Stance." In Bogdan 1991 [13].

522. Corlett, J. A. 1991. "Epistemology, Psychology, and Goldman," *Social Epistemology*, 5, 91–100.

523. Feher, M. 1984. "Epistemology Naturalized vs. Epistemology Socialized." In Hronszky et al. 1984 [66].

524. Gauker, C. 1991. "Mental Content and the Epistemic Division of Labor," *Australasian Journal of Philosophy*, 302–318.

525. Goldman, A. I. 1987. "Foundations of Social Epistemics," *Synthese*, 73, 109–144.

526. Hesse, M. 1984. "Socializing Epistemology." In Hronszky et al. 1984 [66].

527. Kitcher, P. 1990. "The Division of Cognitive Labor," *Journal of Philosophy*, 87, 5–22.

528. Kitcher, P. 1992. "Authority, Deference, and the Role of Individual Reasoning." In McMullin, E., ed., 1992. *The Social Dimension of Scientific Knowledge*, South Bend: Notre Dame University Press.

529. Kornblith, H. 1987. "Some Social Features of Cognition," *Synthese*, 73, 27–42.

530. Moore, J. 1991. "Knowledge, Society, Power, and the Promise of Epistemological Externalism," *Synthese*, 88, 379–398.

531. Schmitt, F. F. 1987. "Justification, Sociality, and Autonomy," *Synthese*, 73, 43–86.

532. Solomon, M. forthcoming. "Social Empiricism," *Nous*.

Other References

The following are additional works cited in the chapters in this book.

Books

533. Abelson, R. P., Aronson, E., McGuire, W. J., Newcombe, T. M., Rosenberg, M. J., Tannenbaum, P. H., eds. 1968. *Theories of Cognitive Consistency*, Chicago: Rand McNally.

534. Alcock, J. 1979. *Animal Behavior: An Evolutionary Approach*, Sunderland, Mass.: Sinauer.

535. Anderson, J. R. and Bower, G. H. 1973. *Human Associative Memory*, Washington, D.C.: Winston.

536. Anderson, R. C., Spiro, R. J. and Montague, W. E., eds. 1976. *Schooling and the Acquisition of Knowledge*, Hillsdale, N.J.: Lawrence Erlbaum Associates.

536a. Attneave, F. 1959. *Applications of Information Theory to Psychology: A Summary of Basic Concepts, Methods and Results*, New York: Henry Holt and Company.

537. Ayer, A. J. 1936. *Language, Truth and Logic*, London: Gollancz.

538. Ayer, A. J. 1940. *The Foundations of Empirical Knowledge*, London: MacMillan.

539. Ayer, A. J. 1956. *The Problem of Knowledge*, London: Penguin.

540. Ayer, A. J., ed. 1959. *Logical Positivism*, New York: Free Press.

541. Ayer, A. J. 1974. *The Central Questions of Philosophy*, New York: William Morrow.

542. Bartlett, F. C. 1932. *Remembering*, Cambridge: Cambridge University Press.

543. Barwise, J., ed. 1977. *Handbook of Mathematical Logic*, New York: North-Holland.

544. Berkowitz, L., ed. 1978. *Advances in Experimental Social Psychology*, vol. 11, New York: Academic Press.

545. Berkowitz, L., ed. 1978. *Cognitive Theories in Social Psychology*, New York: Academic Press.

546. Bernard, E. E. and Kare, M. R., eds. 1962. *Biological Prototypes and Synthetic Systems*, New York: Plenum.

547. Berne, E. 1964. *Games People Play*, New York: Grove Press.

548. Black, A. H. and Prokasy, W. F., eds. 1972. *Classical Conditioning*, vol. 2, *Current Research and Theory*, New York: Appleton-Century Crofts.

549. Bobrow, D., and Collins, A. 1976. *Representation and Understanding: Studies in Cognitive Science*, New York: Academic Press.

550. Bower, G., ed. 1984. *The Psychology of Learning and Motivation*, vol. 18, New York: Academic Press.

551. Brandt, R. B. 1979. *A Theory of the Good and the Right*, Oxford: Clarendon Press.

552. Carey, S. 1985. *Conceptual Change in Childhood*, Cambridge, Mass.: MIT Press.

553. Chisholm, R. M. 1957. *Perceiving: A Philosophical Study*, Ithaca: Cornell University Press.

554. Chisholm, R. M. 1976. *Person and Object*, LaSalle, Ill.: Open Court.

555. Chisholm, R. M. 1977. *Theory of Knowledge*, 2d edition, Englewood Cliffs, N.J.: Prentice-Hall.

556. Christie, R. and Geis, F. L., eds. 1970. *Studies in Machiavellianism*, New York: Academic Press.

557. Church, A. 1956. *Introduction to Mathematical Logic*, vol. 1, Princeton: Princeton University Press.

558. Davidson, D. 1984. *Inquiries into Truth and Interpretation*, Oxford: Clarendon Press.

559. Davidson, D. and Harman, G., eds. 1972. *Semantics of Natural Language*, Dordrecht: Reidel.

560. Demopoulos, W. and Marras, A. forthcoming. *Language Learning and Concept Acquisition*, Norwood, N. J.: Ablex.

561. Dennett, D. 1969. *Content and Consciousness*, London: Routledge and Kegan Paul.

562. Dennett, D. 1978. *Brainstorms*, Cambridge, Mass.: MIT Press. A Bradford Book.

563. Dockx, S. and Bernays P., eds. 1965. *Information and Prediction in Science*, New York: Academy Press.

564. Dold, A. and Eckmann, B., eds. 1975. *Lecture Notes in Mathematics*, 453, Amsterdam: North Holland Publishing Co.

565. Doyle, J. 1980. *A Model for Deliberation, Action, and Introspection*, MIT Artificial Intelligence Laboratory Technical Report 561, Cambridge, Mass.

566. Dummett, M. 1978. *Truth and Other Enigmas*, Cambridge, Mass.: Harvard University Press.

567. Duval, S. and Wicklund, R. A. 1972. *A Theory of Objective Self-Awareness*, New York: Academic Press.

568. Feyerabend, P. 1978. *Against Method: Outline of an Anarchistic Theory of Knowledge*, London: Verso.

569. Feyerabend, P. 1978. *Science in a Free Society*, London: New Left Bank Publishers.

570. Feyerabend, P. 1982. *Realism, Rationalism and Scientific Method: Philosophical Papers*, vol. 1, Cambridge: Cambridge University Press.

571. Flavell, J. H. 1963. *The Developmental Psychology of Jean Piaget*, Princeton: Van Nostrand.

572. Flavell, J. H. 1977. *Cognitive Development*, Englewood Cliffs, N.J.: Prentice-Hall.

573. Flavell, J. H. and Markman, E. M., eds. 1983. *Handbook of Child Psychology*, vol. 3, *Cognitive Development*, New York: Wiley.

574. Fodor, J. 1975. *The Language of Thought*, New York: Thomas Y. Crowell.

575. Fodor, J. 1990. *A Theory of Content and Other Essays*, Cambridge, Mass.: MIT Press.

576. French, P. A., Uehling, T. E., Jr., and Wettstein, H. K. 1977. *Midwest Studies in Philosophy*, vol. 2, *Studies in the Philosophy of Language*, Minneapolis: University of Minnesota Press.

577. Garey, M. and Johnson, D. 1979. *Computers and Intractability*, San Francisco: W. H. Freeman Press.

577a. Garner, W. 1962. *Uncertainty and Structure as Psychological Concepts*, New York: Wiley.

578. Gelman, S. A. 1984. *Children's Inductive Inferences from Natural Kinds and Artifact Categories*, Ph.D. dissertation, Stanford University.

579. Gibson, J. J. 1950. *The Perception of the Visual World*, New York: Houghton Mifflin.

580. Gibson, J. J. 1966. *The Senses Considered as a Perceptual System*, Boston: Houghton Mifflin.

581. Gibson, J. J. 1979. *The Ecological Approach to Visual Perception*, Boston: Houghton Mifflin.

582. Ginet, C. 1975. *Knowledge, Perception and Memory*, Boston: Reidel.

583. Goffman, E. 1959. *The Presentation of Self in Everyday Life*, New York: Doubleday.

584. Goodman, N. 1966. *The Structure of Appearance*, 2d edition, New York: Bobbs-Merrill.

585. Gould, L. and Walker, C. A., eds. 1978. *The Management of Nuclear Wastes,* New Haven: Yale University Press.

586. Gregory, R. L. 1970. *The Intelligent Eye,* New York: McGraw-Hill.

587. Haber, R. N. 1969. *Information-Processing Approaches to Visual Perception,* New York: Holt, Rinehart and Winston.

587a. Haber, R. N. and Hershenson, M. 1973. *The Psychology of Visual Perception,* New York: Holt, Rinehart and Winston.

588. Hacking, I. 1975. *The Emergence of Probability,* Cambridge: Cambridge University Press.

589. Hare, R. M. 1952. *The Language of Morals,* London: Oxford University Press.

590. Hartshorne, H. and May, M. 1982. *Studies in the Nature of Character,* vol. 1, *Studies in Deceit,* New York: Macmillan.

591. Healy, R., ed. 1981. *Reduction, Time and Reality,* Cambridge: Cambridge University Press.

592. Heider, F. 1958. *The Psychology of Impersonal Relations,* New York: Wiley.

593. Higgins, E. T., Herman, P., and Zanna, M. P., eds. 1980. *The Ontario Symposium on Personality and Social Psychology,* vol. 1, Hillsdale, N.J.: Lawrence Erlbaum Associates.

594. Hintikka, J. and Davidson, D., eds. 1969. *Words and Objections: Essays on the Work of W. V. Quine,* Dordrecht: Reidel.

595. Howes, H. E. and Dienstbier, R. A., eds. 1979. *Nebraska Symposium on Motivation,* vol. 26, Lincoln: University of Nebraska Press.

596. Inhelder, B. and Piaget, J. 1964. *The Early Growth of Logic in the Child,* New York: Cambridge University Press.

597. Jeffrey, R. C. 1983. *The Logic of Decision,* 2nd edition, Chicago: University of Chicago Press.

598. Johnson, A. B. 1947. *A Treatise on Language,* Berkeley: University of California Press.

599. Jones, E. E., Kanouse, D. E., Kelley, H. H., Nisbett, R. E., Valins, S., Weiner, B., eds. 1972. *Attribution: Perceiving the Causes of Behavior,* Morristown, N.J.: General Learning Press.

600. Keil, F. C. 1979. *Semantic and Conceptual Development: An Ontological Perspective,* Cambridge, Mass.: Harvard University Press.

601. Kelly, G. 1955. *The Psychology of Personal Constructs,* 2 vols. New York: Norton.

602. Kleene, S. 1967. *Mathematical Logic,* New York: Wiley.

603. Kripke, S. 1980. *Naming and Necessity,* Cambridge, Mass.: Harvard University Press.

604. Kyburg, H. 1961. *Probability and the Logic of Rational Belief*, Middletown, Conn.: Wesleyan University Press.

605. LeBerge, D. and Samuels, S. J., eds. 1976. *Basic Processes in Reading Perception and Comprehension*, Hillsdale, N.J.: Lawrence Erlbaum Associates.

606. Lepore, E. and McLaughlin, B. 1985. *Actions and Events: Perspectives on the Philosophy of Donald Davidson*, Oxford: Blackwell.

607. Levi, I. 1986. *Hard Choices: Decision Making Under Unresolved Conflict*, Cambridge: Cambridge University Press.

608. Lewin, K. 1935. *A Dynamic Theory of Personality*, New York: McGraw-Hill.

609. Lewis, C. I. 1946. *An Analysis of Knowledge and Valuation*, LaSalle, Ill.: Open Court.

610. Lewis, D. 1973. *Counterfactuals*, Oxford: Blackwell.

610a. Lindsay, P. H. and Norman, D. A. 1972. *Human Information Processing*, New York: Academic Press.

611. Lindzey, G., ed. 1958. *Assessment of Human Motives*, New York: Holt, Rinehart and Winston.

612. MacKay, D. M. 1969. *Information, Mechanism and Meaning*, Cambridge, Mass.: MIT Press.

613. Maher, B. A., ed. 1972. *Progress in Experimental Personality Research*, vol. 6, New York: Academic Press.

614. May, E. R. 1973. *"Lessons" of the Past*, New York: Oxford University Press.

615. Michalski, R., Carbonell, J. G., and Mitchell, T. M. eds. 1983. *Machine Learning: Artificial Intelligence Approach*, vol. 2, Los Altos: Kaufmann.

616. Mill, J. S. 1843. *A System of Logic, Ratiocinative and Inductive*, London: Longmans.

617. Miller, R. and Thatcher, J., eds. 1972. *Complexity of Computer Computations*, New York: Plenum Press.

618. Mischel, W. 1968. *Personality and Assessment*, New York: Wiley.

619. Montaigne. 1933. *The Essays of Montaigne*, New York: Modern Library.

620. Morgenbesser, S., ed. 1966. *Philosophy of Science Today*, New York: Basic Books.

621. Munitz, M. K., ed. 1971. *Identity and Individuation*, New York: New York University Press.

622. Neisser, U. 1967. *Cognitive Psychology*, New York: Appleton-Century-Crofts.

623. Neisser, U. 1976. *Cognition and Reality: Principles and Implications of Cognitive Psychology*, San Francisco: Freeman.

624. Newcombe, T. M. 1929. *Consistency of Certain Extravert-Introvert Behavior Patterns in 51 Problem Boys*, New York: Columbia University, Teachers College, Bureau of Publications.

625. Osherson, D. and Smith, E. E. eds. 1990. *Thinking: An Invitation to Cognitive Science*, Cambridge, Mass.: MIT Press.

626. Osherson, D., Kosslyn, S. M., and Hollerbach, J. M. eds. 1990. *Visual Cognition and Action: An Invitation to Cognitive Science*, Cambridge, Mass.: MIT Press.

627. Osherson, D. and Lasnik, H., eds. 1990. *Language: An Invitation to Cognitive Science*, Cambridge, Mass.: MIT Press.

628. Osherson, D., Stob, M., and Weinstein, S. 1985. *Systems that Learn*, Cambridge, Mass.: MIT Press.

628a. Peirce, C. S. 1955. *Philosophical Writings of Peirce*, ed. J. Buchler, New York: Dover.

629. Piaget, J. 1936. *La naissance de l'intelligence chez l'enfant*, Paris: Delachau et Niestle.

630. Piaget, J. and Inhelder, B. 1951/1975. *The Origin of the Idea of Chance in Children*, New York: Norton.

631. Pollock, J. 1974. *Knowledge and Justification*, Princeton: Princeton University Press.

632. Popper, K. 1979. *Objective Knowledge*, New York: Oxford University Press.

633. Putnam, H. 1975. *Mathematics, Matter and Method*, New York: Cambridge University Press.

634. Putnam, H. 1975. *Mind, Language and Reality*, New York: Cambridge University Press.

635. Putnam, H. 1988. *Representation and Reality*, Cambridge: Cambridge University Press.

636. Regan, T. and VanDeVeer, D. eds., 1982. *Individual Rights and Public Policy*, Totowa, N.J.: Rowman and Littlefield.

637. Reichenbach, H. 1938. *Experience and Prediction*, Chicago: Chicago University Press.

638. Riding, A. 1989. *Distant Neighbors: A Portrait of the Mexicans*, New York: Vintage.

639. Rock, I. 1975. *An Introduction to Perception*, New York: Macmillan.

640. Rorty, R. 1982. *Consequences of Pragmatism*, Minneapolis: University of Minnesota Press.

641. Rosch, E. and Lloyd, B. 1978. *Cognition and Catergorization*, Hillsdale, N.J.: Lawrence Erlbaum Associates.

642. Rosenfeld, J., ed. 1974. *Information Processing 74*, Amsterdam: North Holland.

643. Ross, L., Turiel, E., Josephson, J., and Lepper, M. R. 1978. *Developmental Perspectives on the Fundamental Error Attribution*, Stanford University, manuscript.

643a. Rumelhart, D. E. 1977. *Introduction to Human Information Processing*, New York: John Wiley and Sons.

644. Russell, B. 1912. *Problems of Philosophy*, New York: Oxford University Press.

645. Russell, B. 1948. *Human Knowledge: Its Scope and Limits*, New York: Simon and Schuster.

646. Russell, B. 1965. *An Inquiry into Meaning and Truth*, Baltimore: Penguin.

646a. Sayre, K. 1965. *Recognition: A Study in the Philosophy of Artificial Intelligence*, South Bend, In.: University of Notre Dame Press.

647. Schick, F. 1984. *Having Reasons: An Essay on Rationality and Sociality*, Princeton: Princeton University Press.

648. Schank, R. C. 1975. *Conceptual Information Processing*, Amsterdam: North-Holland.

649. Schank, R. C., and Abelson, R. P. 1977. *Scripts, Plans, Goals and Understanding*, Hillsdale, N.J.: Lawrence Erlbaum Associates.

650. Schilpp, P. A. 1942. *The Philosophy of G. E. Moore*, Chicago: Open Court.

651. Schwartz, S., ed. 1977. *Naming, Necessity, and Natural Kinds*, Ithaca: Cornell University Press.

652. Seligman, M. E. P. 1975. *Helplessness: On Depression, Development, and Death*, San Francisco: W. H. Freeman.

653. Sextus Empiricus. 1933. *Outlines of Pyrrhonism*, vol. 1, trans. R. G. Bury, London: Heinemann.

654. Shannon, C. and Weaver, W. 1949. *The Mathematical Theory of Communication*, Urbana: University of Illinois Press.

655. Shisha, O., ed. 1972. *Inequalities—III*, New York: Academic Press.

656. Smart, J. J. C. 1963. *Philosophy and Scientific Realism*, New York: Humanities Press.

657. Smith, E. E. and Medin, D. 1981. *Categories and Concepts*, Cambridge, Mass.: Harvard University Press.

658. Stroud, B. 1977. *Hume*, London: Routledge and Kegan Paul.

659. Traub, J., ed. 1976. *Algorithms and Complexity*, New York: Academic Press.

660. Uhr, L. 1973. *Pattern Recognition, Learning, and Thought*, Englewood Cliffs, N.J.: Prentice-Hall.

661. Warren, N., ed. 1977. *Studies in Cross-Cultural Psychology*, vol. 1, New York: Academic Press.

662. Wason, P. and Johnson-Laird, P. 1972. *Psychology of Reasoning*, Cambridge, Mass.: Harvard University Press.

663. Weber, M. 1930. *The Protestant Ethic and the Spirit of Capitalism*, trans. by T. Parsons, New York: Scribners.

664. Weinberg, S. 1977. *The First Three Minutes*, New York: Basic Books.

665. Winston, P. H. 1975. *The Psychology of Computer Vision*, New York: McGraw-Hill.

666. Wittgenstein, L. 1953. *Philosophical Investigations*, New York: Macmillan.

667. Wittgenstein, L. 1958. *The Blue Book*, New York: Harper and Row.

668. Wittgenstein, L. 1976. *Wittgenstein's Lectures on the Foundations of Mathematics, 1939*, ed. C. Diamond, Ithaca: Cornell University Press.

669. Woodfield, A. 1981. *Thought and Object*, Oxford: Oxford University Press.

Articles

670. Abelson, R. P. 1968. "Psychological Implication." In Abelson et al. 1968 [533].

671. Abelson, R. P. 1976. "Script Processing in Attitude Formation and Decision Making." In Carroll and Payne 1976 [18].

672. Abelson, R. P. 1978. "Scripts," Midwestern Psychological Association, Chicago.

673. Alston, W. P. 1976. "Two Types of Foundationalism," *Journal of Philosophy*, 73, 165–185.

674. Arkin, R. and Duval, S. 1975. "Focus of Attention and Causal Attributions of Actors and Observers," *Journal of Experimental Social Psychology*, 11, 427–438.

675. Averbach, E. and Coriell, A. S. 1961. "Short-Term Memory in Vision," *Bell System Technical Journal*, 40, 309–328.

676. Bem, D. J., and Allen, A. 1974. "On Predicting Some of the People Some of the Time: The Search for Cross-situational Consistencies in Behavior," *Psychological Review*, 81, 506–520.

677. Bem, D. J., and Funder, D. C. 1978. "Predicting More of the People More of the Time: Assessing the Personality of Situations." *Psychological Review*, 85, 485–501.

678. Berwick, R. 1986. "Leaning from Positive-Only Examples: The Subset Principle and Three Case Studies." In Michalski et al. 1986 [615].

679. Biederman, I. 1987. "Recognition-By-Components: A Theory of Human Image Understanding," *Psychological Review*, 94, 115–147.

680. Biederman, I. 1990. "Higher-Level Vision." In Osherson et al. 1990 [626].

681. Bogen, J. and Woodward, J. 1988. "Saving the Phenomena," *Philosophical Review*, 97, 303–352.

682. Bower, G., Black, J., and Turner, T. forthcoming. "Scripts in Text Comprehension and Memory," *Cognitive Psychology*.

683. Braine, M. D. S. 1978. "On the Relation between the Natural Logic of Reasoning and Standard Logic," *Psychological Review*, 85, 1–21.

684. Braine, M. D. S., Reiser, B. J., and Rumain, B. 1984. "Some Empirical Justification for a Theory of Natural Propositional Logic." In Bower 1984 [550].

685. Cantor, N. and Mischel, W. 1977. "Traits as Prototypes: Effects on Recognition Memory," *Journal of Personality and Social Psychology*, 35, 38–49.

686. Cantor, N. and Mischel, W. 1979. "Prototypicality and Personality: Effects on Free Recall and Personality Impressions," *Journal of Research in Personality*, 13, 187–205.

687. Carnap, R. 1932. "Protokollsatze," *Erkenntnis*, 3, 215–228.

688. Carnap, R. 1936. "Testability and Meaning," *Philosophy of Science*, 3, 419–471; 4, 1–40.

689. Castaneda, H.-N. 1967. "Indicators and Quasi-Indicators," *American Philosophical Quarterly*, 4, 85–100.

690. Castaneda, H.-N. 1968. "On the Logic of Attributions of Self-Knowledge to Others," *Journal of Philosophy*, 64, 439–456.

691. Chaitin, G. 1974. "Information-Theoretic Limitations of Formal Systems," *Journal of the Association for Computing Machinery*, 21, 403–424.

692. Cheng, P. W. and Holyoak, K. J. 1985. "Pragmatic Reasoning Schemas," *Cognitive Psychology*, 17, 319–416.

693. Cheng, P. W., Holyoak, K. J., Nisbett, R. E., and Oliver, L. M. 1986. "Pragmatic Versus Syntactic Approaches to Training Deductive Reasoning," *Cognitive Psychology*, 18.

694. Cherry, E. C. 1951. "A History of the Theory of Information," *Proceedings of the Institute of Electrical Engineers*, 98, 383–393.

695. Clarke, T. 1972. "The Legacy of Skepticism," *Journal of Philosophy*, 69, 754–769.

696. Collins, B. E. 1974. "Four Components of the Rotter Internal-External Scale: Belief in a Difficult World, a Just World, a Predictable World, and a Politically Responsive World," *Journal of Personality and Social Psychology*, 29, 381–391.

697. Cook, S. 1971. "The Complexity of Theorem-Proving Procedures," *Proceedings of the 3rd Annual ACM Symposium on Theory of Computing*, 151–158.

698. Cornman, J. 1978. "Foundational vs. Non-Foundational Theories of Empirical Knowledge." In Pappas and Swain 1978 [93].

699. Crandall, V. C., Katovsky, W., and Crandall, V. G. 1965. "Children's Beliefs in Their Own Control of Reinforcements in Intellectual-Academic Achievement Situations," *Child Development*, 36, 91–109.

700. D'Andrade, R. 1982. "Reason Versus Logic," Symposium on Ecology of Cognition, Greensboro, N.C.

701. Davidson, D. 1966. "Emeroses by Other Names," *Journal of Philosophy*, 63, 778–780.

702. Davidson, D. 1970. "The Anomalism of the Mental." In Foster and Swanson 1970 [41].

703. Davidson, D. 1973. "On The Very Idea of a Conceptual Scheme," *Proceedings of the American Philosophical Association*, 47, 5–20.

704. Davidson, D. 1973. "Radical Interpretation," *Dialectica*, 27, 313–328.

705. Davidson, D. 1979. "The Method of Truth in Metaphysics." In French et al. 1979 [42].

706. Dennett, D. 1978. "Intentional Systems." In Dennett 1978 [562].

707. Dennett, D. 1981. "Making Sense of Ourselves," *Philosophical Topics*, 12, 63–81.

708. Dennett, D. 1981. "Three Kinds of Intentional Psychology." In Healy 1981 [591].

709. De Soto, C. B. 1961. "The Predilection for Single Orderings," *Journal of Abnormal and Social Psychology*, 62, 16–23.

710. Donnellan, K. 1977. "The Contingent A Priori and Rigid Designators." In French et al. 1977 [576].

711. Doyle, J. 1979. "A Truth Maintenance System," *Artificial Intelligence*, 12, 231–272.

712. Dretske, F. I. 1977. "The Laws of Nature," *Philosophy of Science*, 44, 248–268.

713. Dummett, M. 1973. "The Justification of Deduction," *Proceedings of the British Academy*, 59, 9–10.

714. Erwin, E. 1974. "Are the Notions 'A Priori Truth' and 'Necessary Truth' Extensionally Equivalent?" *Canadian Journal of Philosophy*, 3, 591–602.

715. Field, H. 1972. "Tarski's Theory of Truth," *Journal of Philosophy* 69, 347–375.

716. Fillenbaum, S. 1975. "If: Some Uses," *Psychological Research*, 37: 245–260.

717. Fillenbaum, S. 1976. "Inducements: On Phrasing and Logic of Conditional Promises, Threats and Warnings," *Psychological Research* 38: 231–250.

718. Firth, R. 1965. "Ultimate Evidence." In Swartz 1965 [132].

719. Firth, R. 1969. "Coherence, Certainty and Epistemic Priority." In Chisholm and Swartz 1973 [20].

720. Firth, R. 1978. "Are Epistemic Concepts Reducible to Ethical Concepts?" In Goldman and Kim 1978 [52].

721. Fischer, M. and Rabin, M. 1974. "Super-exponential Complexity of Presburger Arithmetic," *Complexity of Computation, SIAM-AMS Proceedings, 7,* 27–41.

722. Fischhoff, B. 1975. "Hindsight = Foresight: The Effect of Outcome Knowledge on Judgment under Uncertainty," *Journal of Experimental Psychology: Human Perception and Performance,* 1, 288–299.

723. Fischhoff, B. and Beythe, R. 1975. " 'I Knew it Would Happen'—Remembered Probabilities of Once-Future Things," *Organizational Behavior and Human Performance,* 3, 552–564.

724. Flavell, J. H., Flavell, E. R., and Green, F. L. 1983. "Development of the Appearance-Reality Distinction," *Cognitive Psychology,* 15, 95–120.

725. Fodor, J. 1980. "Methodological Solipsism Considered as a Research Strategy in Cognitive Psychology," *Behavorial and Brain Sciences,* 3, 63–110.

726. Fodor, J. 1981. "Three Cheers for Propositional Attitudes." In Fodor 1981 [37].

727. Fong, G. T., Krantz, D. H. and Nisbett, R. E. 1986. "The Effects of Statistical Training on Thinking about Everyday Problems," *Cognitive Psychology,* 18.

728. Fong, G. T. and Nisbett, R. E. 1986. "The Effects of Statistical Training: Domain Independent and Long-Lived," manuscript.

729. Garcia, J., McGowan, B. K., and Green, K. F. 1972. "Biological Constraints on Conditioning." In Black and Prokasy 1972 [548].

730. Geis, M. C. and Zwicky, A. M. 1971. "On Invited Inferences," *Linguistic Inquiry,* 2, 561–566.

731. Gelman, R. and Baillargeon, R. 1983. "A Review of Some Piagetian Concepts." In Flavell and Markman 1983 [573].

732. Gelman, S. A. and Markman, E. M. 1986. "Categories and Induction in Young Children," *Cognition,* 23, 183–208.

733. Gelman, S. A. and Markman, E. M. 1987. "Young Children's Inductions from Natural Kinds: The Role of Categories and Appearances," *Child Development,* 58, 1532–1541.

734. Gelman, S. A., Collman P., and Maccoby, E. E. 1986. "Inferring Properties from Categories Versus Inferring Categories from Properties: The Case of Gender," *Child Development*, 57, 396–404.

735. Gettier, E. 1963. "Is Justified True Belief Knowledge?" *Analysis* 23, 121–123.

736. Ginsberg, M. L. 1985. "Counterfactuals," *Proceedings of the Ninth Joint Conference on Artificial Intelligence*, Los Altos: Kaufmann.

737. Glymour, C. 1975. "Relevant Evidence," *Journal of Philosophy*, 72, 403–426.

738. Gold, E. M. 1967. "Language Identification in the Limite," *Information and Control*, 10, 447–474.

739. Goldring, E. 1981. "The Effect of Past Experience on Problem Solving," British Psychological Association.

740. Griggs, R. A. and Cox, J. R. 1982. "The Elusive Thematic—Materials Effect in Wason's Selection Task," *British Journal of Psychology*, 73, 407–420.

741. Hanson, N. R. 1966. "Observation and Interpretation." In Morgenbesser 1966 [620].

742. Harman, G. 1982. "Metaphysical Realism and Moral Relativism," *Journal of Philosophy*, 79, 568–575.

743. Hempel, C. G. 1935. "On the Logical Positivists' Theory of Truth," *Analysis*, 2, 49–59.

744. Hempel, C. G. 1945. "Studies in the Logic Confirmation," *Mind*, 54, 1–49, 97–121.

745. Henle, M. 1962. "On the Relation Between Logic and Thinking," *Psychological Review*, 69, 366–378.

746. Higgins, E. T., Rholes, W. S., and Jones, C. R. 1977. "Category Accessibility and Impression Formation," *Journal of Personality and Social Psychology*, 13, 141–154.

747. Hintzman, D. 1986. " 'Schema Abstraction' in a Multiple-Trace Memory Model," *Psychological Review*, 93, 411–428.

748. Hornstein, H. A., LaKind, E., Frankel, G., and Manne, S. 1975. "Effects of Knowledge about Remote Social Events on Prosocial Behavior, Social Conception, and Mood," *Journal of Personality and Social Psychology*, 32, 1038–1046.

749. Johnson-Laird, P. N., Lengrenzi, P. and Lengrenzi, M. 1972. "Reasoning and a Sense of Reality," *British Journal of Psychology*, 63, 395–400.

750. Jones, J. 1978. "Three Universal Representations of Recursively Enumerable Sets," *Journal of Symbolic Logic*, 43, 335–351.

751. Jones, J. 1982. "Universal Diophantine Equation," *Journal of Symbolic Logic*, 47, 549–571.

752. Jones, E. E., and Nisbett, R. E. 1972. "The Actor and the Observer: Divergent Perceptions of the Causes of Behavior." In Jones et al. 1972 [599].

753. Karp, R. 1972. "Reducibility among Combinatorial Problems." In Miller and Thatcher 1972 [617].

754. Karp, R. 1976. "Probabilistic Analysis of Some Combinatorial Search Algorithms." In Traub 1976 [659].

755. Keil, F. C. forthcoming. "The Acquisition of natural kind and artifact terms." In Demopoulos and Marras forthcoming [560].

756. Kelley, H. H. 1972. "Casual Schemata and the Attribution Process." In Jones et al. 1972 [599].

757. Kelley, H. H. 1973. "The Process of Causal Attribution," *American Psychologist*, 28, 107–128.

758. Kelly, G. 1958. "Man's Construction of His Alternatives." In Lindzey 1958 [611].

759. Kim, J. 1984. "Concepts of Supervenience," *Philosophy and Phenomenological Research*, 65, 153–176.

760. Kim, J. 1985. "Psychophysical Laws." In LePore and McLaughlin 1985 [606].

761. Kitcher, P. 1975. "Kant and the Foundations of Mathematics," *Philosophical Review*, 84, 23–50.

762. Kitcher, P. 1978. "The Nativist's Dilemma," *Philosophical Quarterly*, 28, 1–16.

763. Kitcher, P. 1979. "Frege's Epistemology," *Philosophical Review*, 88, 235–262.

764. Klee, V. and Minty, G. 1972. "How Good Is the Simplex Algorithm?" In Shisha 1972 [655].

765. Kolata, G. 1976. "Mathematical Proofs: The Genesis of Reasonable Doubt," *Science*, 1922, 989–990.

766. Kripke, S. 1971. "Identity and Necessity." In Munitz 1971 [621].

767. Kripke, S. 1972. "Naming and Necessity." In Davidson and Harman 1972 [559].

768. Kunda, Z. and Nisbett, R. E. 1986. "The Psychometrics of Everyday Life," *Cognitive Psychology*, 18.

769. Kyburg, H. 1965. "Probability, Rationality, and the Rule of Detachment," *Proceedings of the 1964 International Congress for Logic, Methodology, and Philosophy of Science*, Amsterdam: North-Holland.

770. Lefcourt, H. M. 1972. "Internal vs. External Control of Reinforcement Revisited: Recent Developments." In Maher 1972 [613].

771. Lehman, D., Lempert, R., and Nisbett, R. E. 1986. "The Effects of Graduate Education on Reasoning," manuscript.

772. Lewis, C. I. 1973. "The Bases of Empirical Knowledge." In Chisholm and Swartz 1973 [20].

773. Lewis, D. 1970. "Anselm and Actuality," *Nous*, 4, 175–188.

774. Lewis, D. 1974. "Radical Interpretation," *Synthese*, 27, 331–344.

775. Lewis, D. 1976. "The Paradoxes of Time Travel," *American Philosophical Quarterly*, 13, 145–152.

776. Lewis, H. 1978. "Complexity of Solvable Cases of the Decision Problem for the Predicate Calculus," *Proceedings of the 19th IEEE Symposium on Foundations of Computer Science*, 35–47.

777. Lewis, H. and Papadimitriou, C. 1978. "The Efficiency of Algorithms," *Scientific American*, 238, 96–109.

778. Lovacs, L. 1980. "A New Linear Programming Algorithm—Better or Worse than the Simplex Method?" *Mathematical Intelligencer*, 2.

779. McArthur, L. Z. and Post, D. 1977. "Figural Emphasis and Person Perception," *Journal of Experimental Social Psychology*, 13, 520–535.

780. McArthur, L. Z. and Solomon, L. K. 1978. "Perceptions of an Aggressive Encounter as a Function of the Victim's Salience and the Perceiver's Arousal," *Journal of Personality and Social Psychology*, 36, 1278–1290.

781. McCall, E. 1982. "Performance Results of the Simplex Algorithm for a Set of Real-World Linear Programming Models," *Communications of the Association for Computing Machinery*, 25, 207–212.

782. McNamara, J. 1972. "Cognitive Basis of Language Learning in Infants," *Psychological Review*, 79, 1–13.

783. Mahaney, S. 1980. "Sparse Complete Sets for NP: Solution of a Conjecture by Berman and Hartmanis," *21st IEEE Symposium on Foundations of Computer Science*, 54–60.

784. Manktelow, K. I., and Evans, J. 1979. "Facilitation of Reasoning by Realism: Effect or Non-Effect?" *British Journal of Psychology*, 70, 477–488.

785. Mansfield, A. F. 1977. "Semantic Organization in the Young Child: Evidence for the Development of Semantic Feature Systems," *Journal of Experimental Child Psychology*, 23, 57–77.

785a. Markman, E. M. and Callanan, M. A. 1983. "An Analysis of Hierarchical Classification." In R. Sternberg, ed. *Advances in the Psychology of Human Intelligence*, vol. 2. Hillsdale, N,J.: Lawrence Erlbaum Associates.

786. Markman, E. M. and Hutchinson, J. E. 1984. "Children's Sensitivity to Constraints on Word Meaning: Taxonomic vs. Thematic Relations," *Cognitive Psychology*, 16, 1–27.

787. Markus, H. 1977. "Self-Schemata and Processing Information about the Self," *Journal of Personality and Social Psychology,* 35, 63–78.

788. Medin, D. L., and Schaffer, M. M. 1978. "A Context Theory of Classification Learning," *Psychological Review,* 85, 207–238.

789. Meyer, A. 1975. "Weak Monadic Second-Order Theory of Successor Is Not Elementary Recursive." In Dold and Eckmann 1975 [564].

789a. Miller, G. A. 1953. "What Is Information Measurement?," *The American Psychologist,* 8, 3–11.

790. Miller, G. A. 1956. "The Magical Number Seven. Plus or Minus Two: Some Limits on Our Capacity for Processing Information." *Psychological Review,* 63, 81–97.

791. Minsky, M. 1975. "A Framework for Representing Knowledge." In Winston 1975 [665].

792. Moore, G. E. 1942. "A Reply to My Critics." In Schilpp 1942 [650].

793. Moore, G. E. 1959. "Proof of an External World." In Moore 1959.

794. Neurath, Otto. 1932–1933. "Protolollsatze," *Erkenntnis,* 3, 204–214.

795. Newell, A. and Simon, H. "Computer Science as Empirical Inquiry," *Communications of the Association for Computing Machinery* 19, 113–126.

796. Nisbett, R. E., Fong, G., Lehman, D., and Cheng, P. 1987. "Teaching Reasoning," *Science,* 238.

797. Paris, J. and Harrington, L. 1977. "A Mathematical Incompleteness in Peano Arithmetic." In Barwise 1977 [543].

798. Pastin, M. 1976. "Meaning and Perception," *Journal of Philosophy,* 73, 570–571.

799. Pastin, M. 1976. "Modest Foundationalism and Self-Warrant." In Pappas and Swain 1978 [93].

800. Perry, J. 1977. "Frege on Demonstratives," *Philosophical Review,* 86, 474–97.

801. Perry, J. 1979. "The Problem of the Essential Indexical," *Nous* 13.

802. Pinker, S. 1990. "Language Acquisition." In Osherson and Lasnik 1990 [627].

803. Pollock, J. 1979. "A Plethora of Epistemological Theories." In Pappas 1979 [92].

804. Putnam, H. 1975. "The Meaning of 'Meaning'." In Putnam 1975 [634].

805. Putnam, H. 1975. "What Is Mathematical Truth?" In Putnam 1975 [633].

806. Putnam, H. 1977. "Is Semantics Possible?" In Schwartz 1977 [651].

807. Quine, W. V. 1969. "Reply to Putnam." In Hintikka and Davidson 1969 [594].

808. Quine, W. V. 1978. "The Nature of Moral Values." In Goldman and Kim 1978 [52].

809. Rabin, M. 1974. "Theoretical Impediments in Artificial Intelligence." In Rosenfeld 1974 [642].

810. Rabin, M. 1976. "Probabilistic Algorithms." In Traub 1976 [659].

811. Regan, D. T. and Totten, J. 1975. "Empathy and Attribution: Turning Observers in Actors," *Journal of Personality and Social Psychology*, 35, 49–55.

812. Reich, S. S. and Ruth, P. 1982. "Wason's Selection Task: Verification, Falsification, and Matching," *British Journal of Psychology*, 73, 395–405.

813. Rips, L. J. 1975. "Induction about Natural Categories," *Journal of Verbal Learning and Behavior*, 14, 665–681.

814. Rips, L. J. 1983. "Cognitive Processes in Propositional Reasoning," *Psychological Review*, 90, 38–71.

815. Rorty, R. 1982. "Introduction: Pragmatism and Philosophy." In Rorty 1982 [640].

816. Rosch, E. 1977. "Human Categorization." In Warren 1977 [661].

817. Rosch, E. 1978. "Principles of Categorization." In Rosch and Lloyd 1978 [641].

818. Rosch, E., Mervis, C. B., Gray, W. D., Johnson, D. M., and Boeys-Braem, P. 1976. "Basic Objects in Natural Categories," *Cognitive Psychology*, 8, 382–439.

819. Ross, L. 1978. "Afterthoughts on the Intuitive Psychologist." In Berkowitz 1978 [545].

820. Ross, L. and Anderson, C. 1982. "Shortcomings in the Attribution Process: On the Origins and Maintenance of Erroneous Social Assessments." In Tversky et al. 1982 [68].

821. Ross, L., Lepper, M. R., Strack, F., and Steinmetz, J. L. 1977. "Social Explanation and Social Expectation: The Effects of Real and Hypothetical Explanations upon Subjective Likelihood," *Journal of Personality and Social Psychology*, 35, 817–829.

822. Rotter, J. B. 1966. "Generalized Expectancies for Internal versus External Control of Reinforcement," *Psychological Monographs*, 80.

823. Rumelhart, D. E. 1976. "Understanding and Summarizing Brief Stories." In Lagerge and Samuels 1976 [605].

824. Rumelhart, D. E. and Ortony, A. 1976. "The Representation of Knowledge in Memory." In Anderson et al. 1976 [536].

825. Schlick, M. 1959. "The Foundation of Knowledge." In Ayer 1959 [540].

826. Schlick, M. 1959. "Positivism and Realism." In Ayer 1959 [540].

827. Sinsheimer, R. L. 1971. "The Brain of Pooh: An Essay on the Limits of Mind," *American Scientist,* 59, 20–28.

828. Slovic, P. and Fischhoff, B. 1978. In Gould and Walker 1978 [585].

829. Slovic, P., Fischhoff, B., and Lichtenstein, S. (1977). "Behavioral Decision Theory," *Annual Review of Psychology,* 28, 1–39.

830. Smith, E. E. 1990. "Categorization." In Osherson and Smith 1990 [625].

831. Smith, H. 1983. "Culpable Ignorance," *Philosophical Review,* 92, 543–572.

832. Sosa, E. 1978. "How Do You Know?" In Pappas and Swain 1978 [93].

833. Sosa, E. 1980. "The Foundation of Foundationalism," *Nous,* 14, 547–564.

834. Sperling, G. 1960. "The Information Available in Brief Visual Presentations," *Psychological Monographs,* 74, 1–29.

835. Sternberg, R. J. 1982. "Natural, Unnatural, and Supernatural Concepts," *Cognitive Psychology,* 14, 451–488.

836. Stich, S. P. 1980. "Headaches," *Philosophical Books,* 21, 65–73.

837. Stich, S. P. 1981a. "Dennett on Intentional Systems," *Philosophical Topics,* 12, 39–62.

838. Stich, S. P. 1981b. "On the Ascription of Content." In Woodfield 1981 [669].

839. Stich, S. P. 1982. "Genetic Engineering: How Should Science Be Controlled?" In Regan and VanDeVeer 1982 [636].

840. Stockmeyer, L. and Chandra, A. 1979. "Intrinsically Difficult Problems," *Scientific American,* 240, 140–159.

841. Storms, M. D. 1973. "Videotape and the Attribution Process: Reversing Actors' and Observers' Point of View," *Journal of Personality and Social Psychology,* 27, 165–175.

842. Swinburne, R. G. 1975. "Analyticity, Necessity and Apriority," *Mind,* 84, 225–243.

843. Swinney, D. 1979. "Lexical Access During Sentence Comprehension: (Re)consideration of Context Effects," *Journal of Verbal Learning and Verbal Behavior,* 18, 523–34.

844. Tarski, A. 1969. "Truth and Proof," *Scientific American,* 220, 63–77.

845. Taylor, S. E. and Crocker, J. C. 1980. "Schematic Bases of Social Information Processing." In Higgins et al. 1980 [593].

846. Taylor, S. E., and Fiske, S. T. 1975. "Point of View and Perceptions of Causality," *Journal of Personality and Social Psychology,* 32, 439–445.

847. Taylor, S. E., and Fiske, S. T. 1978. "Salience, Attention and Attribution: Top of the Head Phenomena." In Berkowitz 1978 [545].

848. Tomkins, A. 1979. "Script Theory: Differential Magnigication of Affects." In Howes and Dienstbier 1979 [595].

849. Tversky, A. 1977. "Features of Similarity," *Psychological Review*, 84, 327–352.

850. Tversky, A. 1985. "The Development of Taxonomic Organization of Named and Pictured Categories," *Developmental Psychology*, 21, 1111–1119.

851. van Cleve, J. 1985. "Epistemic Supervenience and the Circle of Belief," *Monist*, 68, 90–104.

852. van Fraassen, B. 1977. "The Only Necessity Is Verbal Necessity," *Journal of Philosophy*, 74, 71–85.

853. Watanabe, S. 1965. "Une explication mathematique du classement d'objets." In Dockx and Bernays 1965 [563].

854. Woodworth, R. and Sells, S. 1935. "An Atmosphere Effect in Formal Syllogistic Reasoning," *Journal of Experimental Psychology*, 8, 451–460.

855. Yilmaz, H. 1962. "On Color Vision and a New Approach to General Perception." In Bernard and Kare 1962 [546].

856. Yilmaz, H. 1967. "Perceptual Invariance and the Psychophysical Law," *Perception and Psychophysics*, 2, 533–538.

Index